The Question of Painting

The Question of Painting

Rethinking Thought with Merleau-Ponty

JORELLA ANDREWS

BLOOMSBURY ACADEMIC
LONDON • NEW YORK • OXFORD • NEW DELHI • SYDNEY

BLOOMSBURY ACADEMIC
Bloomsbury Publishing Plc
50 Bedford Square, London, WC1B 3DP, UK
1385 Broadway, New York, NY 10018, USA

BLOOMSBURY, BLOOMSBURY ACADEMIC and the Diana logo are trademarks
of Bloomsbury Publishing Plc

First published in Great Britain 2019
Paperback edition published 2020

Cover design: Nick Evans
Cover image © Leah Durner, *Rousseau*, 2006, acrylic and oil on canvas, 167.64 x 152.4cm
Courtesy Leah Durner

A catalogue record for this book is available from the British Library.

A catalog record for this book is available from the Library of Congress.

ISBN: HB: 978-1-4725-7428-2
PB: 978-1-4725-7427-5
ePDF: 978-1-4725-7429-9
eBook: 978-1-4725-7430-5

Typeset by Deanta Global Publishing Services, Chennai, India

To find out more about our authors and books visit www.bloomsbury.com
and sign up for our newsletters.

There is a pictorial rationality as there is a rationality of a painter's work, rationality not of completion but of 'investigation'.

(Maurice Merleau-Ponty, 'The Institution of a Work of Art', 1954–55)

CONTENTS

ACKNOWLEDGEMENTS

This book is dedicated, with profound thanks, to the memory of Professor Michael Podro. It was Michael who first introduced me to the work of Merleau-Ponty and who supervised the MA and PhD research I carried out on this topic while at the University of Essex. The original research for this project was supported by funding from a British Academy Scholarship.

I would also like to thank my family members – they know who they are – and my friends and colleagues, including Leah Durner, Walter Hayn, Donna Kehoe, Angela Nicholls, Alex Potts and Diana Stephenson, as well as my editors at Bloomsbury, Liza Thompson, Frankie Mace, Beth Williams and Sweda Deanta, for their wonderful friendship, advice and support.

I thank the publishers of the following works for granting me permission to reproduce substantial extracts for the purposes of analysis and discussion:

From *The Structure of Behavior* by Maurice Merleau-Ponty. Copyright © 1963 by Beacon Press; originally published in French under the title *La Structure du Comportement*, copyright © 1942 by Presses Universitaires de France. Reprinted by permission of Beacon Press, Boston.

From *Phenomenology of Perception* by Maurice Merleau-Ponty. Translated from the French *Phénoménologie de la perception* by Colin Smith. English translation © 1962, Routledge and Kegan Paul Ltd. Reproduced by permission of Taylor and Francis Books UK.

From *Sense and Non-Sense*. Originally published in French as *Sens et non-sens*, © 1948 by Les Éditions Nagel. This translation is based upon the revised third edition, issued by Nagel in 1961. English translation © 1964 by Northwestern University Press. First published 1964 by Northwestern University Press. All rights reserved.

From *Signs*. Originally published in French under the title *Signes*. Copyright © by Librarie Gallimard, Paris. English translation copyright © 1964 by Northwestern University Press. First printing 1964. All rights reserved.

From *The Primacy of Perception and Other Essays*. *L'oeil et l'esprit* © Éditions Gallimard 1964. English translation copyright © 1964 by Northwestern University Press.

From *The Visible and the Invisible*. Originally published in French under the title *Le Visible et l'invisible*. Copyright © 1964 by Editions Gallimard,

Paris. English translation copyright © 1968 by Northwestern University Press. First printing 1968. All rights reserved.

From *Metamorphoses* by Ovid. Translated by A. D. Melville (2008). By permission of Oxford University Press / By permission of Oxford University Press, USA http://www.oup.com.

LIST OF IMAGES

FIGURE I.1 The Louvre during the War: The Rubens Room (Le Museé de Louvre
pendant la guerre: la salle Rubens), *press photograph, n.d., [photographie de presse] /
Agence Meurisse.* © *Bibliothèque Nationale de France.*

FIGURE 1.2 *El Greco*, Christ on the Cross Adored by Donors, *c. 1590, oil on canvas, 248 × 180 cm. The Louvre, Paris. Photo © RMN-Grand Palais (musée du Louvre) / Tony Querrec.*

Introduction –
Painting as thought

Questions

Questions are powerful. At best, they initiate processes of investigation that may change what we take to exist, what we take to be important and what we take to be possible. At worst they provoke defensive withdrawals into earlier but now perhaps decidedly troubled certainties: pseudo-certainties. Normally, though, we think of them as verbalized entities. We ask questions or questions are asked of us, and it is in linguistic terms that these dialogues proceed. Within the realm of philosophy, moreover, these dialogues are conventionally regulated by and carefully articulated within pre-given logical structures; a partial list might include propositional, syllogistic, deductive, inductive, dualistic, dialectical and speculative forms of argumentation. Within each structure certain things can and cannot be said. As will become evident, this issue of the structures of actuality, possibility and limitation that inform our capacities to ask and to think within given situations was of enduring concern to the philosopher whose research provides a primary reference point for this book: the mid-twentieth-century French phenomenologist Maurice Merleau-Ponty. Crucially and unusually though – from a then-conventional philosophical point of view – his investigations in this regard were repeatedly focused on what he defined as the non-dualistic workings of *perception* and *visibility*.

In *The Question of Painting: Rethinking Thought with Merleau-Ponty*, questioning is approached from within the context of twentieth-century and contemporary non-dualistic rearticulations of how thought might be defined, expressed and practised. More particularly, it is associated with the visual and material investigations lying at the heart of the ancient and heterogeneous practice of painting, foregrounding – but not limited to – Merleau-Ponty's engagements with it. As I will show, Merleau-Ponty's reflections on painting were profound even if the range of his interests was relatively narrow, historically and stylistically, given the broader artistic environments of the time. Paul Cézanne was the painter who would remain paradigmatic for him, and on the whole his preferences were focused almost entirely on such other 'classic' figures of modernity as Paul Klee and Henri Matisse, active in the earlier part of the twentieth century. In other words, he would seem to have maintained an intellectual distance not only from the conceptually driven artistic critiques of painting that had been emerging since the start of the century, notably in the work of his compatriot, Marcel Duchamp, but also from the significant ascendency of interest in geometric as well as expressive or 'informal' abstract painting that had been occurring internationally, and in France, from the 1940s and into the 1950s. As the philosopher Véronique Fóti put it in her 1996 essay 'The Evidences of Paintings: Merleau-Ponty and Contemporary Abstraction' – and although she argued that Merleau-Ponty's 'insightful discussion of early modern painting' has much to contribute to an engagement with painterly abstraction – his writing consistently 'gives pride of place ... to figuration'.[1] We find no reflections in his writing on the impact, for instance, of the French art critic and curator Michel Tapié's important book on abstract art, *Un Art Autre* (which has been translated as *Art of Another Kind*), of 1952,[2] or of such key exhibitions as Jackson Pollock's first solo show in Paris at the Studio Paul Facchetti, also 1952, or *Twelve Contemporary American Painters and Sculptors*, which opened at the Musée National d'Art Moderne in Paris in April 1953.[3] Nonetheless, following Fóti and others, I hope to show that Merleau-Ponty's perceptiveness about painting – which, to repeat, I will be framing predominantly in relation to his philosophical quest to rethink the parameters of *thought* – resonate far beyond the specificities of his own investigations.

Over the years and into the twenty-first century, the heterogeneity of painting – conventionally understood as the application of pigment to canvas, paper or some other surface – has continued to expand conceptually, stylistically and in material terms. But the critical value of painting, particularly in its abstract or otherwise non-didactic modes, has been consistently questioned by those modern and contemporary artists, art historians, art theorists and philosophers for whom the art that counts is socially or politically driven and is trans-medial, participatory or activist in orientation. Despite the significant processes of reinvention that painting in even its more conventional formats has undergone in recent decades, it continues regularly to be dismissed as outmoded, reactionary and market-led: an ineffectual medium from the perspective of social and political engagement. At best, it is a contested field. As Anne Ring Petersen put it in her introduction to the 2010 anthology *Contemporary Painting in Context*, recent painting inhabits 'an ambivalent position as a discipline that appears to be simultaneously exhausted and inexhaustible'.[4] Along similar lines, the critic, curator and educator Terry R. Myers has stated in his introduction to the slightly later *Painting: Documents of Contemporary Art* of 2011 that the story of painting 'since the end of the nineteenth century is inextricable from the parallel (if not superseding) story of the perpetual cycle of its deaths and rebirths in the face of photography, conceptual art, installation, digital imaging technologies, the world wide web, or plain lack of interest'.[5] Only more recently has a renewed sense of intellectual hospitality begun to be extended towards this old and still-evolving practice. One reason for this has already been indicated: painting's demonstrable capacity to keep renovating itself. In some cases, fresh interest has been triggered by the proliferation of painterly practices that are actively examining painting's relationship with the wider media-scape and its varied lived implications and impositions, not just referentially but by allowing itself to become visibly and materially changed through such interactions, thus becoming a form of inter-media practice. For others, though, painting is interesting for its capacity to *resist* the increasing dominance of technologically mediated visual modes, not with regressive or conservative intent, but in order to keep alternate image-worlds open and alternate ways of being in play. Indeed, Paul Crowther has argued in the introduction to his 2013 book *Phenomenologies of Art and Vision: A Post-Analytic Turn* that 'to privilege art based on new media embodies a profoundly western bias. The great bulk of visual image-making in non-Western cultures', he wrote, 'continues to involve pictures and sculptures.'[6] In addition, when addressing the perception that 'in the context of globalization and the advent of new technologies, idioms such as painting and sculpture' might be regarded as 'somewhat *passé*' he emphasized the fact that paintings and sculpture have the capacity to *endure* in ways that contemporary forms of visual media, that are dependent upon 'electronic activation', do not.[7] With respect to the latter, Crowther associated their ontological impermanence not only with their dependence on technological systems that are themselves held hostage to inbuilt obsolescence but also with their broader embeddedness in systems of contemporary global consumerism that generate and are fuelled by 'an endless craving for novelty'.[8] By contrast, non-electronically-generated paintings and sculptures

> have an ontological self-sufficiency that allows them to exist alongside us, sharing the same places and being physically present, even though their *raison d'être* is to present virtual meaning. Their visibility and space-occupancy – like ours – are not things that can be switched off. ... As visible products of gestural activity or design, painting and sculpture allow an intimacy of familiar and stable existential contact that electronic media do not.[9]

This is important to Crowther because 'in such works, *the physicality of the medium is integral to the emergence of virtual meaning*'.[10] As such, paintings, thus understood, present a foil to various conceptually driven, post-medium arguments, dominant since the 1960s and championed by such art-practitioners and theorists as Joseph Kosuth, Sol LeWitt and Lucy Lippard (to name the more obvious), in which art-ideas, concepts and meanings were theorized as distinct from, and superior to, artistic concerns with materiality, medium, aesthetics – broadly, the exploration of that which can be perceived and felt – and the activity of art-*making*. Or, as the art historian Erik Verhagen has put it, in which 'the formulae in question' have been thought through 'prior to being given artistic expression'.[11]

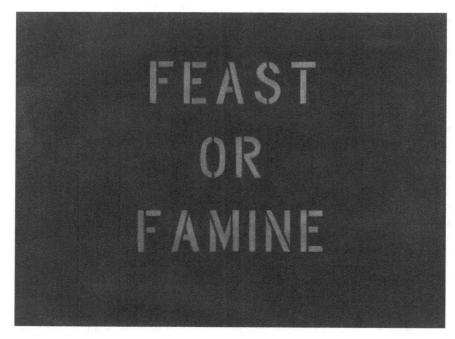

FIGURE I.3 *Leah Durner,* Feast or Famine, *1986, compressed charcoal and graphite on Fabriano paper, 96.52 × 127 cm. Courtesy Leah Durner.*

FIGURE I.4 *Leah Durner,* darkgreylightgreyyellow pour, *2017, from the* Céline *series (2016–present), poured latex enamel on canvas, 182.88 × 152.4 cm. Courtesy Leah Durner.*

FIGURE I.5 *Jan Dibbets,* Perspective Correction – My Studio II, *1969, gelatin silver print on linen. Stedelijk Museum Amsterdam. © Collection Stedelijk Museum Amsterdam / ARS, NY and DACS, London 2018.*

FIGURE I.6 Leah Durner, Studio, New York, NY, *2016, photograph. Courtesy Leah Durner.*

A growing tendency towards integrated and dynamic, non-oppositional understandings of the relations between the conceptual and the aesthetic, between thought and matter, aligns with the often phenomenologically inspired, non-dualistic impulses residing in such newer interdisciplinary and exploratory fields as contemporary critical visual and material culture and in aspects of the 'new materialisms' of such thinkers as Diana Coole, Karen Barad and others. Here, among other quests, the Merleau-Pontean challenge of rethinking the nature and scope of thought outside of its conventional, dematerialized parameters has again been taken up. And it is an understanding that several artists and writers have also been insisting upon, whether the art in question has tended to be defined as 'conceptual' or as 'painterly'. For instance, Marcel Vos – a close friend of the well-known Dutch conceptual photographer Jan Dibbets, who has also written extensively about his work – has challenged the notion of dematerialization that Lippard associated with conceptual art. Dibbets, incidentally, was one of the artists interviewed in Lippard's *Six Years: The dematerialization of the art object from 1966 to 1972*. In his 2001 essay 'Conceptuele Kunst: Een Herinnering' (Conceptual Art: A Reminiscence), Vos remarked that when he reads or hears the claims that are made about mid-twentieth-century conceptual art – about how theory-driven or word-based it was, for instance, at the expense of bodies, matter, intuition, sensuousness and the visual – he feels as though the processes of art-making described are utterly foreign to the ones with which, through his relationships with Dibbets and others, he was so closely involved. Among his remembrances, for instance, Vos recalled a 'lecture' presented by Richard Long in the Vondelkerk in Amsterdam (he and Dibbets had first met Long, along with Hamish Fulton and George Passmore of Gilbert and George, when Dibbets was on a residency in London in 1967). The audience thought they would finally hear the artist provide an explanation of his work, but he didn't utter a word. The 'lecture' consisted only of twenty slides of Long's work and twenty recorded soundtracks of country and western songs: 'Each slide remained visible precisely as long as each song lasted.'[12] Vos wrote that he wanted to foreground this, out of many other possible examples, in order to 'challenge the idea that conceptual art was made by ... disembodied ascetics who preferred to stay in the higher atmosphere of immaterial concepts'.[13] Indeed, he went on to insist that the sensual and sensible aspects of bodily existence played a far greater role in the formation of ideas and concepts within conceptual art than people are now inclined to accept. In the performances of Gilbert and George and in the text-based installations of Lawrence Weiner (who thought of himself more as a sculptor than a conceptualist), to name but two examples, such sensual and sensuous factors were direct sources of reference. For Dibbets too – who had once described his project to Vos in a letter as 'thinking (but not with words)' – to be involved with ideas was not to be distanced from his bodily, perceptual being. Indeed Verhagen – author of *Jan Dibbets: The Photographic Work* (2007) and curator of

Jan Dibbets: Horizons at the Musée d'Art Moderne de la Ville de Paris in 2010 – has said that Dibbets' photographic practice, with its compulsive explorations of such visual phenomena as the horizon line, had led the artist 'to cut free of the dogmatic iconophobia of conceptualism in a return to a more "pictorial" notion of the photographic object'.[14] Vos would no doubt want to qualify this: conceptualism as it tended to be theorized rather than as it was necessarily always practised. Furthermore, with such works as Dibbets' *Perspectiefcorrecties (Perspective Corrections)* – some created in studio settings (Figure I.5), others in the landscape – we see, as Fosco Lucarelli has put it, 'the themes of illusion in art and photography' being addressed. Under scrutiny was

> the gap between perception (what the eye sees) and representation (what the camera sees), the nature of the art object and the role of photography: from a passive medium used by Land artists for documenting ephemeral acts, to an active tool through which to question the intellectual construction of space, an issue that dominated Western art since the Renaissance.[15]

Within what Verhagen has referred to as 'a "hyperconceptual" context a priori, and according to legend, hardly conducive to the emergence of an "iconic" dimension', Dibbets would seem to have returned to 'a more "painterly" image system'.[16]

Conversely, where the work of contemporary abstract painter Leah Durner is concerned – a detail from her large-scale gestural work *Rousseau*, 2006, is on the cover of this book – matter, aesthetics and thought have again always been understood and treated as intertwined. Durner, for whom the non-dualistic, embodied thought of Merleau-Ponty has long been an important source of insight, trained as a painter when debates about the validity of painting were at a height. While studying for an MFA at Rutgers University, New Jersey, between 1983 and 1985, anti-painting debates were a primary focus of discussion, as were ongoing critiques of the visual and of representation. Intriguingly, her teachers during this period were Leon Golub and Martha Rosler. Golub (1922–2004) was a painter who has been associated by art historians with 'new figuration'; this refers to the international revival of representational image-making in the 1960s following a period dominated by varied forms of post-war abstraction. Golub's paintings were strongly political; he has been described as an activist painter. Sourcing his works from newspaper and magazine photographs, and combining an impasto application of paint onto canvases that he also attacked and partially destroyed by scraping and cutting into them 'arbitrarily' and 'irrationally', they consistently dealt with issues of war and violence. Examples include his three enormous *Vietnam* paintings (*Vietnam II*, of 1973, is now part of the Tate, London's collection[17]) and his eleven 'White Squad' paintings (1982–87) which focused on police and vigilante violence. By contrast, Rosler, also a profoundly politicized artist, had a conceptually driven practice that incorporated teaching, writing, photography, video, installation and performance (here again issues of embodiment were important). Key works, by then well-known and still iconic today, included her video performance piece *Semiotics of the Kitchen* of 1975 and her earlier series of anti-Vietnam War collages, *House Beautiful: Bringing the War Home*, produced between around 1967 and 1972. Durner's own early paintings had a strong conceptual and socio-political focus but also foregrounded materiality and aesthetics. As she put it with respect to her *Texts* series of 1985–92:

> Works in the *Texts* series pull common phrases out of the cultural stream. Each piece has multiple meanings that emerge depending on the viewer's physical, political, and psychological point of view. The background (ground) is very heavily built up with compressed charcoal which creates a velvety black matte surface. The text (figure) is very heavily built up with graphite which creates a very shiny surface. The text emerges from the background when light reflects off the shiny surface of the graphite. When light does not hit the graphite, the piece looks like a simple black rectangle and the text nearly disappears into the background. (See Ad Reinhardt.)[18]

The aesthetic and material aspects of these pieces were *conceptually* crucial, specifically the fact that the surfaces of these works were black on black, and evoked both matte and gloss effects. As Durner has put it, 'the light reflecting, or not, off the graphite words evoked subliminal messaging'.[19] This was apt because the words and phrases she was 'pulling from the cultural stream' – such as 'useless' or 'feast or famine' (see *Feast or Famine*, 1986, Figure I.3) are used in everyday speech but rarely attended to in terms of their often complex histories, connotations and effects. To cite Durner again, within her painterly renderings of these expressions, 'when they are lit, brought to attention, we realise the enormity and the multiple meanings of these accustomed phrases: the expression "feast or famine" slips off the tongue but in reality people are dying of hunger while others indulge'.[20]

If works such as *Feast or Famine* pulled 'common phrases out of the cultural stream' and utilized aesthetics (including, as Durner thought of it, 'black as a color') to make them effective, her gestural and poured abstractions begun in the late 1980s, and overlapping with the *Texts* series, might be approached in terms of how they pull out differently rationalized or codified instances of colour usage operative, at a generally unconscious level, within the public sphere – whether in the realms of warfare, the construction industry or fashion – interrogating and then re-presenting them in an alternate, painterly format in order to provoke multivalent aesthetic *and* conceptually nuanced interactions with them. An early example was her *Camouflage* series (1989–92). These works, made either from poured enamel on canvas or acrylic on paper, have an immediately abstract, even decorative, look but they were sourced in – and in critical engagement with – German Second World War camouflage designs as collated and catalogued by the French physician and amateur military historian Jean-François Borsarello. A recent example of a large-scale painting in poured enamel that uses a colour code from fashion is Durner's *darkgreylightgreyyellow pour* of 2017 (Figure I.4). Part of her *Céline* series, begun in 2016 and continuing into the present, it was inspired by the 'rich and unusual' colour of the French fashion house's pre-fall 2016 and spring 2017 collections. Durner tore images of the Céline advertising campaigns from fashion magazines *W* and *Vogue* to which she subscribes. She also visited Céline boutiques to see, touch and try on the clothes herself.[21]

Aptly, at a material level and in terms of its surface qualities, the poured application of paint in *darkgreylightgreyyellow pour* alludes to the flow and fluid, rippling movements of draped cloth. For Durner, its characteristics also have further analogies with the elusive substance and movements of flesh, as evoked within the traditions of European figurative painting and – this is an issue to which I will return later on in this book – as this term was developed and used by Merleau-Ponty in his later writing as a way of articulating the nature of interaction outside of the conventional philosophical opposition of subject and object.[22] The medium of poured enamel also evokes the qualities of shimmer, shine or brilliance that are a dominant visual characteristic of our modern and contemporary built environments and mediascapes, including, of course, the high-gloss images sourced from fashion magazines which provided starting points for Durner's *Céline* paintings. (The phenomenon of shine or brilliance within modern, and particularly metropolitan life and its psychological as well as sociocultural effects was of course intriguingly addressed by the sociologist Georg Simmel (1858–1918) at the beginning of the twentieth century in such essays as his 'Philosophy of Fashion' of 1903.[23]) With respect to Durner's presentation of colour in *darkgreylightgreyyellow pour*, we are given a mix of calmness, vibrancy and turmoil. A smooth and untroubled swathe of powerful, even harshly bright, yellow descends from the top of the painting's upper right-hand quadrant. But upon encountering the turbulent, layered textures of dark and lighter greys that cover the remainder of the canvas, it begins to break up, to destabilize – but crucially also to illuminate – those larger areas of grey as if from within.[24]

As explorations of colour and of the materiality of paint, Durner's poured enamel abstractions unashamedly embrace the often complex dynamics of beauty including, as she has put it, the 'ugly-beautiful-hyper-beautiful juxtapositions of color' to which she is consistently drawn.[25] But this does not mean that her work is a renunciation of the conceptual or a refusal to engage with issues of socio-political concern. At issue instead are reconfigurations of awareness, passion, insight and rhetoric with respect to how the world – including the complex, layered image-worlds in which we are immersed – might be enjoyed, observed, pictured and questioned. As such, her abstract paintings represent an extension of her earlier, more obviously ideas-driven or politically-driven works. For as well as releasing aesthetic pleasure (the virtues of which have tended to be much derided within contemporary art theory), they also have to do with attending to specific, generally unexamined, and often ambiguous culturally embedded systems of expression and thought that impact our lives every day. Specifically, at issue in her abstract works are the *colour*-worlds that structure our surroundings; that is, the sensuous and motivational substrata that unconsciously or subliminally shape our sensibilities and our choices. Her painterly explorations of colour, which, as indicated, often combine beauty and appeal with a sense of aesthetic discordance, make these structures and our interactions with them perceptible, enabling us to think and act with, or at cross-purposes with, or – if required – against them.

This interrogative characteristic to Durner's work, which Merleau-Ponty has termed 'secret science' – of which more later – is reflected in her working methods. On the one hand, the process of applying poured enamel paint onto her canvases is, as she has put it, 'active and physical' as well as necessarily requiring a high degree of focus. In temporal terms, here the artist is inserted within *kairos*, an ancient Greek term that refers to a strategically favourable, one-off, opportunity for decision or action. But the success of the pour depends upon a longer and slower preparatory process involving research, analysis and experimentation. This begins with Durner's discovery and collation of the sources upon which she will base a painting or set of paintings and which will form part of what she calls her 'personal color library'.[26] Here, she remains on the lookout for unusual colour and surface combinations and effects. Then a decision-making process begins during which she develops and finalizes her colour palette. Also taking place during this time, it is worth noting, is a further, ongoing preparatory activity. It is a form of image-making which, on the surface of it, seems far removed, stylistically, from the production of the pours: Durner consistently spends time in museums, studying and making drawings particularly from antique sculpture. Again, thinking in temporal terms, this multifaceted preparatory activity is the work of *chronos*. This is the everyday time of routine, habit and ritual which can feel pedestrian – just plain, hard work – but which readies us for those decisive moments of strategic enactment. In Durner's case, these decisive moments involve a choreography of intentional and practiced movement (developed over a lifetime of painting and drawing), responsive spontaneity and – inevitable for a process of this kind – accident. What finally appears on the canvas is always a surprise.

The Question of Painting, to return to it, is written against the backdrop of the varied philosophical and artistic concerns, positions and repositionings I have just outlined and is in conversation with them. But it is particularly focused on how and why Merleau-Ponty embraced painterly practices as philosophically crucial and reflected upon them. More precisely, this book is about the evolving <u>ways in which practices of painting and</u> different types of painterly self-positioning – as <u>irreducibly embodied,</u> materially grounded and situated on the one hand, while always also enmeshed in the possible, the virtual, the speculative and the imaginative on the other – presented themselves to Merleau-Ponty as figurations of the *inter-corporeal* (later the *intra-corporeal*) investigations he wished to situate at the very centre of philosophy as he was attempting to redefine it. These investigations were inter(intra)-corporeal in the sense that they were neither 'subjectively' nor 'objectively' driven, as these terms are conventionally understood. Here, thought was not defined as that which is produced by a conceptually isolated or autonomous Cartesian cogito (the 'I think', or 'I experience'). They were inter(intra)-corporeal in terms of their capacity to embody and express a profoundly non-dualistic understanding of reality and our access to it. Crucially too – recalling my opening remarks – a nuanced and deeply interconnected, rather than oppositional, relationship was proposed where thought is concerned, between the visual on the one hand and the verbal on the other.

Rethinking thought

In broad terms, the aim of <u>Merleau-Ponty's project, which spanned the mid-</u> <u>1930s to the beginning of the 1960s,</u>[27] was to challenge the viability of so-called Cartesian dualism, that is, René Descartes' *conceptual* distinction between mind understood as non-extended (or non-corporeal) substance, indivisible but finite (*res cogitans*) on the one hand, and on the other hand body/matter understood as extended (or corporeal) substance, divisible and finite (*res extensa*) as set out in the *Meditationes de prima philosophia* (*Meditations on First Philosophy*, 1641/*Méditations Métaphysiques*, 1647). Here, it should be remembered, a rarely discussed third and infinite substance, God – upon which Descartes' two finite substances were dependent – was presented as integral to the coherence of his system; the *Meditations* were subtitled 'In which the existence of God and the immortality of the soul are demonstrated'. Indeed, underlining this point, in their essay 'Descartes' Notion of the Mind-Body Union and its Phenomenological Expositions', Sara Hainämaa and Timo Kaitaro usefully cited Emmanuel Lévinas' reading of Descartes in this regard. 'In *Totality and Infinity* (*Totalité et infini*, 1961) and related works', they wrote, 'Emmanuel Lévinas builds an ethical metaphysics that draws from Descartes' philosophy of infinities and magnitudes and from Kierkegaard's philosophy of faith.' They continued, arguing that for Lévinas

a Cartesian excursion ... allows us to liberate our reflections from the dominant Kantian preconception about the primacy of finiteness in respect to infinity. In *Totality and Infinity*, we read: 'For the Cartesian cogito is discovered, at the end of the Third Meditation, to be supported by the certitude of the divine qua infinite, by relation to which the finitude of the cogito … is posited and conceivable. This finitude could not be determined without the recourse to the infinite, as is the case in the moderns, for whom finitude is, for example, determined on the basis of the mortality of the subject. … This certitude [of consciousness] is due to the clarity and distinctness of the cogito, but certitude itself is sought because of the presence of infinity in this finite thought, which without this presence would be ignorant of its own finitude.'[28]

Of particular concern to Merleau-Ponty, in any case, were the ways in which notions of *res cogitans* and *res extensa*, in isolation from that broader Cartesian context, had been variously taken up or rejected within the ostensibly opposed traditions of rationalism and empiricism.[29] Often referring to these traditions using a variety of terms somewhat interchangeably – on the one hand, idealism, intellectualism and mentalism, and on the other hand, materialism, causal thinking, mechanical thinking, naturalism, behaviourism and positivism[30] – he regarded them as unworkably reductive, indeed fundamentally *non*-rational, due to their disavowals of the complexities and ambiguities of lived experience. Crucially, this included the specific, seemingly intractable challenges presented by post-war current affairs. Merleau-Ponty, by contrast, argued that philosophical propositions could be regarded as viable only insofar as they were rooted *in* our lived engagements with the world and applicable *to* these realities. Philosophical thought must be able to accept the variations of expression, as well as areas of weakness, irreconcilability *and* potential that coexist within even the most difficult aspects of everyday life. These phenomena must be attended to if routes towards positive change are to be found. Indeed, it was into this productively unstable realm of perceptual engagement *with* the world that is prior to the disengaged thoughts we may have *of* it, that Jean-Paul Sartre would later describe Merleau-Ponty as 'always digging'[31] – a territory with which, as Merleau-Ponty saw it, painters – artists – were best acquainted.

Non-dualistic propositions, though philosophically radical in Merleau-Ponty's time, are treated by many thinkers today as over-rehearsed and barely warranting critical attention. But as I see it, these propositions represent unfinished business. It is one thing, nowadays, to regard non-dualistic orientations as *intellectually* normative, as a matter of mental assent. But it is quite another to be capable of embodying them, of fleshing them out in everyday social, cultural, political and communicative contexts and within structures and infrastructures which – for the sake of short-term ease and seeming efficiency – tend still to operate according to norms of mutual exclusivity: either/or; this or that; good or bad. Such mutual exclusivities, Merleau-Ponty argued, are rendered non-viable as soon as we start perceiving and as soon as we start attending to what is given to us in perception. Indeed, in his 1945 essay 'The War has Taken Place', Merleau-Ponty had turned to recent history in order to underline the political as well as broad existential urgency of his argument that perception and thought be brought into a new, critical interrelationship with one another. Writing with considerable passion, he focused on the devastating political consequences for France of an interwar intellectual climate in which the inevitably complex and conflicted evidences of lived perception had been overshadowed by modes of thought conceived of as unambiguous and indubitable due to what was, in fact, their problematically disembodied and historically unsituated character.

At this stage in our discussions, it is worth dwelling on this essay, as well as noting the persistent political commitments that informed Merleau-Ponty's thought-as-a-whole; they ran alongside and would be inflected by his investigations of the questions and insights that emerged from the painterly practices of interest to him. 'We were attending an old school', he wrote, 'in which generations of socialist professors had been trained.'[32] He was most likely referring to the École Normale Supérieure, an elite institution for higher learning and research, established in Paris in 1794 – that is, during the French Revolution. He had studied there from 1926 alongside Sartre (whom he had not yet befriended), Simone de Beauvoir, Claude Lévi-Strauss and Simone Weil. Many of the École's socialist professors, he added, had been killed in action during the First World War.[33] Against these historical facts, however, students were being taught to embrace an 'optimistic philosophy which reduced human societies to a sum of consciousnesses always ready for peace and happiness', a philosophy which was, in reality that 'of a barely victorious nation, an imagined compensation for the memories of 1914'.[34] For Merleau-Ponty, these philosophical expressions of flight from unresolved collective trauma had fostered a widespread incapacity, as well as unwillingness, to discern a new set of dangers – the fact of encroaching German aggression – and respond appropriately:

> We knew that concentration camps existed, that the Jews were being persecuted, but these certainties belonged to the world of thought. We were not as yet living face to face with cruelty and death: we had not as yet been given the choice of submitting to them or confronting them. Outside the peaceful garden of our school where the fountain immemorially and everlastingly murmured, there awaited us for our vacation of '39 that other garden which was France, the France of walking trips and youth hostels, which was as self-evident as the earth itself – or so we thought.[35]

By that time – 1939 – Merleau-Ponty had become well-embedded within the interwar intellectual and educational scene. Nine years earlier, in 1930, he had concluded a first round of studies at the École passing his *agrégation* in philosophy, a competitive examination that qualified him to teach in French state secondary schools, or lycées. Five years on, having first completed his military service, he took up teaching posts in various schools. He then returned to the École as a graduate researcher and tutor. In 1938 he completed an extensive body of research that would finally emerge in published form, in 1942, as _The Structure of Behavior_. As such, the manner in which Merleau-Ponty repeatedly used the term 'we' in 'The War has Taken Place' appears to signal his own acknowledged entrenchment within the philosophical, political and ethical responsibilities, and irresponsibilities, at play in the run-up to the Second World War. This post-war essay also underlined the formative role played by the problems of war in the development and progression of his own thought, notably the intellectual irreconcilabilities and denials that the facts of war had brought to light and his determination to combat them.

For Merleau-Ponty (1908-1961) in person, the facts of war included active service in the infantry from August 1939 until the defeat of France in the summer of 1940. He was wounded just before demobilization and discharged in September 1940. He was awarded the _Croix de guerre_ for heroism.[36] During the German occupation of France, Merleau-Ponty returned to school teaching, research and writing, and participated in the short-lived resistance group _Socialisme et Liberté_ in which Sartre and Albert Camus were leading lights.[37] After the war, and with the book for which he is still best known – _The Phenomenology of Perception_ (1945) – just published, active intellectual engagement with social and political matters remained a priority – a pertinent fact given the surprisingly oft-found scholarly assertion that phenomenology, the philosophical tradition with which Merleau-Ponty was by then principally engaged and was making his own – is intrinsically apolitical or non-political in orientation.[38] Collaborating with Sartre, along with de Beauvoir and others, as well as working within academia, he took on the role of political editor for the newly established journal _Les Temps Modernes_, remaining active in this capacity for a further seven years. Furthermore, although less of a public figure than Sartre, Merleau-Ponty's ideas, including his political ideas, also circulated within the public realm. During the autumn of 1948, for instance, he delivered a series of seven weekly lectures on French national radio in which he presented key ideas from the _Phenomenology_ to a general audience.[39] Later, he would become a regular contributor to the popular weekly magazine _L'Express_. He also took his ideas abroad. Carlos Alberto Sánchez, in his recent book on Mexican existentialism, referred to Merleau-Ponty's visit to Mexico City in January 1949, where he made front-page news as he was welcomed by the philosophers Luis Villoro and Emilio Uranga. According to Sánchez, his visit and lectures on French existentialism were 'a welcome event' for the sake of philosophy due to the fact that Merleau-Ponty's embodied and lived philosophy was 'a philosophy of action, a manner of thinking that could be deployed to confront the needs of a community under siege by the oppressive forces of history'.[40] Indeed, Villoro had written that Merleau-Ponty encouraged 'a conscious project of self-knowledge that gives us the grounding for a subsequent self-transformation'.[41] This was due to not only the embeddedness of Merleau-Ponty's thought within the ambiguities of everyday life, but also his *affirmation* of these ambiguities. As such, his philosophical method involved attending to everyday existence such as it was, and as a site for the discovery of potential solutions, rather than taking the sceptical or despairing route of 'declaring its failure'.[42] Six years later, during October and November of 1955, having accepted the first of two commissions from Alliance Française, Merleau-Ponty went on to visit several African countries including Tunisia, French Equatorial Africa, the Belgian Congo and Kenya, where he lectured on such topics as the concept of race, colonialism and development. He lectured abroad again two years later, during October and November of 1957, this time in Madagascar, Reunion Island and Mauritius, with the intention of also observing at close hand the impact of French reforms to its policies regarding overseas governance. Earlier that year, incidentally, he had declined induction into France's Order of the Legion of Honour. This was most likely in protest of France's record of atrocities particularly in Algiers; the Algerian War of Independence had by then been raging for three years. Closer to home, in 1959, Merleau-Ponty spoke at Manchester University in England where an early interest in continental philosophy was astir. To the reported disappointment of one attendee, his lectures had a political rather than philosophical focus.[43] Interestingly, there are two references to this trip among the working notes included at the end of Merleau-Ponty's last, unfinished book, *The Visible and the Invisible*, which was published posthumously in 1964 by Éditions Gallimard. The more evocative of these (worth citing since it will connect with ideas presented later on) was dated 2 May 1959, and had as its heading the words 'Perception – unconscious – One[44] – retrograde movement of the true – sedimentation (of which the retrograde movement of the true is a part)':

> The taxi driver at Manchester, saying to me (I understood only a few seconds later, so briskly were the words 'struck off'): *I will ask the police where Brixton Avenue is.* – Likewise, in the tobacco shop, the woman's phrase: *Shall I wrap them together?* which I understood only after a few seconds – and *all at once.*[45]

With respect to 'The War has Taken Place' however – originally published over seventy years ago in the first issue of *Les Temps Modernes* – Merleau-Ponty's ideas, indeed his warning, are surely worth heeding in our own at-once contested and distracted times. Recalling Merleau-Ponty's descriptions of the pre-Second World War cultural environment in which he had been immersed, we might ask ourselves where, and what, might be *our* versions of those gardens with their immemorially and everlastingly murmuring fountains, walking trips and youth hostels? Which 'optimistic philosophies' may be underlying *them*? What forms of denial? And what modes of contemporary, dualistically informed thought, apparently enabling, affirming or efficient, may be doing *us* a disservice? Moreover, given the highly visualized and emotive information worlds in which we live, how are the contemporary arts variously playing into such scenarios or helping us seek alternative ways of seeing, thinking and being?

Questions of this kind, which ask us to consider the nature and implications of our individual and collective embeddedness in the world, run through *The Question of Painting*, as do Merleau-Ponty's own responses to them. This is also why the lived, practical techniques of his non-dualistic investigations – the *how* – are consistently foregrounded in this book, and why I focus in particular on Merleau-Ponty's repeated claims that such investigations are, arguably (and perhaps at first sight counter-intuitively), most powerfully figured within painterly practices.[46] As already indicated, this book seeks to become immersed, with him, in the kinds of questions that are asked of and by the hands and eyes of those who paint, of and by the many and varied materials, traditions and evocations of painting, and of and by art-making more broadly. Also of and by the viewers who are being addressed by these works and by the contexts and infrastructures of their display. Following Merleau-Ponty, at issue is painting's capacity both to enter and create territory that is unavailable to cognition as conventionally understood, and which remains unnoticed, unimagined and, therefore, also unquestioned within the exigencies of everyday life. The willingness to enter this under-examined and therefore unfamiliar territory, in which we find ourselves complicit, and in which we may find ourselves subject to challenge, change and what feels like dispossession – rather than the more conventional visual bringing-to-expression of particular ideological positions or critiques; within the Merleau-Pontean model those are secondary practices – I take to be foundational to social and political efficacy at whatever level or intensity this might be required. Crucially, these modes of awareness are fundamental orientations that can be cultivated and practiced, without exclusion, by everyone, everywhere.

To this end, I will turn to both better-known and lesser-known texts by Merleau-Ponty in which questions about or relevant to the issue of painting and/as thought are undertaken. The best known of these include the *Phenomenology of Perception*, as noted, written during the last two years of the Occupation, the essays 'Cézanne's Doubt' (1945) and 'Eye and Mind' (1961), and *The Visible and the Invisible*. But I also regard as pivotal to my project his first book *The Structure of Behavior* (1942) and his essay 'Indirect Language and the Voices of Silence' (1952). In addition, I will refer to such essays as 'Film and the New Psychology' (1945), 'On News Items' (1954) and the now-published course notes relating to his prestigious teaching career at the famous Collège de France in Paris, where, in 1952, aged just 44, he was awarded the chair of philosophy – this was the same year he resigned from his editorial position at *Les Temps Modernes* and broke with Sartre over political and intellectual disagreements, of which more in Chapter 5. Merleau-Ponty would hold his academic position at the Collège de France until his early and unanticipated death in May 1961, aged just 54, counting such now-well-known thinkers as Michel Foucault and Gilbert Simondon among his students. Merleau-Ponty, whose interests and ideas were not only consistently directed towards then-contemporary concerns, but also profoundly interdisciplinary in character, spanning the sciences and the humanities, could not have been better aligned with an institution whose motto was, and is, *Docet Omnia* ('It teaches everything') and whose stated aim was to 'teach science in the making'. In fact, Merleau-Ponty's own description of the Collège's raison d'être, taken from his inaugural lecture of 1952 – 'Not acquired truths, but the idea of a free research' (Non pas des vérités acquises, mais l'idée d'une recherche libre)[47] – was regarded by the Collège as so beautifully in tune that his words were inscribed upon the walls of the college's so-called grand foyer. They remain prominent today on its website. The teaching materials from the Collège de France to which I will refer are Merleau-Ponty's notes for his 1954–55 course Institution in Personal and Public History, including those titled 'The Institution of a Work of Art'.[48] There are also multiple references to painting in a compilation of Merleau-Ponty's writing and teaching published posthumously as *La Prose du monde* in 1969 and in translation as *The Prose of the World* in 1973. Originally intended as part of a substantial book on the topic of truth, Merleau-Ponty had worked on this material while in the position of chair of child psychology and pedagogy at the University of Paris, Sorbonne, between 1949 and 1952. But he never completed the project and according to the collection's editor, his one-time student and lifelong friend Claude Lefort, he may never have done so in this particular form.[49] In the main, I will engage with his writings chronologically and my aim will be to foreground, and think with, the Merleau-Pontean ideas that seem to be especially pertinent in light of the intellectual, social and political challenges that are addressing us today. But as I do so, it will be evident that the unfolding of Merleau-Ponty's thought is by no means that of a linear progression.

My approach – and this constitutes what might be described as a 'visual culture' rather than a more conventionally philosophical strategy – will also be to follow Merleau-Ponty's lead by making painting and, where appropriate, other instances of art practice or visual culture, paradigmatic for my own thought. Drawn to the fecundity of these works, their capacity always to show *more*, and frequently to show *otherwise*, than I, or anyone else, might choose to say *of* them, I will often let them take the lead. My aim is to let the terrain they open up, and the questions they seem to be raising, provide critical contexts that simultaneously ground the specific points I might be making at any given moment *and* extend beyond them. This determination to accept that philosophical work is always a matter of negotiating differently articulated patterns of limitation and possibility is modelled after Merleau-Ponty's own methodologies, and – contrary to what might be expected – is the basis for what I take to be the strength, richness and ongoing applicability of his thought. In some cases, I will revisit visual works, practices or scenarios already explicitly discussed by Merleau-Ponty, although it is important to point out that in his writing Merleau-Ponty tended to focus less on works of art and more on written or recorded testimonies in which painters described their working experiences of looking and making. Émile Bernard's *Souvenirs sur Paul Cézanne* (*Memories of Paul Cézanne*) of 1912, Robert Delaunay's essay 'Sur la Lumière' (On Light) also of 1912 and his *Du cubism à l'art abstrait* (*From Cubism to Abstract Art*) of 1957 were key textual sources, as well as numerous texts by Paul Klee including *Das bildnerische Denken* (known in English as 'The Thinking Eye'), which was translated into French in 1959. Merleau-Ponty did not regard such texts and testimonies as definitive, but as material for further reflection. At other times I will bring into play visual examples from non-Merleau-Pontean or extra-Merleau-Pontean sources, including now-contemporary ones. These are works that seemed insistently to address themselves to me as I was working on this project and had an active role in framing, shaping or repositioning the perspectives presented. Sometimes I will make repeated, perhaps somewhat obsessive, returns to the same work of art, drawing from them fresh observations: a late-sixteenth-century painting by El Greco, for instance, a mid-seventeenth-century Dutch genre painting by Pieter de Hooch or, shifting medium, a contemporary video work by the Austrian artist Barbara Kapusta. Key works will either be reproduced or carefully described in a way that also makes the personal nature of my own engagement with them explicit. I will indicate where they can be seen, whether in public collections or online.

Inevitably, woven throughout *The Question of Painting* will be references to broader scholarship pertinent to the topic of painting and/ as thought. These are by no means intended to be comprehensive; indeed, I am painfully aware of the remarkable and relevant scholarship I will inevitably be omitting. But a brief overview of key works of Merleau-Pontean scholarship with respect to the aesthetic must begin with Galen A. Johnson's classic *The Merleau-Ponty Aesthetics Reader* (1993) which combines translations of Merleau-Ponty's writings on aesthetics with a selection of scholarly essays reflecting on different dimensions of his thought in this regard. Also of note is Johnson's more recent *Retrieval of the Beautiful: Thinking through Merleau-Ponty's Aesthetics* of 2009 which is particularly focused on a reading of 'Eye and Mind' and Rajiv Kaushik's *Art, Language and Figure in Merleau-Ponty* (2013). Other key anthologies are *Difference, Materiality, Painting* of 2000 edited by Fóti, which includes her essay 'The Evidences of Painting: Merleau-Ponty and Contemporary Abstraction' as well as Johnson's insightful 'Thinking in Color: Merleau-Ponty and Paul Klee', Kascha Semionovitch and Neal DeRoo's 2010 edited collection *Merleau-Ponty at the Limits of Art, Religion, and Perception* and Duane H. Davis and William S. Hamrick's recent *Merleau-Ponty and the Art of Perception*, of 2016.[50] Pertinent to this project are the philosopher

Paul Crowther's theorizations of what he calls the 'transperceptual' and *his* reflections on abstract art, found in his 2013 book *Phenomenologies of Art and Vision: A Post-Analytic Turn,* which also contains a chapter on Merleau-Ponty entitled 'Vision in Being: Merleau-Ponty and the Depths of Painting'.[51] Donald A. Landes, in his *Merleau-Ponty and the Paradoxes of Expression* also published in 2013, again focuses on the topic of painting in the book's final two chapters. Among the non-Merleau-Pontean painterly reflections upon which I draw are curator Laura Hoptman's reflections on painting in the catalogue for *The Forever Now: Contemporary Painting in an Atemporal World* (2014), as well as Petersen's introduction to *Contemporary Painting in Context* and her essay 'Painting Spaces'. I will also refer to Peter Osborne's 2013 book *Anywhere or Not at All: Philosophy of Contemporary Art* and to the Dutch art historian Kees Vollemans' book *Het Raadsel van de Zichtbare Wereld: Philips Koninck, of een landschap in de vorm van een traktaat (The Puzzle of the Visible World: Philips Koninck, or a landscape in the form of a treatise)* of 1998.[52] The painting around which Vollemans' book is organized is Koninck's remarkable *An Extensive Landscape, with a River* of 1664, which is part of the Museum Boijmans van Beuningen collection in Rotterdam. (In Dutch it is known as *Vergezicht over een vlak land,* literally *Vista over a Flat Terrain.*) Vollemans' book, together with Graham Ellard and Stephen Johnstone's film *For an Open Campus,* recorded in Japan during 2014,[53] will inform my final reflections on what might productively constitute the creation and shared use of *visual* treatises as crucial contemporary philosophical and pedagogical instruments with respect to rethinking and recreating the spaces of personal and collective learning. To reiterate though, my focus in *The Question of Painting* is above all on how *Merleau-Ponty* navigated painterly territory and how his discoveries might have ongoing philosophical value for us today.

Before embarking on this journey though, I will like to pursue two further introductory routes into his philosophical project as a whole. First, taking an image-led approach in order to present my claims as vividly as possible, I will turn to a historical painting with which Merleau-Ponty was familiar, a late-sixteenth-century crucifixion scene by El Greco whose work and style he discussed in *The Structure of Behavior.* Merleau-Ponty did not write about this painting itself. Nonetheless, I explore it here for the ways in which it evokes in pictorial terms certain consistent features of the new philosophical territory that Merleau-Ponty was trying to enter using *his* chosen material: words. Significantly, and perhaps at first sight surprisingly given Merleau-Ponty's stated agnosticism, the painting in question is a religious work and I will make a case for treating not only its stylistic and compositional aspects, but also its subject matter, as paradigmatic. My rationale for taking this approach will become apparent, I hope, as my discussions of this painting unfold. However, I am entering somewhat contested territory here since Merleau-Ponty's reputed position regarding matters of a transcendental, metaphysical or theological nature is by no means settled. In my view, his writing clearly offers a critique of transcendental idealism, but is it the case that his philosophical interventions are resolutely non-metaphysical, thus non-theological, even anti-theological, in character? Certainly – as Diana Coole has pointed out in her 2010 essay 'The Inertia of Matter and the Generativity of Flesh' – when Merleau-Ponty was in the process of structuring what he called 'My plan' in the final working note appended to *The Visible and the Invisible* (dated March 1961), he wrote, emphatically, that his explorations of (I) The visible; (II) Nature and (III) Logos 'must be presented without any compromise with *humanism*, nor moreover with *naturalism*, nor finally with *theology*'.[54] What should we make of this? Two recent sets of debates associated with Merleau-Ponty's position regarding both transcendental idealism and the theological are also worth referencing. First, in his 2014 essay 'Is Merleau-Ponty's Position in *Phenomenology of Perception* a New Type of Transcendental Idealism?', Christopher Pollard questioned Sebastian Gardner's assertion, recorded in 'Merleau-Ponty's Transcendental Theory of Perception' of 2007, that 'in spite of his critique of "Kantianism," Merleau-Ponty's position comes out as a form of transcendental idealism that takes the perceptual processes of the lived body as the transcendental constituting condition for the possibility of experience'.[55] Second are Richard Kearney's essay 'Merleau-Ponty and the Sacramentality of the Flesh'[56] (upon which I will draw later on in this chapter) and Joseph S. O'Leary's 'Merleau-Ponty and Modernist Sacrificial Poetics: A Response to Richard Kearney',[57] both contributions to the book *Merleau-Ponty at the Limits of Art, Religion, and Perception*. While both texts argue for the reinvigoration of art and theology through the instigation of a renewed dialogue between them, O'Leary seems to support an anti-theological interpretation of the sacramental language that Merleau-Ponty frequently incorporated into his writing, as compared to Kearney's 'anatheistic' position, a non-dogmatic stance in which the dyad of belief and unbelief are taken to be suspended and in which, indeed, 'true belief' and 'non-belief' are found to intersect.[58] O'Leary, in any case, wrote as follows concerning the expressive habits of various modernist writers and painters when treating revelatory and transformative themes in their works: 'It is easy to see why Merleau-Ponty and artists themselves use a religious or quasi-religious terminology of sacrifice, sacrament, metamorphosis, and resurrection to name these phenomena.'[59] But, he added:

> Usually these are metaphors used without any theological intention, or even with the anti-theological intention of secularizing religious discourse by providing its purely this-worldly referent, though some Christian artists, such as Eliot in *Four Quartets*, attest to an intimate link between artistic creation and the religious quest. A phenomenologist would be well advised to bracket initially such religious associations, even practicing a 'methodological atheism', so as to let the inherent dynamic of the work of art come into view. Only then can one go on to ask about its possible

religious significance, which cannot simply be read off from the religious
jargon Merleau-Ponty or artists themselves sometimes use.[60]

Nonetheless, very specific theological terms *are* put to work in Merleau-
Ponty's writing. As such, theological territory, which is so often excluded
from the domain of the 'properly' philosophical, presents itself as one of
the limit-areas which, according to Semonovitch and deRoo, Merleau-Ponty
dared to enter and explore. Indeed, in the section of their introduction,
entitled 'Unlimiting Philosophy', they cite Merleau-Ponty's assertion that
'philosophy's center is everywhere, and its circumference nowhere'.[61]
  Secondly, I will consider various evaluations of the broad trajectory of
Merleau-Ponty's philosophical project. Here I will draw in part on 'An
Unpublished Text by Maurice Merleau-Ponty: A Prospectus of His Work'
from 1951–52. Written with respect to his candidacy to the Collège de
France – having taught at the University of Lyon between 1945 and 1948,
taught supplementary courses at the École Normale Supérieure between
1947 and 1949,[62] and, as indicated above, now holding the chair of child
psychology and pedagogy at the University of Paris, Sorbonne[63] – this was a
mid-career assessment of the important features of his work-to-date which
included two books, *The Structure of Behavior* and the *Phenomenology*,
and more than forty-five essays. Thirteen of these, which treated such
topics as aesthetics and ethics, politics, and the sciences of man, had been
republished in 1948 in the volume *Sens et non-sens* (*Sense and Non-
Sense*).[64] 'An Unpublished Text' also provides an intriguing indication of
the various directions in which he perceived his thought to be developing, a
topic to which I will return.[65]

Merleau-Ponty's trans-
dimensional investigations

In 1908, the Louvre in Paris acquired El Greco's imposing *Christ on the
Cross Adored by Donors* (Figure I.2). In it, the central figure of Christ is
stretched out in crucifixion. Lower down, to his right and left (where the
Virgin Mary and Saint John would traditionally have been positioned)
are half-length portraits of two unidentified men prayerfully gazing up at
him. One wears ecclesiastical garb and the other secular clothing. Created
in about 1590 for a side chapel in the convent of the Hieronymite nuns
in Toledo, Spain – one, if not both, of the men will almost certainly have
commissioned the painting – it is characteristic of the sixteenth-century
painter's now-iconic style which rendered the three figures simultaneously
as flattened *and* subtly pulled and twisted as if through coexistent times and
spaces. This flattening, pulling and twisting also applies to the swathes of
cloud that sweep across the painting's background, rapidly blotting out the

sun so that, in accordance with the biblical accounts, Christ's daytime death will be embedded in inexplicable, untimely darkness.[66]

It was an unsurprising purchase.[67] It is true that El Greco's extreme and idiosyncratic style, admired during his lifetime despite its uncommon character, had suffered from almost three centuries of disrepute under the auspices of what had been a predominantly academically oriented art establishment. But since about 1860 it had been making a comeback. Pioneering modern artists from Manet and Degas to Kandinsky and Picasso were great admirers,[68] and in 1931 the young French writer and critic Jean Cassou – later the first director of the National Museum of Modern Art (Musée National d'Art Moderne) in Paris – wrote a short book on this artist's work simply titled *Le Greco (El Greco)*. Cassou associated the rediscovery of El Greco with the work of such scholars as Manuel B. Cossio in Spain, and, in France, with Maurice Barrès' 1912 book *Greco ou le secret de Tolède* (*El Greco, or the Secret of Toledo*). Such investigations, he wrote, were 'eagerly followed up by artists and psychologists, who found in El Greco's art the assertion of a violently original personality, and a spiritual adventure pushed to its ultimate conclusion, qualities intensely interesting to both in their different fields of research'.[69] Cassou then presented a historically situated exploration of what he called El Greco's 'strangeness', a strangeness 'even carried to excess'.[70] During the later 1930s, Merleau-Ponty would consult Cassou's book while working on *The Structure of Behavior*. Indeed, Merleau-Ponty's first significant discussion of painting, which occurs towards the end of this book and underscores its central argument, convincingly challenged certain then-current positivistic readings of El Greco's style in which El Greco's originality was taken to be a mere symptom of physiological dysfunction. I will discuss this matter in the second chapter of this book.

Since Merleau-Ponty had lived in Paris since his youth, it is likely but not certain that he had viewed El Greco's crucifixion in situ at the Louvre. In any case, it was reproduced, albeit in black-and-white, among the numerous plates in Cassou's book. Within the context of this introduction, the painting is worth reflecting on at length because, alongside its intrinsic points of interest, the territories opened up by its specificities of style and subject matter are remarkably congruent with key aspects of the reconfigured philosophical terrain Merleau-Ponty was trying to articulate, in different ways, throughout his career.

First, the strange spatialities and temporalities displayed in El Greco's painting present a tangible as well as metaphorical sense of the challenging perceptually grounded philosophical possibilities Merleau-Ponty was trying to activate. At issue in the painting is a complex sense of space whose difficult but nonetheless phenomenologically *robust* harmonies and hospitalities are at odds with the rationalized painterly spaces proposed by earlier fifteenth- and then-contemporary sixteenth-century advocates of linear perspective. Indeed, when tracking El Greco's journey from Crete to Spain via Cyprus, Venice and Rome, Cassou contrasted El Greco's engagement with space with

that of the Renaissance and Mannerist masters he had come into contact with –
Titian and Tintoretto in Venice, for instance, and Michelangelo in Rome –
and later of those associated with the baroque. Indeed, Cassou went so far
as to say that El Greco was consistently seeking to escape that space which
'by a tremendous effort the Renaissance painters had finally conquered and
established'.[71] Presumably, El Greco regarded it as inhospitable to his own
pictorial and intellectual purposes:

> The Renaissance and Baroque painters, being masters of spatial
> composition, could deploy their forms in space with sufficient ease to
> allow them a huge field of action. Greco, the Byzantine, abjured space
> and rejected it with violence. ... When he twisted and elongated his forms
> he did so in order to pull them out of space, which he could express only
> at the moment of breaking away from it.[72]

With Cassou, then, refusal and escape were emphasized. By contrast, I think
that Merleau-Ponty perceived the same painterly effort as having more to
do with the creation of *entrances into* spatialities that were alternate to
those Renaissance solutions. But these spaces are difficult to apprehend and
navigate intellectually. Not surprisingly, therefore, until the early twentieth
century Western pictorial traditions would continue to be dominated by the
classical theorems of Euclidean geometry, also taken up by Cartesian and
much post-Cartesian thought. Today, despite well-established theoretical
and empirical evidence to the contrary, the ongoing persuasiveness of these
classical ideas is remarkable. Not only do they shape and indeed homogenize
the look and feel of our contemporary mass-culture image-worlds, as the
philosopher and psychologist Steven M. Rosen (author of the 2006 book
Topologies of the Flesh) has noted, they also often obstruct debates and
developments where advanced research and thought are concerned – even
within the contemporary physical sciences. In his 2013 essay, 'Bridging
the "Two Cultures": Merleau-Ponty and the Crisis in Modern Physics', he
argued for the ongoing importance of Merleau-Ponty's counter-Euclidean
and counter-Cartesian perspectives, given that contemporary physics –
as he saw it – 'in unquestioningly adhering to the classical ontology, is hard
put to deal with the nonlinearities and paradoxes of the phenomena it
encounters'.[73] The 'two cultures' at issue, originally coined by the scientist and
novelist C. P. Snow in his 1959 Rede Lecture at Cambridge University, refer
to the humanities on the one hand and the sciences on the other. Rosen then
turned to a discussion of Merleau-Ponty's teaching, specifically his 1956–57
Collège de France course on Nature, and certain portions of *The Visible
and the Invisible*, remarking that 'Merleau-Ponty well understood how the
phenomena of modern physics uniquely defy the dualisms, objectifications, and
idealizations of Cartesian thought, and how this necessitates a reorientation
of physics' philosophical foundations'.[74] In the remainder of his essay, Rosen
proposed a Merleau-Ponty-inspired phenomenological physics with the

capacity to acknowledge and engage with these difficult phenomena. This would be achieved by enabling an encounter between 'the "soft" intimations of phenomenology and the "hard" facts of physics. Might it be possible', he asked, 'to "soften" physics and "harden" phenomenology in a manner that would bridge the gap between these seemingly irreconcilable endeavours, these "two cultures"?'[75] Rosen's recruitment of Merleau-Ponty is timely and apt. Although it is worth adding that Merleau-Ponty's engagement with nonlinearity, paradox and openness as a matter of *ontological* as well as phenomenological interest may well have represented a shift of perspective and emphasis in his thinking during the 1950s. For in 'An Unpublished Text', written at the beginning of that decade (and to which I will return in more detail shortly), when making a case for the particular capacity of lived perception to accommodate the ambiguous dynamics of lived experience, he had presented 'perceived things' and 'geometrical objects' as necessarily spatially at odds with one another. In other words, in this respect, we see Merleau-Ponty himself thinking oppositionally:

> We find that perceived things, unlike geometrical objects, are not bounded entities whose laws of construction we possess a priori, but that they are open, inexhaustible systems which we recognise through a certain style of development, although we are never able, in principle, to explore them entirely, and even though they never give us more than profiles and perspectival views of themselves.[76]

Clearly, Merleau-Ponty had in mind not only geometric objects of the kind formulated within the Euclidean system but also the definitive forms of knowledge to which they purportedly give access. Nonetheless an assumption of irreconcilability is at issue between the evidences of perception and geometry, between these two systems of things or, more broadly, between those two cultures cited by Rosen and Snow. Today, though, we know that outside of Euclidean logics certain *geometrical* objects, too, may present themselves as paradoxically structured, exhibiting an order that is not periodic in that it lacks translational symmetry. The discovery in 1984 of quasiperiodic crystals (quasicrystals) with their 'forbidden symmetries' provides an intriguing instance of this. But Merleau-Ponty's point is clear. Indeed, already in his early writing we discover the idea that even if classical geometry is theorized as a necessarily closed system, it may not always present itself to us or be engaged with as such. Both in the *Phenomenology* and in 'Cézanne's Doubt' he insisted that even during the High Renaissance, when the use of classical linear perspective was at its height, the greatest works were those operating right at the limits of this system, as if calling its ultimate authority into question – here we have an instance of the flexibility of painterly interrogation and navigation coming to the fore. Certainly, he insisted that linear perspective was only one of several possible structures according to which the world that is opened up through the operations of sight might be experienced, understood and presented, that is, symbolized.

El Greco's painting – to return to it – presents not only a spatial but also a *temporal* scene that is open and ambiguous: at once in and out of time; of its time, and not of its time. Such a multivalent temporality Merleau-Ponty would also explicitly assign to our experiences of painting(s) in general. For him, all paintings, regardless of their age, materiality and style, are more or less porous temporal as well as spatial structures. From an expressive point of view, therefore, each painting could be regarded as an interplay of marks, gestures and meanings that are always at once falling short of, and exceeding, themselves. This phenomenon he also regarded as fundamental to the structures of life itself, of perception and feeling, and also of knowledge and knowledge claims. Clearly – and as I will show in later chapters – whether applied to painting or to life, this was an account that resisted the linear or causal developmental logics of then-conventional histories and biographies. Instead, it was predicated upon the understanding that the primary significance of our creations or discoveries is not tied to the degree to which they supersede existing knowledge but has more to do with the degree to which they bring into play, keep in play, and continue to engage, critically and otherwise, with the widest possible range of existential realities. More often than not, therefore, the questions fuelling these activities may lead not to definitive answers but to what Merleau-Ponty referred to in the *Phenomenology* as a 'kind of attentiveness and wonder'.[77] Merleau-Ponty expressed his position regarding the being of painting most emphatically in the concluding paragraph of the late essay 'Eye and Mind'. He began by stating that no painting may ever definitively be regarded as '*the* painting', and no work ever be regarded as 'absolutely completed and done with'.[78] A little later he restated this point: 'If creations are not a possession, it is not only that, like all things, they pass away; it is also that they have almost all their life still before them.'[79] Despite these fluidities and sense of ongoing incompleteness however, paintings are nonetheless distinguishable relational entities in which visual and material structures operate in and upon one another according to often surprising yet coherent logics of affinity and difference. He wrote evocatively of the ways in which 'still each creation changes, alters, enlightens, deepens, confirms, exalts, re-creates, or creates in advance all the others'.[80] An analogous sensibility may be found in the somewhat earlier 'The Institution of a Work of Art'. Here, Merleau-Ponty wrote that 'institution of a work, like the institution of a love, [intends a] sense as open sense, which develops by means of proliferation, by curves, decentering and recentering, zigzag, ambiguous passage, with a sort of identity between the whole and parts, the beginning and end'.[81] Interestingly, with Merleau-Ponty's evocation of these complex movements, not only do the strange trajectories of El Greco's style come to mind but also the temporal traditions surrounding the central subject matter of the Louvre painting: namely Christ.

In the biblical sources that provide the context for El Greco's crucifixion, Christ – who is also defined as 'Love Incarnate' and as the 'eternal Word made flesh'[82] – is presented as having sacrificed himself as a once-and-for-all sin-offering[83] so that human beings – in different measure always both the perpetrators and the victims of sin, and of long-embedded structures of unrighteousness and injustice that ensnare and entrap – might be empowered both to receive and to release divine forgiveness and in this way pass from spiritual death to life: 'For God so loved the world that he gave his one and only Son, that whoever believes in him shall not perish but have eternal life.'[84] Significantly though, Christ is presented not only as having performed this substitutionary act within historical time,[85] in around 33 CE and in a still-identifiable geographical location. He is also 'the [sacrificial] lamb that was slain from the creation of the world'.[86] In other words, in this scenario the mechanism of divine self-sacrifice was instituted by God *before* human beings had themselves been created. Divine self-sacrifice and salvation were built into God's system from *before* the beginning. This is precisely why Christ directed his followers to emulate him by likewise embodying and extending an everyday economy of grace and faith fuelled by forgiveness and self-forgiveness (the cancellation of all literal and metaphorical debts) and by extravagantly favouring the needs of others above their own. Furthermore, where this issue of strange temporalities is concerned, the legacy of Christ's crucifixion, as both a historical and an ahistorical event, is presented in the scriptures as capable of dramatic reactivation – and indeed retro-activation – in all manner of contexts, including the most sceptical, hostile or indifferent. Such activation is presented as opening up previously sealed-up access points to God, and to life as God intended it. Experiences of the present, memories of the past and expectations of the future may thus be resituated and reshaped. Crucially, then, also exemplified in El Greco's biblically inspired painting is a view of temporality in which modern notions of linear progression, causality and teleology are pre-challenged, and in which 'the new' is not necessarily taken to supersede and invalidate 'the old' just because it is new. It is a mindset in which forms of knowledge or deposits of value that may have become culturally discredited are experienced as reasserting themselves, often offering new inroads into otherwise intransigent problems. One such account of reactivation lies at the heart of Cassou's chronological but non-linear account of the fecundity of El Greco's work; its perceived cultural relevance both in his own day *and* with the emergence of 'modern' art in the nineteenth century. And all of this despite the fact that even at the point of its creation, according to Cassou, El Greco's work proliferated an 'outdated' Byzantinism. In Merleau-Ponty's writing, too, philosophically discredited sources of insight are repeatedly brought to prominence enabling fresh philosophical trajectories to emerge.

Finally, also of interest at this point is how Merleau-Ponty's perspectives about the non-linear temporality of art – in which 'still each creation changes, alters, enlightens, deepens, confirms, exalts, re-creates, or creates in advance all the others'[87] – might compare with certain twenty-first-century artistic and curatorial investigations of similarly complex temporalities, their possible meanings and the challenges posed by them. Here, by way of just one recent example, the Museum of Modern Art, New York's 2014–15 exhibition *The Forever Now: Contemporary Painting in an Atemporal World* might usefully be brought into play.

The Forever Now featured over one hundred works by seventeen culturally diverse albeit mainly American contemporary artists: Richard Aldrich, Joe Bradley, Kerstin Brätsch, Matt Connors, Michaela Eichwald, Nicole Eisenman, Mark Grotjahn, Charline von Heyl (see Figure I.8), Rashid Johnson (see Figure I.7), Julie Mehretu, Dianna Molzan, Oscar Murillo, Laura Owens, Amy Sillman, Josh Smith, Mary Weatherford and Michael Williams.[88] Collectively, the paintings on show, all created between 2006 and 2014, traversed a wide range of painterly styles. Significantly, though, they were stylistically eclectic at an individual level too. This was the case not only with the more overtly appropriationist pieces in the exhibition, by Murillo, Sillman or Williams for instance, but also with less immediately obvious examples such as Connors' bold geometric abstractions, Weatherford's lyrical interplays of stained canvas and neon, the complex gestural compositions created by Eichwald, Johnson and Mehretu, and Eisenman's primal-yet-contemporary mask-like 'portraits'. Indeed, within the context of this exhibition, each work was identified as a differently composed retrieval of 'styles, subjects, motifs, materials, strategies and ideas from an array of periods on the art-historical timeline'.[89] Crucially though – and this accounts for the exhibition curator Laura Hoptman's adoption of the term atemporality from the writing of William Gibson – these retrievals were presented in explicit contrast with both modern and postmodern forms of assemblage or pastiche as those have most commonly been theorized, since they involved neither a quest for artistically or intellectually original, innovative or progressive outcomes, nor an overt engagement in critique, nor even the conveyance of irony or nostalgia. At issue instead was what Hoptman referred to in her catalogue essay as 'a super-charged art historicism ... [that] is closest to a *connoisseurship* of boundless information, a picking and choosing of elements of the past to resolve a problem or a task at hand'.[90] For Hoptman, following Gibson, all of the paintings constituted different expressions of the fact that due to the aggregational character of today's post-internet era – in which her chosen artists and indeed most of us in the developed and developing world are variously immersed – all of this information is regarded as coexistent, regardless of its actual historical or indeed geographic origins and references. At issue is a proliferation of information that is not only deemed to have lost its ties with this or that past, but also cannot be seen to have purchase on a supposed present. Hoptman's use of the term atemporality seems to describe a milieu in which not only a linear, teleological notion of time has ceased to exist but also where time itself may no longer be operative. As she put it in the opening lines of her

FIGURE 1.7 *Rashid Johnson,* Cosmic Slop 'The Berlin Conference', 2011, *black soap, wax, 184.2 × 245.11 × 5.1 cm.* © *Rashid Johnson. Courtesy of the artist and Hauser & Wirth. Photo: Martin Parsekian.*

FIGURE I.8 *Charline von Heyl,* The Colour Out of Space, *2013, acrylic and oil on canvas, 209.6 × 182.9 cm. Courtesy of the artist and Petzel, New York.*

essay, the differently visualized and materialized paintings on show were all responses to a 'cultural moment at the beginning of this new millennium' characterized by 'the inability – or perhaps the refusal – of a great many of our cultural artefacts to define the times in which we live'.[91] She described this as 'an unsettling and wholly unique phenomenon in Western culture' adding that 'it should come as no surprise that it was first identified by a science-fiction writer – Gibson – who in 2003 used the word *atemporality* to describe a new and strange state of the world in which, courtesy of the internet, all eras seem to exist at once'.[92] She continued: 'Since that time, atemporality has been observed in literature, popular music, and fashion, and subsequently called many different names, including *retromania, hauntology, presentism*, and *super-hybridity*.'[93]

How then might Merleau-Ponty's 'pre-internet age' ideas about spatiality, temporality, and the questions of painting compare? One point of difference might be that Hoptman's theorizations seemed to present *The Forever Now*'s painterly practices as involved in a form of escape from time, much as Cassou described the art of El Greco as an escape from space. Indeed, Hoptman went on to define time as having become spatialized. At first sight, the image she presented of this in her essay was homogeneous and unobstructed: 'Instead of an information superhighway', she wrote, 'we can picture the eternal present as an endlessly flat surface with vistas in every direction – not unlike the surface of a painting.'[94] While her words speak of far-showing and far-seeing, in actuality such surfaces are never endlessly flat, neither the 'bare' canvas of a not-yet-embarked-upon project nor indeed the myriad differently worked actual surfaces on show in *The Forever Now*. At issue is always a wealth of layered textures and references embedded within different ecologies of revelation and hiddenness. And while in a *conceptually* abstract sense it may be possible for everything in a painting to be given at once, it can never be experienced as such from a phenomenological perspective or from the perspective of making. In Merleau-Ponty's writing, therefore, the emphasis was first on how, in lived perception-and-thought, temporality and spatiality are experienced as proliferating, intertwining, colliding, entering into prominence and receding from it in ever-varied ways. Secondly, he was interested in structures of possibility as well as limitation, and the varied trajectories that are being proffered within and by these scenarios; how processes of inhabitation, navigation, communication and forms of renewal are proposed and worked through. It is precisely such rich terrain that is opened up by the works in *The Forever Now* themselves. Take, for instance, the most 'abstract' or 'minimal' works in the exhibition, Rashid Johnson's five panoramically scaled *Cosmic Slop* paintings, which are nonetheless replete with cultural as well as art-historical associations. Part of a large series, in each instance a thick ground composed not of traditional canvas but of African black soap and wax is scored and scratched, in some cases with a delicacy that recalls the lyrical gestures of a Cy Twombly, in other instances with violent abandon – Hoptman remarked that *Cosmic Slop: 'The Berlin Conference'* of 2011 (Figure I.7) 'looks as if it was drawn with a sword rather than a paintbrush handle'.[95] But what are we to make of those marks? Are they expressions of anger and aggression, a fighting back? – the Berlin Conference was a meeting of major European powers held in that city during 1884–85 at which their respective claims to territory in Africa were negotiated and formalized. Is Johnson referencing the whipped and slashed bodies of slaves? Are these the desperate clawings of those seeking freedom from incarceration? Or all of these and more? Are there also other, anarchically productive energies at play? *Cosmic Slop*, incidentally, is also the name of a studio album released by George Clinton's funk band Funkadelic in 1973 and refers to a fictional dance. At first sight Johnson's and Clinton's aesthetics couldn't be further apart but as Johnson has explained in interview: 'I like the idea that this dance has something to do with the performance of making a painting. When I make these works in the studio, I move around them on the floor, on the wall, back on the floor, and I realize the movement ends up becoming something like a dance that the painting comes out of.'[96] Significantly too, the African black soap of Johnson's ground speaks of cleansing and restoration: originating in Ghana and made from the ash of local plants and barks – plantain, cocoa pods, palm tree leaves and shea tree bark – mixed with water and various plant oils, it is reputed to have significant healing properties and to be especially beneficial for delicate, sensitive and irritated skin. Certainly, as with Johnson's large-scale sculptural installations (Figure 5.4) which again incorporate culturally loaded items relating to black domestic and popular culture and black history, these paintings, through their complex materiality, might also be described as amalgamations of compressed and expressed emotion, with anxiety, and its urgent resolution, often looming large. Also of note where questions of making and meaning are concerned are the ways in which various dualisms are disrupted, not only those associated with wounding and healing as just described, but also, at a fundamental level, between figure and ground, both of which are presented as having been formed together and as being in ongoing dialogue. Here too questions seem to be at issue, surely, regarding conditions of ending and starting over; Johnson's dark, monochromatic surfaces cannot but remind us of such proto-abstract works as Kazimir Malevich's iconic *Black Square* of 1915 or Ad Reinhardt's aforementioned 'black', or 'ultimate' paintings from the 1960s. Johnson's works, then, are as intensely art historical and intellectual as they are emotive.

At this point, we might also turn to Charline von Heyl's expansive canvases. Not only do they seem to be places of encounter between diverse visual and formal entities – places where their associated sensibilities and histories might get acquainted. Again, there is also a profound sense of ontological uncertainty about where 'ground' finishes and 'figure' or 'figuration' begins. In *The Colour Out of Space* of 2013, for instance (Figure I.8), the monochromatic portions look as if they have been transferred there, as if von Heyl's canvas had once been lying somewhere, long forgotten, absorbing into itself dust, dirt and traces of debris. Other marks, such as the four hard-edged, black-and-white geometric forms in the painting's upper left-hand section, have the appearance of being intentionally conceived and positioned additions. By contrast, an only partially completed, circular, diagrammatic structure somewhat lower down and to the right seems to be a crystallization of the dark, vague markings surrounding it. Finally, an extraordinary cluster of swirling pastel pinks, blues, ochres, greys, blacks and whites might be growing on the painting's surface like an organic, ornamental encrustation. Here, it seems, are many different ways in which visual things – and Hoptman records von Heyl as saying that 'everything exists as image'[97] – might come to, or be brought to, appearance.

And now a further remark regarding Hoptman's theorization of *The Forever Now* since it both connects and contrasts with further themes in El Greco's painting and in Merleau-Ponty's thought. When searching for the right concepts and terminology to convey the sense of restorative energy associated with the 'atemporal' practices of pastiche embodied in her chosen works – the ways in which they might be described as raising the dead – she turned not to religious language, as she might have done, but to a zombie metaphysics in which a clear distinction between what is dead and what is alive is no longer operative: 'The undead are the perfect embodiments of the atemporal', she wrote.[98] As such, she categorized von Heyl, along with Eichwald, Weatherford, Mehretu and others, as reanimators of forms and ideas associated with past traditions. Despite von Heyl's 'deliberately open references' Hoptman wrote that her work nevertheless 'conjures the existential *Weltschmetz* of Sartrean Europe with bold, Informal calligraphies surrounded by tenebrous, Wolsian lines (see Figure 3.2) layered atop biomorphic shapes redolent of the age of nuclear anxiety'.[99] Johnson, due to the performativity of his practice, she categorized as a re-enactor. 'Re-enactment', she wrote, 'is another strategy under the rubric of zombie painting. … Though both reanimators and reenactors raise the dead, it is only the latter who don another's skin, allowing their gestures to propel a hollow body to life.'[100] As such, these works are also opening up embodied mind- and memory-scapes in ways that are aligned not only with Merleau-Pontean sensibilities, but also with the enlarged sense of insight *and* mystery that contemporary research in neuroscience and neuroaesthetics is beginning to articulate.[101] Here, arguably, rather than – or as well as – making a case for 'the biological basis for aesthetic experience', an argument for 'the aesthetic basis for biological functioning' might equally be evidenced,[102] the latter being the territory that these paintings and Merleau-Ponty's project differently enter and explore. I might add that my own organically evolving, visual-cultural-philosophical method also finds its home here, with its combinations of description, analysis, argumentation, possibly unanticipated juxtapositions, densities and detours.

And this brings me to my next point. Within this exhibition's particular engagement with painting, temporality and thought – and although phenomenological sources are by no means referenced – we discover affinities with the questions lying at the heart of *The Question of Painting*: What kinds of thinking, learning, knowing and indeed relations are possible once traditional teleological, as well as dualistic, infrastructures for thought have been abandoned and alternatives sought? For despite *The Forever Now*'s stated acriticality it was nonetheless positioned as an intellectual project and Hoptman described the artists she had brought together as having contributed to its artistic and intellectual development by means of their art-making and through debates. Of particular interest to me is the fact that Hoptman described the works, and the working methods exemplified by these artists, as painterly opportunities to 'roam around'[103] in an (over)-abundant informational and stylistic territory. In this regard, Hoptman cited Connor who had described his own multi-referential abstract works in terms of 'a redirection of artistic inquiry from strictly forward moving into a kind of super-branched-out questioning'.[104] Hoptman went on to associate this with what we might call a laissez-faire ethics grounded in a kind of freedom of-and-or-from use, attribution and interpretation where the work of others is concerned. She cited Murillo: 'We have everything available and we can just use what's there and around, but not feel concerned by it.'[105] Hoptman continued:

> Murillo is not saying that there are no stakes involved in borrowing from the freighted language of Euro-American modernism. Rather he is reminding those of us with long memories of the opening salvo of postmodern critique: that the stakes have irrevocably changed. The transfer of styles, of motifs, of ideas, from a historical context to the present one does not reinforce their obsolescence. In fact, the opposite occurs. In the atemporal present, they are resurrected and made newly relevant. At this moment in time we can look back at the condition of postmodernism and say, 'Yup, that happened.' And then we can observe, 'Now, there's this.'[106]

She added:

> A work of art that refutes the possibility of chronological classification offers a dramatic challenge to the structure that disciplines like art history enforce – the great ladder-like narrative of cultural progress that is so dependent upon the idea of the new superseding the old in a movement simultaneously forward and upward.[107]

What are we to make of all of this with respect to the issue of painting as/ and thought? Given that the art-making in *The Forever Now* is presented as operating in a non-critical, non-distancing connoisseurial mode,[108] must it therefore be seen as operating in a milieu where visual and material forms are proliferating but where thought itself, as this is generally understood, has either ceased or not yet begun? Should we forge a connection between Hoptman's reference to roaming around and Merleau-Ponty's problematization, in 'The War has Taken Place', of those perceptually and politically unaware and perhaps even unwittingly indifferent involvements in 'walking trips and youth hostels' which were 'as self-evident as the earth itself – or so we thought?'[109] More generally, do the attitudes described with respect to the production, and by extension the viewing, of these paintings smack of the political redundancy and irrelevance with which the practice of painting in general has repeatedly been charged over the last one hundred years or so? At best, is this roaming around, this picking up and repositioning or recomposing without any clear goal in mind, a more or less empty gesture, a contemporary manifestation of the French idiom, 'bête comme un peintre' (stupid as a painter)[110] to which Marcel Duchamp famously sought to react by means of his conceptualism? Duchamp, of course, was reacting above all to the then still normative associations of art-making or image-making with imitation and illusionism.

It will come as no surprise that my response is at once a 'yes' and a 'no' and that I see this response not as paradoxically problematic but as paradoxically productive. But in order to justify this 'yes-and-no', the question of what we might mean by thought, and where and how we understand it to occur, must be extended outside of the still-conventional boundaries within which it has become encased. As I hope I have already begun to show, Merleau-Ponty's writing plays a crucial role in this regard. Certainly though, returning to that notion of painterly roaming around with respect to the working methods of the artists exhibiting in *The Forever Now*, one great contrast at issue with the pre-war activity of vacationing described by Merleau-Ponty is that, far from being escapist in a perceptual and political sense, this contemporary work may be regarded as a great, collective venture of cultural retrieval and creation – sometimes carried out with seemingly furious speed (Grothahn, Murillo), sometimes through the use of a schematic shorthand (Bradley), sometimes obsessively (Mehretu, Molzan) and sometimes slowly and with deliberation (Sillman has spoken about the long, slow processes of making, looking, thinking and waiting that are involved as she builds up her canvases).[111] Arguably at issue in each case is an effort at expanding our understanding of, and engagement with, being in its multiple and always to some extent overlooked manifestations. New and varied infrastructures *for* thought are being constructed in which, recalling Hoptman's references to the connoisseurial, the immediate challenge is not to judge, but to see, to become immersed, and to do so in a way that is heartfelt even if not always experienced as entirely pleasurable. Such a sensibility was in play in both Johnson's and von Heyl's works. And so I turn to the next set of observations I wish to make about key constancies in Merleau-Ponty's writing, still using El Greco's Louvre crucifixion as a point of reference.

An incarnational logic

The subject matter of El Greco's painting also helps turn our attention towards a further characteristic of Merleau-Ponty's thought, one that is inextricably connected with the spatial and temporal issues just discussed. For the figure of Christ – understood as the eternal (or atemporal) God in the form of man; the eternal (or atemporal) 'Word made flesh' – may also be regarded as synonymous with the *incarnational* logic that is consistently at the heart of Merleau-Ponty's writing. It is also at the heart of *his* understanding of the nature, methods and manifestations of valid philosophical thought. My focus in this book is on Merleau-Ponty's repeated recourse to *painterly* paradigms to bring this profoundly non-dualistic self-positioning to expression. At this point, however – returning to Kearney's observations referenced earlier – it is important to note that despite Merleau-Ponty's religious agnosticism as an adult he repeatedly 'chose to describe his phenomenology of the sensible body in sacramental language'.[112] Here I am again drawing on Kearney's 2010 essay 'Merleau-Ponty and the Sacramentality of the Flesh', the 'flesh' being a term Merleau-Ponty developed in his late writing to describe the trans- and intra-corporeal modes of lived being he was prioritizing. Kearney presented this sacramental logic as prefigured in the thought of Edmund Husserl, notably in Husserl's *Ideas Part II* of 1913 with its theorizations of the 'living body' (*das Leib*). As Kearney put it, against the entrenchments of Western metaphysics which, since Plato, had largely ignored non-dualistic notions of incarnate, or embodied, thought with its accompanying complexities and ambiguities, 'it would take Edmund Husserl and the phenomenological revolution to bring philosophy back to the experience of "sacramental flesh," that is, the possibility of acknowledging Spirit in our prereflective lived experience'.[113] Then, with respect to *Merleau-Ponty*'s use of sacramental language, and by way of example, Kearney referenced a telling description of sense experience – specifically hearing and seeing – found in the *Phenomenology*. In order to clarify the nature of the transaction at issue here, Merleau-Ponty had referred to the Christian sacrament of Holy Communion and to the Roman Catholic doctrine of transubstantiation according to which ordinary bread and wine (the elements central to this sacrament), once they have been consecrated by the priest, are mystically transformed into the real body and real blood of Christ and are consumed as such by the faithful. Merleau-Ponty's words are worth citing at some length.

> I give ear, or look, in the expectation of a sensation, and suddenly the sensible takes possession of my ear or my gaze, and I surrender a part of my body, even my whole body, to this particular manner of vibrating and filling space known as blue or red. Just as the sacrament not only symbolizes, in sensible species, an operation of Grace, but is also the

real presence of God, which it causes to occupy a fragment of space and communicates to those who eat of the consecrated bread, provided that they are inwardly prepared, in the same way the sensible has not only a motor and vital significance, but is nothing other than a certain way of being in the world suggested to us from some point in space, and seized and acted upon by our body, provided that it is capable of doing so, so that sensation is literally a form of communion.[114]

As it turns out, the reversals at issue here – 'I give ear, or look, in the expectation of a sensation, and suddenly the sensible takes possession of my ear or my gaze' – are ones that Merleau-Ponty also found recorded, again and again, in the written testimonies of the painters he was drawn to with respect to their embodied experiences of perceiving and painting. Interestingly, too, remaining with this theme of communion, it was precisely the performance of this sacrament that provided the original context of display for the El Greco crucifixion. For this large painting, measuring 2.48 m × 1.80 m, was created to hang behind and above the altar of a side chapel in the Hieronymite convent where the Eucharist was regularly enacted in commemoration of Christ's death and subsequent resurrection. In other words, the original staging of this painting opened up a doubled scenario: the imminent transformation from death to life that is heralded by the subject matter of El Greco's painting was made corporeally available to those participating in the Eucharist by means of another transformation, namely, the mystery of transubstantiation. This ancient idea that ordinary substances, once consecrated, might be perceived and consumed as now also having become wholly divine, operates like a materialized, literalized metaphor – X *really is* Y – and can be received as such; the symbolic and the real are experienced as nested one within the other. Of course, this makes no sense to minds schooled solely by rationalism and old-fashioned materialism. But it was entirely relatable then, and remains so, to those whom Merleau-Ponty would describe as having allowed themselves to become appropriately prepared and attuned. For at the core of his phenomenological philosophy was the call to cultivate a perceptual, that is, intellectual as well as sensuous receptivity to everyday instances of transformative potential. As was seen earlier, in Villoro's testimony, it was this that made his philosophy existentially viable. Indeed, it was the role of philosophical questioning, as Merleau-Ponty saw it, to facilitate such encounters. As already indicated, he regarded painters – and painterly interrogation – to be particularly attuned to these phenomena, capable not only of inhabiting them but also of making them visually and materially available to others. The phenomena of exchange at issue – which he insisted were not exceptional occurrences but are so fundamentally embedded within everyday perceptual life that we are generally unaware of them – are dramatized by the practice of painting. They are writ large and brought to our attention, including our critical attention. He emphasized this last point in 'The Institution of a Work of Art'. On the one hand, he insisted that acts of painting are neither governed by chance nor conducted with the pre-knowledge of what is being done and where these efforts will lead.[115] As such, as he put it in a later set of notes, paintings may be experienced as partaking in what he called a 'subterranean logic'.[116] But on the other hand – and no matter how personal, idiosyncratic or indeed apparently inconclusive a painter's immersion within this logic might be – this was by no means an internalist or esoteric activity. On the contrary, and in contrast with our everyday, non-reflexive, perceptual ways of being, art-making, he wrote, 'is usually a conscious, deliberate relation to public history'.[117] Here, consciousness must again be understood as embodied, situated consciousness. Indeed, it was precisely this broad and embedded relationality that Merleau-Ponty associated with the term 'institution' as explored in his Institution in Personal and Public History course. In contrast with the Kantian notion of 'constitution' ('the constituted depends entirely on the me who constitutes'[118]) as well as with 'constitution' as it was variously used by Husserl ('even if we grant that certain of the objects are "never completely" constituted (Husserl), they are at each moment the exact reflection of the acts and powers of consciousness'[119]), institution for Merleau-Ponty was an ambiguously located, inter- or intra-corporeal phenomenon. As Lefort put it in the 'Foreword' to Institution and Passivity, it has a doubled meaning. It is that which 'provides a beginning' and it is 'a state of the thing established, for example, the state of being social, political, or juridical'[120] – and here I cannot help but find an analogy in the extraordinarily weighty-but-still-formative socio-political presence of Rashid Johnson's African black soap and wax paintings with their evocative proto-calligraphy. With respect to the crucial gaps and fissures, the asymmetries, at the heart of institution in both of its modes, Merleau-Ponty wrote, beautifully, that

> if the subject were instituting, and not constituting, we would understand … that the subject is not instantaneous and that the other person is not merely the negative of myself. … An instituting subject is able to coexist with another because the instituted is not the immediate reflection of the activity of the former and can be taken up by himself or by others without a total re-creation being at issue. *Thus the instituted exists between others and myself, between me and myself, like a hinge, the consequence and the guarantee of our belonging to one self-same world.*[121]

Where Merleau-Pontean notions of institution are concerned, therefore, sequences of dispossession are at issue and these are also intrinsic to his incarnational understanding of perception, thought and communication. As I will show, these three are understood as vitally interconnected in Merleau-Ponty's writing as a whole. The receptivity and the transformations that are central to the institution rather than constitution of knowledge, for instance, testify to what we might call a sacrificial logic necessitating surrender of certain culturally or personally sedimented, carefully constructed, or cherished, understandings of ourselves and all that we regard as belonging to us. Again, this is precisely the sensibility that is portrayed in El Greco's crucifixion. Here, thematically and compositionally, self-dispossession is presented as the fundamental characteristic of life itself which, in the Christian tradition, is not a conceptually abstract or impersonal force but, precisely, love, this being another designation for Christ. Indeed, in Merleau-Ponty's words, cited earlier, analogous connections were made: 'Institution of a work, like the institution of a love, [intends a] sense as open sense, which develops by means of proliferation, by curves, decentering and recentering, zigzag, ambiguous passage, with a sort of identity between the whole and parts, the beginning and end.'[122] These words which, as already noted, seem almost literally to evoke the compositional dynamics of El Greco's work also remind us that just as crucifixion precedes resurrection, so self-dispossession is both a risk and the prerequisite for change and enlargement – of a particular kind. For at issue is an understanding of enlargement that is uncompromisingly at odds with the various forms of hubris, including so-called Faustean and Promethean impulses, that have asserted themselves philosophically as well as politically and personally throughout history.[123] Observe, by contrast, the utter vulnerability of Christ's outstretched and abandoned, that is, self-forgetting, bodily gesture of embrace – an embrace freely offered regardless of consequence.

All in all, therefore, Merleau-Ponty's mid-twentieth-century notions of materialized, incarnate thought beg comparison not only with historically located theological models aimed at resisting egocentricity and hubris but also with the recent non-ego-centric (or non-subject-centred) modes of thought that are gaining increasing philosophical respectability. I am thinking, of course, of the burgeoning scholarship that is associated with the so-called new materialisms, as well as, somewhat differently, with Speculative Realism and Object-Oriented Ontology. It is not the aim of this book overtly to pursue such comparisons, nor to tease out what might be taken to be fundamental irreconcilabilities. This complex territory requires focused interrogation in its own right. But given the various criticisms of phenomenology that characterize both Speculative Realism and Object-Oriented Ontology – for instance, Graham Harman's claim, contra his own championing of 'inanimate relations', that phenomenology remains 'too attached to human being as the centerpiece of philosophy', or his critique of phenomenology's prioritization of 'sensuous' rather than 'real' objects[124] – it is worth making the following observation. As already indicated, Merleau-Ponty's thought is perceptually grounded and therefore profoundly and unapologetically relational ('we are through and through compounded of relationships with the world'[125]). Furthermore, what it means to operate humanly and politically and ethically remain crucial throughout. Certainly Merleau-Ponty's ongoing concern, as expressed during the early 1950s, was with 'the general problem of human interrelations'.[126] But the traditional philosophical idea of the human being as subject was by no means at the heart of his thinking. Phenomenologically speaking there are no isolable subjects,[127] or indeed isolable objects. Nor, finally, was the notion of intersubjectivity a central point of focus. This traditionally grounded terminology did recur particularly in Merleau-Ponty's earlier writing. But I think it is fair to say that this usage was testament to his ongoing struggles with and against the traditional vocabulary of philosophy; in his quest to communicate his own thinking as clearly as possible he repeatedly found himself simultaneously using and redefining traditional philosophical terms – a point to which I will return in this book. Rather, as already indicated, more accurately at issue were innumerable inter- and intra-corporeal infrastructures and entanglements where the world, in which we ourselves are already embedded, is never stripped of 'its opacity and its transcendence'.[128] This was a recurrent albeit differently articulated theme in his writing as a whole. It was embedded into the logics of *The Structure of Behavior* as I will show. It is also already emphasized in the 'Preface' to the *Phenomenology* when, for instance, Merleau-Ponty contrasted the experiences of the world's facticity that are opened up by phenomenology with the impoverished perspectives that lie at the heart of then-conventional empiricist and idealist thought. As he put it: 'Sensationalism "reduces" the world by noting that after all we never experience anything but states of ourselves.'[129] But transcendental idealism is also reductive. He wrote that 'in so far as it guarantees the world, it does so by regarding it as thought or consciousness of the world, and as the mere correlative of our knowledge, with the result that it becomes immanent in consciousness and the aseity of things is therefore done away with'.[130] Years later, in 'Eye and Mind', akin to his critique of transcendental idealism here, he would critique the 'classical idea of intellectual adequation' which holds that the human intellect, with its capacity for logical truth, is capable of progressively attaining to ontological truth (the world as it 'really' is) and of articulating the totality of this truth.[131] Merleau-Ponty – returning to the portion of the *Phenomenology*'s 'Preface' under discussion – then referred to the phenomenological perceptual-imaginative methodology of 'eidetic reduction' as first elaborated in the writing of Husserl, defining it as 'the determination to bring the world to light as it is before any falling back on ourselves has occurred, it is the ambition to make reflection emulate the unreflective life of consciousness'.[132]

Having opened up this point, there is much more that could be said at this stage about the dynamics of El Greco's Louvre crucifixion in relation to the consistent characteristics of Merleau-Ponty's thought. Certainly, given Merleau-Ponty's enduring commitment to issues of a perceptual-visual nature (a commitment, as noted, at odds with the anti-ocular discourses that would dominate continental philosophy and art theory after his death), we could examine how this painting might present us with a visual and material treatise on the dispossessive, transformational intimacies of devotional sight. Here, parallels may be found with Merleau-Ponty's own explicit account of gazing-as-surrendering cited earlier. To repeat: 'I give ear, or look, in the expectation of a sensation, and suddenly the sensible takes possession of my ear or my gaze, and I surrender a part of my body, even my whole body, to this particular manner of vibrating and filling space known as blue or red.'[133]

In El Greco's painting, a divinely inspired transaction is pictured. Christ, gazing up towards the turbulent heavens with a look of agonized yet trusting appeal, is in the process of carrying out 'the work' he had repeatedly told his disciples he had come to perform: that substitutionary act already described in which, as God incarnate, he would lay down his life so that human beings could be freed from sin and its consequences. But what of El Greco's depiction of the two donors? Faces raised, their eyes fixed on Christ, it is clear that we are not being presented with a figuration of 'the Gaze' as this has been negatively theorized within twentieth-century and contemporary thought – the 'Gaze' as objectifying, oppressive or belittling. In the biblical tradition as pictured by El Greco, to look devotionally upon the crucified Christ would be to embark upon a process of surrender and renewal – both men would be choosing to let go of their old lives which – sometimes overtly, sometimes subtly – would have tended towards death and deadliness. They would now be venturing to partake in the imperishable life of the resurrected Christ. But when their pious looks are considered alongside the comportment of their bodies, a moment of possible withholding, of as-yet incomplete surrender, might be indicated. Both bodies seem to convey degrees of ambivalence and hesitation. Take their hands. Although they are pressed together in prayer they also seem to gesture a desire for self-containment precisely when, through their looking, they are at the point of being taken elsewhere: into the divine economies that Christ's soon-to-be-dead and soon-to-be-resurrected body is opening up. Perhaps they understood only too well that to take this route would render their worldly status, their secular as well as religious power, insignificant. Or perhaps the divine gift of freedom that was being proffered seemed too good to be true and therefore to trust?

Here though, the role of the visual is key: for devotional seeing – wherever and however it is enacted, for better or for worse – is a practice in which those who look aspire towards and become *like* that at which they look. Today, arguably, devotional seeing is most prevalently activated by advertising. Devotional seeing is a process of attunement and recomposition in which the realms of the perceptual, aesthetic and ethical have become intertwined in ways that tend to bypass propositional logic. What these alterations mean in Merleau-Pontean terms, how these modes of aesthetic transfer and recreation are embedded in painterly practice and thought, and how they are made explicit by them, are matters to which we will return repeatedly in this book. In 'An Unpublished Text', for instance, Merleau-Ponty referred to 'a mimic usage of our body'[134] that is nonetheless not mimetic, as this term is commonly understood, since it is governed not by a logic of exact replication but by a logic of metamorphosis.

'Digging in the same place' – Merleau-Ponty's broad project

I remarked earlier that in *The Question of Painting* I am taking a chronological but non-linear approach to the development of Merleau-Ponty's thought as it applies to the question in hand: painting and/as thought. In this regard, however, my reading of his thought cannot and will not be exhaustive; it is a route through, intended to be considered alongside other treatments of Merleau-Ponty's aesthetics, and other reflections on the nature, scope and possibilities associated with painting, understood both as sets of practices and as particular visual and material entities with which we share space. The book is organized into four broad sections. The first section, 'Painting – Rethinking Thought beyond Dualism and Positivism' focuses on insights derived from *The Structure of Behavior* (1942) and is proportionately longer than the subsequent sections. This is because, as with this introduction, it aims also to describe broad philosophical challenges and methodological strategies that were relevant to Merleau-Ponty's project as a whole. The second section, 'Painting – Rethinking Thought as Perceptual and Embodied' draws insight from the *Phenomenology of Perception* (1945) and related essays, in particular 'Cézanne's Doubt'. The third section, 'Painting – Rethinking Thought as "Silence" and "Speech"', focuses, as indicated, on 'Indirect Language and the Voices of Silence' (1952) and the fourth section, 'Painting – Rethinking Thought as "Secret Science"', on 'Eye and Mind' (1961) and *The Visible and the Invisible (followed by Working Notes)* (1964). These sections do need to be read in order because information, analyses and interpretations presented in earlier chapters are either directly referenced or implied within later parts of the book. But now, having presented a sequence of introductory reflections on consistently important themes in Merleau-Ponty's writing as these relate to the topic of painting and/as thought, I turn finally to questions concerning the overall trajectory of Merleau-Ponty's thought-in-general.

In 1961, shortly after Merleau-Ponty's death, Sartre wrote a commemorative essay called 'Merleau-Ponty Vivant' ('Merleau-Ponty Lives').[135] Here, as already indicated, one of the ways in which he summarized Merleau-Ponty's philosophical quest was that it was into the realm of lived engagement *with* the world which is prior to the disengaged thoughts we may have *of* it, that he was 'always digging'.[136] But this was not to imply that Merleau-Ponty's thought was therefore always the same. On the contrary, this 'always digging' testified to the enormity, indeed inexhaustibility, of the territory that was his focus of philosophical attention, the intractability of the dualistically oriented modes of investigation his own explorations were attempting to counter, and the variety of ways in which this profoundly interdisciplinary thinker approached and re-approached the issues of particular concern to him.

FIGURE I.9 *Paul Cézanne,* Mont Sainte-Victoire Seen from the Bibémus Quarry, *c. 1897, oil on canvas, 25 5/8 × 32 inches (65.1 × 81.3 cm), The Baltimore Museum of Art: The Cone Collection, formed by Dr Claribel Cone and Miss Etta Cone of Baltimore, Maryland. BMA 1950.196. Courtesy Baltimore Museum of Art.*

FIGURE I.10 *Paul Cézanne*, Mont Sainte-Victoire, *c. 1902–6, watercolour and graphite on paper. Sheet (sight): 18 1/2 × 12 1/16 inches (47 × 30.7 cm). Credit: Philadelphia Museum of Art. Made possible by the families of Helen Tyson Madeira and Charles R. Tyson, 2015-42-1.*

Or, one might say that if his overall quest was the same, it was so only in the way that his favoured painter Paul Cézanne's diverse, serial explorations of a particular location, the Mont Sainte-Victoire, for instance, were the same. For if we consider just three from among the forty-four oil paintings and forty-three watercolours Cézanne produced of the mountain – the panoramic *Mont Sainte-Victoire*, from about 1886 to 1888 (part of the Courtauld Collection, London) with its subtle contradictions of perspectival and non-perspectival space,[137] his *Mont Sainte-Victoire seen from the Bibémus Quarry*, from about 1897 (Figure I.9), which seems itself to approximate, in places, the materiality of a cross section of rock face, and finally the late watercolour *Mont Sainte-Victoire* from about 1902 to 1906 (Figure I.10) which is all fluidity and vapour – it is true that the familiar motif of the mountain is clearly discernible in each one. However, each work displays radical differences (or as Merleau-Ponty would put it, 'divergencies') of point of view and context, of texture, of colouration and mode of expression. The same holds for Merleau-Ponty's writings. In each case, of interest are the ways in which specific constellations of similarity and difference are played out, and to what end.

Merleau-Ponty scholars have taken a variety of positions concerning the nature and degree of the alterations in his thought, and the way in which his writings interrelate. An early commentator, Theodore F. Geraets, whose *Vers une nouvelle philosophie transcendantale* of 1971 was focused on Merleau-Ponty's early work, identified the key turning point to occur between *The Structure of Behavior* and the *Phenomenology of Perception* due in large part to Merleau-Ponty's increased exposure to, and incorporation of Husserl's thought from 1939 onwards. Another point of transition is also often associated with the texts focused on language mainly written during the early 1950s, including 'Indirect Language and the Voices of Silence', which demonstrate Merleau-Ponty's active engagement with questions of a linguistic and semiotic nature, this being a broad area of emphatic interest within French thought during this period. Generally, the most significant shift in Merleau-Ponty's thought is located in the late works, 'Eye and Mind' and *The Visible and the Invisible*, these being described as displaying a movement from phenomenology to ontology, and from a concern with perception to a foregrounding of visibility. Gary Brent Madison in his 1981 book *The Phenomenology of Merleau-Ponty: A Search for the Limits of Consciousness* saw the late work to be corrective of the earlier texts, more successfully articulating a non-dualistic philosophy.[138] But Martin Jay, in his well-known compendium *Downcast Eyes: The Denigration of Vision in Twentieth-Century French Thought* of 1993, read in 'Eye and Mind' a 'less enthusiastic endorsement of the visual – understood in any of its conventional senses – than appears at first glance'.[139] In fact, he argued that Merleau-Ponty's 'later work can be interpreted as anticipating some of the themes of later contributors to the antiocularcentric discourse'.[140] As he saw it, Merleau-Ponty had 'hesitantly started to explore the ways in which language worked at cross-purposes with perception',[141] this project being cut short by his death. Jay cited in confirmation the following words from 'An Unpublished Text': 'The study of perception could only teach us a "bad ambiguity", a mixture of finitude and universality, of interiority and exteriority. But there is a "good ambiguity" in the phenomenon of expression.'[142] Crowther, in *Phenomenologies of Art and Vision*, by contrast, has argued that there is 'significant conceptual continuity' between Merleau-Ponty's earlier and later thought, a position with which I am in agreement.[143]

Given that the main focus of *The Question of Painting* is, precisely, on various manifestations of painterly interrogation and of the painting and/as thought relationship in his writing, it is important to return to the question raised by Jay about the significance of the visual in Merleau-Ponty's work as a whole. For instance, what did Merleau-Ponty mean when he wrote in 'An Unpublished Text' that, having 'sought to restore the world of perception' in his first two books, his works in preparation now aimed to show 'how communication with others, and thought, take up and go beyond the realm of perception which initiated us to the truth'?[144] At this mid-career stage, the works he had in mind most likely included *The Prose of the World* which, as already indicated, he was then drafting but which he would abandon in around 1959; the incomplete manuscript would later be edited by Lefort and was published in 1969. At this stage he may also already have been beginning to conceive of the project that would be published, again in incomplete form, and under the direction of Lefort, as *The Visible and the Invisible*. It is possible that this material was to be part of a more extensive project with a working title of *Être et Monde* (*Being and World*) for which draft manuscripts titled *La Nature ou le monde du silence* (*Nature or the World of Silence*)[145] and *Introduction à l'ontologie* (*Introduction to Ontology*) have been found. And what of the quotation from the end of 'An Unpublished Text' cited by Jay, about the study of perception being able to teach us only a 'bad ambiguity'? How are these statements to be understood in relation to the rest of that essay and, indeed, in relation to Merleau-Ponty's subsequent published works in which visual themes became increasingly dominant? Here, I would like to make three points.

First, if Merleau-Ponty really was implying that a philosophical concern with communication should be identified with an abandonment of concern with the visual, he would have been aligning himself with the very position which, in the opening lines of 'An Unpublished Text', he had just described his philosophical work as determined to combat. The position he was challenging was that of 'critical thought' which, he had stated emphatically, was problematic precisely because it had 'broken with the naïve evidence of *things*' that are given to us in perception. Capable only of encountering 'bare propositions',[146] this mode of thought was closed to the ways in which perceived things – visual entities – resist, undermine or go beyond the ideas we may have of them. Again, at issue here was Merleau-Ponty's philosophical concern with questions of the institution rather than constitution of knowledge[147] and with the fact that critical thought had abandoned or forgotten its origins within lived experience. Merleau-Ponty's philosophical journey, by contrast, located its interrogations in the realm of the perceptual and there is bountiful evidence, in his earlier *and* in his later writing, that to 'take up and move beyond' perception was in fact to enter into a much more complex and nuanced understanding of the visual structures and economies in which we are embedded. This brings me to my second point.

Already in the *Phenomenology* Merleau-Ponty had presented perception and expression as primordial and intertwined aspects of embodied being. In this regard, therefore, to 'take up and go beyond perception' enabled an understanding of the visual, outside of the usual dyadic logics of seeing-and-being-seen, as itself fundamentally expressive: as self-showing – this is a topic I have examined at length in my 2014 book *Showing Off! A Philosophy of Image*. As Merleau-Ponty put it in the *Phenomenology*, 'to see is to enter a universe of beings which *display themselves*'.[148] Later, in 'An Unpublished Text', he reflected on the insights that his research thus far had yielded in this regard. 'It seems to me', he wrote, 'that knowledge and the communication with others which it presupposes not only are original formations with respect to the perceptual life but also they preserve and continue our perceptual life even while transforming them.'[149] To reiterate: this taking up and going beyond is not about abandonment, but rather metamorphosis. In the chapters that follow, the various contexts and manners in which Merleau-Ponty explored these perceptual-expressive entanglements and transformations will be pursued; for Merleau-Ponty, after all, this was painterly territory par excellence. Significantly, as I have already indicated, a key issue in what follows will be not only *what* Merleau-Ponty had to say at different junctures but also *how* he did so. Of concern – and this became increasingly apparent in his late writings – were alterations of both perspective *and* mode of expression. In *The Visible and the Invisible* and to a lesser extent in 'Eye and Mind' he experimented with philosophical 'neologisms' ('flesh', 'chiasm', 'dehiscence' and 'wild being') as part of his struggles to develop a philosophically viable terminology free from dualistic associations.[150] Given this issue of use of language, throughout *The Question of Painting*, I will cite rather than paraphrase him wherever possible. Even in translation, a powerful sense of his voice is communicated.[151] Indeed, in general I will seek to cite rather than paraphrase the words of others as much as possible in order to dominate their thought as little as possible. Where Merleau-Ponty is concerned, my use of citation is not always unproblematic; for instance, it means retaining what we would now consider to be his gendered use of language. All in all, my method, in terms of my use of the work of others will be that of the 'treatise', a format discussed at the end of Chapter 8 of this book in a section called 'Visual Treatises'. There, having detoured briefly to the thought of Walter Benjamin as discussed by Vollemans, treatise 'in its canonic form' is presented, following Benjamin, as having dispensed with 'the coercive proof of mathematics'. As such, its 'only element of intention – and it is an educative rather than a didactic intention – is that of the authoritative quotation. Method', as Benjamin put it, 'is a digression. Representation as digression – such is the methodological nature of the treatise.'[152]

Returning to Merleau-Ponty's late experiments with language, though, it is important to reiterate that these did not so much represent a radical departure from his earlier thought, as a re-articulation, recomposition, even at times an apparent reversal or inversion of it. Just as Cézanne's late watercolour, *Mont Sainte-Victoire* (Figure I.10) with its airiness and evocative gaps, has the appearance of being the inverse of the earlier, densely textured *Mont Sainte-Victoire seen from the Bibémus Quarry* (Figure I.9) so Merleau-Ponty's treatments of visibility in 'Eye and Mind' and *The Visible and the Invisible* might be regarded as invaginating, or turning inside-out, his earlier treatments of embodiment and perception.

There is a third and final pertinent issue, raised by Merleau-Ponty in 'An Unpublished Text', that is crucial to the question of painting understood as thought. It is one to which I have already made reference in this introduction. For in 'An Unpublished Text', and in a way that strengthens the case for Merleau-Ponty's ongoing philosophical commitment to questions of a perceptual nature – even though these would be increasingly reframed by a growing prioritization of an ontological as well as phenomenological concern with *visibility* – he highlighted a particular relationship between perception and truth that his researches thus far had revealed to him. In his words:

I found in the experience of the perceived world a new type of relation between the mind and truth. The evidence of the perceived thing lies in its concrete aspect, in the very texture of its qualities, and in the equivalence among all its sensible properties – which caused Cézanne to say that one should be able to paint even odors. Before our undivided existence the world is true; it exists. The unity, the articulations of both are intermingled. We experience in it a truth which shows through and envelops us rather than being held and circumscribed by our mind.[153]

Merleau-Ponty continued by stating that this issue of our perceptual initiation into truth was the key question raised in the early essays on painting and literature, 'Cézanne's Doubt' and 'Metaphysics and the Novel' (also 1945), as well as in his thesis on politics, *Humanism and Terror: An Essay on the Communist Problem* which was published in 1947. In addition, it should be noted that in his descriptions of the theories of mind that are delivered via our visual engagements with the world, he challenged a further still-persistent dualism: between the concrete, or the actual, and the virtual.[154] As he put it: 'The insertion of our factual situation as a particular case within the system of other possible situations begins as soon as we designate a point in space with our finger.'[155] Again, against anti-ocular understandings of the visual that would become increasingly dominant after Merleau-Ponty's death, our visual modes of being are particularly well-disposed to navigating this territory of the actual-virtual. Seen from this perspective, painting, too, is a mode of pointing; a specific instance, or announcement of modes of being that are, as he put it, 'capable of redesigning an infinite number of situations'.[156] This phenomenon was first discussed by Merleau-Ponty at length in *The Structure of Behavior* under the auspices of what he called the symbolic forms of behaviour. It is to this work that we now turn, albeit my means of a short detour. For – perhaps surprisingly – I will set the scene for those early Merleau-Pontean explorations by describing and discussing a compelling piece of contemporary art (*not* in this instance a painting) with which certain comparisons may be made: the Austrian artist Barbara Kapusta's short video-piece *O's Vocalization*.

PART ONE

Painting – Rethinking thought beyond dualism and positivism

FIGURE 1.1 *Barbara Kapusta, Still from* O's Vocalization, *2016, HD 16:9 video transferred to PAL 4:3, sound Chra, 10:56 mins. Courtesy Barbara Kapusta.*

FIGURE 1.2 *Pieter de Hooch*, A Woman Carrying a Bucket in a Courtyard (Eine Magd mit Eimer in einem Hinterhof) *c. 1658–60, oil on canvas, 44 × 42 cm. Staatliche Kunsthalle Karlsruhe. Credit: bpk / Staatliche Kunsthalle Karlsruhe / Wolfgang Pankoke.*

CHAPTER ONE

'Nature' and 'consciousness' – Merleau-Ponty's critical encounter with dualism

Broken?

In free fall
we meet,

O and (.

Our bodies
move – thrown,
gravity pulling us.

Time slows down, O.

In slow motion
we start to move
to turn, and to crack.

Our bodies open
and break into parts,
into pieces.

We begin to hum
and to beat ... .[1]

These are some of the words that accompanied Barbara Kapusta's short black-and-white film *O's Vocalization* (see Figure 1.1)[2] when it was shown as part of her installation for the Kunsthalle, Vienna's 2016 exhibition, *The Promise of Total Automation*. I have turned to them, in the first instance, because they convey a scene akin to that found in Merleau-Ponty's early writing: a scene of breakage – in his case, breakage from philosophical tradition – from which an emphatically generative energy is gently released. Usefully, too, Kapusta's words connect us with a set of contemporary concerns and a contemporary art practice through which to consider Merleau-Ponty's initial attempts at reformulating philosophical thought in non-dualistic, non-linear and non-causal terms. They also connect us with early Merleau-Pontean insights gleaned from his considerations of painterly interrogation, understood as resolutely inter-corporeal, in terms of its situation, outlook, methods and ethical implications.

The *Promise of Total Automation* – to begin with this – was a group venture in which artists reflected on a pressing topic: How might the shifting relations between machines, nature, humans and objects be understood in a cybernetic age in which processes of production, communication and the circulation of capital are increasingly driven by algorithms whose speeds of calculation and execution exceed unaided human apprehension?[3] At issue here is a focus on communication and control theory – whether referencing artificially constructed or coded mechanical-electrical systems on the one hand, or, on the other hand, the automatic control systems operative within non-human as well as human physical and psychological functioning. The latter include what Merleau-Ponty would refer to in the *Phenomenology of Perception* as the 'habit-body' as well as the deep structures of so-called anonymous being in which embodied beings are also involved. As I will show, these concerns provide an apt backdrop against which to consider *The Structure of Behavior*'s key themes (Merleau-Ponty's comparative explorations of the 'syncretic', 'amovable' and 'symbolic' forms of behaviour, for instance, to which I will return in the following chapter) and his motivations for writing it. For although cybernetics was then not yet a named field as such – Norbert Wiener's inaugurating book *Cybernetics: Or Control and Communication in the Animal and the Machine* would be published some years later, in 1948[4] – it was precisely within the context of analogous phenomena, and their implications for learning, change and freedom, that Merleau-Ponty's early philosophical thought and his first sustained engagement with painterly practice took place. Indeed, a notable feature of *The Structure of Behavior* is the fact that his philosophical arguments, and his discussion of El Greco's art practice in the book's penultimate chapter, entitled 'Naturalism', occur alongside close and prolonged readings of work carried out in the field of ethology, the scientific study of animal behaviour, where explorations of the involuntary reflex, the conditioned reflex and causation were central. Merleau-Ponty engaged with the work of Pavlov and others and, as Brett Buchanan argued in his 2008 book *Onto-Ethologies: The Animal Environments of Uexküll, Heidegger, Merleau-Ponty, and Deleuze*, Merleau-Ponty's thought was shaped in important ways by the legacy of the 'father' of ethology, the Swiss biologist Jakob Johann Baron von Uexküll (1864–1944). Significantly, where notions of causality were concerned, Uexküll's work sought to navigate a route between a Darwinian reduction of biological processes to physical mechanisms on the one hand and, on the other hand, the then-proliferating critiques of Darwinism found in vitalism.[5] Uexküll was also the originator of the term *Umwelt* – the environing or surrounding world – which would become so important within phenomenology. About half way through *The Structure of Behavior*, when discussing 'the vital structures' (structures of awareness that are located somewhere between reflex actions and symbolic functioning in terms of their flexibility), Merleau-Ponty cited an evocative quote by Uexküll as recorded in the psychologist F. J. J. Buytendijk's 1930 essay 'Les Différences essentielles des fonctions psychiques de l'homme et des animaux' ('Essential differences in the psychic functions of man and animals'): 'Every organism is a melody which sings itself.'[6] More fundamentally, when contextualizing his own philosophical position and aims at the beginning of *The Structure Behavior*, Merleau-Ponty referred overtly to the fact that within the intellectual milieu of his time – the late 1930s – an attachment to *two rival control systems*, defined by him as 'consciousness' and 'nature', were in problematic coexistence. Each system, an offspring of Cartesian dualism,[7] tended to present itself as indubitable and complete. Within this context he also drew attention to the then-conventional but problematic philosophical and scientific habit of associating 'nature' with classical notions of causality and reflex behaviour:

> Our goal is to understand the relations of consciousness and nature: organic, psychological or even social. By nature we understand here a multiplicity of events external to each other and bound together by relations of causality. ... [A]mong contemporary thinkers in France, there exist side by side a philosophy, on the one hand, which makes of every nature an objective unity constituted vis-à-vis consciousness and, on the other, sciences which treat the organism and consciousness as two orders of reality and, in their reciprocal relation, as 'effects' and as 'causes'.[8]

I will return to *The Structure of Behavior* shortly and to how Merleau-Ponty intervened in and challenged this state of affairs. But if we reflect on our own early twenty-first-century contexts, and return to Kapusta's film *O's Vocalization* in particular, its significance is that at a visual and thematic level it is doing something akin to what Merleau-Ponty was also seeking to present as philosophically viable: it immerses us in an inter-corporeal scenario in which classical notions of causality seem to have lost their dominance. In Kapusta's film, the inter-corporeal scenario is focused around objects and their interactions. In other words, although we cannot pretend that human subjectivity and agency were not involved in the making of this artwork, agency at its most active is presented as having been displaced from the human realm to that of things – in the exhibition's documentation these things are referred to as 'fictitious object-persons' – not in an anthropomorphic sense but with the intention that our conventional ideas about agency, action and interaction might be extended.[9]

In visual terms, Kapusta's film opens with a field of black. Were it not for the sound accompanying this blackness, we might assume that nothing was happening; that nothing – rather than this rich *something* – was there. The soundtrack is difficult to describe. Sourced from a composition by the Austrian musician, DJ and founder of the label Comfortzone, Christina Nemec aka Chra – a piece called *Il_Liquid* created for *Spectral Sounds*, a site-specific sound art exhibition held at the Musikpavillon in Innsbruck's Hofgarten during January 2016[10] – it is rhythmic rather than melodic. But its texture has a rather disrupted quality. It is somewhat like an electronic sea, its acoustic tides surging in and out unevenly, between dimensions. Or it is like the slightly wavering pulse, beat or breath of a part-industrial, part-organic being. Or it is as though we are in an echo chamber or positioned against some kind of sound barrier witnessing a strange mechanical transmission fade in and out.

But then, abruptly, the black screen erupts into activity, albeit in mesmerizing slow motion; *O's Vocalization* was filmed at a high speed of up to 1,500 frames per second. We see a cluster of c-shaped, oval and circular forms surge upwards with anti-gravitational force as if of their own accord – whether they are links removed from once-existent chains or the components of not-yet-existent ones is undetermined. A few of these elements appear to be awkwardly joined but most exist as independent entities. Nonetheless they appear to act with mutual awareness and as something of a cohort. In the sequences that follow, the familiar downward force of gravity has been restored and, over and over again, falling links glint against that surrounding blackness, so continuous that it is difficult to establish precise spatial references. Again, most of the links descend singly although a few are interconnected. To begin with, they are presented as if somewhat at a distance, then up-close, and it is evident that several are not the mass-produced, metallic objects we might have anticipated but have a handcrafted look. At the very least they seem to be partially machined or cast *and* partially handmade – they were in fact individually created from unfired, painted clay. In *The Promise of Total Automation* similarly crafted clay objects were on view, positioned here and there, as part of Kapusta's installation.

> Your surface is
> covered with
> dents and scratches
> and fingerprints.[11]

Midway through the film – which has a total duration of around eleven minutes – there is a thematic shift and a point of temporary climax: individual links now reappear in the form of a long, flexible chain, swinging and twirling, like a necklace, swaying as if lifted from an invisible display box or as if hanging from an invisible neck. As a consequence, too, the film's black background suddenly obtains a new sense of texture and suggestiveness; it is now reminiscent of the soft, dark velvet against which jewellery is often both protected and displayed. But darker associations also now come to the fore: those which connect chains with heavy industry and heavy labour (notably slavery) and with the conditions of bondage, weight and constraint. Forms of social brokenness, in other words, that are at once hidden by, embedded in and facilitated by a structure – the chain – that may nonetheless also be described as conveying forms of connectivity, flexibility and coherence.

In the film's final portion, a fragile loop of chain falls and spreads out onto the black ground. Then, once again, we are in the realm of discrete, falling bodies as individual c-shaped, oval and circular links slowly descend, land and bounce upwards, sometimes breaking but nonetheless spinning, twisting and turning in what might most appropriately be described as a carefree choreography of bits and pieces in potentially endless recombination.

Regarding her own motivations in relation to this film, Kapusta has said that she was interested in 'the point and moment where things start to come into our focus and become visible'. Then, shifting her references from the visible to the audible, she continued: 'The title points to the moment of vocalization, the change of a sound into a vowel and in general to speech, communication and exchange.'[12] In order to facilitate this, she created a filmic *Umwelt* in which it became possible for the capacities, actions and desires of these objects – or 'object-persons – to come into ear- and eyeshot in ways that have not already been predetermined by their human counterparts. There is space and time for revelation, surprise and mutual adjustment, with Kapusta's role, and ours too, closest to that of witness-facilitators. As indicated, this type of sensibility is one that is also generally extended and encouraged by Merleau-Ponty's own approach to seeing, thinking and writing.

Within the context of my introduction to, and interest in, Merleau-Ponty's *The Structure of Behavior*, I am particularly drawn to the fact that in Kapusta's film our attentiveness is directed towards a communicative scenario that is organized around and animated by the debris of broken chains. For this is also how Merleau-Ponty's philosophical venture might be described – not only in broad terms but also as it is expressed in this early and still relatively disregarded philosophical text. As already noted, it is immediately clear from the opening lines of this book that Merleau-Ponty is setting out to break chains of philosophical and scientific argumentation in which, to repeat, 'nature: organic, psychological or even social' [is erroneously understood as] 'a multiplicity of events external to each other and bound together by relations of causality'.[13] It is this erroneous understanding, and the unresolvable contradictions to which it had given rise, that Merleau-Ponty sought to counter in this, and subsequent, writings. But in so doing, of course, he was dismantling long-established rational infrastructures for thought that were regarded as foundational and indubitable if not sacred. In this sense, therefore, Merleau-Ponty was *breaking* philosophy. And it is for this reason that he has frequently been described by commentators as a non-foundational thinker, a post-structuralist *avant la lettre*, and a non-philosopher.[14] Therefore – and here I am returning to an issue already opened up in the introduction to *The Question of Painting* – a key question that his work provokes, and which he specifically sought to address, is this: What kinds of thinking and learning, what transformations, if any, become possible if the dualisms and linear causalities that form the infrastructures for traditional philosophical and scientific thought are dismantled?

Eighty years later – again I am repeating a point already made in the introduction – the traditional infrastructures challenged by Merleau-Ponty have tended to remain in place largely due to their clear (but arguably deceptive) logic and their (arguably fraudulent) ease of application in a range of practical contexts. Thus Merleau-Ponty's broad concerns in this regard remain current and are shared by a variety of differently positioned thinkers today. One of several possible contemporary expressions of concern, for example, may be found in the 'realist metaphysician' Graham Harman's 2007 essay 'On Vicarious Causation'. Harman (whose object-oriented ontological thought was grounded in but then relocated outside of the domains of Heideggerean – rather than Merleau-Pontean – phenomenology) opened his essay by claiming that 'causality has rarely been a genuine topic of inquiry since the seventeenth century' and needs urgently to be re-examined and reformulated. He continued (and he is worth citing at some length):

> The supposed great debate over causation between sceptics and transcendental philosophers is at best a yes-or-no dispute as to whether causal necessity exists, and in practice is just an argument over whether it can be known. What has been lacking is active discussion of the very nature of causality. This is now taken to be obvious: one object exerts force over another and makes it change physical position or some of its features.[15]

For Harman, of course, an obstacle to a radically reconfigured understanding of the nature of causation was the 'correlationism' that is at the heart of the phenomenological project, including that of Merleau-Ponty:[16]

> No one sees any way to speak about the interaction of fire and cotton, since philosophy remains preoccupied with the relational gap between humans and the world – even if only to deny such a gap. Inanimate relations have been abandoned to laboratory research, where their metaphysical character is openly dismissed.[17]

Acknowledging the inevitably (and I would argue unapologetically) 'correlational' character of Merleau-Ponty's thought, I would argue, nonetheless, that the terrain described by Harman – that of 'the interaction of fire and cotton' – as well as that opened up by Kapusta's film, accords in important ways with that towards which Merleau-Ponty was also oriented when he was researching and writing *The Structure of Behavior* in the late 1930s. For he was interested in immersing himself in, and expounding upon, the inter-corporeal rather than subject-centred or conventionally ego-centric nature of our perceptual engagements in and with that which we call 'the world'. If, as Sara Hainämaa had pointed out in her 2015 essay 'Anonymity and personhood: Merleau-Ponty's account of the subject of perception', Merleau-Ponty's position is one in which a sense of selfhood is maintained – he is not proposing an ego-less system[18] – it is nonetheless the case that this self is understood and experienced as being embedded within various inter-corporeal structures of being and functioning as an irreducible part of them.

There is a second reason why Kapusta's film is significant within the context of my introductory reflections on Merleau-Ponty's project in *The Structure of Behavior*, and indeed subsequently. Not only does it present a scene characterized by different forms of brokenness but it also enables us to inhabit this scene perceptually, in a slow and unintimidated way. The workings of the camera enable our own eyes to draw near to this brokenness rather than pull away from it. In addition, the flickering allure of the film's dark surface – what we might like to call its ornamental aspect – through which the movements of Kapusta's non-human actors (or actants) are brought to visibility as they descend and sometimes break is captivating.

As a philosopher, Merleau-Ponty too was prepared to enter and explore challenging territory in a slow and unthreatened way. From *The Structure of Behavior* onwards, when engaging with philosophical or scientific positions he regarded as irreconcilable with his own, his response was neither simply to dismiss them (as, for instance, traditional thought had done with respect to the lived world of perception) nor quickly to turn away. On the contrary, he displayed a high degree of attentiveness towards them. As James Edie put it in his 1987 essay 'Was Merleau-Ponty a Structuralist?', Merleau-Ponty 'always puts *himself* into an argument [he wants to destroy] and presents it in its most appealing and forceful form'[19] – much as Descartes had done by employing his 'method of doubt' in order to overcome the scepticism of his sixteenth-century interlocutor, Michel de Montaigne (1533–92).[20] Merleau-Ponty's strategy had its strengths and what would conventionally be described as its points of weaknesses or vulnerability. On the one hand, the embedded nature of Merleau-Ponty's attentiveness made him all the more alert to spaces of internal contradiction to which a more immediately oppositional stance (a critique from the outside) would not have been attuned. As an embedded investigator, he was able to subvert or undo those positions all the more convincingly, from within, on their own terms. In *The Structure of Behavior* (and later in the *Phenomenology*) we see this approach adopted again and again. As indicated, his first book consists of extensive accounts of experiments conducted within the behavioural sciences that in fact challenge reductive notions of causality as they set out to explain the mechanics of adaptation, learning and inventiveness occurring within various, *differently* complex forms of non-human and human behaviour, including the domain of the reflex. On the other hand, however, Merleau-Ponty's habit of addressing the positions he regarded as problematic from the 'inside', and *as if* from their position, meant that his own thinking often remained problematically entangled within their logics, especially, as already observed, at the level of language. Merleau-Ponty was acutely aware of this as an issue. A further repercussion is that his thought has sometimes been misunderstood, with readers mistakenly identifying his thought with the positions he was 'ventriloquizing' in order to contest them from within. This sense of entanglement Merleau-Ponty would later describe as 'chiasmic' and, in fact, as something that can never finally and absolutely be overcome within the context of any embodied, inter-corporeal or relational practice of thought. For at issue here are scenarios in which seeming oppositions are undone and strange reversals and processes of mutual implication are experienced between investigator and investigated, seer and seen, the up-close and the far-off.[21] In *The Visible and the Invisible*, for instance, he would write that 'the world is what I perceive, but as soon as we examine and express its absolute proximity, it also becomes, inexplicably, irremediable distance'.[22] As Geraldine Finn pointed out in her 1992 essay 'The Politics of Contingency', what Merleau-Ponty was advocating was the art of arguing from a position that has no place within traditional philosophical schemata, nor a definitive place of its own elsewhere.[23] And returning to Kapusta's film in this regard, we cannot help but recall those uncertain and often suddenly radically altered and altering spaces and perspectives that it, too, repeatedly brings to expression.

A related point is also worth reiterating about Merleau-Ponty's philosophical self-positioning, already in evidence in *The Structure of Behavior*. As well as entering into and arguing from the established philosophical and scientific positions he wished to challenge by breaking them open and revealing their inconsistencies, as noted in the introduction he was also able to develop his own counter-position because he willingly entered and examined those territories that classical philosophy regarded as invalid: the realms of the perceptual and, within this context, those of painterly engagement and experience which he regarded as fundamental sites of genuine questioning and knowledge formation. Crucially, too, he treated them not as illustrative of the new forms of philosophical thought and philosophical positioning he was trying to formulate but as paradigmatic for them. This also meant, for instance, that as he sought to discover the flexible rather than static perceptual foundations for truth, he rejected the traditional distinction between appearance and reality and turned specifically to a close examination of the phenomenal realm. In *The Structure of Behavior*, as already indicated, the phenomenal world is presented to us in terms of three sets of observable lived behaviours: the 'syncretic', the 'amovable' and the 'symbolic' forms. In other words – to repeat – Merleau-Ponty insisted upon the philosophical worth of interrogating that which traditional thought has consistently regarded as without value for reflection, and even detrimental to it. This is also why, in his critiques of empiricism and positivism, he insisted upon the need to acknowledge the limits of scientific explorations of lived behaviours when these were enacted or re-enacted in the 'artificial', controlled conditions of the laboratory. Citing Finn's politically inflected, and in this case also religiously inflected language, in so doing he took 'the standpoint of the oppressed [and] the "unredeemed"'.[24]

It would also appear that throughout his career, Merleau-Ponty remained more than aware of the persistent nature of the difficulties, the traditionally perceived weaknesses, associated with his project of making painting paradigmatic for thought as he wished to recompose it. As he put it in the late 'Eye and Mind': 'We are so fascinated by the classical idea of intellectual adequation that painting's mute "thinking" sometimes leaves us with the impression of a vain swirl of significations, a paralyzed or miscarried utterance.'[25] But 'Eye and Mind' also testifies to his conviction about the crucial possibilities inherent in 'mute' painterly thought and what he also called a 'figured philosophy'. Indeed, one way of expressing their importance would be to say that for Merleau-Ponty this 'mute' painterly thought, and this 'figured philosophy' – sometimes, indeed, barely more than a materialized exclamation – provoked scenarios in which the domain and dimensions of questioning itself were experienced as stretched well beyond their usual parameters.

This brings me to a third aspect of Kapusta's film of especial interest to me in the context of these discussions. Earlier, when describing the final portion of the film, I referred to a realm of discrete, falling bodies (those c-shaped, oval and circular links) which were seen to 'slowly descend, land, and bounce upwards, sometimes breaking but nonetheless spinning, twisting and turning in what might most appropriately be described as a carefree choreography of bits and pieces in potentially endless recombination'. In other words, what seems to be emphasized at the end of the film is a condition in which brokenness and recomposition coexist and interact. The energy is positive and productive even if the outcome is as yet unpredictable. I also noted that in the opening portion of the film a cluster of these links was seen to 'surge upwards with anti-gravitational force' as if of its own accord in a way that seemed to indicate a sense of their operating as a cohort and as if with mutual awareness. In other words, the terrain that is opened up here has affordances with the *symbolic* forms of behaviour with which *The Structure of Behavior* culminates; it is significant because it enables the creation of new forms of integration in contexts that may at first present themselves as irremediably dysfunctional. Significantly – and this again aligns with the key elements and characteristics of Kapusta's film as just described – the word symbol has its etymological roots in the assimilation of *syn-* (together) and *bole* (a throwing or casting), hence, a throwing or casting together. Merleau-Ponty's explorations of the symbolic forms of behaviour will be the focus of the second chapter of this book. But first, in this chapter, it will be necessary to explore in greater depth Merleau-Ponty's critical engagements with the rival systems of rationalism and empiricism which he described as existing, incompatibility, side by side. As already indicated in the introduction, this will mean turning to what is by now a philosophically well-trodden topic: the problem of Cartesian dualism as the paradigm from which rationalism and empiricism were off-shoots. Of particular interest here, however, will be *how* Merleau-Ponty – who may fairly be described as a forerunner in this regard – took up that challenge.

The problems of rationalism and empiricism

As indicated, Merleau-Ponty's philosophical goal in *The Structure of Behavior* was to understand 'the relations of consciousness and nature'. This places his project at, or near, the beginning of a long line of twentieth-century philosophical attempts to resolve problems raised by Descartes' mind/body dualism as presented in the *Meditations*, problems that Descartes had himself recognized. As Hainämaa and Kaitaro have pointed out, however – in the essay already cited in the introduction, 'Descartes' Notion of the Mind-Body Union and its Phenomenological Expositions' – critiques of Cartesian dualism have tended 'to emphasize one element of Descartes' philosophy but neglect another central factor',[26] namely, his arguments for the union, or intermingling, of body and soul in actuality. This intermingling, he claimed, 'can be known very distinctly only by the senses' of which the human mind was also composed – in Descartes' writings, mind comprised not only will and intellect but also the passions (sensations, perception, emotion) and imagination.[27] In both the *Meditations* (specifically the Sixth Meditation) and in the earlier *Discours de la méthode pour bien conduire sa raison, et chercher la vérité dans les sciences (Discourse on the Method of Rightly Conducting One's Reason and of Seeking Truth in the Sciences)* of 1637, wrote Hainämaa and Kaitaro, Descartes had contrasted 'the holistic metaphors of intermingling explicitly with the traditional Platonic images of piloting and control' and had argued that 'we cannot make sense of our sensations unless we let go of the imagery of mental piloting'.[28] From these observations they built an argument to demonstrate the formative role played by Descartes' conceptual distinction of mind and body for further thought, including Husserlian and Merleau-Pontean phenomenology.

Nonetheless, Descartes' philosophical position may justly still be described in terms of its prioritization of the non-extended or non-corporeal *cogito* from which, as already discussed, a well-ordered argument could be derived for the mind's belief in the existence first of God and then of the corporeal world of bodies, other people and things.[29] And on a practical level, despite Descartes' consistent arguments to the contrary, the difficulty for then-contemporary and subsequent commentators remained that of having to explain how the non-corporeal *cogito*, as his source of reasoning, meaning and purposefulness, could affect material existence conceived of in wholly mechanistic and causally predetermined terms. This problem, expressed in terms of the relationship between soul and body, was raised early on by Princess Elizabeth of Sweden in her correspondence with Descartes: 'I beg of you to tell me how the human soul can determine the movement of the animal spirits in the body so as to perform voluntary acts – being as it is merely a conscious (*pensante*) substance', she asked, continuing:

> For the determination of movement seems always to come about from the moving body's being propelled – to depend on the kind of impulse it gets from what sets it in motion, or again, on the nature and shape of this latter thing's surface. Now the first two conditions involve *contact*, and the third involves that the impelling thing has extension; but you utterly exclude extension from your notion of soul, and contact seems to me incompatible with a thing's being immaterial.[30]

Thus, the question was this: How can consciousness operate as an effective or intervening force within the realm of physical facts and events if it is non-extended? And if it cannot operate upon the physical order in this way, what practical purpose does it fulfil? As the philosophers José Luis Bermúdez and Naomi Eilan, and the psychologist Anthony Marcel, put it in their 1995 book *The Body and the Self*: 'If Descartes's dualism is wrong, then the body, contra Descartes, is arguably integral to some aspects of self-consciousness and/or of the use of 'I'. The question is, In what way?'[31]

Since the time of Descartes – if I may approach this issue in the most rudimentary of terms for now, bearing in mind that my aim in this chapter is to contextualize Merleau-Ponty's engagement with this issue during the late 1930s – a traditional response has been to try to bypass questions about the interrelations of nature and consciousness when explaining our perception of the world and our capacities to respond to or act in that world. This has been done from those two basic positions already referenced: rationalism and empiricism. In each case, either consciousness or nature is privileged at the exclusion or expense of the other. For rationalism, with its prioritization of the disembodied mind, nature cannot be accessed but only constituted by consciousness. Perception understood as a function of the physical organism is unintelligible. Instead, our capacities for perception and action – which, within this scheme, refer to the functioning of consciousness – are seen to be governed by judgement and free will, that is, by the power to make choices that are not determined by laws of an external nature. From the empiricist position, on the other hand, perception and thought are wholly physiological operations and our actions, as embodied beings ultimately governed by determinism, are the necessary outcome of preceding events or states of affair. Here, it is the notion of (disembodied) consciousness that is unintelligible. This brings us back to Merleau-Ponty's reference to the problematic coexistence of these positions within the then-contemporary intellectual climate in France. At issue was not only a scenario of apparent irreconcilability in which certain thinkers were advocates of rationalism while others, their intellectual opponents, were advocates of empiricism. Also at issue was that a coexistence of both positions could be found within the intellectual project of a single thinker. A case in point was Merleau-Ponty's older contemporary and former teacher, and one of his interlocutors, Léon Brunschvicg (1869–1944), an idealist philosopher and professor at the Sorbonne since 1909 who would be forced from his position by the occupying Nazis once war broke out, and who died in Paris six months before the city was liberated. Brunschvicg's writings focused on the place of judgement in our knowledge of the world, and he taught that the true universe of the intelligence is that of science. In *The Structure of Behavior* (and indeed in the *Phenomenology*) Merleau-Ponty made specific reference to Brunschvicg's *L'Expérience humaine et la causalité physique* (*Human Experience and Physical Causality*) of 1922. He also referred to his *Spinoza et ses contemporaines* (*Spinoza and his Contemporaries*), published a year later in 1923. In the words of John Bannan, an early commentator on Merleau-Ponty's work, what Merleau-Ponty regarded as problematic here was a reductionism that threatened 'the variety in consciousness and in things': not Nietzsche's biological reductionism but 'an intellectualism with enough affinities with physical science to regard itself as a scientific naturalism. Intellectualism turns perception, art, sentiment, and religious behaviour into rigid and uniform objects of scientific observation'.[32] As Bannan noted, Merleau-Ponty was not the only thinker to regard this as problematic. The philosopher Jean Wahl (1888–1974), a younger colleague of Brunschvicg's at the Sorbonne from 1936, whose tenure would also be interrupted by the Nazi occupation, had 'already asserted the incompetence of such a view to deal with the fullness of what exists'.[33] He had done so particularly in his *Vers le concret* (*Towards the Concrete*) of 1933 – also cited by Merleau-Ponty – in which he had meditated on affinities in the work of three then-contemporary thinkers, William James, Alfred North Whitehead and Gabriel Marcel – thinkers, incidentally, whose work has been gaining renewed attention today, in the early decades of the twenty-first century. Ten years before the appearance of Wahl's book, in 1923, Marcel had made analogous claims in his *Journal Métaphysique* (*Metaphysical Journal*).

Marcel was another important source for Merleau-Ponty. In contrast to Descartes' and the rationalists' identification of selfhood and self-reflexivity wholly with the disembodied consciousness, Merleau-Ponty was committed to an understanding of the human self as embodied, to Marcel's 'I am my body' (*je suis mon corps*). Indeed, Merleau-Ponty had already aligned himself to this position in his 1936 essay on Marcel's *Être et avoir* (*Being and Having*) of 1935, which was published in the journal *La Vie Intellectuelle* in October of that year.[34] In addition, as already indicated in the introduction, this commitment also was already evident in Husserl's conception of the 'living body' as found in *Ideas II*, although it should be noted that while Merleau-Ponty referenced key works by Husserl in *The Structure of Behavior*, *Ideas II* was not one of them.[35] In any case, in *The Structure of Behavior* Merleau-Ponty was now keen to explore the further implications of this equation of the self with the body and, by extension, the world. Specifically, at issue was whether behaviour – which he took to refer both to perception and action – must necessarily be understood following the empiricist logic as 'a multiplicity of events external to each other and bound together by relations of causality'[36] or whether he could account for it *as* embodied without taking this route. Could consciousness and extension be tied together in a way that was philosophically, empirically and, indeed, existentially convincing? But this task was combined with another. It was necessary for him to clarify his objections to rationalism and to empiricism as he understood them, and he did this in two broad ways. On the one hand, he argued that the routes taken by rationalism and empiricism must be regarded as empty because they both failed, in different ways, to help us comprehend our practical, everyday experiences of perceiving and acting in the world. On the other hand, he argued that empiricism, the position with which, superficially, his perceptually grounded approach was more closely aligned, was intrinsically unsound because of the false, objectivist presuppositions upon which it has been built.

Since rationalist and empiricist theories of behaviour formed an important ground against which Merleau-Ponty's own theories were figured, and in contrast to which painting-as-practice – that is, painting as a particular set of behaviours – offered alternate models for thought, it is with his diagnosis of their respective positions and problematics that I now proceed. And, in order to give this discussion a concrete point of reference, I again draw upon a work of art. It is a painterly depiction of behavioural interaction with the world, independent of Merleau-Ponty's own case studies but illuminating when considered alongside them, since it is derived from the period and culture in which Descartes, Merleau-Ponty's chief interlocutor in this regard, wrote his key philosophical works: the Dutch Republic of the mid-seventeenth century. The painting in question is Pieter de Hooch's *A Woman Carrying a Bucket in a Courtyard* from around 1658 to 1660 (Figure 1.2).[37] And here a further point must be made regarding the philosophical usefulness of considering this work. Crucially, as art historians have evidenced and argued, genre paintings of this kind may justifiably be regarded not only as visual meditations on aspects of everyday life in a culture undergoing rapid social development but also as visual treatises which used the languages of figuration, colour and composition to address epistemological questions, and questions about the role and functioning of sight, light, thought and action, akin (or certainly adjacent) to those that Descartes was also pursuing in his way.

A Woman Carrying a Bucket in a Courtyard, now in the collection of the Staatliche Kunsthalle Karlsruhe, was previously privately owned but had entered the public realm for a short period when it was on loan to the Scottish National Gallery in Edinburgh during the 1990s. This was where I first came to know it, and where it took on a significant mediating role in terms of my engagement with Merleau-Ponty's thought. Measuring just 44 × 42 cm, it is a luminous and polished piece. At first sight, it conveys an air of quietude. The woman, who has entered the courtyard to carry out an everyday domestic task, is portrayed not hard at work but in a mood of deep introspection. Upon longer consideration, though, the image reveals itself as riven with tension at a representational level between an apparently self-imposed condition of containment, on the one hand, and an apparently unheeded, discounted or rejected promise of freedom on the other. As already indicated, this tension between freedom and constraint and the question of to what degree, if at all, it might be negotiated was one that Merleau-Ponty, writing from within and contributing to debates associated with pre- and post-war philosophical existentialism, was constantly examining. But it was also a matter of profound philosophical concern during the period in which de Hooch was painting. Expressed in terms of free will versus determinism, it was the subject of heated theological debate where quandaries concerning Calvinistic doctrines of predestination were at issue, Calvinism being the doctrinal position that had most forcefully shaped the post-Reformation Republic's officially approved religious denomination: the Dutch Reformed Church. Also implicit here are those questions of causality that have already been opened up.

The painting's immediate point of interest, then, is the woman who is positioned towards the centre of the image. She has emerged from a place of relative darkness seen through the gateway behind her, and has just stepped over a patch of light that is entering the courtyard through the large open doorway to her right. She carries a bucket and broom, and her overskirt has been hitched up in readiness for work. To the left of the image, ahead of her, chickens are depicted, pecking at the ground. So, what are we to make of her pensiveness? And what of the inclusion of that 'pathway' of light over which she has stepped as if it were a form of virtual intersection? Had she hesitated a moment earlier in that patch of sunlight and considered putting down the bucket and mop, un-hitching her overskirt, and allowing the sunlight to lead her outside? (Courtyards were then regarded not as external but as interior spaces.) More pointedly, again responding imaginatively to the way in which the work seems to present itself to us, how might her perception of the light that bathes parts of her body and parts of the environment affect her subsequent actions – her apparent decision to continue with her duties?[38]

Taking the empiricist position first, a person believing perception and action to be determined by the accumulative effect of external stimuli would see the woman's eventual behaviour as the inevitable outcome of a physical and measurable causal process. According to this scheme, if the woman had indeed hesitated before going about her task, this hesitation would have to be regarded, precisely, *as* an appearance. It could not be interpreted as a moment of conscious debate or decision-making prior to choosing a course of action since central to this way of thinking is the insistence that human functioning is purely a matter of physiology. We would be mistaken in wanting to invest in her the power or self-awareness to make physiologically unconditioned choices. Such powers or capacities would be at worst illusions, and at best phenomena that in humans only accompany mechanical functioning, without power or influence (epi-phenomena). Here, in Merleau-Ponty's words, 'organism and consciousness' are regarded as 'two orders of reality and in their reciprocal relation, as "effects" and "causes"'.[39] Indeed, it could be argued that such a mechanistic view of humanity appears to be represented in the painting. Certainly, the woman's posture – head down with apparent resignation and body tilted slightly forward – echoes that of birds towards which she is moving, creatures whose functioning would be described within the logic of traditional empiricism as governed solely by external conditions and an inbuilt, non-reflective instinct for survival. In the final analysis, even if her functioning *were* read as operating differently from that of those other creatures depicted, to say that it displayed uniqueness or distinctiveness at the level of meaning would be regarded as an empty statement. This was precisely the type of viewpoint to which Merleau-Ponty objected. As he put it in *The Structure of Behavior*, correlation by laws 'leaves a residue in the phenomena of life' and 'nothing justifies postulating that the vital dialectic can be integrally translated in physico-chemical relations and reduced to the condition of anthropomorphic appearance'.[40]

For Merleau-Ponty, a fundamental problem with the empiricist position as he understood it was that by eliminating from its account of behaviour what we would normally understand as consciousness, it left the issue of meaning unresolved and did so on two levels. First, both where behaviour is observed in others and where it is experienced by the subject, intention, desire, fear, and adherence to a personal belief system or to a set of culturally embedded values were discounted as effective factors. Referring back to the painting, from such a perspective the personal and social significance of the woman's behaviour would have meaning only in an impoverished form as the *necessary* result or effect of pre-existing conditions. Indeed, these conditions could in principle be reduplicated or reconstructed – in a laboratory setting for example – to produce the same outcome. For the woman to have behaved differently, the physical and chemical stimuli acting upon her organism would have had to be different.

In the second place, the empiricist approach also leaves unexplained the phenomenon of the empirical quest itself. How is this to be understood if not as a quest for knowledge and order, requiring the ability to stand back from a situation, to question it, and to consider its meaning and implications?

Is it possible to posit a self that is capable of doing so without a notion of consciousness? Indeed, *who* does the empiricist researcher think is carrying out the investigations in question? From Merleau-Ponty's point of view, empiricism could be maintained as a position only so long as investigators resisted making themselves the object of study.

Someone opposed to the doctrine that behaviour is always governed by laws of physical causality, someone believing, on the contrary, that the challenge facing human beings is to throw off limitation in all of its guises, whether physiological, historical, social or political, might respond to the subject matter of de Hooch's painting as just described with frustration and impatience. It might be felt that by failing to respond to the play of light on her face and body, by stepping over the path of light which leads the eye through the open doorway to a sun-filled landscape with distant city (traditionally symbolic of an heavenly or utopian ideal), the woman has literally passed by the opportunity to reject the drudgery demanded and expected of her. She has failed to exchange a life of duty and restriction for one of freedom and in so doing is equating her options with the instinctive behaviour of the fowl who share her space. According to this view, truly human behaviour comprises projects or indeed projections of the will or desire. They are modes of being of an entirely different order to the physiological and, since they have to do only with the mind and its contents, need take no serious account of material conditions or limitations.

The naïve consciousness and its reconstructive powers

In de Hooch's painting, an instance of everyday human behaviour is pictured as occurring against, and with reference to, a 'virtual intersection' of bright sunlight that has inserted itself within the scene. As it turns out, this visual presentation has affinities with an important moment in Merleau-Ponty's intervention into the empiricism/rationalism dyad within *The Structure of Behavior*. Merleau-Ponty had begun by presenting rationalism and empiricism as mutually exclusive projects since each regards itself as providing a (potentially) complete explanation of the relations between self and world and of the nature of the will. From this position, however, he moved on to a further analysis in which he showed them to be deeply congruous. He prepared the ground for this analysis strategically by bringing into play a third manner in which the relationship between self and world has been understood, namely, the everyday, non-self-reflexive experiences of the 'naïve consciousness':[41]

> If I am in a dark room and a luminous spot appears on the wall and moves along it, I would say that it has 'attracted' my attention, that I

have turned my eyes 'toward' it and that in all its movements it 'pulls' my regard along with it. Grasped from the inside, my behavior appears as directed, as gifted with an intention and a meaning.[42]

The voice speaking in this passage is that of the naïve consciousness. It describes in non-philosophical and uncritical terms what it feels like to be in relationship with a world of apparently externally existing things and events. In this instance, this world comprises a dark room in which a luminous spot has suddenly appeared on one of its walls.

The naïve consciousness perspective as it is expressed here has several characteristics. In the first place, it provides a description of experience 'from the inside'. Contrary to the objectifications by which the empiricist position justifies itself, here, the speaker – let us imagine that it is Merleau-Ponty himself – acknowledges the personal character of this perspective on the world. It is the world as this speaker experiences it.

In the second place, the speaker describes a relationship with an entity (the luminous spot) that is perceived as having external reality, to be mind-independent and therefore to have a status of 'otherness': 'I have turned by eyes "*toward*" it.'[43]

In the third place, contact with the world is described as relational in character. The speaker feels invited, even strongly invited, to respond to this other, which is before him. He speaks of it as attracting his attention and pulling his regard along with it as it moves along the surface of the wall. And yet, the words '*I have turned my eyes* "toward" it'[44] indicate that he feels his behaviour to have an initiatory and willed component. He *gives* his attention; it does not automatically emanate from him. The implication, then, is that he can also *retract* it. However responsive he may be to the stimulus before him, he retains the capacity to turn away, to lose interest, to resume an abandoned activity or embark upon a new one. He would not say that his perceiving and acting were controlled by this other, that his behaviour was blind and inevitable. Instead, he evidently experiences it as having been called forth by the other. Hence Merleau-Ponty's reference to the naïve consciousness's experience of behaviour as '*gifted* with an intention and a meaning'.[45]

For Merleau-Ponty a fundamental strength of the naïve consciousness position was its non-dualistic stance: it acknowledges in an immediate, albeit unformulated, manner the already intertwined nature of what we conventionally call mind, body and world. As Merleau-Ponty put it towards the end of *The Structure of Behavior*, from the naïve consciousness perspective:

The body proper and its organs remain the bases or vehicles of my intentions and are not yet grasped as 'physiological realities'. ... The unity of man has not yet been broken; the body has not yet been stripped of human predicates; it has not yet become a machine; and the soul has not yet been defined as existence for-itself (*pour soi*). Naïve consciousness does not see in the soul the *cause* of the movements of the body nor does it put the soul in the body as the pilot of his ship. This way of thinking belongs to philosophy; it is not implied in immediate experience.[46]

This also means that where experiences of freedom versus constraint, or free will versus determinism, are concerned, again at issue is not a duality, an opposition, but variations of experience located along a spectrum of possibilities. In the instance described above of an interaction with the spot of light appearing on a wall, the active and receptive components of this experience are presented as more or less equally balanced. Nonetheless, upon examination a certain tension is apparent within this reciprocity between openness to possibility and choice *and* an experience of real limitation. In contrast to the rationalist and empiricist positions, however, neither possibility nor limitation is regarded as absolute. In the most restricted of circumstances certain choices remain open, however limited these might be. Alternatively, even in the most open-ended or apparently unbounded circumstances, one is never in a position wholly to impose one's will or realize one's desires. This tension, which Merleau-Ponty defined as an integral structural characteristic of human behaviour, may be exemplified through a re-reading of the de Hooch in which, now, its composition (or structure) is primarily taken into account. Before proceeding with this, though, it is worth emphasizing that the notion of relative limitation or 'finitude' that is opened up here is one that would remain vital to Merleau-Ponty's ongoing thought, and, as I will show, to the ethics that emerged from it.

Returning to de Hooch's painting, there is an evident contrast between the artist's representation of the courtyard in which the woman stands and the way in which the landscape beyond has been depicted within the painting's background. In visual terms, the courtyard presents itself as the most open structure in the painting but only a small portion of it is visible. It is impossible to judge how far it might project into the viewer's space, making it a realm of possibility and unknowability, an ambiguous space. The painting's background, on the other hand – the expanse of landscape with the barely perceptible city in the distance – is presented as rigidly contained by the symmetrical form of the open doorway leading from the courtyard. Compositionally, not only is the space of the open doorway fairly small but this area is also further sub-divided, vertically by the two tree trunks and horizontally by the canal and dark edge of field further back, thus evoking a strong metaphorical sense of access to the outside being considerably restricted.

Then there is the house, depicted as a solid mass covering more than a third of the canvas. Presented from the rear, and partially obscured by dark foliage, it appears near impenetrable. Yet it is by no means entirely closed or bounded. A window is visible, set high in a bright wall to the left, perpendicular to the surface of the canvas. Further windows are just discernible in a section of wall facing us below the building's pointed roof.

The light which illuminates the left-hand wall may well, if the window is unshuttered, be streaming into the unseen room to which it gives access. There are, then, both ways in and ways out. Thus, while the composition of this painting confirms that limitation is an ever-present reality it also affirms that scenarios are never so enclosed as to be entirely imprisoning.

This reading of the painting's composition may now be re-applied to the question of the woman's functioning. As noted above, she appears to be stepping forward to fulfil a predetermined task while physically aware of the warm invitation of the light and the open doorway to do otherwise – the doorway constitutes a part of her visual field even though she does not look directly at it; we also see the play of light on her face and body, implying the recognition on her part that other possible behaviours run alongside her own. Her behaviour may thus be read not as mechanical or slavish in nature but as occurring within the context of a deeper recognition that to have ceased working and to have gone outside would *not* have been to exchange mindless duty for freedom but rather one set of limitations and possibilities for another. Extrapolating from this third reading, then, interaction with the world does not revolve around the alternatives of free will or determinism but occurs with the awareness of both limitation and possibility as inherent to any given or potential situation.

Returning more pointedly, then, to what Merleau-Ponty saw to be the strengths of the naïve consciousness position and its implications for his own thought, it is nonetheless the case that, while sentient, this position is itself, precisely, naïve and non-reflective. In the first place, while it describes relationships with entities or phenomena that are perceived as having mind-independent reality, insufficient unawareness is expressed regarding the embodied, and therefore mediating, perspectival nature of viewpoints; the naïve consciousness takes for granted that contact is with the world as it is 'in itself'. Secondly, alongside its sense of the interrelatedness of self and world (its non-dualistic position), the naïve consciousness recognition of the apparently reciprocal nature of behaving (of perceiving and acting), the sense that it is neither wholly determined by external conditions nor wholly able to transcend them, remains unproblematic within its processes of looking and acting. But when these experiences are reflected on, or if such behaviours are observed by a third party, certain paradoxes become apparent. In what sense can behaviour be both a response to externally existing conditions and yet also appear initiatory in character, having the capacity to affect events? The naïve consciousness does not raise these questions for itself. Although capable of *describing* its experiences of interrelationship with the world, it does not analyse these descriptions or draw from them conclusions of a philosophical nature concerning either the nature of its perceiving or the nature of the perceived.[47] As Merleau-Ponty wrote later on in *The Structure of Behavior*: 'One can say, if you like, that the relation of the thing perceived to perception, or of the intention to the gestures which realise it, is a magical one in naïve consciousness.'[48]

As indicated, a central aspect of Merleau-Ponty's task in *The Structure of Behavior* was precisely to reflect upon such experiences of interrelationship and take them from the realm of the untheorized, un-reflected, or 'magical' into the realm of the philosophically articulate. However, at this early stage his concern was primarily to show the non-viability of both the rationalist and the empiricist positions with respect to behaviour. The introduction of this third model of behaviour played a key role because it allowed him to discuss those two positions from a new perspective. Specifically, he was able to show that instead of standing in *opposition* to one another as conventionally assumed, rationalism and empiricism could now be seen to stand *together* (a second interpretation of the words 'side by side'[49]) in respect of their responses to the naïve consciousness.

The first way in which they 'stand together' is in their shared criticisms of the naïve consciousness position – although each provides different solutions to the perceived problems and regards itself alone as the necessary corrective. The second, and more important way in which they 'stand together', relates to certain commensurabilities on an unacknowledged pre-suppositional level concerning the nature of their respective positions towards the world. In Merleau-Ponty's view, these commensurabilities outweighed what might be regarded as the more obvious differences between them. For while the empiricist and rationalist positions seemed radically opposed to one another when considered only in relation to each other (as *thesis* and *antithesis* as it were), when examined from this third perspective, the apparently rigid boundaries that seemed to distinguish them collapse and the associations connected with each term de-stabilize.

The immediate point of similarity between rationalism and empiricism is the fact that both actively disregard the naïve consciousness understanding of what it is like to perceive and to act in the world. This lack of engagement leads to the production of philosophical and scientific theories that fail to articulate our everyday, lived experiences. In each case, the naïve consciousness position is dismissed as offering no profitable material in the search for truth concerning our relationship with the world. The reason for this lies in the *reciprocal* nature of the naïve consciousness model, which both empiricism and rationalism regard as unintelligible. As a consequence, the reciprocal model is exchanged for a linear one in each case: interactions that *appear* to the naïve consciousness to be fundamentally reciprocal are presented as if *in reality* they have a point of initiation either wholly within the physical world or wholly within the disembodied mind. From such an active and initiatory position a responsive process is triggered, in the one case, determined, in the other, free. The priority of the naïve consciousness point of view is thus refuted. Empiricism at its most crude prioritizes a situation in which a discrete active component or a complexity of active components, namely, the world, acts upon a passive component: the self as physical organism. For rationalists the active component is the disembodied self or *cogito* which constitutes for itself a world. According to this model, the active component has primary or positive value, the passive one, secondary or even negative value.

Another deep similarity between empiricism and rationalism became apparent when Merleau-Ponty contrasted empiricist and naïve consciousness perspectives in detail. He articulated this in the passage referred to above where the naïve consciousness describes 'from the inside' its interaction with the spot of light. For surrounding that description is the following commentary in which the event is interpreted by a notional third person, an onlooker, in the guise of an experimental psychologist:

> The scientific analysis of behavior was defined first in opposition to the givens of naïve consciousness. ... Science seems to demand that we reject these characteristics as appearances under which a reality of another kind must be discovered. It will be said that seen light is 'only in us'. It covers a vibratory movement, which movement is never given to consciousness. Let us call the qualitative appearance 'phenomenal light'; the vibratory movement, 'real light'. Since the real light is never perceived, it could not present itself as a goal towards which my behavior is directed. It can only be conceptualized as a cause which acts on my organism. The phenomenal light was a force of attraction, the real light is a *vis a tergo*.[50]

The first point is that the scientific mindset, as characterized here, cannot negotiate with the naïve consciousness account of behaviour because one of the ways in which the latter experiences its perceiving and its acting is as intentional or purposive: the light is said to have presented itself as 'a goal' towards which behaviour is directed. But intention as a factor governing behaviour takes behaviour out of the arena of predetermined physical causality. How can purpose, or desire, or notions of attracting as well as being attracted by something adequately be reconciled with a view of organisms, including human organisms, as passive responders to external stimuli, even stimuli of a highly complex nature? For 'science', therefore, the naïve consciousness experience is rooted in an illusory or mistaken understanding of how self and world relate perceptually, one which must be peeled away to reveal a hidden and prior state of affairs. Thus, science sets up an absolute distinction between appearance and reality, the former being the province of the naïve consciousness, the latter of science. The task of science, in this case, is to show that intention, rather than governing and directing behaviour, is in fact only the by-product of a physiological operation. 'Phenomenal light' (*lux*), which is said to appear as a 'force of attraction', is distinguished from 'real light' (*lumen*), this being regarded as the prior physical and physiological reality: a 'vibratory movement, which movement is never given to consciousness'. According to this view, to repeat, since 'the real light is never perceived, it could not present itself as a goal towards which my behavior is directed. It can only be *conceptualized* as a cause which acts on my organism'.[51] Empiricism's rejection of the world of appearance in favour of a 'real' state of affairs associated wholly with the physiological is thus a move governed by *a priori* factors. Like rationalism, the empiricist position is rooted within the realms of the purportedly invisible and conceptual. While, superficially, it presents itself as a mode of investigation based on the unprejudiced observation of phenomena, in reality it too rejects attention to the perceptual world and fails to acknowledge its priority for further thought. As Merleau-Ponty saw it, instead of turning *towards* a realm of foundational, all-embracing realities as it purports, it turned *away* from it to a much more narrowly defined place from which it produced mis-representations of what human beings are, and what it means to see, to act, to think and, indeed, to search for knowledge.

For Merleau-Ponty, however, the most important way in which empiricism and rationalism were aligned is that in both positions there is a split between the world which is regarded as the object of philosophical or scientific investigation and the individual who is taken to be the subject of those investigations. In each case, to reiterate, the 'world' that is posited is a world distinct from a self who either constitutes it or observes and analyses it. *Both* rationalism and empiricism may in fact be said to take an outside view, rationalism with its disembodied cogito, empiricism with its disengaged observer. For Merleau-Ponty the fundamental flaw of empiricism was that it failed to take seriously the embodied nature of its own seeing. As Bannan put it, 'Each is a form of the *natural attitude*, which he also calls *la pensée objective*, or "objectivist thinking"', the function of which is 'to reduce all phenomena which bear witness to the union of subject and world, putting in their place the clear idea of the object as *in itself* and of the subject as pure consciousness. It therefore severs the links which unite the thing and the embodied subject.'[52]

Here though a further observation must be made. Interestingly, it is with respect to rationalism's *and* empiricism's failure to take into account the embodied nature of their seeing that a connection (but not a correlation) may now also be made between those positions and that of the naïve consciousness. Earlier I observed that in the naïve consciousness description of interaction with the spot of light it is unclear to what degree the subject was aware of the embodied and therefore perspectival nature of its viewpoint: the subject seemed not only to have a sense of interacting purposefully with an externally existing world from within its midst but also to feel that this contact was a direct, transparent and 'unmysterious' one. As it turns out, later on in *The Structure of Behavior* when Merleau-Ponty reflected upon the nature of our everyday, naïve descriptions of engagement with the world, he observed that while the naïve consciousness position is clearly a non-dualistic one, it nonetheless bears witness to a naïve form of the natural attitude: 'The bodily mediation most frequently escapes me: when I witness events that interest me, I am scarcely aware of the perpetual breaks which the blinking of the eyelids imposes on the scene, and they do not figure in my memory.'[53]

In this regard, not only rationalism and empiricism but now also the naïve consciousness may be seen to stand 'side by side'. Significantly, however, rationalism and empiricism, while rejecting those aspects of naïve consciousness experience Merleau-Ponty regarded as promising for philosophical reflection, appeared (unwittingly) to have absorbed and elevated to the level of theoretical truth the one aspect of that position which Merleau-Ponty regarded as misleading.

The significance of Gestalt

Having discussed the basic positions adopted by rationalism and empiricism with respect to human functioning, positions which Merleau-Ponty argued are deeply analogous, I turn now to consider the empirical position in more detail. Merleau-Ponty demonstrated that empiricism reduces to the status of epi-phenomena those aspects of behaviour we would naïvely describe as intended, emotional or governed by values and beliefs. Nonetheless, it could be argued that 'sacrificing' these kinds of meaningfulness would be justified if the causal or reflex model of behaviour proved to be viable on its own terms. But in the first half of *The Structure of Behavior*, Merleau-Ponty's exploration of then-recent developments in physiology and experimental psychology, particularly Gestalt theory[54] – which challenged the classical notion of the organism as a passive responder to stimuli – showed this to be unlikely. In other words, these researches were undermining empiricism's project from within.

As noted, empiricism (as it was encountered by Merleau-Ponty) placed behaviour at the end of a chain of events, starting with external stimuli, on to receptors in the body, and from there on to effectors. With the exception of the lowest life forms, the route from receptor to effector was mediated by some kind of information processing centre or centres. According to this model, the differences we notice in everyday life between human functioning and that of animals were differences of degree or quality but not of kind; humans simply have more complex capacities for processing information than do animals. Behaviours that appeared to contradict the causal model, behaviours that seem unpredictable or capricious, were still regarded as explainable in terms of stimulus and response. It was merely a matter of digging deeper in order to finally account for them.

This process of digging deeper on the part of reflex theory so that these more complex connections might be discovered led exponents of this approach to construct explanatory theories of ever-increasing subtlety. Merleau-Ponty observed, for example, that one way of seeking to account empirically for the apparently unaccountable in human functioning was the notion of competition between external stimuli, on the one hand, and certain inbuilt physiological systems with the power to 'over-rule' the otherwise immediate effect of those stimuli on the organism, on the other. The appearance of apparently unexpected behaviour was seen as evidence that a more complex physiological operation was in play. Such operations might be governed by the organism's natural and overriding propensity for equilibrium having final sway, or the body's propensity to inhibit painful excitation. A third notion, as seen in the theories of Pavlov, concerned the manner in which conditioning imposed upon a subject from without (as opposed to innate or instinctual responses) trained the reflexes to regard certain stimuli unfavourably so that they functioned as inhibitors, and others favourably and therefore to be enacted. An alternative to all of these positions was to regard apparently initiatory behaviour as evidence of mechanical/physiological dysfunction. In any case, whichever strategy was adopted, the fact remained that irreconcilabilities between observable phenomena and presupposition or theory (i.e. the theory that all behaviour is purely mechanistic and causally determined), were deemed to be explicable through an increase in complexity in the model. Even for human beings, to act in the world was, in the final analysis, to be acted upon.

Merleau-Ponty's examination of the claims of reflex theory takes up more or less the first half of *The Structure of Behavior*. His conclusion was that processes of devising ever more sophisticated causal theories to account for the complications and complexities of human behaviour would never satisfactorily be resolved. Fuelling his claim was evidence obtained from the field of experimental psychological research itself. Indeed, as indicated at the beginning of this chapter, it was in large part due to developments of this kind that Merleau-Ponty was inspired to embark upon the work that would become *The Structure of Behavior*. In his proposal for this project, then referred to as a study of the nature of perception (his *Projet de travail sur la nature de la Perception* of 8 April 1933), Merleau-Ponty had not only outlined his objections to what he called *une doctrine d'inspiration criticiste* (a mode of thought that treats perception as an intellectual operation in which non-extensive sensations are ordered and explained in such a way as to constitute an objective world) but also presented findings from the experimental researches of Gestalt theory which demonstrated that perception is not such an intellectual act. Among the Gestalt sources referenced in *The Structure of Behavior* was what is often regarded as Gestalt theory's founding text, Max Wertheimer's groundbreaking 1912 paper 'Experimentelle Studien über das Sehen von Bewegung' (Experimental Studies concerning the Perception of Movement). It examined phi-motion, an optical illusion (upon which cinema depends, and before that such instruments as the stroboscope) in which still images, when viewed in rapid succession, are perceived as being in continuous motion.[55] To cite the experimental psychologist Johan Wagemans, Wertheimer understood that

> perceived motion was not just added subjectively after the sensory registration of two spatio-temporal events (or snapshots) but something

special with its own phenomenological characteristics and ontological status. Indeed, based on the phi phenomenon, Wertheimer argued that not sensations but structured wholes or Gestalten are the primary units of mental life. This was the key idea of the new and revolutionary Gestalt theory.[56]

Merleau-Ponty also referenced neurological findings that indicated that activities traditionally associated with the intellect (memory and judgement, for instance) were actually integral to the workings of the nervous system itself, and he wrote about the role of *mouvements naissants* (incipient movements) that are associated with the nervous system and which accompany perception. These findings again challenged the notion of non-extended sensations which need to be 'converted' by the intellect in order to construct the world of extension as it is supposed to exist in 'reality'. In the light of this, Merleau-Ponty wrote of the need to examine the recent literature on '*la perception du corps propre*'. Referring to the work of the English and American realists, he wrote that 'the universe of perception will not be assimilated into the universe of science'.[57]

Of particular importance to him in this respect, were once again the findings of Gestalt theory. Although in his view Gestalt theory was problematic in that it proposed a wholly physiological model of perception, it nonetheless rejected the linear and piecemeal sensationalist model proposed by classical empiricism in favour of a reciprocal and holistic one. Gestalt researchers had discredited the theory that in perception discrete sensations are configured and thus made intelligible via the activities of a separated memory and the capacity to make associations. They demonstrated instead that sensations are from the first perceived in configurations, as 'wholes', 'forms', or 'Gestalts'. They also demonstrated that such patternings do not simply reflect how the world might be taken to be 'in itself' at a given moment but arise relationally within the process of perceiving – we witnessed this phenomenon in the introduction, in auditory terms, with Merleau-Ponty's description of becoming attuned to spoken English during his visit to Manchester: 'Likewise, in the tobacco shop, the woman's phrase: *Shall I wrap them together?* which I understood only after a few seconds – and *all at once.*'[58] As Madison put it, 'Forms are not *real* properties of things but their way of presenting themselves to a perceptual consciousness; they are not therefore real but perceived things.'[59] Although Merleau-Ponty did not see Gestalt theory as going far enough in its explications of perception[60] it did provide him with a justification for making behaviour as it *appears* to the investigator a focus of his own philosophical reflections. He found its claims suggestive; indeed multiple references to Gestalt theory also occur in his late writing, notably, in several working notes appended to *The Visible and the Invisible*. As Wagemans has stated, Gestalt theory has been generally regarded as outmoded since the 1940s in the light of later discoveries within the field of psychology (electrical field theory in the 1950s, and developments in cognitive science and neuroscience from the 1960s).[61] He has also remarked that 'one of the issues that did not fit the Gestalt approach well was language. The reason for this is clear', he has added. 'In psychologies and epistemologies based on rationalist categories, language constitutes meaning. For Gestalt theory, in contrast, language expresses meaning that is already there in the appearance or in the world.'[62] Wagemans concluded that 'although it may be true that the Gestalt theorists failed to develop a complete and acceptable theory to account for the important phenomena they adduced, it is also true that no one else has either. The challenges for contemporary vision scientists are still significant'.[63] Indeed, he has stated that since the turn of the twenty-first century research themes such as perceptual grouping and figure-ground organization – central to the work that Max Wertheimer and his younger colleagues Kurt Koffka and Wolfgang Köhler were conducting in Berlin from the 1920s – have returned to centre stage.

Describing behaviour – Its limitations and scope

Merleau-Ponty's position, then, was to reject not only the theories of behaviour – particularly perceptual behaviours – proposed by both rationalism and empiricism but also the way in which they were conceived. His overall objection was that the systems of thought produced in each case failed to articulate the richness of our everyday experiences of what it is like to live in the world of other people, things and events. Those factors which failed to fit predetermined rationalist or empiricist models were relegated to the realm of the irrational or illusory and a chasm was created between a 'false' world of appearances and a 'real' or 'true' world of *a priori* truths, laws or principles. Indeed, as Merleau-Ponty saw it, in the end both rationalism *and* empiricism – despite the latter's ostensible claims to found its theorizations upon the careful observation of externally existent physical facts – reject the perceptual world favouring that of the intellect. In each case, intellection as a *discrete* act is prioritized and it is to this discreteness that Merleau-Ponty objected.

For Merleau-Ponty, then, both empiricism and rationalism were inadequate with respect to articulating the 'relations of consciousness and nature' in behaviour. But having attempted to show the degrees to which these positions were flawed (on their own terms as well as in relation to our everyday experiences), Merleau-Ponty's strategy was not to attempt some kind of synthesis between them. He did not adopt a dialectical approach. Instead, he pursued the nature/consciousness question from a wholly other starting point.[64] Importantly, before attempting to account for the factors *governing* behaviour (which ended up being the starting point taken by both rationalism and empiricism), he proposed an approach that began by *describing* the phenomenon of behaviour itself in order to better understand it.

> We will come to these questions by starting 'from below' and by an analysis of the notion of behavior. This notion seems important to us because, taken in itself, it is neutral with respect to the classical distinctions between the mental and the physiological and thus can give us the opportunity of defining them anew.[65]

The first characteristic of this approach was Merleau-Ponty's determination to take perception and our spontaneous way of talking about it seriously as a route towards gaining knowledge of what behaviour is and is like. Secondly, his investigative stance, in contrast to that of empiricism, was that of an *engaged* and embedded observer, who was as concerned with the nature of his own perceptual behaviour as with the behaviour of that which he was observing. Needless to say, though, this perception-based approach had repercussions when it came to questioning the kind of philosophy – if any – that could evolve from it. His necessarily situated point of view would inevitably be partial and perspectival, as would any theorizing based upon those observations. This led to a philosophical stance – Paul Ricoeur would, arguably incorrectly, criticize it as a 'philosophy of finitude'[66] – that could claim neither completeness not transparency with respect to its understanding of behaviour and of the world within which those behaviours were installed. Merleau-Ponty had identified the difficulties that arise when the problem of behaviour is approached from a disengaged or disembodied position. But he still needed to demonstrate how and why a philosophy that is incapable of providing complete answers or making ultimate claims for a closed system of truths might nonetheless be regarded as rational and reasonable.[67]

A further way of describing Merleau-Ponty's investigative starting point is to say that his intention was to take seriously the naïve consciousness experience of interaction with the world that was rejected by rationalism and empiricism and to find a way of theorizing it. To do so seemed reasonable if, once again, then-recent scientific findings with respect to behaviour were taken into account, particularly, as noted, the reciprocal model proposed by Gestalt theory. Why? In the first place, despite the apparent paradox that the naïve consciousness seemed to see the world as existing both independently *and* in interrelationship with itself, its understanding of our relationship with the world was a suitably complex one. Here, behaviour is neither wholly determined by externally existent causal factors nor is it the free expression of the mind's untrammelled intentions. This recognition that behaviour is governed in part by factors which we cannot control guarantees the sense of a world that is experienced as having a crucial degree of independent existence, which is therefore capable of arousing genuine curiosity, and which may be interacted with in ways that are both responsive and purposive. This is in contrast to rationalism, on the one hand, which was unable properly to account for responsiveness *to* the world, and to empiricism, on the other, which failed to account for the possibility of changing it – despite its activities clearly having been recruited to bring about a great many such changes – and of being capable of both turning towards and withdrawing from it. Importantly, too, as described, this non-dualistic understanding of behaviour (in which, for instance, curiosity and purposiveness, indeed thought itself, are connected not to the functioning of a disembodied *cogito* but to the activity of an embodied being *in* the world) Merleau-Ponty found to be backed up by recent scientific research into developmental psychology.[68] As he put it, for the naïve consciousness

> thinking can be 'in the throat', as the children questioned by Piaget say it is,[69] without any contradiction of confusion of the extended and the non-extended, because the throat is not yet an ensemble of vibrating cords capable of producing the sonorous phenomena of language, because it remains that privileged region of a qualitative space where my signifying intentions manifest themselves in words.[70]

In the second place, Merleau-Ponty saw the naïve consciousness position as having philosophical possibilities because its route to knowledge was based in perception, a perception which, in keeping with the Gestalt understanding of it, is intuitively understood to be already meaningful; it does not require the activity of a separated intellect to make it so. He backed this up with findings from developmental psychology, referring, in this case, to a late nineteenth-century source, namely, research carried out by the American developmental and educational psychologist Milicent Washburn Shinn (1858–1940):

> Perception is a moment of the living dialectic of a concrete subject; it participates in its total structure and, correlatively, it has as its original object, not the 'unorganized mass', but the actions of other human subjects. ... Nascent perception has the double character of being directed toward human intentions rather than toward objects of nature or the pure qualities (hot, cold, white, black) of which they are the supports, and of grasping them as experienced realities rather than as true objects. ... It is a known fact[71] that [in contrast to the 'hypothesis of sensations'] infantile perception attaches itself first of all to faces and gestures, in particular to those of the mother ... it is possible to perceive a smile, or even a sentiment in this smile, without the colors and the lines which 'compose' the face, as one says, being present to the consciousness or given in an unconscious. Thus the frequently noted fact that we can know a physiognomy perfectly without knowing the color of the eyes or of the hair, the form of the mouth or of the face should be taken quite literally.[72]

The point Merleau-Ponty saw as vital was that the perception of behaviour, both as described by the naïve consciousness and as evidenced in the findings of developmental psychologists, was presented above all as the apprehension of *structures*. It was this fact that led him to develop an approach to behaviour that involved identifying and describing behaviour in terms of the different *forms* it takes. He regarded this approach as productive with respect to the nature/consciousness relationship in human perceiving and acting. According to Merleau-Ponty, rationalism and empiricism had assumed that these terms, 'nature' and 'consciousness', referred to two different kinds of substance, the first belonging to the realm of extension and the second to that of non-extension, with the result that the notion of real interrelationship between them remained unintelligible. Merleau-Ponty, on the other hand, saw that it is possible to treat consciousness and nature as terms descriptive of *different forms of engagement* that might be displayed by an organism (or parts of an organism) with respect to its milieu. The advantage of this was, first, that consciousness now becomes embodied and therefore observable (nature and consciousness are thus no longer regarded as essentially distinct) and secondly, that perception could genuinely be instated as the primary faculty by which knowledge may be gained. In the final paragraph of *The Structure of Behavior* he wrote as follows:

> If one understands by perception the act which makes us know existences, all the problems which we have just touched on are reducible to the problem of perception. It resides in the duality of the notions of structure and signification. A 'form', such as the structure of 'figure and ground', for example, is a whole which has a meaning *and which provides therefore a base for intellectual analysis*. But at the same time it is not an idea: it constitutes, alters and re-organizes itself before us like a spectacle. The alleged bodily, social and psychological 'causalities' are reducible to this contingency of lived perspectives which limit our access to eternal significations.[73]

Indicated in this passage, once again, is the necessarily incomplete nature of the philosophy Merleau-Ponty would derive from such an approach. On the one hand, to repeat, as embodied beings, 'the contingency of lived perspectives … limit our access to eternal significations'. On the other hand, the objects of investigation themselves, namely the many forms that behaviour takes, are not the stable, mind-dependent ideas posited by traditional science and philosophy but may be perceived as mobile and fleeting, provoking wonder as much as understanding, as they 'constitute', 'alter' and 're-organize' themselves before us depending on the nature of our – and their – modes of embeddedness and orientation.

CHAPTER TWO

The symbolic forms and the question of integrated being

Obstacles

It is on the basis of the given obstacle that I will learn.

(*Maurice Merleau-Ponty*)[1]

It is now time to focus on those aspects of *The Structure of Behavior* that have the most direct bearing on the questions at the heart of this book. In what sense might painting be regarded as a mode of interrogation? And, how did painting – as a particular type of object and as a practice, a form of behaviour – enable Merleau-Ponty to reformulate traditional understandings of philosophy and cast new light on its capacity to address the personal, social, political and creative challenges that are presented to us in everyday life?

As indicated, in *The Structure of Behavior* Merleau-Ponty identified and sought to validate his new conceptions of thought through a committed, embedded encounter with the philosophical 'obstacles' inherent to rationalism and empiricism. Contra rationalism, a fundamental task with respect to the Cartesian consciousness/nature dyad was to recast consciousness no longer as non-extended and immaterial but as an observable structure of behaviour. Contra empiricism, it was also recast as operating outside of the stimulus–response model, however elaborately that model might be conceptualized. This was where behaviour in its 'symbolic' mode would come into play. Towards the end of his book, Merleau-Ponty presented painterly practice as an instance of this par excellence. Given the challenge that Merleau-Ponty had set himself, and the fact that it was particularly from the empiricist position that he had to distinguish his own thought, one way of framing his discussion of the behavioural structures surrounding painterly-practice-as-thought is to compare them with the investigative structure that was most consistently examined by him elsewhere: that of the scientific experiment. Significantly, as I will show – and in contrast to the investigative strategies of science that conventionally investigate phenomena in order to discover their principles of repeatability – Merleau-Ponty presented painterly investigation as characterized by the creation of new structures. Or, to recall Merleau-Ponty's words in 'An Unpublished Text', as an orientation 'capable of redesigning an infinite number of situations'.[2] Crucially, again contra rationalism, this achievement was not the result of mental projection or imposition but of responsiveness. As already indicated, the painterly practice that Merleau-Ponty made his point of focus in *The Structure of Behavior* was that of El Greco. It is with the discoveries Merleau-Ponty derived from his engagement with empirical modes of investigation that I begin.

Merleau-Ponty drew on an impressive range of scientific case studies from the experimental and behavioural sciences in order to substantiate the philosophical argument he was trying to forge in *The Structure of Behavior*. One such case study found in the central portion of the book – an experiment by the American psychologist Henry Alford Ruger (1872–1947) and published as 'Psychology of Efficiency' in 1910 – was particularly significant in supporting Merleau-Ponty's own reconfigured understanding of core human behaviour outside of the stimulus–response model.[3]

Ruger's work as a whole focused on the study of individuality and motivation – topics analogous with those already explored from a painterly perspective with respect to de Hooch's *A Woman Carrying a Bucket in a Courtyard*, and indeed with the naïve consciousness description, also discussed earlier, of being in a dark room and responding to a luminous spot that had appeared upon one of its walls. The experiment recorded in 'Psychology of Efficiency' examined approaches to problem-solving. Specifically, it was concerned with how learning obtained in one situation might successfully be applied within a related but novel situation. Ruger's test materials were mechanical puzzles of varying complexity, made from wire, with titles ranging from 'Fan Wire', 'Bicycle', 'Semicircle and Ring' to 'Jiujitsu', 'Twisted Wire', 'Six-piece Cross Long' and 'Race War'. His test subjects were men and women from different cultural and educational backgrounds whom he tasked with the challenge of dismantling the puzzles. This challenge – fortuitously apt given the broad focus of the previous chapter on processes of philosophical disassemblage and themes of apparent incarceration and release – typically involved the removal of some part of the apparatus, such as a ring, star or heart, from the rest. Also significant, given the non-dualistic orientation of Merleau-Ponty's understanding of thought, was the fact that both mental and manual dexterity were required in discovering solutions to these puzzles. In Ruger's words, 'the movements required for solution were, in general, rather complex. In certain cases the degree of complexity could be indefinitely increased, and yet a single rule be developed for solution in the various resulting forms'.[4] In a typical scenario, then, Ruger would start by training individuals in certain methods of dismantlement taking a systematic but piecemeal approach. In other words, at this stage of the experiment, subjects were allowed to perceive and work only with parts of a puzzle. Ruger then presented them with the entire puzzle to dismantle and discovered that they behaved as though the skills they had just learned in piecemeal fashion were unfamiliar to them. Ruger's finding, cited by Merleau-Ponty as especially significant, was that

> learning acquired with respect to a 'part' of a situation is not acquired with respect to this 'same' part assimilated into a new whole. In other words, the real parts of the stimulus are not necessarily the real parts of the situation. The efficacy of a partial stimulus is not tied solely to its objective presence. It must make itself recognised as it were by the organism in the new constellation in which it appears. There is reason for distinguishing the presence of the stimulus in-itself (*en soi*) and its presence for the organism' which reacts.[5]

Merleau-Ponty continued by writing that since 'the decomposition into real parts can never be completed, it is never as an individual reality that the stimulus becomes reflexogenic; it is always as a structure'.[6] Therefore, he argued against the established habit of classifying behaviour according to the rubric of elementary versus complex, proposing instead that behaviour be classified 'according to whether the structure in behavior is submerged in the content or, on the contrary, emerges from it to become, at the limit, the proper theme of activity'.[7] What Merleau-Ponty meant by this, and what he paid attention to, was the organism's *typical* mode of spatio-temporal interaction with its environment and the degree to which it was able to withdraw from a concrete situation (albeit not according to the traditional logic and language of disembodiment), to dominate and to learn from it. It is to the key aspects of this argument, which constitute the bulk of *The Structure of Behavior*, that I now turn.

The three forms of behaviour

Referencing experiments that used both animal and human subjects – experiments whose findings were then valid and in most cases have remained so, but are of enduring interest now in terms of how Merleau-Ponty engaged with them – Merleau-Ponty named three basic forms of behaviour: the syncretic, the amovable and the symbolic. The degree of flexibility evidenced in each depended on whether behaviour occurred mainly in response to stimuli, to signals, or was symbolic in nature. The syncretic forms he described as the most 'submerged' and inflexible. They correspond to mechanical, automatic kinds of functioning, and occur in organisms that respond *mainly* to stimuli; he was quick to point out, however, that 'there is no species of animal whose behavior *never* goes beyond the syncretic level'.[8]

The stimulus/response relationship was understood by him according to the Gestalt model, where the particular nature and orientation of the organism is included in the definition of the stimulus. Citing such experiments as Buytendijk's work with toads, Merleau-Ponty noted that creatures of this kind remained locked into certain inbuilt patterns of behaviour and were unable to over-ride them, even when they were clearly inappropriate or inefficient. As Bannan put it, 'his instinctual equipment allows him no improvisation, and he must adhere strictly to the concrete situation'.[9] He also noted that for a given response to be triggered, a complex set of stimuli needed to be in place (or simulated) at the same time – hence the term 'syncretic'. Conditions needed to be very specific and exact. 'The simplest forms of behaviour, those for example that are found in invertebrates, are never addressed to isolated objects and always depend upon *a large number of external conditions*', wrote Merleau-Ponty:

> An ant placed on a stick allows itself to fall on a white paper marked with a black circle only if the sheet of paper is of definite dimensions, if the distance from the ground and the inclination of the stick have a definite value, and finally if there is a definite intensity and direction of the lighting. This complex of conditions corresponds to natural situations which release the 'instinctive' acts of the animal.[10]

As it turns out, then, reflex behaviour is in fact highly specialized, and it is its highly specialized nature that makes it so inflexible. Not only that, Buytendijk's research showed it to be an *advanced* mode of behaving: 'Functioning by separated parts represents a late acquisition in animal ontogenesis. Reflexes properly so called are found only in the adult salamander; the embryo executes movements of the ensemble, global and undifferentiated movements of swimming.'[11] Indeed, Merleau-Ponty continued: 'It may even be that pure reflexes will most easily be found in man because man is perhaps alone in being able to abandon this or that part of his body separately to the influences of the milieu.' His assessment, then, was that 'the reflex ... cannot be considered as a constituent element of animal behavior except by an anthropomorphic illusion ... the reflex exists; it represents a very special case of behavior, observable under certain determined conditions. But it is not the principal object of physiology'.[12]

A greater degree of flexibility with respect to the milieu is observed in behaviours that typically accord with the amovable forms. Here, behaviour is principally governed by the capacity to respond to *signals* which 'are not determined by the instinctual equipment of the species'.[13] Learning is now a possibility because signals are perceived as providing cues about the structure of a given situation to which the organism can respond, and for which it can develop an aptitude.[14] To cite Merleau-Ponty again, such behaviours are 'founded on structures which are relatively independent of the materials in which they are realized'.[15]

The symbolic forms are the behavioural structures that display the greatest degree of flexibility with respect to the milieu and were associated by Merleau-Ponty only with human – although by no means inevitably humane – functioning; crucially, the capacity to symbolize is not intrinsically ethical; it produces bad as well as good fruit. Merleau-Ponty also made the further point, to which I will return, that the other two forms of functioning are also highly developed in humans: 'There is no species of animal … whose behavior *never* descends below the symbolic forms.'[16] The most obvious instances of the symbolic forms of behaviour are displayed in our facility to create and deploy 'use-objects' such as 'clothing, tables [and] gardens', and to interact by means of 'cultural objects' such as 'books, musical instruments [and] language'.[17] We might add to this the impulse to create and communicate by means of visual imagery. The flexibility that the symbolic forms of behaviour make possible is due to the complex networks of connection that the symbol makes perceptible to organisms so oriented as to apprehend them: not only is the symbol related to the thing or events for which it stands but it is also related to other symbols.[18]

Most importantly, the realm of the symbolic as the milieu of the human being is one in which both actual and potential spatio-temporalities are perceptible and thus made accessible, and here there is a connection with the themes already opened up in the introduction. Merleau-Ponty insisted that whether we are thinking about the signification of speech, suicide or revolution, 'these acts of the human dialectic all reveal the same essence: *the capacity of orienting oneself in relation to the possible, to the mediate, and not in relation to a limited milieu*'.[19] Thus it was within this generative context that he accounted for consciousness (i.e self-reflexivity) defining it as 'a network of significative intentions which are sometimes clear to themselves and sometimes, on the contrary, lived rather than known. Such a conception', he added, 'will permit us to link consciousness with action by enlarging our idea of action.'[20] Moreover, this relationship between the concrete and the possible within the symbolic forms is of a special kind: a grasp upon the specificities of a given situation is always *maintained* while unspecified alternative possibilities, scenarios or points of view are *also* envisaged in relation to it.

Experimentation revealed that symbolic functioning thus defined was exclusive to human beings. With animal activity certain limits were revealed. Drawing on Köhler's 1921 study, translated as *The Mentality of Apes*, Merleau-Ponty reported that, like the human, a chimpanzee could use the branch of a tree as a stick in order to accomplish a desired goal – to reach a piece of fruit hanging out of reach, for instance. However – and again at issue for us now is not the validity of the human/animal distinctions Merleau-Ponty was making here but the behavioural differences being foregrounded – Köhler's research revealed that the chimpanzee could see this object under a *single* aspect only: either as a tree branch or, when it was being used as such, as a stick, but never as both. Such 'single-aspect' perception and the activity that accompanies it, Merleau-Ponty wrote, 'loses itself in the real transformations which it accomplishes and cannot reiterate them'[21]. The chimpanzee's functioning occurred only in relation to *concrete* situations. In animal behaviour 'signs always remain signals and never become symbols'.[22] For humans, on the contrary, 'the tree branch which has become a stick will remain precisely a tree-branch-which-has-become-a-stick, the same *thing* in two different functions and visible *for him* under a plurality of aspects'.[23] In other words, the object's continuity is maintained even when alterations occur with respect to its function or position within the milieu. This is known as object constancy.[24]

The different ways in which it is possible to relate to objects has consequences where the capacity to learn is concerned. Animal activity, to repeat, 'loses itself in the real transformations which it accomplishes and cannot reiterate them'. According to the research cited by Merleau-Ponty, the chimpanzee might, on one occasion, have used a tree branch to reach an inaccessible piece of fruit. But in order to do so on subsequent occasions with different tree branches and different pieces of inaccessible fruit this possibility would once again need to be signalled to him.[25] Such signalling need not occur for human learning to occur. Although learning through signals – through the instruction of others, for instance, as in Ruger's experiment – is an important aspect of our development, the innovative learning that is so characteristically associated with the symbolic forms is possible because, from the beginning, situations and configurations present themselves to us as replete with possibility. This means, first, that we can improvise within given situations. Secondly, we can learn from them, repeating and making successful behaviours dispositional, while avoiding unsuccessful ones. (We may of course also choose to do the inverse, thus creating bad habits.) Thirdly, we can generalize from given situations.

Merleau-Ponty wrote that the unique manner in which humans are able to relate to the milieu (the way in which we are able to hold together a sense of the concrete with a sense of the possible or virtual) has its foundations in the equally unique manner in which we are able to relate to ourselves as embodied beings. In animal behaviour, he wrote,

> the external object is not a thing in the sense that the body itself is – that is, a concrete unity capable of entering into a multiplicity of relations without losing itself. What is really lacking in the animal is the symbolic behavior which it would have to possess in order to find an invariant in the external object, under the diversity of its aspects, *comparable to the immediately given invariant of the body proper and in order to treat, reciprocally, its own body as an object among objects.*[26]

Again, he wrote that 'the animal cannot put itself in the place of the movable thing and see itself as the goal'.[27]

In both respects, there are points of similarity and distinction between human and animal behaviour as Merleau-Ponty presented them here, drawing of course on then-current research. The experiments to which he referred demonstrated that, like humans, animals perceive *themselves* as remaining the same individual despite even radical alterations in behaviour, experience and situation. For both, the body is experienced as a concrete unity capable of entering into a multiplicity of relations without losing itself.[28] Again, both humans and animals are united in being able to regard the world (or more precisely certain objects, organisms or events) as goals towards which their behaviour is directed. And this leads to a further key observation. Where the behaviour of humans and animals are taken to differ is that humans have the capacity to treat the things in the world ('the external object') according to the model provided by our own body. External things can be seen to be *like* our own body (despite various obvious differences) and, conversely, the body is also seen to be like things: it can be treated as 'an object among objects' – or indeed, parts of the body as objects among objects. This capacity to regard or represent ourselves as objects – which includes being able to regard ourselves as if from the point of view of others,[29] also known as the substantive self-consciousness – has a number of behavioural implications. For instance, it means that humans are able to regard ourselves not only as the instigators of an action but also as the goal of a particular action. It also means we have the capacity to treat the body or parts of the body as (detachable) instruments. Indeed, as noted earlier, this explains the success of those modes of human behaviour displayed within laboratory contexts which led Merleau-Ponty to observe that pure reflexes are most likely to be found in us.

As already emphasized, this does not mean that human behaviour is therefore governed and explainable by the reflex. Rather it reveals that our ability to symbolize must be prior and innate; this is why we are able to regard our own bodies as taking on multiple meanings, articulations and corporeal schemata in relation to the world, including fragmented and piecemeal ones. The laboratory, as an artificial space created specifically for testing hypotheses, is itself an outcome of this primordial human capacity. The laboratory's creation and use, like that of all objects, depends upon 'the recognition, beyond the present milieu, of a world of things visible for each "I" under a plurality of aspects, the taking possession of an indefinite time and space... the capacity of orienting oneself in relation to the possible, to the mediate'.[30]

Beyond inherited structures

We have seen that Merleau-Ponty associated 'consciousness' with the symbolic forms of behaviour, and 'nature' above all with the syncretic and amovable forms, stating that all three forms of behaviour occur in human functioning. Humans respond to stimuli, signals and symbols and, indeed, as noted, it is in us that 'pure reflexes will most easily be found'. Having made these claims, he proceeded to clarify how he took these three forms of behaviour to interrelate in humans. It is here, through Merleau-Ponty's positioning of the symbolic forms as both the highest *and* the most primordial form of behaviour in humans, that we find the first articulation of what would become a key philosophical theme in his later writing: the priority of creativity within specifically human modes of behaviour. 'What defines man', he wrote, 'is not the capacity to create a second nature – economic, social or cultural – beyond biological nature; it is rather the capacity of going beyond created structures in order to create others.'[31] Here, again, he overturned a conventional hierarchy in which creative behaviour is defined as an add-on rather than a prerequisite, as secondary rather than primary. In this way he also refuted the idea of there being absolute distinctions between notions of nature (associated, by empiricism above all, with the syncretic forms of behaviour) and consciousness (associated, by Merleau-Ponty, with the symbolic forms and creativity). From this perspective, 'biological nature' must itself be understood as a construct, a creation, derived from our capacity to symbolize.

Merleau-Ponty went on to present the interrelationship of the three forms in the human context as a matter of varying degrees of integration with the highest degree of integration between them being preferable. Indeed, a propensity towards integration appears to be another function of consciousness as he understood it and it is again enabled by the human capacity to symbolize. Now, making a shift in terminology, and referring to the three forms of behaviour just discussed as the 'physical', 'vital' and 'human' orders, he expressed this idea as follows:

> The relation of each order to the higher order is that of the partial to the total. A normal[32] man is not a body bearing certain autonomous instincts joined to a 'psychological life' defined by certain characteristic processes – pleasure and pain, emotion, association of ideas – and surmounted with a mind which would unfold its proper acts over this infrastructure. The advent of higher orders, to the extent that they are accomplished, eliminate the autonomy of the lower orders and give a new signification to the steps which constitute them. This is why we have spoken of a human order rather than of a mental or rational order.[33]

A further crucial Merleau-Pontean point was that for cohesive and unified human functioning to occur, the integration between the three forms of behaviour had to be accomplished internally. In the section of *The Structure of Behavior* entitled 'The Physical Order; The Vital Order; The Human Order' he attributed to the symbolic forms the ability to create internal linkages between what he called 'situation' and 'reaction' in a way that refuted the logics of causality and linearity that were foundational to traditional empirical thought. Where symbolic behaviour is concerned, he wrote: 'Situation and reaction are linked internally by their common participation in a structure in which the mode of activity proper to the organism is expressed. Hence they cannot be placed one after the other as cause and effect: they are two moments of a circular process.'[34]

What makes this internal linkage of situation and reaction possible is, again, the uniquely human capacity to create new structures by which to interrelate with the world of other people or things, and, concurrently, new ways of perceiving and interacting with the self. This matter was explored with particular focus in the section of *The Structure of Behavior* called 'The Relations of Body and Soul and the Problem of Perceptual Consciousness'. It was here that the question of painting and painterly practice arose in a sustained way through Merleau-Ponty's suggestive discussion of the 'novelty' of El Greco's style, revealed in how he rendered 'the form of the body'[35] in his paintings.

As indicated in the introduction, El Greco had become a focus of art-historical interest from the second half of the nineteenth century. Among the various ways in which his work was discussed were attempts to present a wholly physiological interpretation of his style. This was part of a broader attempt to validate art history as a field of study by subsuming it under a positivistic logic. This interpretation – which came to be known as the 'El Greco Fallacy' – posited that the elongated forms depicted in his paintings were the outcome of a physical dysfunction: the perceptual elongation of objects caused by astigmatism.[36] Merleau-Ponty, by contrast, interpreted the 'form of the body' in El Greco's paintings as a significant pictorial instance of the creation of new integrative structures. In Merleau-Ponty's alternate interpretation, for the sake of argument, the situation requiring integration remained that of the physical condition (astigmia) which purportedly affected the artist's vision. The 'reaction' referred to the particular way in which El Greco, thus afflicted, may be thought to have perceived and engaged with the world – specifically how he perceived the world of other bodies and represented them in his paintings. The questions Merleau-Ponty raised were focused on the nature of the relationship between these two phenomena and the meaning of the work produced:

If one supposes an anomaly of vision in El Greco, as has sometimes been done, it does not follow that the form of the body in his paintings, and consequently the style of the attitudes, admit of a 'physiological explanation'. When irremediable bodily peculiarities are integrated with the whole of our experience, they cease to have the dignity of a cause in us. A visual anomaly can receive a universal signification by the mediation of the artist to become for him the occasion of perceiving one of the 'profiles' of human existence. The accidents of our bodily constitution can always play this revealing role on the condition that they become a means of extending our knowledge by the consciousness which we have of them, instead of being submitted to as pure facts which dominate us.[37]

Here, then, we return explicitly to the theme – and to scenes – of brokenness and revivification with which the previous chapter opened by means of its discussions of Kapusta's *O's Vocalization*, and which were also explored in the introduction particularly with respect to El Greco's *Christ on the Cross Adored by Donors*. In *The Structure of Behavior*, the point of focus for Merleau-Ponty, to repeat, was El Greco's 'broken' body as a body that continued to paint. Merleau-Ponty's proposition was that by painting in the way that he did, El Greco reconfigured his own purported disability into a new mode of enablement. Here, the dualism of disability and ability also lost its viability and force.[38] Indeed, it is worth noting that even though the main philosophical context for Merleau-Ponty's discussion of El Greco was his broad refutation of empirical, causally grounded attempts at explaining human behaviour, his alternate reading also provided invaluable resources for an issue that has become increasingly urgent within late-twentieth-century and twenty-first-century debate: our need, in a world characterized by much brokenness, to think productively about all of those bodies that are deemed to be 'disabled' – our own, or those of others – and to situations that are deemed to be hopelessly and repeatedly 'dysfunctional'.

As indicated earlier, in the empiricist interpretation of the relationship between El Greco's physical condition and the way in which he represented the body artistically, the latter was regarded as wholly accounted for by the former. Here, situation and reaction were *externally* related: they were 'placed one after the other as cause and effect'.[39] The procedure of painting was thus regarded as an imitative operation in which the artist literally recorded in paint the sensations received by his damaged perceptual apparatus: El Greco painted the body as elongated and twisted because he was a sufferer of astigma, and this was how he *saw* it. This position suggested that the painter was enslaved by the particularities of his irremediable bodily condition and had no option other than passively to submit to them. It also carried with it a necessarily impoverished interpretation of El Greco's paintings, with their main significance now revolving around their signalling of physiological symptoms and potential diagnoses.

Merleau-Ponty's objection in challenging the physiological explanation was not primarily to the belief that the artist may have suffered from an 'anomaly' of vision – whether from birth or from a certain point in his life onwards – or indeed that this might have affected the appearance of the body in his work. Rather, it was with the explanation provided by empiricism about the nature of El Greco's response to this physical condition and with the suggestion that this was the only option available to him. This led Merleau-Ponty to supply an alternative reading of El Greco's mode of representing of the body. Far from being a symptom of dysfunction, he argued, it expressed the painter's *active* navigation of his condition, and of the world, *by means of* this altered mode of seeing. Thus, for Merleau-Ponty, the 'novelty' of El Greco's style pointed, first, to El Greco's successful integration of his condition into the whole of his experience, and, secondly, to it having become a means of *extending* his knowledge of the world by providing him with *another way* of seeing it. As Merleau-Ponty put it, the accident of his bodily constitution played a 'revealing role' with respect to the world as opposed to being that which cut him off or permanently estranged him from it. 'When irremediable bodily peculiarities are integrated with the whole of our experience', he wrote, 'they cease to have the dignity of a cause in us. A visual anomaly can receive a universal signification by the mediation of the artist to become for him the occasion of perceiving one of the "profiles" of human existence.'[40] Merleau-Ponty's point was that a condition such as this, assuming that it could not be rectified, need not therefore be perceived as a pure fact which would 'dominate' the subject as if from the outside, either by 'enforcing' submission to it, or by provoking resistance to or flight from it:

> Ultimately, El Greco's supposed visual disorder was conquered by him and so profoundly integrated into his manner of thinking and being that it appears finally as the necessary expression of his being much more than a peculiarity imposed from the outside. It is no longer a paradox to say that 'El Greco was astigmatic because he produced elongated bodies'.[41] Everything which was accidental in the individual, that is, everything which revealed partial and independent dialectics without relationship to the total signification of his life, has been assimilated and centred in his deeper life. Bodily events have ceased to constitute autonomous cycles, to follow the abstract patterns of biology and psychology, and have received a new meaning.[42]

Having conquered his visual disorder not by eliminating it but by so profoundly integrating it into his manner of thinking and being that 'it appears finally as the necessary expression of his being', El Greco's disorder was no longer a disorder for him. Conversely, it would have remained so had this integration failed to occur. The question, then, is how this alternative, productive and, indeed, liberating route of integration came to be accomplished.

As Merleau-Ponty saw it, the challenge in the first place was for the subject (here, El Greco) to acknowledge who he was, what had happened to him physiologically and the effect this had on the way the world appeared to him. By being faithful to *this* world, and bringing *it* to expression (by thus creating a new structure of being) he was not closed off from the world as he had experienced it in the past, or as he supposed it still to be for others. Instead, he experienced his own particular mode of seeing as the entrance *into* a world that was distinctive but remained intersubjectively open. Because of the nature of painterly activity – the complex ways in which hands, eyes, matter, structure, tradition and novelty combine and express – painting is a particularly powerful (albeit by no means the only) sphere in which navigations and readjustments of this kind can take place.

While this was not an observation that Merleau-Ponty made explicit at this stage, it would become increasingly so as his writing developed. Here too, given his focus on the capacity to symbolize, to perceive and, thus also, to conceive or think under multiple profiles, the roots of Merleau-Ponty's lifelong exploration of painting-as-thought are in evidence.

This leads to another aspect of Merleau-Ponty's thought that would become increasingly prominent. It is the generalization that the basis for communication is *not* the assurance of having access to a world that has a single persisting appearance and meaning for all of us. For as is evidenced by our innate capacity to symbolize, and whether we have a recognized bodily dysfunction or not, we all perceive, approach and describe the world in ways that are necessarily situated and individualized. There are many ways for the world to be a world. Similarly, there are many ways for our bodies to be bodies – the ambiguous, shifting or mutating nature of El Greco's bodies may be seen to testify to this understanding. Additionally, there are many ways for a given cultural (or symbolic) entity like language to be a language.[43] As Merleau-Ponty saw it, it is precisely this fact that presupposes our propensity to communicate in the first place. Since, as symbolizing beings, we are capable of perceiving *as if* from the point of view of others, since we regard the world and the things in the world 'under a plurality of aspects', our different modes of perceiving overlap in our own experience, and, by extension, in the experiences of the group. All members of a group, whatever its nature, size or complexity, can adjust their own points of view and imagine seeing their world differently. They can join others in seeing as they do. Thus, as a viewer of El Greco's painting I do not need to suffer from astigma in order for it to take on meaning for me. I can so adjust my vision as to comprehend his world as a variation of mine, as one of its possible manifestations.

The second requirement for productive integration is that its accomplishment be genuine: it must not be an 'apparent' or 'stereotyped' unity – and here, as above, the implications of these discussions for our own still urgent questions about the nature, perception and nurturing of true community within fractured times are more than apparent.[44] In Merleau-Ponty's words:

> Unity does not furnish an adequate criterion of the liberty which has been won, since a man dominated by a complex, for example, and subject to the same psychological mechanism in all his undertakings, realises unity in slavery. But here it is only a question of an apparent unity, of a stereotyped unity, which will not withstand an unexpected experience. It can be maintained only in a chosen milieu which the sick person has constructed for himself precisely by avoiding all situations in which the apparent coherence of his conduct would be disorganised. True unity on the contrary is recognised from the fact that it is *not obtained by a restriction of the milieu.*[45]

Merleau-Ponty continued:

> The same sensory or constitutional infirmity can be a cause of slavery if it imposes on man a type of vision and monotonous action from which he can no longer escape, or the occasion of a greater liberty if he makes use of it as an instrument. This supposes that he knows it instead of obeying it. For a being who lives at the simple biological level, it is a fatality.[46]

Genuine integration is not merely the capacity to conform to circumstances which are first experienced as externally originating intrusions upon the self: the indignities of an illness, for instance, the destabilizing impact of 'foreign bodies' – however we might interpret these – or of the wounds inflicted by an injustice. As already observed, it requires that we consciously, and most likely painfully, acknowledge and 'know' them and in this way assume responsibility for them. Old attachments to self and world must be lost, and new ones gained – here again is a recurrence of that theme of renunciation or sacrifice already discussed. It is only in this way that the intrusion can lose its dominance over us. It must no longer be perceived as an external force acting upon us. Rather, it must undergo a transformation such that, as Merleau-Ponty insisted, it becomes for us an *instrument* for changing the structure of the world, fluently and, as 'the necessary expression of [our] being', unconsciously. Again, given contemporary current affairs, the relevance of, and need for, such reconfigured understandings hardly needs pointing out.

In the case of a false or superficial unity, an intrusive set of circumstances retains its dominance and its externality. This has the effect of making the sufferer – the one who has been intruded upon – *its* instrument or expression, a reality that can be hidden from awareness only through the subject's adherence to 'monotonous' self-deceptive devices which must be perceived by him as having an *external* rather than self-derived source. Both the individual nature of the subject's perspective and the possibility that the world could be otherwise than it is now conceived of must be suppressed. The subject's world and *the* world must be felt to coincide. In a situation of false unity, the creation of new structures does not occur since this would constitute a threat to the subject's precarious sense of equilibrium. As Merleau-Ponty put it, superficial forms of integration are obtained 'by a restriction of the milieu'. All situations in which 'the apparent coherence of his conduct would be disorganised' must be avoided. This position he described as 'unity in slavery', and as the evidence of repression:

> One will say that there is repression when integration has been achieved only in appearance and leaves certain relatively isolated systems subsisting in behavior which the subject refuses both to transform and to assume. A complex is a segment of behavior of this kind, a stereotyped attitude, an acquired and durable structure of consciousness with regard to a category

of stimuli. A situation which could not be mastered at the time of an initial experience and which gave rise to anguish, and the disorganisation which accompanies failure, is no longer experienced directly.[47]

Merleau-Ponty's position, then, was that enslaving or repressive conditions have an absolute force upon us only if we collude with them to such a degree that we are no longer aware of them. Thus, the important work of consciousness is to reveal and resist such acts of collusion. The flexibility of vision and action that is intrinsic to symbolic functioning must be awakened. And finally, there is the call – and, if the mysterious pleasures of painterly and other acts of creation are made paradigmatic, the joyous call – to instigate processes through which unacceptably limiting articulations of self, world, and their interrelationship, may be transformed into promising ones.[48] A cautionary remark to conclude, however. To describe such transformations as promising is not to make a moral claim; their outcomes should not be regarded as inevitably or unambiguously in service of the good; they might be the inverse. But having been born from integrity they *will* be persuasive.

PART TWO

Painting – Rethinking thought as perceptual and embodied

FIGURE 3.1 *Wols (Alfred Otto Wolfgang Schulze)*, Untitled (Paris – Palisade) (Ohne Titel [Paris]), *1932–3, gelatin silver print on paper, 7.7 × 4.6 cm. © ADAGP, Paris and DACS, London 2018 / Kupferstich-Kabinett, Staatliche Kunstsammlungen Dresden. Photo: Herbert Boswank.*

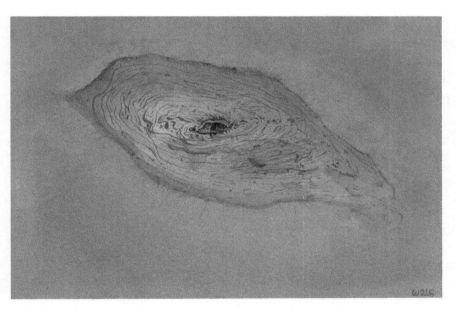

FIGURE 3.2 Wols (*Alfred Otto Wolfgang Schulze*), Untitled, *c. 1944–5, graphite, watercolour and gouache on paper, 9.2 × 13.5 cm. Tate, London. © ADAGP, Paris and DACS, London 2018 / Tate, London, 2017.*

CHAPTER THREE

Description and the re-education of sight

How to start again

A question that was being asked again and again within the immediate post-war period was this: 'Is it possible to start again?' It lies at the heart of Merleau-Ponty's *Phenomenology of Perception* and other key essays written during this period, including 'Cézanne's Doubt' – indeed, for Merleau-Ponty the trajectory of Cézanne's art-making was paradigmatic in this regard. Crucially, as demonstrated by Frances Morris and Sarah Wilson in the catalogue for the Tate, London's 1993 exhibition *Paris Post-War, Art and Existentialism 1945–55*, it was also a problem being addressed in visual and material terms by then-contemporary artists, using pictorial languages that ranged from the figurative and realist, to the primitivist, and to the lyrically and geometrically abstract – despite the fact that, as Morris put it, 'the image presented by the *fonctionnaires* of the artistic community in post-war Paris ... was one of cultural continuity and of the resurgence of pre-war masters'.[1] She continued:

> Museums and critics lionised Picasso, Braque, Léger and Matisse, originators of the French traditions of Cubism and Fauvism (as opposed to the more international phenomena of Expressionism, Surrealism and Abstraction). Their status was confirmed by prizes awarded at successive Venice Biennales from 1948, to Braque, Matisse and Dufy. Such apotheoses encouraged a proliferation of Cubist and Fauvist styles among the next generation. One such, the young painter André Marchand, now barely remembered, was widely considered the worthy successor to Picasso and Braque.[2]

Before turning more pointedly to Merleau-Ponty's thought, I would like to linger for a moment with the *abstract* art-making practices emergent in the 1940s and 50s. Why? Because abstraction constitutes perhaps the most

emphatic artistic expression of starting over. Among these practices was
what Tapié, in *Un Art Autre* (already referenced in the introduction), had
coined 'L'art informel' due to the spontaneous and improvised nature of
its mark-making. Associated with L'art informel – in which the surrealist
technique of automatism played a significant role and which also included
such subgroupings as 'taschisme', 'matter painting' and lyrical abstraction –
were works by artists such as Jean Dubuffet, Jean Fautrier, Karel Appel,
Alberto Burri, Willem de Kooning, Georges Mathieu, Jean-Paul Riopelle,
Henri Michaux, Hans Hartung, Pierre Soulages and Wols (Alfred Otto
Wolfgang Schulze; 1913–1951). Wols' watercolours, for instance (see
Figure 3.2), had attracted critical attention within intellectual circles due to
a one-man show, his first, at the Galerie René Drouin in December 1945.[3]
He had previously been a photographer. Characteristic of Wols' paintings, as
with works by Giacometti, Dubuffet, Fautrier, Germaine Richier and others,
was a materially and perceptually embedded entrance into the physical and
psychological anguish of a world torn open – by the war, of course but also
by post-war privations and the effects of the post-war processes of *épuration*
(the purging of French society of Nazi collaborators) that were taking place.
Although it was Sartre rather than Merleau-Ponty who would write about
Wols' work,[4] the latter's approach and the terrain his work evokes is well-
aligned with important aspects of Merleau-Ponty's project. This is certainly
the case where perspectives on the primacy and expansiveness of embodied
perception are concerned but affinities may also be found between the
inter-corporeal and arguably non-anthropocentric energies associated with
Wols' formations and Merleau-Ponty's explorations of what he called
'anonymous being' and the operations of the habit-body – a topic I will
explore in greater detail in the next chapter. Take the small untitled work on
paper from 1944 to 1945 which is part of the Tate collection, made using
graphite, watercolour and gouache (Figure 3.2). Moving between figuration
and abstraction, like most of Wols' works, it evades clear identification. It
looks bloody, coagulated and as if torn from a larger body. According to
the description provided by the Tate, a source for the image 'might be a
photograph taken by Wols that shows a cut of meat, exposing the joint'.[5] It
also looks like a torn-out eye, uncannily alive and furtively viewing the world
around it. But as an image it is also well-formed and visually coherent; and,
alongside its more gruesome visual associations, it may also be interpreted
as seed-like in form and thus suggestive of growth. Indeed, whether Wols'
images are apparently self-enclosed, as here, or wildly explosive as is often
the case with his drawings and later paintings, they always also convey a
formative and energetic quality. However small in size, they always seem
to evoke large-scale scenarios – an effect, I'd argue, produced by Wols'
incorporation of immense detail, texture and layering into his works, which
provoke close, absorbed and thus expansive viewing. This tendency was
also evident in his earlier photographic work. For Wols, reputedly, the
camera lens was a means of expressing the rhythm and movement of the

visual world; he had a painterly engagement with the camera. Thus in an untitled pre-war photograph of a Paris palisade from which the ripped debris of one or more notices or posters or billboards furl and flap (Figure 3.1), we see his attentiveness towards a surface marked by brokenness, damage and demolition. But the work's overall composition again testifies to an underlying sense of order. Furthermore, the photograph's more obvious subject matter – the palisade – signals the boundaries of a terrain that is not directly visible but in which something is either being constructed or is deemed worthy of protection. To repeat, despite the centrality given to the textures of torn-ness, and indeed to material and information that is now absent, there is an overall sense of cohesiveness, a gestalt, a sense of aliveness and a sense of structure in which the viewer's eye is being exercised and our vision expanded. And in this respect, a short, interwar review of Wols' photography by Hector E. Henry van Loon makes interesting reading. Having first referred to Ferdinand Léger (also an important source for Merleau-Ponty) who, he wrote, had 'termed the eye the most important organ because it assumed myriad duties', van Loon added:

A consciousness of the multiple duties of vision is evident in the work of WS [sic], who, considering his young age, has already produced a large oeuvre. This consciousness in premised on a deeper connection between viewer and viewed than in the usual sense: the work of Schulz [sic] expresses a feeling for the essence of objects in their unity with the searching, meditative eye.[6]

Here, of course, we find a deep connection with Merleau-Ponty's discussions of the multiple profiles of being in *The Structure of Behavior*. Sartre, in his reflections on the work of Wols, would adopt a more alienated position akin to that found in his 1938 novel *Nausea*. He characterized the artist as seeing with the eyes of an outsider, from a place of isolation, and representing 'anguish in plastic form, revealing the continuous struggle of the artist to define himself in the world'.[7] In van Loon's review, arguably, we also find an evocation of what Crowther, in *Phenomenologies of Art and Vision*, referred to as the 'transperceptual', namely, 'the space of those unnoticed or hidden details that subtend immediate experience'; the space – and indeed the 'cognitive background' – that provides a sense of the 'possibilities and transformations that might emerge to perception if we changed our current spatial and temporal position'.[8] Also evoked are Crowther's discussions of abstract tendencies in art, which he most forcefully associated not with phenomena of abstracting-from but with *abstracting-as*, thus proffering an expansive understanding of the perceptual experiences abstract art in its varied modes can open up. Despite the fact that, as indicated in the introduction, Merleau-Ponty did not himself reflect philosophically upon abstract art, I hope that by considering it briefly now, especially as treated by Crowther, pertinent connections with important aspects of

Merleau-Ponty's thought and its wider application will be evident. Indeed, Fóti, in her own treatment of the significance of Merleau-Ponty's ideas for abstract art-making, had put it as follows:

> Given that Merleau-Ponty's thought remains fascinated by vision and that, as Lefort puts it 'he interrogates vision as no one else has done', a mode of painting that arises out of vision itself as a purely visual interrogation of vision should be particularly important to him. One would expect his discussions of painting to prepare for a form of abstract painting. ... His texts on painting do indeed offer insights crucial for a philosophical study of abstract painting. Prominent among these is the point that the painter's signifying intention is not guided by pre-given significations or that 'conception' cannot, for the painter, precede 'execution'.[9]

Crowther – to return to him – derived his notion of abstracting-as from his reading of the first (1968) edition of Richard Wollheim's book *Art and its Objects* and from the notion of 'seeing-as' presented within it: seeing-as 'in the Wittgensteinian sense of perceiving something under one of its aspects – a perception that can sometimes "dawn" upon one rather than always be immediately recognized'.[10] Thus, the expansiveness associated with abstracting-as emerges, for instance, when one particular aspect of the abstract tendencies in art-making is attended to and pursued, and then perhaps another.

In the opening paragraph of the chapter in Crowther's book dedicated to this topic, 'Abstract Art and Transperceptual Space: Wollheim and Beyond', he had identified five aspects under which painterly abstraction – that is, work that does not 'present some recognizable specific kind of three-dimensional entity or state of affair'[11] – might present itself. His list began with 'self-referential' works by which he meant those involving various 'minimal and post-painterly idioms'. Secondly, he listed works that alluded to but did not represent three-dimensional forms, as in biomorphic and technomorphic abstraction. Thirdly, he referred to 'idioms of spatial structure and its perception' as in colour field painting, geometric abstraction and 'op' art. Fourthly he referenced works in which two or more of the modes of abstraction just listed might be combined and, fifthly, those in which one or more abstract modes might be combined with figuration, that is, with 'specific recognisable three-dimensional forms'.[12] (Wols' paintings would certainly fall into, but not necessarily be contained by, the biomorphic category. We might also want to think about the paintings of Durner, Johnson and von Heyl in relation to this overall scheme.) Then, with respect to the expansiveness of 'seeing-as', which he saw to be particularly useful when applied to discussions of abstract art, he wrote that

> seeing-as – in the sense of seeing an aspect of something – involves the *selective* perception or imagining of some specific feature of that

something. This can be exemplificational, as when we focus on one aspect (to the exclusion of others) that is presently available to perception, or it can be imaginative – as in those cases when we think of an aspect that is presently hidden but which could in principle become directly accessible to perception under certain circumstances. Such imaginative seeing-as might, indeed, involve the projection of hypothetical aspect perception (i.e. possible appearances of the item or state of affairs, encompassing, indeed, relations as well as qualities). Indeed, it is possible to project things or aspects that do not actually exist, by means of imaginatively intending aspects (in the form of mental imagery).[13]

For Merleau-Ponty, writing in the *Phenomenology*, the question of how to start again was applied to the realm of philosophy but here too the way forward was posited in terms of refreshed and remobilized perceptual orientations. As he had already begun to make explicit in *The Structure of Behavior*, a renewed philosophical thought *must* begin with practices of looking and describing – practices which not only classically oriented philosophers of Merleau-Ponty's era but also, within the still largely anti-ocular contexts of contemporary visual culture scholarship today, many artists and theorists of the visual are reluctant to engage in. Hence, his increasingly active and intensive interest in the work of those painters who did look intently at the world and seek to bring those experiences of looking to material expression. In contrast to Sartre, however, who would write seminal essays on the work of then-contemporary artists – Giacometti (1947) and, as noted, Wols (1963) – Merleau-Ponty insisted on returning to the late nineteenth-century endeavours of Cézanne as foundational for a diversity of twentieth-century departures from tradition.[14]

I will return to this matter. But with this reference to foundations, and before also turning to those themes in the *Phenomenology* that are of particular pertinence to the painting-as-thought issues that are at the heart of this study, I must make another introductory point. It concerns an area of contention among thinkers about the *kind* of philosophical foundations upon which Merleau-Ponty was seeking to establish his own thought, a certain misreading of which would negatively impact the reception of his thought after his death. For as Derek Taylor pointed out in his 1992 essay 'Phantasmic Genealogy',[15] later commentators, including Foucault, would seem to have misunderstood and misrepresented Merleau-Ponty in this regard. In 'Theatrum Philosophicum' of 1972, a review essay of Gilles Deleuze's *Difference and Repetition* (1968) and *The Logic of Sense* (1969). Foucault contrasted Deleuze's 'anti-phenomenology' with Merleau-Ponty's phenomenology. In Taylor's words, Foucault, having claimed that Deleuze's thought in those two books

is the only successful anti-Platonic strategy ... goes on to say that Deleuze's innovative approach liberates us from the restrictive confines of the old subject/object debate to finally give us free reign for the 'play of surfaces'. Deleuze's 'anti-phenomenology', according to Foucault, consists precisely of this refusal to seek stable truths beneath these surfaces and thereby place limitations upon the meaning of experience, particularly of the body. What is targeted here, then, is the foundationalism inherent in the phenomenological approach which 'reduces' the meaning of experience to an originary presence or origin.[16]

Taylor continued to say that, according to Foucault, 'Deleuze's works "can be read as the most alien books imaginable from the *Phenomenology of Perception*".'[17] As will become apparent, such a claim could only arise from a comprehensive misapprehension of the *Phenomenology*. In the introduction, I have already explained how and why Merleau-Ponty's own non-oppositional and embedded modes of argumentation, unless carefully attended to, may well have provoked this. A year later, in his 1993 essay 'Merleau-Ponty in Retrospect' – and, like Taylor, in a corrective mode – Madison described Merleau-Ponty as 'a hermeneuticist *avant la lettre*', defining his position as 'anti-foundationalist':

> Merleau-Ponty was an anti-foundationalist (in the sense in which the term is used today, to designate one of the main thrusts of postmodern thought, in both its hermeneutical and post-structuralist variants) throughout his philosophical career. In the *Phenomenology of Perception* he characterised phenomenology as a discipline without foundations or, as he put it, one which 'rests on itself, or rather provides its own foundation ('*se fonde elle-même*').[18]

Embodied perception – Our *only* access to the real?

The *Phenomenology of Perception*[19] appeared in 1945, three years after the publication of *The Structure of Behavior*, and shares aspects of its content and approach. Indeed, both works may be considered part of the same project. Organized in three main sections, 'The Body', 'The World as Perceived', and 'Being-for-Itself and Being-in-the-World', Merleau-Ponty again positioned his own thought against a backdrop of the problems and irreconcilabilities endemic to rationalism and empiricism. The *Phenomenology*, it might be said, was where Merleau-Ponty worked out and justified his philosophical position; the subsequent essays, broadly speaking, were where he put this thought to work, pointedly, in relation to then-contemporary cultural and political affairs.[20] In the book's substantial, four-chaptered introduction, titled 'Traditional Prejudices and the Return to Phenomena', Merleau-Ponty's first move was to challenge empiricist theories of perception founded upon the notion of pure, internally apprehended 'sensations' as their primary building blocks:

> At the outset of the study of perception, we find in language the notion of sensation, which seems immediate and obvious: I have a sensation of redness, of blueness, of hot and cold. It will, however, be seen that nothing could in fact be more confused, and that because they accepted it readily, traditional analyses missed the phenomenon of perception.[21]

In the first chapter of the introduction to the *Phenomenology* ('The "Sensation" as a Unit of Experience'), Merleau-Ponty enlarged upon territory already opened up in *The Structure of Behavior* and presented evidence drawn from Gestalt theory to show that the sensationalist view of perception characteristic of empiricism (and specifically of classical psychology) was unjustified. He contrasted the traditional internalized, sensation-based model with his notion of 'phenomenal field', this also being the title of his fourth and final introductory chapter. 'The perceptual "something"', he wrote, 'is always in the middle of something else, it always forms part of a "field".'[22] In the fourth chapter of the introduction, Merleau-Ponty elaborated upon this field and described his project in the rest of the *Phenomenology* as that of entering this ambiguous domain. His stated aim would be to interrogate the findings of experimental psychology in particular, not by adopting an objectivist, scientific mindset but by being led by what he called 'the psychologist's self-scrutiny'.[23] Thus, he would arrive 'by way of a second-order reflection, to the phenomenon of the phenomenon' by which the phenomenal field would be 'decisively' transformed into a transcendental one.[24] Indeed, he had already explained that a philosophy 'becomes transcendental, or radical' not by 'taking its place in absolute consciousness without mentioning the ways by which this is reached but by considering itself as a problem'.[25] Hence the requirement for self-scrutiny. The approach taken should not postulate 'a knowledge rendered totally explicit' but rather recognize 'as the fundamental philosophic problem this *presumption* on reason's part'.[26] It was crucial, he continued, that the investigations in question begin with the perception and description of the phenomenological field in order to avoid 'placing ourselves, from the start, as does reflexive philosophy, in a transcendental dimension assumed to be eternally given'.[27]

Merleau-Ponty would go on to present painters – specific painters such as Cézanne – as the pioneering interrogators par excellence of this terrain, and of these transformations from the phenomenal to the transcendental, and throughout his philosophical project he consistently prioritized the explorations of painters over those of experimental scientists in this regard. Therefore, it is worth reflecting, a little longer, on the tenor of Merleau-Ponty's introductory remarks. For instance, preceding his first reference to the notion of 'perceptual field' and its importance, he had summoned up a scene akin to the naïve consciousness experience of being-in-the-world that he had presented in *The Structure of Behavior*: the scenario of the luminous spot appearing on a dark wall. That is, in the *Phenomenology*, Merleau-Ponty asked his readers to imagine 'a white patch on a homogenous background'.[28] Such a patch, and such a background – which, following Gestalt theory, Merleau-Ponty defined as 'the simplest sense-given available to us' – might as easily relate to a first mark made by a painter upon paper or canvas.[29] Alternatively, or additionally, we might want to think of the paper or canvas itself as a figure positioned against a complex historical and cultural background of its own, not to mention the specificities of the spatial background of its literal setting. In any case, here, the realm of painterly actively is indirectly yet actively evoked. He continued:

> All the points in the patch have a certain 'function' in common, that of forming themselves into a 'shape'. The colour of the shape is more intense, and as it were more resistant than that of the background; the edges of the white patch 'belong' to it, and are not part of the background although they adjoin it: the patch appears to be placed on the background and does not break it up.[30]

But not only that. 'Each part', he wrote, also, 'arouses the expectation of more than it contains, and this elementary perception is already charged with a *meaning*.' As already noted, Merleau-Ponty would turn to Cézanne's explorations of this perceptual field as a way of guiding and shaping his own methods and observations but we might equally return to, and reflect on, the various contemporary examples of fundamental, and already fundamentally complex mark-making, as seen, for instance, in the work of Durner, Johnson and von Heyl and the ways in which Crowther's 'transperceptual' phenomena are called forth. Again, referencing the ambiguity that inevitably characterizes the phenomenal field:

> We must recognize the indeterminate as a positive phenomenon. It is in this atmosphere that quality arises. Its meaning is an equivocal meaning; we are concerned with an expressive quality rather than with logical signification. The determinate quality by which empiricism tried to define sensation is an object, not an element, of consciousness, *indeed it is the very lately developed object of scientific consciousness*. For these two reasons, it conceals rather than reveals subjectivity.[31]

Here, to reiterate, subjectivity as treated by Merleau-Ponty was a subjectivity that had already been revealed to be an intersubjectivity; he would later describe this as inter- or intra-corporeality.

Continuing with our comparison of the *Phenomenology* and *The Structure of Behavior*, there are, however, also important shifts in emphasis to be found in the *Phenomenology*, as well as developments in Merleau-Ponty's thought.

Crucially, as indicated it its title, in this work he advanced arguments in *The Structure of Behavior* concerning 'the primacy of perception' for thought, by elaborating on the connection he saw to exist between perception and the philosophical quest for knowledge.[32] Although, as already established, his position was greatly informed by the findings of Gestalt theory, a specific characteristic of the *Phenomenology* was the *explicit* positioning of his investigations within the context of the phenomenological tradition of Husserl.[33] Alongside his engagements with key scientific findings, it was within the context of his own profoundly embodied inroads into the phenomenological tradition – of which more shortly – that his explorations of perception unfolded.

In the *Phenomenology*, as in *The Structure of Behavior*, Merleau-Ponty insisted that whatever the specificities of our engagement with the world might be at any given time – whether we are in a garden cutting wood, out shopping, in a laboratory conducting a psychological experiment or at our desks battling with a philosophical question – our contact with it is primarily and inescapably a bodily and therefore a perceptual one.[34] The descriptions of everyday behaviour just listed are purposefully in keeping with the pre-internet period in which Merleau-Ponty was writing. But today, everyday behaviour for significant portions of the global population is digitally mediated and screen-based; our handheld tools are largely tools for communication. But these relations with technology, while typically defined and discussed in terms of their virtuality, retain crucial embodied and inter-corporeal dimensions which have lived consequences especially in terms of shaping personal and public, or shared, time and space. Given, too, that perception always traverses the concrete and the virtual, in this respect the albeit significant differences between electronically based and non-electronically based activities, and between online and offline experiences, are arguably differences of proportion and scale. In any case, whatever we are doing, and no matter how mechanical or unconscious our actions might be, no matter how all-absorbingly technical or abstract might be our thoughts, and even though it is in the nature of perception itself to be self-effacing, this bodily, perceptual contact with the world cannot be eradicated. Perception, then, cannot be the *product* of a discrete intellectual capacity to judge, to analyse or to rationalize. In fact, perception is not something we *do* but that which makes possible our varied activities, including our intellectual ones. 'Perception is not ... an act', he wrote, 'it is the background from which all acts stand out and is pre-supposed by them.'[35] This is what he meant by the term 'the primacy of perception', also the title of a paper produced a year after the publication of the *Phenomenology* and in defence of it. Since perception is not merely optional, he regarded a careful exploration of the perceptual world as foundational for philosophy.

This had consequences. Merleau-Ponty's position concerning the primacy of perception insisted upon a contact with the world that is inescapably partial, always dependent upon where the one who perceives is located bodily and by extension also historically, culturally, politically, emotionally and so on. Thus Merleau-Ponty's embodied, perceptual consciousness made no pretence at being able to access reality as it might exist 'in-itself', nor could it make claims to universal validity as this was, and is, conventionally and reductively understood.[36] These conditions were reflected in his reconceptualized understanding of the proper nature, limits and possibilities of philosophical thought.

Given the incomplete nature of our perceptual grasp of things, an important aspect of the *Phenomenology* was Merleau-Ponty's elaboration of the kind of world that is thus available to us. He explored this matter within the context of what we would ordinarily call the 'meaningfulness' of the world, its implications and its importance for us. For Merleau-Ponty, then, our first perceptual contact with the world (defined not as an 'in-itself' but precisely *as* that which we perceive), was apprehended as already 'pregnant' with meaning.[37] In 'The Primacy of Perception' he expressed this by saying that 'the matter of perception' is '"pregnant with its form"'.[38] Indeed, it would be worth citing Merleau-Ponty at some length on this point.

The unprejudiced study of perception by psychologists has finally revealed that the perceived world is not a sum of objects (in the sense in which the sciences use this word), that our relation to the world is not that of a thinker to an object of thought, and finally that the unity of the perceived thing, as perceived by several consciousnesses, is not comparable to the unity of a proposition [*théorème*], as understood by several thinkers, any more than perceived existence is comparable to ideal existence.

As a result we cannot apply the classical distinction of form and matter to perception, nor can we conceive the perceiving subject as a consciousness which 'interprets', 'deciphers', or 'orders' a sensible matter according to an ideal law which it possesses. Matter is 'pregnant' with its form, which is to say that in 'the final analysis every perception takes place within a certain horizon and ultimately in the 'world'.[39]

In classical thought, form and matter are regarded as distinct, with 'form' (*eidos*) referring to that which makes a thing intelligible, to that which is grasped by the intellect. By contrast, in perception as understood by Merleau-Ponty, no such distinction is made. Rather, the world in its visual and material being immediately presents itself to us as significant,[40] even if that significance is unresolved. The implications of particular objects or states of affair are not presented to us unambiguously or with their own theory defining them – although we may *choose* to read them in this way. They are suggested, outlined, indicated to us. Specific meanings are not created by us ex nihilo and superimposed upon a supposedly unintelligible perceptual world, nor are they uncovered by us, as if they exist, in themselves, in an unambiguous form beneath or beyond the flux of appearances. They are the consequence of a reciprocal interaction between embodied perceiver and the perceived.

We experience meaning as coming to birth *for* us within the context of our perceptual explorations of the world. If we will continue to observe and describe, we witness its inexhaustible unfolding before us. Thus, perception always occurs within contexts that are both spatial *and* temporal. Hence, the significance of Merleau-Ponty's explorations of temporality in the final section of the *Phenomenology* and, alongside his examinations of painterly interrogation in 'Cézanne's Doubt', his discussions of film in 'The Film and the New Psychology', which was first delivered in the form of a lecture at the Institut des Hautes Études Cinématographiques in 1945.[41] There, Merleau-Ponty began by introducing the principles of Gestalt theory (the so-called new psychology) in relation to our perception of visual phenomena, including ambiguous figure-ground puzzles and camouflage, and our perceptions of movement and sound understood, non-sequentially, as temporal forms involving the interworkings of perception, memory and anticipation. He then stated that film is best conceived of not as 'a sum total of images' but rather as a 'temporal *gestalt*' in which the meaning of a shot 'depends on what precedes it in the movie, and this succession of scenes creates a new reality which is not merely the sum of its parts'.[42] Towards the end of the essay he wrote, evocatively, and in a way that also recalled the fundamental argument of *The Structure of Behavior*, that

A movie is not thought; it is perceived.

This is why the movies can be gripping in their presentation of man: they do not give us his *thoughts*, as novels have done for so long but his conduct or behavior. They directly present to us that special way of being in the world, of dealing with things and other people, which we can see in the sign language of gesture and gaze and which clearly defines each person we know. If a movie wants to show us someone who is dizzy, it should not attempt to portray the interior landscape of dizziness, as Daquin in *Premier de cordée* and Malraux in *Sierra de Terruel* wished to do. We will get a much better sense of dizziness if we see it from the outside, if we contemplate that unbalanced body contorted on a rock or that unsteady step trying to adapt itself to who knows what upheaval of space. For the movies as for modern psychology dizziness, pleasure, grief, love, and hate are ways of behaving.[43]

At issue here is consciousness understood as 'thrown into the world', as intermingled in the world and coexistent with others.[44] This brings us back to the portion of 'The Primacy of Perception' under discussion (regarding matter–form relations and Merleau-Ponty's claim that 'every perception takes place within a certain horizon and ultimately in the "world"'.[45]), for it clarifies his understanding of how meaning is not only given to us but also constituted *by* us *not* – as already discussed in the introduction with respect to his later teachings on the phenomenon of institution – in the rationalist, Kantian or Husserlian sense but because, collectively, we are embodied beings whose inherence in the world is always *situated* within certain physical, emotional, historical and social contexts, and because, as intentional beings, we always approach it with particular desires and goals in play. This is a key point of the *Phenomenology*. As Bannan put it, in the *Phenomenology* the 'central phenomenon of perceptual life [is] the constitution without any ideal model, of a significant grouping'.[46] And indeed, in 'The Primacy of Perception', referring to Husserl, Merleau-Ponty referred to the emergence of meaning as a 'synthesis of transition' and as a 'horizontal synthesis', as opposed to an 'intellectual synthesis'.[47] Whereas an 'intellectual synthesis' produces meanings that are supposedly complete and unambiguous such that further exploration is obviated, those constituted by a 'synthesis of transition' are incomplete. Our perceptual explorations give rise to a world that takes on specific meaning(s) for us while continuing to exist for us in its 'pregnant' state, making the search for understanding inexhaustible and leaving space for further knowledges or truths to emerge.

Acknowledging the incomplete manner in which the world is given to us in perception, Merleau-Ponty argued in the *Phenomenology* that it is nevertheless from the starting point of our perceptual explorations of the world, and from these alone, that access to what may properly be called knowledge is possible. Here, as in *The Structure of Behavior*, to repeat, Merleau-Ponty's position contrasted sharply with those espoused by rationalism and empiricism where in each case, as noted earlier but for different reasons, the argument for a direct connection between lived perception and knowledge was philosophically incomprehensible. Such a quest was seen to undermine philosophy, indeed to run counter to it. Indeed, in a discussion of Merleau-Ponty's work held in 1946, one of his older contemporaries, the classical philosopher and historian of philosophy, Emile Bréhier, one of several thinkers in attendance who objected to Merleau-Ponty's project, declared that

> philosophy was born of the difficulties encountered in ordinary perception [*perception vulgaire*]. It was from ordinary perception and by getting away from it that men began to philosophise. The first philosophers and Plato, our common ancestor, philosophised in this way. Far from wanting to return to an immediate perception, to a lived perception, he took his point of departure in the insufficiencies of this lived perception in order to arrive at a conception of the intelligible world which was coherent, which satisfied reason, which supposed another faculty of knowing other than perception itself.[48]

Although this objection was made subsequent to the *Phenomenology*'s publication, Merleau-Ponty had attempted to anticipate such responses at the time of writing. His criticisms of rationalist and empiricist claims to knowledge were elaborated throughout the work, and they were presented most coherently in the *Phenomenology*'s introduction. As in his earlier work, the basic problem he attached to both positions was their objectivist stance: by choosing not to explore the embodied and perspectival nature of their own explorations, adherents thought that the world with which they had to do was the world in-itself.[49] He called this 'the prejudice in favour of the objective world'.[50] At the beginning of the third chapter, '"Attention" and "Judgement"', having addressed what he saw to be the inadequacies of empiricism but insisting that 'it was not empiricism alone that we were attacking', he wrote:

> We must now show that its rationalist antithesis is *on the same level* as empiricism itself. Both take the objective world as the object of their analysis, when this comes first neither in time nor in virtue of its meaning; and both are incapable of expressing the peculiar way in which perceptual consciousness constitutes its object. *Both keep their distance in relation to perception instead of sticking closely to it.*[51]

It is fair to say, then, that whether Merleau-Ponty was overtly addressing empiricism or rationalism, at issue in each case was the intellectualism displayed, an intellectualism that thought it was dealing with first-order principles but, according to Merleau-Ponty, was instead immersed in philosophical abstractions and in a second-order reality (as indicated earlier, processes of philosophical and painterly abstraction differ significantly in terms of their modus operandi and their effects). In 'The Primacy of Perception' he presented his reasons for rejecting such intellectualism as follows:

> What prohibits me from treating my perception as an intellectual act is that an intellectual act would grasp the object either as possible or as necessary. But in perception it is 'real'; it is given as the infinite sum of an indefinite series of perspectival views in each of which the object is given but in none of which it is given exhaustively. It is not accidental for the object to be given to me in a 'deformed' way, from the point of view [*place*] which I occupy. That is the price of its being 'real'.[52]

In this text Merleau-Ponty contrasted the way in which the world is known in perception treated as an intellectual act and the way in which it is known in perception as he understood it. He had already rejected the idea that either his own approach or that of traditional thinkers could give us access to things 'in-themselves'. But he argued that it is our *perceptual* experience of the world which brings us into the closest possible contact with that which we *experience* as being *real* or, as he puts it in the *Phenomenology*, as '*for us* an *in-itself*' – I will return to this concept in the following chapter.[53] Perception treated as an intellectual act, in common with all intellectual acts, he saw as incapable of achieving this. At best, it gives us access to a world that is either necessarily or possibly real. It provides us with a world of things and people whose reality can be posited or inferred but which can never be *experienced* as such.

For Merleau-Ponty, the reality of an object for some possible subject of experience was connected to the way in which it is given to that subject in perception. To repeat, for it to be experienced as real, it must be given as 'the infinite sum of an indefinite series of perspectival views in each of which the object is given but in none of which it is given exhaustively'. This was a phenomenon he recognized in the mature paintings of Cézanne. A paradigmatic example, not specifically referenced by Merleau-Ponty, would be Cézanne's much-discussed, multi-perspectival *Still Life with Plaster Cupid* of 1894, which is part of the Courtauld Collection, London.[54] In order to be experienced as real, it must be presented to that subject 'in a "deformed" way, from the point of view [*place*] which I occupy'. Indeed, this idea of deformation or deformity, which should not be interpreted with its usual negative connotations, was important in Merleau-Ponty's thought, and it is opened up powerfully in Cézanne's multifaceted paintings. Merleau-Ponty's point was that we experience the perceptual world as real not in spite of the incomplete way it is apprehended by us as embodied beings but *because* of it. In the first place, because the object is given in this way, we know it inhabits the same spatio/temporal framework as we do and can therefore be approached, picked up, examined and used – here we might recall Crowther's comments, referenced in the introduction, about the significance of the physicality, presence and duration of paintings in this regard as contrasted with the very different physicality, presence and duration of electronic image-communication formats. In the second place, because the object reveals new, often unanticipated aspects of itself as we perceive it from different points of view, we know it exists independently of us. In the third place, since we know that its existence or reality does not wholly depend on or derive from us as individuals, we know that other people can also perceive and approach it, although their perspectives upon it will differ in certain ways from our own. We experience it as real because we experience it as being intersubjectively available. Concerning the 'deformations' that occur in perception, Merleau-Ponty made the related point in the *Phenomenology* that an object reveals itself to the embodied perceiver as real because, with other objects, it forms 'a system in which one cannot show itself without concealing others. More precisely', he continued, 'the inner horizon of an object cannot become an object without the surrounding objects becoming a horizon. … The horizon, then, is what guarantees the identity of the object throughout the exploration.'[55] Therefore:

> The object-horizon structure, or the perspective, is no obstacle to me when I want to see the object: for just as it is the means whereby objects are distinguished from each other, it is also the means whereby they are disclosed. To see is to enter a universe of beings which *display themselves*, and they would not do this if they could not be hidden behind each

other or behind me. ... [Furthermore, w]hen I look at the lamp on my table, I attribute to it not only the qualities visible from where I am but also those which the chimney, the walls, the table can 'see'. ... I can therefore see an object in so far as ... each one treats the others round it as spectators of its hidden aspects and as guarantee of the permanence of those aspects.[56]

For Merleau-Ponty, then, *real* rather than inferred knowledge or truth is something we can apprehend only as embodied, perceiving beings. Knowledge or truth that is intelligible only to our thought, as for traditional philosophy, has no such status. If I believe with the empiricists that my perception of the world is made comprehensible only through the deciphering and ordering of discrete sensations by the intellect, then the person I take to be seated opposite me is given to me as a representation. According to Merleau-Ponty, such a representation can only be regarded as *possibly* real, and its intersubjective status is unclear. But if a rationalist approach is taken, I would regard my perception as an intellectual act, free from the perspectival restrictions of space and time, and capable of presenting to me in their entirety not only objects or people but also their surroundings. While I might be convinced of the *necessary* existence of such objects or persons, this certainty would be of a constructed rather than an experienced nature.

Description – The first philosophical act

Merleau-Ponty critiqued rationalism and empiricism as positions which display repression or forgetfulness about their origins in the realm of the world-and-self as perceived. Philosophy, as Merleau-Ponty saw it, must be a corrective in this respect and begin by installing itself in this 'forgotten' realm. Perception, as he put it, must be reawakened. 'True' philosophy starts with *relearning* what it is to look at the world. It is archaeological in nature but its task is not to dig beneath appearances to uncover universal truths-in-themselves. On the contrary, it must dig beneath the rational constructions we have erected and rediscover behind these 'figures' the 'ground' of appearances upon which they depend:

The first philosophical act would appear to be to return to the world of actual experience which is prior to the objective world, since it is in it that we shall be able to grasp the theoretical basis no less than the limits of that objective world, restore to things their concrete physiognomy, to organisms their individual ways of dealing with the world, and to subjectivity its inherence in history. Our task will be, moreover, to rediscover phenomena, the layer of living experience through which other people and things are first given to us, the system 'Self-others-things' as it comes into being; to re-awaken perception and foil its trick of allowing us to forget it as a fact and as perception in the interest of the object which it presents to us and of the rational tradition to which it gives rise.[57]

The 'first philosophical act' referred to in this passage consists of *describing* our experience of the world instead of presupposing it, and it occurs *before* becoming involved in processes of analysis or explanation. Analysing and explaining are intellectual acts, describing is an expressive one tied to our identity as perceptual beings. It is through description that perception is 'awakened'. The 'world of actual experience which is prior to the objective world' is a world that we experience not as being possible or necessary but as being *real*.

The task of description is to explore the individual ways in which each of us experiences and deals with the world, the specific ways in which the world both takes on a particular meaning *for* us and is constituted *by* us (in the Merleau-Pontean understanding of this term). In contrast to the explanations and analyses of traditional thought, its focus is not on how knowledge of the world and communication with it, or with others, are possible from a place of initial separation from it. Nor at issue is how the perceived world takes on meaning for us from an initial state of incomprehensibility. We are 'through and through compounded of relationships with the world' and, because we are embodied, situated beings and not disembodied minds, we are, as he put it 'condemned to meaning'[58] – here he was likely reformulating Sartre's well-known assertion in *Being and Nothingness* that 'man is condemned to be free'. Rather, what the process of describing reveals, and what the philosopher must then seek to articulate, is first how and why what I *now* perceive to be the world is for me the *same* world I perceived on previous occasions when its (*specific*) meanings for me, my perspectives upon it and intentions towards it may have been radically different. Secondly at issue is how and why I take my world, now, to be *the* world, that is, a shared world not only in the present but also in historical or trans-temporal terms. As Merleau-Ponty saw it, then, to philosophize was first to provide a description of the phenomenal world, and then to reflect upon it such that its transcendental value – as defined earlier – is made explicit.[59] Hence: *phenomenology*.

In the preface to the *Phenomenology* – which opens with the question 'What is phenomenology?' – Merleau-Ponty defined his position in relation to the broader phenomenological tradition in explicit terms. As already discussed, this mode of investigation was already implicit in *The Structure of Behavior*, and an interest in phenomenology was also in evidence in his 1936 essay on Marcel's *Etre et avoir*.[60]

One of his first observations was that although phenomenology had only fairly recently been identified and labelled as a specific branch of philosophy, it had a longer history as a term and as an orientation as evidenced not only in the writings of Hegel and Kierkegaard but also in Marx, Nietzsche and

Freud. He wrote that 'the opinion of the responsible philosopher must be that *phenomenology can be practised and identified as a manner or style of thinking, that it existed as a movement before arriving at complete awareness of itself as a philosophy*'.[61] Given that his writing was not uncontroversial within philosophical circles, he may have wanted to show by this that his methods had credentials, being prefigured in the works of notable thinkers. His own interest was particularly with the phenomenology of Husserl as he understood it and there is evidence that between the completion of *The Structure of Behavior* and the writing of the *Phenomenology* – that is, during the years of Nazi Occupation – his exposure to the works of Husserl was greatly increased, particularly where the latter's late writings and the unpublished texts housed at Louvain were concerned.[62] (As an aside – and this may have much to do with the universalist values with which philosophical thought tends to be accorded – it is worth observing that Merleau-Ponty seems to have felt no conflict, as a French thinker embedded within the political circumstances of the day, in immersing himself in, and being shaped by, the work of a German intellectual.[63])

One aspect of Husserl's thought regarded by Merleau-Ponty as crucial was Husserl's 'phenomenological reduction',[64] that is, his insistence that his philosophical investigations be founded upon a description of the world as it is first 'given' to consciousness – his rejection, in other words, of objectivist thinking.[65] Merleau-Ponty wrote in this regard that phenomenology

> does not expect to arrive at an understanding of man and the world from any starting point other than their 'facticity'. It is a transcendental philosophy which places in abeyance the assertions arising out of the natural attitude, the better to understand them; but it is also a philosophy for which the world is always 'already there' before reflection begins – as an inalienable presence; and all its efforts are concentrated upon re-achieving a direct and primitive contact with the world, and endowing that contact with philosophical status.[66]

By placing 'in abeyance the assertions arising out of the natural attitude', phenomenology is concerned with the world as we live it. Husserl, in his late writing, named this the *Lebenswelt* or lifeworld. Merleau-Ponty saw this to be an area of agreement between himself and Husserl.[67] But for Merleau-Ponty, and in contrast to Husserl, this lifeworld, or realm of phenomena, was that which is apprehended by the *embodied* self from its place of immersion in the world as opposed to that of the disembodied consciousness in relation to its (mental) contents. Moreover, the world that presents itself and is experienced in this embedded way is one that precedes reflection: Merleau-Ponty's 'inalienable presence'. It is experienced as being real because it is experienced as having existence in connection with but also apart from us – thus it is not an intellectual construct – and as having the power to reveal or give itself *to* us. This mode of engagement with the world he described as 'direct and primitive' and his use of these terms must not be misunderstood. Phenomenology, he continued:

> offers an account of space, time and the world as we 'live' them. It tries to give a direct description of our experience as it is, without taking account of its psychological origin and the causal explanations which the scientist, the historian or the sociologist may be able to provide. Yet Husserl in his last works mentions a 'genetic phenomenology',[68] and even a 'constructive phenomenology'.[69]

What is meant here by 'direct'? As Merleau-Ponty saw it, the 'phenomenological reduction' involves setting aside questions concerning both causality and finality. This does not mean that physical, historical, social or psychological factors are irrelevant to the way we perceive the world. For a philosophy to be truly rational it must take into account our lived and therefore *situated* nature in all of these respects. Neither was he suggesting that it is possible for us to describe our perception of the world, or indeed to perceive the world, in a way that is literally uninformed by certain inherited or already existent values, assumptions, ideas, intentions and experiences. His point was that these factors cannot be regarded as decisive or explanatory. The world as we experience it now, the fact that it has both specific and suggested implications for us, is not merely the consequence of identifiable pre-existing, predetermined conditions. In fact there are no discrete previous conditions that the philosopher can 'go back' to. This would be to misrepresent the way in which necessarily embodied and perspectival beings experience time. We are never in a position to isolate a present from its past: its relation is not that of effect from cause. Except in the case of certain disorders, the past is always integrated into the present and thus transformed by it. Experientially, it cannot be called upon to explain the present. On the contrary it is the past that is accessed, 'read', or interpreted through the present and continually assigned new meanings.[70] This is why Merleau-Ponty identified as significant in Husserl's late writings his mention of 'a "genetic phenomenology," and even a "constructive phenomenology"'. What phenomenology's 'direct' and 'primitive' contact with the world reveals is a world that is being continually re-formed.[71] It is always in a state of *origination*, and it was this figuration and bringing-to-awareness of origination that drew him to the painterly projects he was interested in. Therefore, for Merleau-Ponty – and in contrast to the claims of certain detractors past and then-present[72] – phenomenology by no means represented 'the return to a transcendental consciousness before which the world is spread out and completely transparent'.[73] Referencing Husserl:

> The most important lesson which the reduction teaches us is the impossibility of a complete reduction. This is why Husserl is constantly re-examining the possibility of the reduction. If we were absolute mind,

the reduction would present no problem. But since, on the contrary, we are in the world, since indeed our reflections are carried out in the temporal flux on to which we are trying to seize (since they *sich einströmen*, as Husserl says) there is no thought which embraces all our thought. The philosopher, as the unpublished works declare,[74] is a perpetual beginner, which means taking for granted nothing that men, learned or otherwise, believe they know.[75]

The consequence of the reduction for Merleau-Ponty (and he saw the late Husserl to be making the same point) was that just as there is no 'absolute mind' and 'no thought which embraces all our thought'[76] neither is there absolute (in the sense of absolutely-graspable) truth. What persists, nonetheless, is the inexhaustible task of bringing an emergent, non-absolutist notion of truth into being. We must understand rather than evade the paradox that what we call 'true' are those things that are both given to us *and* constituted by us, both radically our own but, because not absolutely or completely so, also accessible to and shareable by others – in some cases through communicable acts of describing.[77] Importantly, for Merleau-Ponty, this was not a task of philosophy alone, understood in the traditional sense. To repeat, it is already being carried out by everyone who is willing to approach the perceived world as such a beginner, in an attitude of at least provisionally relinquishing inherited knowledge and belief, and with the ability to convey, in words, imagery or gesture, the meanings that arise, thereby making them available for exploration (and reinterpretation) by others. Thus, it is a task that philosophy shares with art.[78]

In 'Metaphysics and the Novel',[79] also published in 1945, Merleau-Ponty wrote in no uncertain terms that the task of both phenomenological and existentialist philosophy was not that 'of explaining the world or of discovering its "conditions of possibility," but rather, through description, of formulating an experience of the world, a contact with the world which precedes all thought *about* the world'.[80] He again contrasted this position with that of traditional philosophy which regards our relationship with the world as one of having thoughts about it. And in 'Cézanne's Doubt',[81] he made a direct connection between the active and exemplary ways in which phenomenological (and existentialist) ideas are articulated, and the way in which paintings, and works of art more broadly, also seek to communicate:

> It is not enough for a painter like Cézanne, an artist, or a philosopher, to create and express an idea; they must also awaken the experiences which will make their idea take root in the consciousness of others. A successful work has the strange power to teach its own lesson.[82]

Here, two points are important. In the first place, he saw the project and methods of phenomenology, including his own, as coinciding with those of artists, and he identified Cézanne as a case in point. He made a similar claim in 'Metaphysics and the Novel' about philosophy and literature, with acts of description again playing an important role: 'For a long time', he wrote, 'it looked as if philosophy and literature not only had different ways of saying things but had different objects as well. Since the end of the nineteenth century, however [that is, with the rise of phenomenology and existentialism as recognized philosophical approaches, and *specifically* with their rejection of absolutist system-building], the ties between them have been getting closer and closer.'[83] He identified as the 'first sign of this reconciliation ... the appearance of hybrid modes of expression, having elements of the intimate diary, the philosophical treatise, and the dialogue',[84] and cited the works of Charles Péguy as a good example of this.[85] He wrote a little later on that philosophical expression 'assumes the same ambiguities as literary expression, if the world is such that it cannot be expressed except as "stories" and, as it were, pointed at'.[86] Thus philosophy and literature could no longer be regarded as having to do with two discrete worlds. There was no longer a 'real' world, stable and certain, accessible only to the intellect, which is the province of philosophy, and, distinct from it, a second, shifting world of appearances and ambiguous, everyday realities, which is the province of literature. There is only one world with which an embodied being can have to do: the latter. And it is a world that can only be spoken of in a particular way: incompletely but evocatively, in stories; it cannot be fully explained but can be brought to our awareness through description. Thus, for Merleau-Ponty, description was a methodology of primary philosophical importance. In the *Phenomenology*, therefore, discussions of the power of description found in *The Structure of Behavior* in relation to the naïve consciousness and its evocations were scaled up.

Merleau-Ponty also claimed that the criterion for judging the success of a work of philosophy and that for judging the success of a work of art, visual or literary, was the same. To repeat, both must 'so awaken the experiences which will make their idea take root in the consciousness of others', with consciousness, for Merleau-Ponty, of course, being irremediably embodied. Such works must evoke in recipients not merely intellectual assent but, through their 'story-telling', enable them to live for themselves that which is being conveyed. But here, since what is being expressed is not some kind of absolute or transparent truth, it is open to interpretation and redesign.[87] Therefore the most important impact of the work of art is the way it can enable recipients to witness for themselves, from their own unique perspectives, the birth of a truth that is, as Merleau-Ponty put it, *for them* an *in-itself*. Its chief value is the way in which, by 'pointing', it can awaken perception in others and initiate a process in which accepted notions about self and world become destabilized, require questioning and are reconfigured. What is thus revealed is wonder not only at the intersubjective or inter-corporeal, that is, already communicative value of phenomena that are necessarily ambiguously presented within these creative situations but also at the new meanings that thereby become apparent. 'Cézanne's Doubt' is most effectively approached with this in mind.

In 'A questionnaire, *Mes Confidences*',[88] Cézanne was asked what his greatest aspiration was. His answer? *'Certainty'*. Nonetheless, as Merleau-Ponty saw it, based upon his reading of the artist's conversations with the French painter and writer Émile Bernard, the artist was not prepared to acquire this certainty by second-hand means:

> Cézanne was always seeking to avoid the ready-made alternatives suggested to him: sensation versus judgement; the painter who sees against the painter who thinks; nature versus composition; primitivism as opposed to tradition. ... Rather than apply to his work dichotomies more appropriate to those who sustain traditions than to those men, philosophers or painters, who initiate these traditions, he preferred to search for the *true meaning of painting, which is continually to question tradition*. Cézanne did not think he had to choose between feeling and thought, between order and chaos. He did not want to separate the stable things which we see and the shifting way in which they appear; *he wanted to depict matter as it takes on form, the birth of order through spontaneous organisation*. He makes a basic distinction not between 'the senses' and 'the understanding' but rather between the *spontaneous* organisation of the things we perceive and the *human* organisation of ideas and sciences. We see things; we agree about them; we are anchored in them; and it is with 'nature' as our base that we construct our sciences. Cézanne wanted to paint this primordial world, and his pictures therefore seem to show nature pure. ... He wanted to put intelligence, ideas, sciences, perspective, and tradition back in touch with the world of nature which they must comprehend. He wished, as he said, to confront the sciences with the nature 'from which they came'.[89]

According to this passage – and it must be emphasized that here 'nature' is clearly *not* equated, as it was in *The Structure of Behavior*, with the empirical notion of 'a multiplicity of events external to each other and bound together by relations of causality'[90] – Merleau-Ponty saw Cézanne's explorations of the world as parallel to his own, Cézanne's process being tied into the task of questioning and surpassing already-established ideas and practices. He saw Cézanne as someone who questioned habit and tradition, understood in a general sense as applying to the whole range of acquired ideas which, unless challenged, shape our thinking. These include not only the various intellectual or theoretical models that traditional philosophy and science impose upon the world in order to explain it ('the human organisation of ideas and sciences') but also the assumptions and expectations we so easily adopt in our everyday, practical modes of being:[91]

> We live in the midst of man-made objects, among tools, in houses, streets, cities, and most of the time we see them only through the human actions which put them to use. We become used to thinking that all of this exists

necessarily and unshakeable. Cézanne's painting suspends these habits of thought.[92]

On the other hand, he saw Cézanne particularly challenging traditional dualistic thinking as it might be applied (in theory) to the painter and to the practice of painting. Merleau-Ponty referred in particular to the false distinction he saw this tradition creating between 'the [inferior] painter who sees against the [superior] painter who thinks'.[93] By stating that Cézanne, in his search for certainty, 'did not think he had to choose between feeling and thought, between order and chaos [or between ...] the stable things which we see and the shifting way in which they appear', he regarded this painter's investigations of the world and his relationship with it *through* painting as an integrated one, involving the whole of his being. He saw Cézanne as someone, like himself, seeking to reconnect ways of approaching and understanding the world that had become fragmented and had lost a sense of their intrinsic relatedness and interdependence: 'He wanted to put intelligence, ideas, sciences, perspective, and tradition back in touch with the world of nature which they must comprehend. He wished, as he said, to confront the sciences with the nature "from which they came".'[94]

For Merleau-Ponty, then, Cézanne's investigations were invaluable not only where painting is concerned but for all our attempts at exploring the world, since it was an approach that sought certainty not by denying or avoiding all that is perceived as uncertain or ambiguous but, precisely, by grappling with it. However, his decision not to sacrifice the 'chaos' of lived vision to the 'order' of classical perspective, or to 'separate the stable things which we see and the shifting way in which they appear' did not result in images that are fragmented, intangible and incomprehensible.[95] In the Courtauld's *Still Life with Plaster Cupid*, for instance, Cézanne's use of multiple vantage points to describe the space of display – including the surprise of the steep, upward tilt of what is most likely the floor – and the multiple outlines used to delineate such elements as the fruit and vegetables arranged throughout the composition, combine to produce a certainty of another kind. What is presented is a scene that has been (or could have been) explored by any embodied, mobile being. Instead of pinning viewers to a single, ideal and distanced point of inspection as proposed but not always necessarily delivered by classical Western painting, it gives us a sense of being in contact with a world that is real – approachable, handle-able, full of possibility and accessible to further exploration – precisely because of its open appearance.[96] Importantly, by challenging traditional formulae for representing objects in space on a flat surface, his investigations through painting reveal what the 'human organisation of ideas and sciences' obscures, namely, 'the spontaneous organisation of the things we perceive',[97] their presence to us as 'an indivisible [and fertile] whole'.[98] Of concern again is that dualism, referenced earlier, and challenged by Gestalt theory, between matter, on the one hand, and form or meaning, on the other:

It is Cézanne's genius that when the overall composition of the picture is seen globally, perspectival distortions are no longer visible in their own right but rather contribute, as they do in natural vision, to the impression of an emerging order, of an object in the act of appearing, organising itself before our eyes. ... To trace just a single outline sacrifices depth – that is, the dimension in which the thing is presented not as spread out before us *but as an inexhaustible reality full of reserves.*[99]

For Merleau-Ponty, then, Cézanne's project could be defined in terms of his attempts to 'reawaken perception' and thus re-establish contact with that perceptual world of 'inexhaustible reality' by suspending (or, in phenomenological terms, 'bracketing') our preconceived notions of some world in-itself and by relinquishing the ingrained habits of thought to which we find it convenient to succumb.

A further dimension of the essay is his argument that Cézanne's particular way of approaching the world has a bearing not only upon how we may ourselves learn to approach the world but also upon how we approach works of art. First, we must avoid reading the latter through the application of certain pre-established formulae of a psychological or art-historical nature.[100] Secondly, by treating works of art as objects which challenge presupposed schemata and create new ones (which will in turn be challenged), we may regard them as exemplary for further creativeness.

Into the base of 'inhuman' nature

Merleau-Ponty's discussions in 'Cézanne's Doubt' concerned not only the particular ways in which Cézanne used line and colour to describe the spatiality of objects but also the meaning of the 'world of nature' his works opened up. Merleau-Ponty described this world as evoking the pre-personal. By means of Cézanne's practices of painterly description,

nature itself is stripped of the attributes which make it ready for animistic communions: there is no wind in the landscape, no movement on the Lac d'Annecy; the frozen objects hesitate at the beginning of the world. It is an unfamiliar world in which one is uncomfortable and which forbids all human effusiveness.[101]

For Merleau-Ponty, a similar sensibility was at work in Cézanne's portraits. Early on in the essay he referred to the 'inhuman' character of Cézanne's works[102] and to the painter's comment that 'a face should be painted as an object'.[103] Here, we might turn to an image not referenced by Merleau-Ponty: *La Femme à la Cafetière* dating from around 1890–95, which is now in the Musée d'Orsay but in 1945 was in the private collection of the

Pellerin family.[104] In it, items on a partially revealed table positioned next to a seated woman – a cup and saucer with a spoon and a coffee-pot – appear to be no more inanimate than she does. For however moved we might be by the artist's nuanced application of colour in this painting, and by the luminosity of the blues and greens, pinks and ochres, the woman's aspect is disturbing. She has a monumentally object-like appearance. She is immense, immovable, inscrutable. Her eyes are like holes.

Earlier in this chapter, as well as in my discussions of the form of the body in El Greco's paintings as discussed by Merleau-Ponty in *The Structure of Behavior*, I referred to traditional modes of investigation that sought to *explain* experiences or states or affair either in terms of their 'psychological origin' or in terms of 'the causal explanations which the scientist, the historian or the sociologist may be able to provide'. As Merleau-Ponty indicated in 'Cézanne's Doubt', art too, including that of Cézanne, had traditionally been approached in these ways. Accordingly, one way in which the 'inhuman' aspect of his works – the representation of the woman in *La Femme à la Cafetière*, for instance – has been accounted for has been as symptomatic of the artist's problematic psychological make-up: his reputed 'fits of temper and depression', his preoccupation with death, his flights into isolation and his paranoia that people were trying to get their 'hooks' into him.[105] Merleau-Ponty wrote that 'an observer of Cézanne's life such as Zola, more concerned with his character than with the meaning of his painting, might well consider it "a manifestation of ill-health"',[106] and thus interpret the nature of his attentiveness to the world, as revealed in his paintings – his intense focus on colour, for instance, his attempts, in a portrait such as that of the collector Victor Chocquet,[107] to paint 'all the little blues and all the little maroons'[108] – as representing 'a flight from the human world, the alienation of his humanity'.[109] From Merleau-Ponty's point of view, while the details of Cézanne's life (problematic or otherwise) were by no means irrelevant to the way in which he chose to approach and depict the world, the exact nature of the connection between the two was impossible to ascertain. It was merely conjectural. As he wrote at the end of this essay, 'The life of an author can teach us nothing [... and yet] if we know how to interpret it – we can find everything in it, since it opens onto his work'.[110] Moreover, such biographical speculations failed to provide 'any idea of the positive side of his work.'[111]

Merleau-Ponty went on to write that art-historical explanations of artistic style based on its likely sources of artistic influence, were no more satisfactory:

> [The meaning of Cézanne's work] will not become any clearer in the light of art history – that is, by bringing in the influences on Cézanne's methods (the Italian school and Tintoretto, Delacroix, Courbet and the Impressionists) – or even by drawing upon his own judgement of his work.[112]

It is possible to show that Cézanne went regularly to the Louvre and drew from the old masters. Likewise that it was through his contact with impressionism, and particularly his friendship with Camille Pissarro, that working from nature and making a study of appearances became important to his own practice. But to suggest that it was in such contacts, influential though they may be, that the meaning of his own work might be found again failed to illuminate its positive value. To account for a present circumstance (in this case, a painting) as the explicit product of certain previously existing ones was non-viable as far as Merleau-Ponty was concerned. To take this approach would obscure the manner in which Cézanne's paintings questioned that which had gone before, challenged inherited schemata and testified to the artist's attempts to 're-learn' how to see – that is, to learn how to see the world in in terms of the specificities of his own inherence in it. Indeed, for Merleau-Ponty, the real value of Cézanne's explorations of the works of other painters – his practice of drawing from the old masters, for instance – was that it served above all to throw up the *divergencies* of perception and expression existing between them. This definition of painterly practice in terms of challenging and questioning convention was also implied in Merleau-Ponty's schematic outline of what might be regarded as the progression of Cézanne's work from early fantastical pieces ('the projection of dreams outward'[113]), through impressionism (the concern with nature and with appearance), to his quest to 'find [the object] again behind the atmosphere'.[114]

Merleau-Ponty's point was not that it is inappropriate to explore connections between the works of Cézanne and those of other artists, or to deny that such connections existed. For instance, he would, I think, regard it as quite reasonable first to perceive Cézanne's representation of the woman in *La Femme à la Cafetière* (and, indeed, his other paintings of seated women) as a 'multi-profiled figure' set against the equally complex ground of those many other seated women with which European art and, indeed, world art is replete, and then to consider how the 'inhuman' aspect of Cézanne's woman, her monumentality and inscrutability, might differ in its meaning from the not dissimilar aspect of the Virgin in, say, Duccio's *Madonna Enthroned*.[115] Indeed, by noting the contrast between the former's empty arms and lap, and the arms of the latter, which support the Christ child, the 'inhuman' aspect of Cézanne's woman could, as a consequence, be read not necessarily as symptomatic of the painter's paranoid flight from humanity but – in the context of this particular juxtaposition – as evoking reflection on the alienation of a humanity without faith and as a challenge to such a humanity to bring to birth, from a place stripped of traditional religious preconceptions, a new conception of truth. For Merleau-Ponty, however, such an argument, while it might be plausible and even valuable, would not represent an *explanation* of *La Femme à la Cafetière*. It would represent instead one possible interpretation of the work, revealing as much about the commentator as it would about the painting. This is why not even

Cézanne's own verbal assessments of the meaningfulness of his works can be regarded as definitive. Works of art, and indeed all forms of expression, have no definitive meaning but have the potential to take on new meanings each time they are approached. This is why they retain their fascination, why a single work can be endlessly explored and discussed, whether in the form of conversations, works of criticism or further paintings.

Merleau-Ponty's argument, with respect to a productive engagement with Cézanne's paintings, was that if we were to resist providing definitive explanations of them and pursue instead a 'pure' description of his project, emphasis might than be placed upon their positive value. For instance, positive value could be placed upon the strangeness of his people, upon the unfamiliar worlds his paintings opened up and upon his attempts at revealing what Merleau-Ponty described as 'the base of inhuman nature upon which man has installed himself'.[116] As a consequence, the importance of such a work as *La Femme à la Cafetière* would revolve around the kinds of experiences and insights contact with it might provoke in its viewers. For Merleau-Ponty the first point of importance was how an image, through its very unfamiliarity, would provoke us to *scrutinize* it and, in so doing, to scrutinize ourselves also. Specifically, by identifying the appearance of such works with Cézanne's task of 're-learning' how to see, and with what Merleau-Ponty also referred to in this essay as the difficulties of 'the first word',[117] their meaning-for-Merleau-Ponty lay in their capacity to provide him with particular insight into the related processes of communication, description and creativity/institution.

In the first place, Merleau-Ponty's attentiveness to the 'pure', 'primitive' and 'inhuman' nature that he saw Cézanne's works to uncover, brought to him the realization that what is revealed is not a realm cut off from all that is humanly or personally relevant. It is a realm that disturbs because we do not immediately recognize or know it. But in so doing it *communicates* nonetheless. Through such works, then, the primordial nature of communication is revealed, communication not as something *we* do but as that which is always already taking place.[118] Cézanne understood this. As he opened himself up to the 'world which precedes all thought *about* the world' by looking and painting, he found himself on the receiving end of its communications and infiltrated by them. Indeed, Cézanne, attempting to perceive the natural word as if for the first time, is reputed to have said that 'the landscape thinks itself in me and I am its consciousness'.[119] The 'thought' to which Cézanne referred was not that which, according to traditional philosophy, appealed to the intellect but that which appealed to his eyes and hands and provoked new painterly activity.

Likewise, that disconcerting visual phenomenon, the woman in *La Femme à la Cafetière*, communicates. She speaks to me, for instance, of the mysteriousness of the people and things I think I know best and of the need for continual reassessment. She also reminds me of those rare moments I share with others when, unknowingly catching sight of our reflections in a mirror or shop window, we see an uncanny stranger. In more general terms, this image and others like it, reveal the non-oppositional nature of the known and the unknown, of knowing and not-knowing, and, as Merleau-Ponty put it, of sense and non-sense. It connects, again, with those aspects of human existence and experience that Merleau-Ponty, writing in the *Phenomenology*, discussed in terms of 'anonymous being' and the functioning of the sedimented 'habit-body'.

In the second place, Cézanne's acts of expression confirmed the power of description, whether manifested visually in his paintings or verbally in his statements, to reveal the emergence of things and meanings, leading Merleau-Ponty to consider the relationship between communication (expression/description) and knowledge or understanding. Because, as he put it, Cézanne painted as if no one had ever painted before and spoke 'as the first man spoke', his works could not, therefore, 'be the translation of a clearly defined thought, since such clear thoughts are those which have already been uttered by ourselves or by others'.[120] '"Conception" cannot precede "execution"', he insisted.[121] And with these words we have the reverse of Sol LeWitt's later claim, in 'Paragraphs on Conceptual Art', that

> in conceptual art the idea or concept is the most important aspect of the work. When an artist uses a conceptual form of art, it means that all of the planning and decisions are made beforehand and the execution is a perfunctory affair. ... It is usually free from the dependence on the skill of the artist as a craftsman.[122]

For Merleau-Ponty, by contrast, 'there is nothing but a vague fever before the act of artistic expression, and only the work itself, completed and understood, is proof that there was *something* rather than *nothing* to be said'.[123] And indeed, ironically, where conceptual art is concerned, one of its most enduring and interesting legacies was, precisely, its proliferating experimentation with materials and processes which changed prevalent ideas of what art should look like and how it should, or could, be interacted with. This brings us back to those earlier discussions about art opened up in the introduction.

For Merleau-Ponty, then, Cézanne's paintings, and his statements about the experience of painting, did not retrospectively record completed processes of thinking, perceiving or learning, or retrospectively point to the birth of new meanings but rather *enabled* them. Communication through description, which Merleau-Ponty regarded as the necessary starting point for all attempts to investigate the world and our relationship with it, was thus identified as a creative reconfiguring of the world. The intersubjective nature of these reconfigurations was, likewise, revealed.

> The painter recaptures and converts into visible objects what would, without him, remain walled up in the separate life of each consciousness: the vibration of appearances which is the cradle of things.[124]

The shared, intersubjective or, more properly, inter-corporeal world is thus not a world that is perceived (or conceived of) as that which is the same for everyone. It is a world that is 'talked about', verbally and visually, because it is different for each of us and because it is always present to us ambiguously and incompletely. Our desires to express our own engagements with this realm, and our interests in the experiences and expressions of others, presuppose that there is also a general aspect to the differently configured perceptual worlds that are opened up for each of us in this way. This theme would become a focus of Merleau-Ponty's later writing on language, notably in his 1952 essay 'Indirect Language and the Voices of Silence', which will be considered at length later on.

CHAPTER FOUR

Embodied thought

How do bodies think?

The body is to be compared, not to a physical object, but rather to a work of art. In a picture or a piece of music the idea is incommunicable by means other than the display of colours and sounds.

(*Maurice Merleau-Ponty*)[1]

A powerful idea within the *Phenomenology*, carried over from *The Structure of Behavior*, is that both perception and thought are observable forms of behaviour and thus modes of *display*. In and of themselves, they are already expressive and communicable. A second powerful idea is the alignment Merleau-Ponty proposes between human bodies as perceiving, thinking entities and works of art. But not only does our contemplation of works of art illuminate what bodies are and can be; the reverse is also the case. In this chapter, therefore, my aim is to examine three key Merleau-Pontean claims about the body's self-reflexivity in order, in this way, also to obtain a greater sense of how painting – particularly in its thingly aspects – might be regarded as thoughtful and how its often unaccountable agencies might be better understood. Where painting is concerned, it is again particularly abstract art or what we might call the abstract substrata (the abstract qualities and energies) of figurative art that will be *evoked* even if they are not directly addressed. In what follows the implicit foundations for an ethics also present themselves.

According to 'An Unpublished Text', Merleau-Ponty's stated aim in the *Phenomenology* was to produce an in-depth description of the embodied subject's 'exceptional' perceptual relationship with self and world.[2] This involved a redefinition of the term 'body'. It was not to be understood according to scientific and philosophical norms as 'an object in the world, under the purview of a separated spirit' but 'on the side of the subject ... our point of view on the world, [and] the place where the spirit takes on a certain physical and historical situation'.[3]

At issue in treating the body as 'on the side of the subject' was, again, the rejection of the classical distinction between matter and form, understood here as the distinction between body and (disembodied) mind or consciousness. Merleau-Ponty's task was to show how it is that human beings, as wholly embodied, are capable of self-reflexivity. Crucially – indeed, Bannan identified this as the central problem of the *Phenomenology*[4] – Merleau-Ponty had to provide an account of the body as *for us* an *in-itself*. This was vital because, as Merleau-Ponty put it in the chapter of the *Phenomenology* titled 'Experience and Objective Thought: The Problem of the Body', 'the whole life of consciousness is characterised by the tendency to posit objects, since it *is* consciousness, that is to say self-knowledge, *only in so far as it takes hold of itself and draws itself together in an identifiable object*'.[5] Indeed, the task at issue was to 'discover the origin of the object at the very centre of our experience',[6] without, in so doing, closing off those possibilities for change and growth which also characterize conscious functioning. Thus Merleau-Ponty's notion of the body also needed to be suitably flexible and open.

In the *Phenomenology*, Merleau-Ponty treated embodiment as it relates to self-reflexivity in at least three important ways. First, he examined the significance of what might be called the body's 'peculiar' permanence for us. Defining it as a 'middle term between presence and absence',[7] he claimed that it was here that the foundations for self-reflective, embodied consciousness were to be found.[8] It is within this context that an important discussion occurs concerning the 'habit-body', aspects of which, in its relationship with the 'body-at-this-moment', need to be cultivated but, when necessary, also surrendered. Secondly, following Husserl, Merleau-Ponty focused on the reciprocally intentional nature of our embodied relationship with the world. Intertwined into these discussions are his examinations of the body's sense of being a dynamic whole comprising what in traditional philosophical language would be termed both subject and object, this again – as noted, and without positing an opposition between them – being a prerequisite for consciousness or self-knowledge. At issue here are scenarios that are aptly described as inter-corporeal. Thirdly, he reflected on the social implications of these complex and often ambiguous bodily self-understandings. I begin with the issue of the body's peculiar permanence for us.

Peculiar permanence

My body, regarded as an object in the traditional sense, would require, like other such objects, some*thing* else or some*one* else to direct and use it. Empiricism, in a crude form (making as its focus not the body of the investigator but those of the other people or entities being examined), attempted to posit a something else: impersonal, physical forces which act upon it. Rationalism, on the other hand, grappled unsuccessfully with the problem of trying to show how a 'someone else', namely, my disembodied mind, could influence the body I regard as mine.[9] In the chapter of the *Phenomenology* entitled 'The Experience of the Body and Classical Psychology', Merleau-Ponty pointed out that my body regarded as such an object would have to have other characteristics as well. I would have to be able to experience it as 'standing in front of me' under my gaze and under my hand. In particular, it would need to have the capacity to move away from me and 'ultimately disappear from my field of vision. Its presence ... [would have to be] such that it entails a possible absence'.[10] Merleau-Ponty went on to insist that, as classical psychology had already begun to show and as contemporary psychology and psychopathology confirmed, such a view of the body was unjustified:

> The permanence of my body is entirely different in kind: it is not at the extremity of some indefinite exploration; it defies exploration and is always presented to me from the same angle. Its permanence is not a permanence in the world, but a permanence on my part. To say that it is always near me, always there for me, is to say that it is never really in front of me, that I cannot array it before my eyes, that it remains marginal to all my perception, that it is *with* me.[11]

My body has a peculiar permanence and an opacity that makes my relationship with it different to the relationship I may have with an object lying on the desk where I am working. I can pick up the pen and use it, or I can leave it lying in a bag or in another room, away from me. Even though the significations and usages of such an object are potentially inexhaustible, and my explorations of it at any one time always incomplete, even though it still has a kind of general presence for me when it is out of sight, in principle I can nonetheless examine it from all angles, inside and out, take it apart and put it together again. I cannot handle or explore my body in the same way. Nor – however much, at times, I might wish to do so – can I leave it behind. In other words, referring to Crowther's ideas as outlined in the previous chapter, transperceptual space, as this is explicitly foregrounded in abstract art, occurs and is experienced at the core of our relationships with and understanding of ourselves.

My body, then, is not an object like other objects and I can never become literally disconnected from it. Nonetheless, it is the case – not only where rationalist thinking is concerned but also often in everyday experience – that we have the capacity, indeed the propensity, to attempt such detachments, or, at least, to live *as if* these were possible. In the chapter of the *Phenomenology* entitled 'The Body as Object and Mechanistic Physiology', Merleau-Ponty referred to an instance of recognized dysfunction in which this phenomenon occurs, a condition known as anosognosia which entails the inability or refusal to recognize a defect or disorder that is clinically evident.[12] Thus he wrote of 'subjects who systematically ignore their paralysed right hand, and hold out their left hand when asked for their right, [and] refer to their paralysed arm as "a long, cold snake"'.[13] In the causal explanations of traditional physiology and psychology, in which the body is approached mechanistically, he wrote, anosognosia would be accounted for 'as the straightforward suppression ... of "interoceptive" stimulations. According to this hypothesis, anosognosia is the absence of a fragment of representation which ought to be given, since the corresponding limb is there'.[14] On the other hand, a psychological account of the phenomenon would define anosognosia as 'a bit of forgetfulness, a negative judgment or a failure to perceive'. In the first case, he concluded, anosognosia is 'the actual absence of a representation'.[15] In the second case, it is the representation of an actual absence. In both cases, 'we are imprisoned in the categories of the objective world, in which there is no middle term between presence and absence'.[16]

By treating the body as a mechanism, these explanations failed to take into account the human factors that are at issue for sufferers of this disease. In contrast to both the mechanistic and psychological diagnoses of anosognosia, Merleau-Ponty saw the problem as an existential one in which a vital sense of coexistence and thus tension had been lost between two bodily modes of being, that of the habit-body and that of the body-at-this-moment. Indeed, this was another way of indicating that the embrace of peculiar permanence is required for the proper functioning of embodied self-consciousness. Merleau-Ponty wrote that organisms, and not only human organisms, display 'the impulse of being-in-the-world'.[17] The ways in which we immediately respond to the world and our situation within it are tied to 'a [pre-objective] intention of our whole being' which determines 'what our reflexes and perceptions will be able to aim at in the world, the area of our possible operations, the scope of our life'.[18] This is what is absorbed into the habit-body and it was this that the anosognosic patient was unwilling to let go. The implicit relationship between our capacity to grapple with such pre-objectively-situated challenges and our more general ethical, social and political capacities is evident; here too we find the basis for insisting upon the generally unacknowledged centrality of those practices, notably within the arts, which install themselves in this terrain, intervening in and interrogating those borderlands already referred to between the verbally articulate and what is generally regarded as the 'inarticulate', between the 'representational' and the 'non-representational'. For Merleau-Ponty, as noted, Cézanne was paradigmatic in this respect.

For Merleau-Ponty, then, the refusal of the body in anosognosia was above all the refusal of perceived limitation, or what he called disablement,[19] that is, the refusal to accept that a bodily alteration had occurred which, if acknowledged, would require an alteration in the subject's mode of being in the world – and here we cannot but recall Merleau-Ponty's discussions of El Greco in *The Structure of Behavior*. At issue here, was a repression of the disabled body-at-this-moment in favour of the habit-body:

> What it is in us which refuses ... disablement is an *I* committed to a
> certain physical and inter-human world, who continues to tend towards

his world despite handicaps ... and who, to this extent, does not recognise them *de jure*. The refusal of the deficiency is only the obverse of our inherence in a world, the implicit negation of what runs counter to the natural momentum which throws us into our tasks, our cares, our situation, our familiar horizons.[20]

However, while the body-at-this-moment is repressed in anosognosia, it cannot be *wholly* repressed. The success of such an explicit attempt at detachment is dependent upon an unacknowledged recognition of a present but undesired condition and of the impossibility of really leaving it behind. It is this recognition that enables effective defence and avoidance strategies to be constructed, and it is this recognition that also refutes a purely physiological diagnosis of the condition:

> In reality, the anosognosic is not simply ignorant of the existence of his paralysed limb: he can evade his deficiency only because he knows where he risks encountering it, just as the subject, in psychoanalysis, knows what he does not want to face, otherwise he would not be able to avoid it so successfully.[21]

Having made these points, however, Merleau-Ponty was insistent that while the body cannot be left behind, while there is no place of disembodiment to which we may retreat, our functioning as self-reflective beings nonetheless requires the capacity to gain sufficient distance from ourselves such that a perspective upon ourselves, albeit an incomplete one, may be taken. This capacity must be a primordial one. Our immediate experience of our own embodied selves must be something other than absolute coincidence (absolute presence) or absolute disconnection (absence).[22]

One of the ways in which Merleau-Ponty attempted to articulate what I will call this 'vital existential space' between absolute presence and absolute absence, was in terms of the capacity for often uneasy, ongoing interaction or cooperation between the habit-body and the body-at-this-moment, such that each becomes 'contaminated' and altered by the other. This would culminate in an altered habit-body and an altered body-at-this-moment – either of which might be experienced as a 'stranger', even an 'interloper', within – not merely in terms of content but also in terms of *structure*.[23] Clearly, this is highly charged but again often repressed emotional terrain. In order for these recompositions to occur, however, neither must be inappropriately prioritized over the other. Crucially, the importance of the *habit-body* must not be minimized. In the first place, the habit-body provides for the body-at-this-moment a context or background of generality or 'impersonal being' to which it can refer and in the context of which it can distinguish itself.[24] In the second place, it is due to the modes of unconscious awareness and action characteristic of the habit-body that the possibility is opened up for that other aspect of our being, the body-at-this-moment, to engage flexibly and creatively with the world and to acquire new perspectives upon it. As Merleau-Ponty saw it, genuine creativity arose not with the suppression of the habit-body (the implication being that the body-at-this-moment would then be free to express itself spontaneously). Rather, the habit-body has a crucial contribution to make. For,

> it is by giving up part of his spontaneity, by becoming involved in the world through stable organs and pre-established circuits that man can acquire the mental and practical space which will theoretically free him from his environment and allow him to *see* it. ... *It is an inner necessity for the most integrated existence to provide itself with an habitual body.*[25]

While the importance of the habit-body must be maintained, however, it is vital that it does not become resistant to the influence of its counterpart, the body-at-this-moment, as in the case of anosognosia. For where this resistance *does* occur, wrote Merleau-Ponty, 'the subject remains open to the same impossible future, if not in his explicit thoughts, at any rate in his actual being'.[26] Subjects must thus learn to recognize and accept that a lack of 'fit' frequently occurs between the two and be prepared, time and again, to make the kinds of compromises and adjustments necessary for a renewed structural integration to occur. In certain circumstances, to repeat, this might require 'giving up part of [their] spontaneity', in others, giving up already-rehearsed ways of behaving. Here, the additional point may be made that a persistent theme in the *Phenomenology* and in later writings is that – as with Freud, for whom the unconscious functioning of the mind was taken most powerfully to dictate behaviour – in our everyday functioning, and unless challenged by the body-at-this-moment and its awakened perception, it is the automatic, and indeed anonymous,[27] modes of being of the habit-body that tend to dominate. Contra Freud, however, it would seem that for Merleau-Ponty it was not unconscious but *conscious* behaviour, associated here with the body-at-this-moment, that presented what might initially be perceived as the greater threat to our equilibrium. For it is the task of the body-at-this-moment to bring to awareness our ongoing perceptual contact with actual and continually altering states of affair.

A second way in which Merleau-Ponty sought to describe the peculiar permanence of the body was in terms of the body experienced as both sensing and sensible.[28] In the chapter entitled 'The Experience of the Body and Classical Psychology' he wrote:

> When I press my two hands together, it is not a matter of two sensations felt together as one perceives two objects placed side by side, but of an ambiguous set-up in which both hands can alternate the roles of 'touching' and being 'touched'. What is meant by talking about 'double sensations'

is that, in passing from one role to the other, I can identify the hand touched as the same one which will in a moment be touching. In other words, in this bundle of bones and muscles which my right hand presents to my left, I can anticipate for an instant the integument or incarnation of that other right hand, alive and mobile, which I thrust towards things in order to explore them. The body catches itself from the outside engaged in a cognitive process;[29] it tries to touch itself while being touched, and initiates 'a kind of reflection'.[30]

Here, two points are important. The first concerns the ambiguous because reversible nature of the body, or parts of the body, as both sensing and sensible, as in the case of the two hands pressed together. The second concerns the quality of anticipation that is involved in such an experience such that the body-part now functioning and experienced as object – the hand which presents itself as 'a bundle of bones and muscles' – may, in the next instance, take on the role of subject – the hand 'alive and mobile' – reaching out and exploring its environment.

Although the body as both sensing and sensible was discussed here in terms of touch, Merleau-Ponty referred also to visual experience in this regard: the body as both seeing and seen, either by the self, by other people or, more generally, as seeable.[31] And there are, of course, the other senses that would need to be taken into account.[32] In each of these instances, the ways in which the body experiences itself and its world are different; they are instances of the varied ways in which our body can be a body. And yet, as Merleau-Ponty wrote in the chapter entitled 'Sense Experience', these different experiences are integrated in normal functioning so that subjects 'know' not only that the world that is seen, touched, heard and so on is the *same* world but also that this is the same world to which other beings are, differently, open:

Every sensation is spatial; we have adopted this thesis, not because the quality as an object cannot be thought otherwise than in space, but because as the primordial contact with being, as the assumption by the sentient subject of a form of existence to which the sensible points, and as the co-existence of sentient and sensible, it is itself constitutive of a setting for co-existence, in other words, of a space. We say *a priori* that no sensation is atomic, that all sensory experience presupposes a certain field, hence co-existences, from which we conclude, against Lachelier, that the blind man has the experience of a space. But these *a priori* truths amount to nothing other than the making explicit of a fact: the fact of the sensory experience as the assumption of a form of existence. Moreover, this assumption implies also that I can at each moment absorb myself almost wholly into the sense of touch or sight, and even that I can never see or touch without my consciousness becoming thereby in some measure saturated, and losing something of its availability.[33]

Later, concerning the interaction of these spaces, with reference to auditory space and visual space, he wrote that

> the two spaces are distinguishable only against the background of a common world, and can compete with each other only because they both lay claim to total being. They are united at the very instant in which they clash [... even though I may] try to shut myself up in one of my senses and, for instance, project myself wholly into my eyes ... the experience of separate 'senses' is gained only when one assumes a highly particularised attitude, and this cannot be of any assistance to the analysis of direct consciousness.[34]

Merleau-Ponty presented various models of the dual, or doubled, body – the body as sensing and sensible, the body as 'habit-body' and 'body-at-this-moment', the body as 'objective' and 'phenomenal'. His position was that this sense of duality can never be suppressed to such a degree that we are wholly present to one and wholly absent from the other. The two are mutually dependent and in their often disconcerting and destabilizing crossings-over provide us with the 'existential space' that is required for self-awareness and reflexivity. Such self-awareness or reflexivity is unavailable to a self conceived of as having a complete or unambiguous grasp of itself. As Merleau-Ponty put it in the chapter of the *Phenomenology* entitled 'The Cogito', it is impossible for such a being to 'recognise [within itself] the junction of the *for itself* and the *in itself*',[35] that is, to recognize itself as the place where subjective and objective, personal and impersonal, self and world first emerge as entities which find definition in relation to each other. Thus, what Merleau-Ponty attempted to reveal was the primordially decentred and open character of the self. There is no 'pure' or self-contained subject.[36]

A third way in which Merleau-Ponty described the peculiar permanence of the body was in terms of its ambiguous inherence in the social world. In the 'Preface' to the *Phenomenology*, he had already written that 'man is in the world, and only in the world does he know himself'.[37] The body, regarded as an isolated, self-contained and context-less entity, cannot know itself. Not only that. Picking up on discussions from *The Structure of Behavior*, in order to exhibit the characteristics of consciousness its relationship with the world must be sufficiently flexible to allow a range of behaviours to be perceived as possible, thus enabling self-transformation to occur:

> If man is not to be embedded in the matrix of that syncretic setting in which animals lead their lives in a sort of *ek-stase*,[38] if he is to be aware of a world as the common reason for all settings and the theatre of all patterns of behaviour, then between himself and what elicits his action a distance must be set.[39]

Indeed, such setting at a distance is one of the several functions of the symbolic, in which relations are reimagined and reinvigorated, including relations with what one takes to be the self. This idea of setting and seeing oneself in the context of what we might call a vista, where one is not at the centre of things but an entity among many others, is one to which I will return at the end of Chapter 8. But for now it is worth adding that the setting up of such distances is always a matter of scale, not size, and does not preclude intimacy. Rather it has the capacity to extend intimacy. Here we might recall Wols' miniscule drawings and paintings which consistently seemed to open up deeply felt infinities.

The body in its intentional being

In the *Phenomenology*, a particular way in which Merleau-Ponty examined the nature of our inherence in the world was with respect to the body in its intentional being. 'I am a body', he wrote, 'which rises *towards* the world.'[40] This intentional stance towards the world is prefigured within the body's own relationship with itself, experienced as both subject and object. Indeed, as noted, in *The Structure of Behavior*, in the context of his treatment of the symbolic forms of behaviour, Merleau-Ponty had already referred to our primordial awareness of ourselves as both the subject and object of goal-directed or purposive behaviour.[41] In the *Phenomenology* this became thematic, now explored through the notion of intentionality as found in the writing of Husserl and elaborated upon:

> Husserl takes up again the *Critique of Judgement* when he talks about a teleology of consciousness. It is not a matter of duplicating human consciousness with some absolute thought which, from outside, is imagined as assigning to it its aims. It is a question of recognising consciousness itself as a project of the world, meant for a world which it neither embraces nor possesses, but towards which it is perpetually directed – and the world as this pre-objective individual whose imperious unity decrees what knowledge shall take as its goal.[42]

Merleau-Ponty was careful, here, to define exactly what he saw to be Husserl's position. In the first place, he saw Husserl to be equating consciousness with intentionality. As he understood Husserl, the purposes we have as human beings with respect to the world do not represent the outworking of goals embedded within some universal consciousness, or indeed some Hegelian Spirit. Neither do these purposes find their origin solely within an individual consciousness, then to be imposed onto the world, however this is understood. This would be to idealize subjectivity, precisely what Merleau-Ponty – who saw himself to be following the late Husserl in this respect – sought to avoid. Hence his descriptions of the dual body which experiences itself as both subject and object and his definition of the world, just cited, as a 'pre-objective individual whose imperious unity decrees what knowledge shall take as its goal'. When he wrote that it is 'a question of recognising consciousness itself as a *project of the world*, meant for a world which it neither embraces nor possesses',[43] he understood this to mean that individuals find themselves embedded within structures of intentionality as both subject and object. There is, therefore, no 'I'-with-intentions prior to or distinct from the 'I' who is in the world and knows itself only in and through its entangled relationships with other people, things and events.

First, then, Merleau-Ponty presented intentionality as the project of both self *and* world. Secondly, in the chapter of the *Phenomenology* entitled 'The Spatiality of One's Own Body and Motility', again in keeping with his description of the symbolic forms in *The Structure of Behavior*, he also defined it as the body's openness not only to a given 'concrete setting' – a job in hand, for instance – but also to an unspecified number of 'verbal or imaginary situations'.[44] And here it is immediately apparent how such intertwined modalities are foregrounded and made examinable within the relatively bounded but always still open contexts of specific artistic practices or within specific works of art. Two points are important with respect to Merleau-Ponty's position. First, openness to the possible or virtual means that the body-in-the-world has a particular kind of spatial awareness. I do not experience my body as a discrete object definitively located within a closed, homogenous, geometric space of which I have an unambiguous grasp – the rationalized space proposed by linear perspective, for instance. It is not towards such an understanding of self-and-world that we should fundamentally aspire and seek to conform, although it is one of several possible profiles or modes of being that we might imaginatively adopt and experiment with. Rather, I am a mode of being *flexibly* inhering in a specific geographic, intellectual and emotional environment that I perceive as figuring against a background of potential contexts, and I can anticipate this 'realm of the potential'[45] as itself becoming the concrete focus of my actions and desires. Citing the psychologist F. Fischer's 1930 paper 'Space-time structure and thought disorder in schizophrenia' ('Raum-Zeitstruktur und Denkstörung in der Schizophrenie'), Merleau-Ponty called this space in which we inhere, this 'milieu' with both its concrete and its potential aspects, an 'intentional arc':[46]

> the life of consciousness – cognitive life, the life of desire or perceptual life – is subtended by an 'intentional arc' which projects round about us our past, our future, our human setting, our physical, ideological and moral situation, or rather which results in our being situated in all these respects. It is this intentional arc which brings about the unity of the senses, of intelligence, or sensibility and motility. And it is this which 'goes limp' in illness.[47]

But if this intentional arc 'goes limp' in illness, it should be added that aspects of it can also be amplified within experiences conventionally defined as dysfunctional or anomalous. Here we might recall Merleau-Ponty's reflections on the meaning of a supposed visual dysfunction in El Greco and how this became philosophically paradigmatic for him (in *The Structure of Behavior*), his explorations of the multidimensional renderings of space (and time) found in Cézanne's paintings (in 'Cézanne's Doubt'), *and* his broader explorations of the vital role of distortion and deformation in the presentation of truth (in the *Phenomenology*). From this, it would appear that Merleau-Ponty regarded experiences of time and space defined as pathological to be constitutive of the broad range of possibilities available to consciousness, of which our habitual, linear or teleological understanding are a subset. Indeed, in this regard, and from a now-contemporary perspective, research in the field of mathematical physics is pertinent here. That of Metod Saniga, for instance, who is based at the Astronomical Institute, Slovak Academy of Sciences, and counts among his many publications the 2003 volume *The Nature of Time: Geometry, Physics & Perception* co-written with R. Buccheri and W. M. Stuckey.[48] In an early presentation on this topic, delivered in Rome in 1998 and titled 'Unveiling the Nature of Time: Altered States of Consciousness and Pencil-Generated Space-Times', he described various pathologies of time and space, as reported in near-death experiences, drug-induced states, mental psychosis and mystical states, and proceeded to outline a 'simple' model whereby these phenomena could be visualized in geometrical terms and thus made amenable to further analysis. He concluded by stating that these ideas and findings

> provide us with strong evidence that there are forms of human consciousness entirely different from our waking state and experiences of them may represent important phenomenological resources whose contents may, when properly mathematically classified and analyzed, provide valuable insights into the nature of the human mind. Although the interpretation of unusual (or anomalous) mental states, of which those mentioned ... represent only a tiny fraction, has up to now been the domain of psychologists, psychiatrists, philosophers and/or theologians, the time is ripe now for a more general assault, demanding physical and mathematical scrutiny as well.[49]

Saniga, incidentally, had also drawn on Fischer's early twentieth-century research on space-time structure and schizophrenia in making his case.

A second, related point with respect to intentionality, defined as openness to/directedness towards concrete situations and to the 'realm of the possible', is that it is first and foremost an openness displayed by the body – here Merleau-Ponty's position differed from that of Husserl. Specifically, it is presupposed by the body's motility, our capacity to spontaneously move in relation to our surroundings in their concrete and virtual aspects.

Indeed, Merleau-Ponty defined motility as 'basic intentionality'.[50] Here, his discussions revolved particularly around the performance of what he called 'abstract movement'. By this, he meant our ability to project or throw ourselves into tasks and situations that are not *demanded* by actual or pre-existing conditions. Abstract movement is, in the first place, brought into play – largely but not wholly – by our own initiative. Needless to say, his discussions in this regard offer material with which to consider the varied implications and possibilities, including, I would argue, the broader philosophical and political implications of artistic engagements with, and interrogations of, painterly abstraction in its many modes. As Crowther has put it, painterly activity understood as 'abstracting-as'.

In the second place, intentionality as here defined has the significance of transforming our present milieu in some way. Here, again, it is the openness of our stance within the context of the actual or the concrete that is crucial. In Merleau-Ponty's words:

> The abstract movement carves out within that plenum of the world in which concrete movement took place a zone of reflection and subjectivity; it superimposes upon physical space a virtual or human space. Concrete movement is therefore centripetal whereas abstract movement is centrifugal. The former occurs in the realm of being or of the actual, the latter on the other hand in that of the virtual or the non-existent; *the first adheres to a given background, the second throws out its own background.* The normal function which makes abstract movement possible is one of 'projection' whereby the subject of movement keeps in front of him an area of free space in which what does not naturally exist may take on a semblance of existence.[51]

From our earlier discussions in this book, it will be clear that Merleau-Ponty was not referring here to an impositional, non-porous or literally self-centred notion of projection.

In the *Phenomenology*, the stress Merleau-Ponty placed on the body's motility as the basic intentionality upon which all modes of intentional behaviour are modelled was, in part, a consequence of his reflections on an account of morbid motility and its broader behavioural implications. The patient in question was one Schneider, whose condition was documented in works by the Gestalt psychologists Gelb and Goldstein in the 1920s.[52] Schneider had been wounded by a shell splinter to the back of the head. As a result of this injury, a radical alteration had occurred in his basic awareness of his body and in his manner of being in the world. In the first place, as Merleau-Ponty described it, Schneider no longer had an immediate awareness of how and where the various parts of his body were located in relation to each other and to the environment. In the second place, although he was still able to function with reasonable efficiency within already-familiar concrete situations, he was no longer able to perform abstract movements with his eyes shut, either of an initiatory nature or in response to a verbal command. He *could* do so with his eyes open but only with great difficulty. Schneider himself was recorded as saying that he was scarcely aware of 'any voluntary initiative' and that it 'all happens independently of me'.[53] Merleau-Ponty took this to indicate that when motility and an immediate sense of the spatiality of our own bodies is no longer an aspect of self-awareness, also lost is an intentional, imaginative and creative stance towards the world. He wrote that where abstract movement is concerned 'the patient must first of all "find" his arm, "find" by ... preparatory movements, the gesture called for, and the gesture itself loses the melodic character which it presents in ordinary life, and becomes manifestly a collection of partial movements strung laboriously together'.[54] Thus, what Schneider's strange, piecemeal functioning displayed, in fact, is 'normal' behaviour as defined within the empiricist model.

Another point of interest identified by Merleau-Ponty related to the fact that, for Schneider, those categories of the subjective and the objective, discussed earlier, were seen to have become relatively ineffectual. Schneider 'is conscious of his bodily space as the matrix of his habitual action but not as an objective setting; his body is at his disposal as a means of ingress into a familiar surrounding but not as the means of expression of a gratuitous and free spatial thought'.[55] Later on Merleau-Ponty wrote:

> Whereas in the normal person every event related to movement or sense of touch causes consciousness to put up a host of intentions which run from the body as the centre of potential action either towards the body itself or towards the object, in the case of the patient, on the other hand, the tactile impression remains opaque and sealed up. It may well draw the grasping hand towards itself, but does not stand in front of the hand in the manner of a thing which can be pointed out.[56] The normal person *reckons with* the possible, which thus, without shifting from its position as a possibility, acquires a sort of actuality. In the patient's case, however, the field of actuality is limited to what it met with in the shape of a real contact or is related to these data by some explicit process of deduction.[57]

For Merleau-Ponty, then, 'bodily space and external space form a practical system' and, although ordinarily our attention is so taken up with 'things' regarded as external to us that we are rarely aware of the fundamental role played by our bodies in this respect, bodily space is nonetheless 'the background against which the object as the goal of our action may stand out or the void in front of which it may *come to light*'.[58] This tendency to forget the role that the body plays in our various perceptual behaviours is, in fact, a consequence of our character as intentional beings. In an important respect, then, Merleau-Ponty's position was that we must be careful not to allow this capacity for positing objects to mislead us about the kind of world we inhabit and the kinds of beings we are. Furthermore, he stressed that it is the fluid, two-sided character of the motile body as receptive both to actual *and* possible situations that enables an open and creative relationship to exist between individuals and the world. The connection between this fluidity – which gives rise to a sense of self as shifting and in an important respect unknowable – and the issue of bodily motility, was stressed by Merleau-Ponty later on in the *Phenomenology* as follows:

> It is true neither that my existence is in full possession of itself, nor that it is entirely estranged from itself, because it is action or doing, and because action is, by definition, the violent transition from what I have to what I aim to have, from what I am to what I intend to be.[59]

Merleau-Ponty's use of the word 'violent' here is significant; it applies even in instances of positive transformation.

There is, finally, a third point of importance concerning Merleau-Ponty's discussions of intentionality here, namely how in its display of openness towards the realms of the concrete and the virtual a reciprocally constituted sense of world comes into being – as noted in the introduction, in his slightly later writing Merleau-Ponty would use the term 'institution' to express this. Again, the case of Schneider played a key role in his arguments. In the first place, as noted above, Merleau-Ponty wrote that abstract movement 'carves out within that *plenum* of the world in which concrete movement took place a zone of reflection; it *superimposes* upon physical space a virtual or human space'.[60] By using the term 'plenum' (one meaning of which, especially in the philosophy of the Stoics, is a space regarded as filled with matter), and by using the term 'superimposes', the impression that is given is of a closed space being opened out or, indeed, being replaced by an expanded one. What the motile body may be read as bringing about is a disruption to the way in which a restricted, concrete situation is configured so that an environment may be facilitated in which new modes of being – those which we would refer to as initiatory – can begin to offer themselves for consideration. To repeat: 'The subject of movement keeps in front of him an area of free space in which what does not naturally exist may take on a semblance of existence.'[61] Here, again, I cannot but also think of those endlessly differentiated 'fundamental' spaces opened up by means of painterly abstraction.

A little later on, this model of a closed space being expanded was presented alongside a second model in which the activity of constituting identifiable objects was associated with the capacity to mark out boundaries or to impose limitations upon a world in accordance with specific practical intentions. What was described was a narrowing and defining of possibilities – also a crucial aspect of any creative process – enabled by the intentional subject's immediate perception of the environment not as an 'in-itself' but as an 'in itself *for* me'. This, again, was something Schneider, and patients like him, cannot do:

One knows of patients with powers less seriously affected than Schneider's who perceive forms, distances and objects in themselves, but who are either unable to trace in objects the directions which are useful from the point of view of action, or to arrange them according to some principle, *or generally to assign to the spatial scene delimitations in human terms which make it the field of our action.*[62]

This inability to take the initiative of setting limits in order to perform a task or to fulfil a specific verbal instruction[63] is tied to the particular way in which the body is itself experienced. Merleau-Ponty wrote concerning Schneider that 'the patient finds in his body only an amorphous mass into which actual movement alone introduces divisions and links. In looking to his body to perform the movement for him he is like a speaker who cannot utter a word without following a text written beforehand'.[64] Schneider's body was not experienced by him as being a 'for me', that is, he could not delineate or configure his body so as to enjoy it in a variety of ways 'as the mood takes [him]',[65] imaginatively, non-compulsively or playfully. In Schneider's words, cited earlier, it 'all happens independently of me'.

Intersubjectivity, inter-corporeality and otherness – Foundational hospitality

Finally, I turn to the social implications of Merleau-Ponty's understanding of embodied self-reflexivity in the *Phenomenology*. A particular context for these discussions are my earlier references in this chapter to Merleau-Ponty's understanding of embodied self-reflexivity as proto-sociality requiring the capacity to embrace certain felt tensions, irreconcilabilities and impositions. In the 'Preface' he had written, evocatively, that

> if the other is truly for himself alone, beyond his being for me, and if we are for each other and not both for God[66] we must necessarily have some appearance for each other. He and I must have an outer appearance, and there must be, besides the perspective of the For Oneself – my view of myself and the other's view of himself – a perspective of For Others – my view of others and theirs of me. Of course, these two perspectives, in each one of us, cannot be simply juxtaposed, *for in that case it is not I that the other sees, nor he that I should see.* I must be the exterior that I present to others, and the body of the other must be the other himself.[67]

For Merleau-Ponty, genuine communication with, and knowledge of, other people – as was the case with the self – requires that they be apprehended by us *as* Other. In order for this to occur it is not sufficient to have thoughts about them. This would be to understand them as deriving from the self, and to be the product of reflection, imagination or projection. As Merleau-Ponty saw it, the apprehension of otherness is not available to the disembodied mind but only to beings who take their own embodiedness into account and thus consider their contact with others to be of a perceptual nature. For at issue here are encounters between beings who have an *appearance* for one another and therefore experience themselves as 'expose[d] ... to the gaze of others'.[68] I will reflect further on this notion of exposure shortly.

Later, he made a connection between this phenomenological, perceptually grounded understanding of how people communicate and are understood by each other and how works of art communicate. As noted at the start of this chapter: 'The body is to be compared, not to a physical object but rather to a work of art. In a picture or a piece of music the idea is incommunicable by means other than the display of colours and sounds.'[69] This was a suggestive observation, revealing that for Merleau-Ponty it was not only differently articulated modes of painterly interrogation on the part of painters and viewers that had important philosophical implications but also paintings themselves, as particular kinds of self-showing entities.

The second point he made about the nature of our embodied, perceptual contact with the genuinely – but never radically or absolutely – Other was its grounding in our acceptance that, as embodied beings, our existence is never in full possession of itself – that the 'true' cogito or 'incarnated mind'[70] necessarily gives me only a partial grasp even of myself. As he put it, and again he is worth citing at some length:

> Unless I learn within myself to recognise the junction of the *for itself* and the *in itself*, none of those mechanisms called other bodies will ever be able to come to life. ... The plurality of consciousness is impossible if I have an absolute consciousness of myself. ... If it is perfect, the contact of my thought with itself seals me within myself and prevents me from ever feeling that anything eludes my grasp; there is no opening, no 'aspiration'[71] towards an Other for this self of mine, which constructs the totality of being and its own presence in the world, which is defined in terms of 'self-possession',[72] and which never finds anything outside itself but what it has put there. This hermetically sealed self is no longer a finite self.[73]

It is at this juncture that the social, political and ethical dimensions of Merleau-Ponty's thought in this regard become apparent. The fact that contact with the Other depends, firstly, on our having an appearance for each other and, secondly, on our having an incomplete grasp of our own existence has implications not only for the kind of communications we can have with others and the kinds of knowledges we can have of them but also for the contexts in which such communications and knowledges must occur. According to Merleau-Ponty, we can be known and communicated with only incompletely. First, as embodied beings, we present ourselves to other embodied beings as appearances, situated within albeit complex given contexts and visible only from particular points of view. Thus certain aspects of ourselves are revealed to others, while others remain hidden from them (and we can never be completely certain which are which). The truth about ourselves and other people is never given immediately or fully. Paraphrasing Merleau-Ponty, the price we pay for being 'real'[74] is that we cannot expect either to be wholly known or to wholly know another. Crucially, though, incorporated into this being-seen-by-the-Other in which much remains hidden is the reality that, as well as potentially delivering a diminished viewpoint (in which we feel that we are less in their eyes than we are in our own), this Other is as likely to obtain a more expansive and multidimensional understanding of our being than is available to us. This is in large part because Others experience our situatedness differently than we do; for them, we figure against a backdrop of people and things that we can never perceive – or never perceive quite as they do – since it is always 'behind' us. Likewise, to this Other, our more submerged modes of being, associated for instance with the habit-body whose behaviours we barely register, may be more than evident.

Appearances count. But, secondly, the significance of these appearances, like that of a painting, can never be regarded as definitive. Although incomplete, however, our knowledge of others, and theirs of us, may expand and alter – even to the degree of becoming contradictory – as perceptual acquaintance continues and as we attempt to approach and consider one another from different points of view.

Merleau-Ponty made a third, related point. Embodied beings, inhering in and displaying intentionality towards the world, can be known only in the context of their modes of behaving in this world. To gain understanding of each other we must pay attention above all to how we relate to the wider environment and interact with one another. Here, intersubjectivity and inter-corporeality are found to be inextricably intertwined:

> For the 'other' to be more than an empty word, it is necessary that my existence should never be reduced to my bare awareness of existing, but that it should take in also the awareness that *one* may have of it, *and thus include my incarnation in some nature and the possibility, at least, of a historical situation*.[75] The *Cogito* must reveal me in a situation, and it is on this condition alone that transcendental subjectivity can, as Husserl puts it,[76] be an intersubjectivity.[77]

A fourth and final point is that communicating with, and knowing, others involves allowing them to reveal themselves to us, rather than imposing our interpretations onto them. The ethical implications of this are clear. Indeed, in the *Phenomenology* and in his defence of it, published as 'The Primacy of Perception', his discussions of perception and intersubjectivity culminated in discussions of morality. In 'The Primacy of Perception' he defined 'true' morality not as the public or private adherence to a set of pre-established rules but as 'generously meeting the other in the very particularity of a given situation'.[78] In such encounters we may find that 'our perspectives are irreconcilable'. Therefore, radical disagreement must remain a possible, although not necessarily permanent, factor of communal life. This, Merleau-Ponty insisted, was preferable to a superficially less problematic notion of community in which agreement is achieved through dogmatism, that is, through collective adherence to a set of external principles and the active suppression of irreconcilable points of view. He implied that in a situation where such irreconcilabilities *are* given space for expression, the possibility arises for individuals either to display hospitality or generosity by voluntarily submitting to the position of another, *or*, should this be regarded as inappropriate, to search together for an as-yet unanticipated vantage point about which some degree of productive or practical agreement could be reached.[79] As he put it in 'Metaphysics and the Novel', within such contexts, old habits would be found to have exploded.[80] Hostility, of course, is the other option; as thinkers from Kant to Carl Schmitt, Jacques Derrida, Richard Kearney and others have reminded us, hospitality and hostility are intimately as well as etymologically related.[81]

In any case, returning to Merleau-Ponty and remaining with 'Metaphysics and the Novel', we see that the issue of morality is in fact central to this work. Merleau-Ponty had written it primarily in response to the negative critical reception of Simone de Beauvoir's recently published novel *L'Invitée*.[82] The fact that her characters were involved in a ménage à trois, he wrote, had 'provoked the literary critics to censure them for immorality'.[83] Or rather, not the *fact* of this ménage à trois but first the fact that de Beauvoir had presented her characters as involving themselves in it in all ignorance and honesty,[84] and, secondly, because she set about only to *describe* their interrelationship and not to judge it in accordance with predetermined values. In Merleau-Ponty's view, on the contrary, it was because de Beauvoir refused to subject her characters to standards of judgement conceived of as absolute and as existing wholly externally to the individuals concerned that she not only displayed generosity towards them, allowing them to reveal themselves but also, more generally, presented her readers with the challenge of rethinking, on a more nuanced level, the issues of what makes for genuine community and morality.[85]

And so, in the final paragraph of this essay, Merleau-Ponty defined communication as he understood it and distinguished the true morality which he saw de Beauvoir's characters display from the false morality of the censors:

Communication exists between the moments of my personal time, as between my time and that of other people, *and in spite of the rivalry between them. It exists, that is, if I will it, if I do not shrink from it out of bad faith, if I plunge into the time which both separates and unites us, as the Christian plunges into God.* True morality does not consist in following exterior rules or in respecting objective values: there are no ways to be just or to be saved. One would do better to pay less attention to the unusual situation of the three characters in *L'Invitée* and more to the good faith, the loyalty to promises, the respect for others, the generosity and the seriousness of the two principals [Françoise and Pierre]. For the value is there. It consists of actively being what we are by chance, of establishing that communication with others and with ourselves for which our temporal structure gives us the opportunity and of which our liberty is only the rough outline.[86]

Here, Merleau-Ponty was writing about literature. But analogous sensibilities of hospitality and generosity (as opposed to the types of censure and critical opposition just described) might be perceived within the types of painterly activity that were of particular interest to Merleau-Ponty. While such works might have the immediate appearance of being thematically unconcerned with questions of the social and political they nonetheless may be seen to play an essential role in terms of emphasizing the centrality of the aesthetic realm – understood in terms of activating appropriately flexible sensibilities, perceptual orientations and emotional capacity – for motivating real social and political change. This is because change of this kind requires levels of adjustment and genuine self-relinquishment that are relatively easy to proclaim but less easy to put into practice. It generally involves addressing those recalcitrant ways of being that are embedded within the structures of the habit-body. Later, in 'Eye and Mind', Merleau-Ponty would present an interesting twist on the potential of painting-in-general to generate hospitality or, at the very least, to generate an attitude in which outright censure and opposition are withheld. Comparing the painter with the writer, from whom an opinion is expected and repeatedly elicited, he began by stating that 'only the painter is entitled to look at everything without being obliged to appraise what he sees. For the painter, we might say, the watchwords of knowledge and action lose their meaning and force'.[87] He then continued (and here memories of the war were surely at the forefront of his mind): 'Political regimes which denounce "degenerate" painting rarely destroy paintings. They hide them, and one senses here an element of "one never knows" amounting almost to a recognition.'[88]

PART THREE

Painting – Rethinking thought as 'silence' and 'speech'

FIGURE 5.1 Merleau-Ponty and his Daughter, La Canebière, Marseille, *summer 1948, photograph. © Archives Merleau-Ponty. Disclaimer: Every effort has been made to obtain permission to reproduce this image. The publishers will be pleased to make the necessary arrangement at the first opportunity.*

FIGURE 5.2 *Katharina Grosse,* This is Not Dogshit, *2007, acrylic on wall, windows and floor, 600 × 1200 × 100 cm. Leeuwarden / Franchise Foundation. Photo: Harold Koppmanns.* © *Katharina Grosse and VG Bild-Kunst, Bonn / DACS 2018.*

CHAPTER FIVE

The being of language, reconceived

A new index of curvature

Expression is a matter of reorganizing things-said, affecting them with a new index of curvature, and bending them to a certain enhancement of meaning.

(Maurice Merleau-Ponty)[1]

These words from the introduction to Merleau-Ponty's *Signs* – a collection of essays spanning the late 1940s and 1950s published by Éditions Gallimard, Paris, in 1960 – encourage us to ask how, during the middle period of his philosophical career, Merleau-Ponty himself reorganized the statements he had made in *The Structure of Behavior*, the *Phenomenology* and related essays.

In the early works, his claims about the primacy of embodied perception for thought and his exemplifications of painting in this regard were situated within a broad understanding of consciousness as behavioural and visible, thus expressive, and of thought, therefore, as intertwined with perception and motility. From the late 1940s, one of the important ways in which Merleau-Ponty rearticulated these ideas was by bringing them into conversation with philosophical and anthropological debates in which meaning – including the emergence of visual and social meaning – was increasingly taken to be modelled, constructed or codified according to deeply embedded linguistic structures as well as more localized language games. A case in point was his remarkable essay 'Indirect Language and the Voices of Silence' with which *Signs* opens. It was first published in two parts in the June and July 1952 issues of *Les Temps Modernes*.[2] In *Signs* it is followed by a second, slightly earlier essay also explicitly on language to which I will also turn: his 'On the Phenomenology of Language' of 1951.[3]

Given Merleau-Ponty's already clearly expressed focus on questions of structure and expression in his early writing, his turn to an immersive study of the nature and workings of language should come as no surprise. In fact, Merleau-Ponty had begun reading 'scientific linguistics', particularly the work of Ferdinand de Saussure, shortly after completing the *Phenomenology* and he had taught on the topic of language during his last year at Lyon (1947–48).[4] But during his tenure as chair of child psychology and pedagogy at the University of Paris, Sorbonne, this became an increasingly important area of academic focus. A case in point was his 1949–50 course *Consciousness and the Acquisition of Language*.[5] A sense of the content of this course is available to us, in posthumously published form, thanks to the use made of his students' notes. During his lifetime he published at least ten essays that dealt directly with language, the earliest being 'Language and Communication' of 1948.

As I have already indicated, rather than disavowing the perceptual and the visual, Merleau-Ponty's researches into language significantly enriched his thought in this regard by enabling previously underemphasized or underexposed aspects of it to become apparent. To re-cite his own words from the introduction to *Signs*, we see his already-articulated perspectives being bent to 'a certain enhancement of meaning'. But there is more. His approach, especially as presented in 'Indirect Language and the Voices of Silence', offered a rich, non-oppositional understanding of the relations between the visual and the verbal. This challenged, *avant la lettre*, the anti-ocular 'logocentrism' within philosophy that would become increasingly dominant in the decades after his death and which would so forcefully impact developments within art history and art theory. Indeed – remaining with the short portion of text under discussion from the introduction to *Signs* – it is significant that Merleau-Ponty evoked this crucial sense of expressive-linguistic complexity through a use of powerful visual-spatial metaphors: those processes of bending and of being affected by 'a new index of curvature'. And with these words, familiar territory is recalled, that is, the shifting, transformative presentations of space and time that were already integral to Merleau-Ponty's philosophically-fuelled – as well as existentially- and politically-fuelled – insistence that thought be reconceptualized upon non-dualistic, non-causal foundations. A provocative variation of such trans-dimensionality was pictured in El Greco's *Christ on the Cross Adored by Donors* as the environment in which the dying Christ was embedded and which, simultaneously, his approaching death seemed also to be generating.

Notably, Merleau-Ponty's orientations also prefigured certain twenty-first-century attempts at reconceptualizing and repositioning thought outside of the enduring legacies of dualism and causality in which in practice, if not always in theory, it is still deeply entrenched. Among these efforts at reconceptualization are certain new directions taken, and territories opened up, within the realm of post-1990s painting. Here, we might look again at certain discussions raised in *The Forever Now* where Hoptman took inspiration from, and activated, Gibson's notion of atemporality in order to conceptualize current trends. This time though it is worth also considering Anne Ring Petersen's slightly earlier and somewhat differently positioned reflections in *Contemporary Painting in Context*, in which she turned to the well-known notion of 'expanded field' – also the title of the third section of Petersen's anthology – from Rosalind Krauss' 1979 essay 'Sculpture in the Expanded Field'.[6] Petersen used it as a point of departure for reassessing recent histories of, and developments within, *painting*. Regarding the proposition at issue – and it is worth remembering that Krauss' thought, while significantly influenced by phenomenological insights and orientations[7], was in this case informed above all by semiotics – Petersen wrote in her introduction that

> The expansion that Krauss is talking about is not a merely quantitative expansion, an inclusion of the sculptural materials and means of expression that makes it possible to construct sculptures out of mirror glass, soil or felt and enlarge them to the size of Robert Smithson's *Spiral Jetty* (1969–70). It is not synonymous with an expansion of the discipline 'sculpture' in itself. What Krauss identifies as 'the expanded field' is *a new set of relations between 'sculpture' and two other categories that are not 'sculpture' and cannot be subsumed under the category of 'sculpture': 'architecture' and 'landscape'*. Thus, in Krauss's terminology 'the expanded field' is an expression that refers to the exploration of innovative interrelations and combinations between categories that are fundamentally different, not the limitless and eclectic assimilation of new stuff. Thus, the primary thing that the explorations added to sculpture was not greater variety, *but a new set of cultural terms and structural principles with which to work.*[8]

Of course, Crowther's theorizations of abstract painting – outlined earlier, in Chapter 3 – organized around the notions of seeing-as and abstracting-as, could again be brought into play. Seeing-as and abstracting-as were described as sharing the capacity to be either exemplificational or imaginative; thus at issue again are modes of perception and, by extension, embodied thought that are expansive not because they are assimilative but because they involve genuine, multimodal repositionings at the level of perception, cognition and expression. From these new constellations of meaning and possibility, new constellations of revelation and hiddenness may be derived. Also of note is Crowther's own brief reference in *Phenomenologies of Art and Vision* to Krauss' notion of 'expanded field' in the context of his broader discussions of art. In the chapter 'Space, Place and Sculpture: Heidegger's Pathways', Crowther stated that post-1960s 'postmodern' sculpture is now regarded, 'broadly speaking ... as a visual idiom based on the hewing, carving, digging, casting or *arranging* of three-dimensional material'[9] – a characterization that may be seen to have crossed over into much contemporary (Petersen would say post mid-1990s) painterly practice too, where questions of facture and installation are concerned. I will return to this point in a moment. In a footnote, Crowther referenced the impact in this regard of Krauss' 'Sculpture in the Expanded Field', merely describing it as identifying a shift in sculpture from the production of 'certain kinds of objects to ... modes of cultural intervention'.[10] But in his earlier book, *Phenomenology of the Visual Arts (even the Frame)* of 2009, he had already set out what he saw to be the limitations of the then-emergent semiotically driven approaches to art history that also underpinned Krauss' 1979 essay. It occurred in a chapter entitled 'Against Reductionism' and in the context of his critique of the 'social history of art' which – in critical counterpoint to what were regarded as reductive 'formalist', so-called 'art-for-art's-sake' histories of modern art – now foregrounded the social, political and economic circumstances governing the production and reception of art. The importance of such ventures notwithstanding, Crowther wrote that they were generally presented by advocates as providing 'a *sufficient* characterization of meaning in the image', such that the significance of the image was reduced to 'its informational content and persuasive effects, and to the social and other circumstantial elements which enable these'.[11] Crowther described these approaches to art history, except for their occasional discussions of 'technique and artists' materials', as 'consumer and historical-context orientated'.[12] '*Social reductionism* of this kind', he added, 'is combined often with a tendency to assimilate art's visual dimension on the basis of models derived from literary analysis' – namely, *semiotic reductionism*.[13] Arguably, a more recent variant of this type of approach, certainly in terms of an understanding of art-as-information, was referenced by Hoptman in her introduction to *The Forever Now*. Citing the art historian David Joselit's 2011 *Artforum* essay 'Signal Processing', she described him as 'recasting contemporary painting as "essentially a broadcast medium" [thus transforming] an individual painting from an object to a transmitter of information'.[14] This is again reductive although, as I will show, aspects of this reading of contemporary painting – and contemporary art more generally – are useful when considered alongside other factors and when notions of objecthood, transmission and motility are held and thought together.

Also pertinent to our discussions of how the painting of today might be approached and understood are Peter Osborne's reflections in his 2013 book *Anywhere or Not at All: Philosophy of Contemporary Art*.[15] The book is organized around the assertion that in order for contemporary art effectively and robustly to become 'the object of some kind of reflective philosophical experience'[16] fundamental ontological questions must first be asked about the designation 'contemporary' beyond the merely temporal. Not all art produced now counts as contemporary. A critical-historical designation is required:

> 'Contemporary' is, at base, a critical and therefore a selective concept: it promotes and it excludes. To claim something is contemporary is to make

a claim for its significance in participating in the actuality of the present – a claim over and against that of other things, some of which themselves may make a similar claim on contemporaneity.[17]

This led to Osborne's proposition that 'contemporary art is post-conceptual art',[18] which he described as an art 'premised on the complex historical and critical legacy of conceptual art, broadly construed, which registers its fundamental mutation of the ontology of the artwork'.[19] Like the term 'contemporary', 'post-conceptual' was defined by him as a critical category that eschewed theorizations of art 'at the level of medium, form or style'.[20] Post-conceptual art constitutes a radical, critical destruction of notions of medium and medium-specificity as foundational art-historical categories. Among other things, it is necessarily trans-categorical and trans-medial. According to this view, the notion of 'post-conceptual *painting*' would make little sense, if painting, whether as object or practice, is taken to be a fundamentally medium-specific designation.

In the chapter 'Art Beyond Aesthetics', Osborne went on to present a six-point, sequentially evolving account of the characteristics of post-conceptual art, each aspect of which must be in evidence. They are worth reproducing here because they raise points with which this book's explorations of painting-as-thought will need to engage. The first point is self-evident since it relates to art's 'necessary conceptuality'. The second point refers to arts 'ineliminable – but radically insufficient – aesthetic dimension', 'ineliminable' because 'all art requires some form of materialization; that is to say, aesthetic – felt, spatio-temporal – presentation'.[21] In the book's introduction, Osborne had already written that contemporary art, as he defined it, 'is not an aesthetic art in any philosophically significant sense of the term'.[22] The third point he described as a conjunction of the first two. It consisted of the 'critical necessity of an anti-aestheticist use of aesthetic materials' and was 'a critical consequence of art's necessary conceptuality'. At issue, here, is a polemical opposition of the aesthetic and the conceptual, which is clearly in discord with the Merleau-Pontean position that I am presenting. But Osborne's fourth, fifth and sixth points move in the direction of expansiveness. Fourthly, then, at issue is an 'expansion to infinity of the possible material forms of art'. This is an important point since, as discussed in my introduction, it counters the commonly asserted association of conceptual art practices (*à la* Lippard) with a condition of dematerialization. Osborne's fifth point is significant and will resonate with the discussions of art to which I will turn in a moment, since it refers to a 'radically distributive – that is, irreducibly relational – unity of the individual artwork across the totality of its multiple material instantiations, at any particular time'. His final point references a 'historical malleability of the borders of this unity'.[23]

Of particular affinity to the discussions in this chapter about painting and language, image and word, and 'the reorganization of things-said' are Osborne's discussions of what he called the 'radically distributive – that is, irreducibly relational – unity of the individual artwork across the totality of its multiple material instantiations, at any particular time'; his claims regarding 'a historical malleability of the borders of this unity' are also of particular interest.[24]

Finally, within the context of our current discussions regarding notions of the 'expanded field' of art (and of painting) also worth remarking upon is Osborne's insightful evaluation – in the chapter 'Transcategorality: postconceptual art' – of Krauss' model. His objections are akin but not identical to those of Crowther. Specifically at issue is her use of a semiotic resource, Algirdas Greimas' semiotic square. While this did enable her to position contemporary sculpture within a critical context that included the non-sculptural realms of architecture and landscape, the expansive trajectories of the model were also restricted, nonetheless, to just those two non-sculptural realms. As he remarked, this model was 'a transitional account, between medium-specificity and what Krauss would later acknowledge to be a much more various – and, for her, critically irrecuperable – "post-medium condition"'.[25]

Now, though, having made these observations, I would like to return to *Contemporary Painting in Context* and, particularly, to Petersen's essay 'Painting Spaces',[26] in which, at some length, she applied the insights *she* had gained from Krauss's theorization of the expanded field of sculpture to the question of painting. She began by reiterating the point she had made in the introduction about the important difference between assimilative notions of painterly expansion, which she associated with much pre- and post-1960s inventiveness, and the new types of spatial exploration she saw as emergent in the 1990s, paradigmatically in the many, now-iconic, architecturally scaled, industrially spray-painted installations by Katharina Grosse begun in 1998. More recent examples of Grosse's work, situated in non-gallery public spaces, include *This is Not Dogshit* of 2007 sprayed onto the exterior of a building in the Dutch city of Leeuwarden (Figure 5.2) and Grosse's 2016 transformation of an old aquatics building, and the pavement, sand and foliage surrounding it, for the *Rockaway!* arts programme at Fort Tilden in New York. This was a collaborative venture begun by MoMA PS1 staff and volunteers in 2012 in the aftermath of Hurricane Sandy in order to aid the local community.[27] Petersen also examined other examples of painterly space-creation in works by such artists as Julian Opie, Peter Bonde, Torgny Wilcke (who works at the 'interstice between painting and design' making 'modular' paintings that can be assembled after the model of mass-produced, self-assembly furniture[28]), Franz Ackermann and Jessica Stockholder. According to Petersen, until the 1970s 'painters usually extended the traditional domain of figurative painting by exploring *abstraction* or by assimilating images from popular culture and the mass media, that is, by working with and reflecting on the *mediation* of images in modern society'.[29] With her reference to mediation, she was specifically referencing concepts formulated by Peter Weibel in his 1995 catalogue essay and exhibition 'Pittura/Immedia: Die Malerei in den 90er Jahren zwischen mediatisierter Visualität und Visualität im Kontext' ('Pittura/ Immedia: Painting in the Nineties between Mediated Visuality and Visuality in Context').[30] Petersen described these extensions to the 'vocabulary of painting' as having 'established a long and rich tradition that continues to this day',[31] and here again we might want recall the assimilative painterly recombinations foregrounded by Hoptman in relation to the post-2006 works exhibited in *The Forever Now*. But Petersen went on to argue that since the mid-1990s a major change had taken place in the field of painting:

> A remarkable number of painters have begun to explore the possibility of developing painting in a third direction and redefining what 'space' is in relation to painting. Today, much of the experimental energy is put into exploring the *spatiality* of painting, not as a product of illusionism, but as something physical and tangible. Artists are investigating painting's relations to objects, space, place, and the 'everyday', and in so doing they are expanding 'painting' physically as well as conceptually. In many cases, one can hardly say that the artist is painting pictures; he or she is rather painting or creating spaces. This rethinking of space in painting, or of painting *as* space, brings about changes in the relationship of painting to the viewer, the exhibition space, the art institutions, the market, and the other contexts of the artwork.[32]

Where the work of Grosse is concerned, one of the things Petersen particularly attended to, in the portion of her essay entitled 'Paintings to Walk Into',[33] was the impact of the artist's in situ use of the industrial spray gun such that the exhibition space as a whole became 'a surface to be painted on'.[34] 'To Grosse', she wrote 'everything is a potential ground for her paintings: walls, ceilings, windows, doors and the everyday objects and materials that she sometimes brings into the room.'[35] And, of course, to this list can also be added large portions of the built environment, as in the case of the *Rockaway!* installation or in such earlier works as *Untitled Berlin* of 2003, where the 'ground' comprised an entire external corner elevation of an office block belonging to an old glass factory. Usefully, Petersen's observation clarified foundational issues that relate to Merleau-Ponty's own re-evaluations of thought and of painting-as-thought: namely, that *expression*, understood as 'a matter of reorganizing things said, affecting them with a new index of curvature', produces altered perceptions and thus altered conceptions not only of what might constitute 'figure' but also of what might constitute 'ground'. Also clarified was the fact that here acts of expression do not merely inhabit existing space but create and recreate it. In alignment with what Merleau-Ponty wrote in the *Phenomenology* about the spatiality of the human body, here too painted or painterly bodies and space are experienced as being produced together. Again, both the ambiguity and the peculiar permanence of these bodies are

FIGURE 5.3 *Katharina Grosse*, The Poise of the Head und die anderen folgen, *2004, acrylic on wall, floor, soil and canvas, 900 × 900 × 1100 cm. Photo: Nic Tenwiggenhorn and VG Bild-Kunst, Bonn. © Katharina Grosse and VG Bild-Kunst, Bonn / DACS 2018.*

FIGURE 5.4 *Installation view,* Rashid Johnson. Within Our Gates, *Garage Museum of Contemporary Art, Moscow, Russia, 2016.* © *Rashid Johnson. Courtesy the artist and Hauser & Wirth. Photo: Alexey Naroditsky.*

seen to be irreducibly intertwined. To cite Petersen again: 'Grosse's in situ works are not objects'.[36] And indeed, in Grosse's own contribution to this anthology – a photoessay entitled *The Poise of the Head und die anderen folgen*, also the title of an installation created in 2004 for the Kunsthalle Düsseldorf which I will discuss later (Figure 5.3) – Grosse described how making her first spray-gun painting (*Untitled, Bern*, 1998), with its indirect approach to applying pigment to ground, produced new iterations and understandings of the nature of painterly space.

> This was the first time I used a spray gun to make a painting in relationship to space and its volume. Until then I had used paintbrushes to cover the full wall space, going in regular movements from left to right or up and down thus creating different overlaying color segments. When showing canvases I also used to make them correspond to the given wall dimensions until I thought that this was a too sculptural interpretation of the situation. Painting evokes illusionistic space that follows different rules than built space; that's why it should make different use of the space it is shown in.[37]

Grosse went on to write that this new approach enabled her paintings to display 'independence from the surrounding set-up by underscoring an incongruent relationship to it'.[38] There is a lack of fit that the installation visualizes and materializes and thus makes strangely enterable – again there is that sense of peculiar permanence as conventional figure-ground or pigment-ground relationships are relinquished. With respect to *Untitled, Bern*, where green acrylic paint had been spayed expansively across a corner of one of the Bern Kunsthalle's exhibition spaces to create a rough and improvised rectangular form (inevitably reminiscent of some sort of window and of some sort of view?), she focused on how it had 'optically destabilized the corner of the room, letting it appear soft or even dissolved'.[39] This sense of expansiveness she experienced as going further: 'The phthalo green of my painting reflected in a very artificial way the outside context and despite its monochrome nature developed a polychrome character'.[40] Then, regarding the reorganized *lived* experience of making these works:

> Spraying paint on a wall has a very different effect on the working method than using a paintbrush. There is no physical contact with the wall anymore. The brush not only feeds back the disposition of the surface linking the painter more strongly to the surface's construction, but it also covers what is being painted at that very moment. The painter only sees a little later what they did a moment before.[41]

By contrast:

> The spray gun's movement is less related to body or support but it allows the activity of painting and looking to happen at the same time

and to coincide. The movement of the spray gun is more related to the movement of the eyes than to the movement of the body in space. In a way it dematerializes the painter. The body-size/painting-size relationship is given up. The eye movement places painted areas in out-of-body-size relationships. This is why the artificial enlargement of the painter's body (ladders, scissor lifts) goes along with the continuous development and expansion of the work.[42]

Here then, as is the case in Merleau-Ponty's writing, an environment was being created in which all manner of too easy, conventional oppositions were disrupted. These oppositions include those between what is conventionally regarded as material and immaterial, or between the realms of the visual, the material and thought. By extension, in crude art-historical terms, it also includes conventional oppositions between image-making traditions categorized as 'painterly', 'formalist' or concerned with material process, on the one hand, and those designated as ideas-based or 'conceptual', or politicized, on the other hand.

Painterly approaches, such as Grosse's, which use an abstract and gestural language, are generally positioned as apolitical in character. Indeed, her *Rockaway*! installation might be accused of aestheticizing a site of adversity. But – reversing the opening lines of Charles Dickens' *A Tale of Two Cities*, which read: 'It was the best of times. It was the worst of times' – arguably the installation is doing work that is foundational to the possibility of social and political change. Literally and lavishly, with pigment of vibrant red and white and with all that those gestures and colours signify, it is evidencing, within the realms of perception and thought, that an otherwise stultifying opposition between adversity and possibility – with adversity appearing to have gained the upper hand – has been disrupted. Through their visual and material traces, actions of this kind, though easily and frequently dismissed as superfluous, address and re-energize the deep heart of the matter – those territories that cannot easily be named, talked about or thought about when only conventional formats and logics are to hand. As such, they are vital to the task of reimagining relationships between community, self and an altered environment. Crucially, here, as in her earlier installations, the work's site-specificity did not entail perfectly adjusting to and reflecting that which was given. At issue instead was enabling a specific disjunction – and thus an openness – between the already given and the new to emerge, one that could not come into being anywhere else in exactly the same way. And here, surely, a powerful metaphor is materialized with respect to what it might mean to dwell and constructively contribute to a place or a community: an expansive and revelatory understanding of integration which recalls Merleau-Ponty's explorations of this matter in *The Structure of Behavior*. Here, to fit in is not to be absorbed into a pre-established situation without leaving a trace. On the contrary, a bigger, as-yet unanticipated pattern is being constructed in relation to which all concerned may also differently understand themselves, their capacities and their connections with others. Not just a new construction but a construction site in which – again akin to so many of Grosse's installations – yet-to-be used raw materials are found to have piled up!

This brings me to a further, final, introductory context from which to consider the texture and implications of Merleau-Ponty's reorganizations of things-said during this period. Again at issue is that forms of social and political (or properly speaking pre-political or politically enabling?) openness to transformation are facilitated here, akin to those just touched upon. This time, before turning to a discussion of Merleau-Ponty's treatment of language and visuality in 'Indirect Language and the Voices of Silence', my aim is to position *the fact* of his interest in language in relation to the other topics collated in *Signs*, topics which he described in his introduction as seemingly 'ad hoc' and even 'downright incongruous' in terms of their varied content.[43] For as well as those two essays specifically focused on language, *Signs* contained philosophical reflections on the work of other thinkers, among them Mauss, Lévi-Strauss, Bergson, Einstein, Montaigne and Machiavelli, as well as explorations of relationships between philosophy and the social sciences, psychology and Christianity. Significantly, though, *Signs* also contained, in its concluding section, twelve essays and two interviews on politics and then-current affairs. Of particular concern were questions associated with Marxism, communism and their legacies set against the backdrop of the Cold War as well as with various post-war, postcolonial struggles aimed at redrawing the lines of political power and authority. These matters had inevitably provoked fervent debate within philosophical circles, particularly those shaped by Marxism and existentialism, and Merleau-Ponty's own phenomenologically grounded reflections had led him to rethink and reject his earlier political allegiances as untenable, to disagree with Sartre in this respect and to resign as political editor of *Les Temps Modernes*. Merleau-Ponty's political essays in *Signs*, some written before but most after his resignation, covered such matters as the political state of affairs in places where communism was the ruling ideology (notably the Soviet Union), the facts of communist aggression in various parts of the world and – as was foregrounded in the work of Merleau-Ponty's contemporary Frantz Fanon in Algeria from 1953 – the rise of socialist revolution and post-war decolonization movements, particularly in regions that had once been subject to French colonial rule, namely, North Africa, Indo-China and Madagascar, a colony between 1897 and 1958, which Merleau-Ponty visited during October and November of 1957.[44] As already shown, a central Merleau-Pontean concern had to do with the human capacity to perceive and uncomfortably embrace shifting lived experiences of self, community and environment in order best to understand and navigate them. He had insisted on this in 'The War has Taken Place'. And in *Signs*, in what might be described as a short meta-political text written in December 1954 entitled 'On News Items', this territory between perception, expression and the political was opened up in a manner that is particularly pertinent to claims also made in 'Indirect Language and the Voices of Silence'. Merleau-Ponty's perspectives as presented in 'On News Items' are worth briefly reflecting on now.

The essay opens with the line: 'There is perhaps no news item which cannot give rise to deep thoughts.'[45] It would appear that by 'deep thoughts', Merleau-Ponty meant transformative self-reflexive thought – thought provoked by some occurrence within public space which we allow to loop back onto, and challenge, our own lives. A bit further on, though, he wrote that there is 'a good and a bad use of news items, perhaps even two kinds of news items, according to the type of revelation they bring'.[46] In the essay Merleau-Ponty provided two negative instances. The first was an event he claimed to have witnessed himself in 'Fascist Italy'.[47] This was an institutionally driven act of concealment within public space – the 'railway police' in Genoa pushing back crowds in the wake of a messy suicide: 'This blood disturbed order; it had to be quickly wiped away, and the world restored to its reassuring aspect.'[48] Merleau-Ponty went on to describe this act of concealment as defending the witnesses of this event, above all, from self-reflexively learning 'to judge' their own lives in relation to what had just happened, terrible though it was. The second negative instance he presented was a fictionalized, filmic scenario:

> What is hidden is first of all blood, the body, linen, the interiors of houses and lives; the canvas underneath the flaking painting, materials beneath what once had form; contingency; and finally, death. The street accident (seen through a window), a glove on the sidewalk, a razor next to the eye, the pins and needles of desire and its paralysis – Buñuel's *Le chien andalou* described all of these encounters with the pre-human. And we can always obtain the same dreamlike lucidity, the same stupefying emotion, *each time we cut ourselves off from ourselves and make ourselves a stranger to ourselves*. That air of derisory intelligence, those nuances in the absurd of a man talking on the telephone are, if I do not hear what he is saying, a fascinating spectacle – *but after all they teach us only our bias of looking without understanding.*[49]

Merleau-Ponty contrasted these modes of encouragement not to see, and not to think, with the kinds of revelatory situation he regarded as crucial. Again he turned to an example drawn from the arts: the writing of the great French novelist Stendhal who, as he put it, 'passionately loved to look but who surveyed himself' and who 'understood very well that even indignation is at times suspect'.[50] In particular, Merleau-Ponty referred to Stendhal's use of his 'true little incidents', small, sometimes objectively insignificant encounters or happenings that he presented as having witnessed, that had enraptured him and which he then ruminated upon.[51] In fact, the unnamed author of 'The Analysis of Stendhal', a 1952 review of *To the Happy Few:*

Selected Letters of Stendhal, which had just been translated into English, described them well: Stendhal, we read, 'gives us sidelights on everything, a full view of almost nothing. But these little incidents, these sidelights, are the seeds from which spring the great scenes of the novels'.[52] In Merleau-Ponty's words (and again in the context of distinguishing Stendhal's 'true little incidents' from the negative, non-revelatory evocations and usages of news items, such as those he had just described: his experience in fascist Italy; the approach taken in Buñuel's film):

> Stendhal's true little incidents must be set aside from or above these. His reveal not just the underside, the dust, dirt, and residues of a life, but rather what is incontestable in a man – what he is in limiting cases, when he is simplified by circumstances, when he is not thinking of creating himself, in good fortune or bad.[53]

And here, by way of further exemplification, the words of intercultural communication theorist Mark Orbe, in his 1998 book *Constructing Co-Cultural Theory: An Explication of Culture, Power and Communication*, are worth turning to, specifically a section titled 'Conflicting Standpoints on the World'. In this section, he drew both on Merleau-Ponty's 'On News Items' and on the more recent writing of the sociologist Mary E. Swigonski, whose work includes arguments for the necessity of perceiving the patterns of assumed privilege and superiority that are operative within society and the need 'to step outside of those patterns'.[54] Orbe's observations have the additional pertinence of highlighting what would be the future significance of Merleau-Ponty's work and that of other phenomenologists for the social sciences. Particularly at issue is how phenomenological priorities would impact the development of social research strategies that would be especially oriented towards garnering rich, situated, even self-contradictory or conflictual experiential data, namely standpoint theory[55] and muted group theory, and, derived from them, the co-cultural communication theory that Orbe himself played a foundational role in developing during the 1990s.[56] This was in contrast to the generally still-preferred, superficially precise but existentially inaccurate standardized category-driven procedures of quantitative data gathering. Insisting that the life perspectives of both non-dominant and dominant group members develop from 'their daily – often indiscernible, but nonetheless meaningful – activities', he specifically referenced 'On News Items'. In his words: 'Merleau-Ponty confirms the relevance of scrutinizing the daily, seemingly insignificant, experiences of others since "true little incidents" are not life's debris but signs, emblems, and appeals.'[57] Orbe continued:

> The appropriate perspective for research activities is exploration of the occurrences of everyday life. A focus on the everyday life experiences helps to reveal *the ways in which the public world structures the private,*

everyday/everynight lives of persons in ways that are not immediately visible as those lives are lived. Giving consciousness to these daily practices allows scholars to question the larger 'taken-for-granted' assumptions that guide our communicative behaviors. Besides a crucial point of understanding the conflicting life perspectives between dominant and nondominant groups, this focus of inquiry also allows a discernment among the various standpoints within a specific co-cultural positioning.[58]

From these preliminary discussions, then, it is clear that works of art, novels, reportage – indeed, the full range of visual and linguistic behaviour that we might employ – all may set out, or be set up, to provoke self-reflection or they may assist us in evading it. Indeed, it may be the case that our personal and institutionalized habits, including, it is again implied, the linguistic habits of much reportage and much art-making, tend towards concealment, teaching us, as Merleau-Ponty put it, 'only our bias of looking without understanding'.[59] Nonetheless, phenomenology insists that the impetus of being towards revelation (or self-showing) cannot be entirely contained or disciplined, nor, therefore, its capacity to produce counterorientations and counteractions geared towards increased personal and collective self-awareness. Bearing in mind Orbe's Merleau-Pontean observation that 'the public world structures the private, everyday/everynight lives of persons in ways that are not immediately visible as those lives are lived',[60] it is all the more vital that the public realm, however and wherever this might be manifested, is consistently configured and reconfigured so as to make such self-showings effective. Here we cannot also but recall Merleau-Ponty's words in the 'Preface' to the *Phenomenology*:

> The world ... is the natural setting of, and field for, all my thoughts and all my explicit perceptions. Truth does not 'inhabit' only 'the inner man', or, more accurately, there is no inner man, man is in the world, and only in the world does he know himself. When I return to myself from an excursion into the realm of dogmatic common sense or of science, I find, not a source of intrinsic truth, but a subject destined to the world.[61]

Merleau-Ponty and the priority of expression

In the *Phenomenology*, Merleau-Ponty's investigations into the nature of our inescapably embodied, perceptual relationship with the world led him to observe its primordially communicative nature. In making this connection it became apparent to him that language and perception have important characteristics in common. In the first place, not only the world of perception but also that of language is apprehended by us as 'pregnant' with meaning. In the second place, like perception, language has an instituting[62] role which has implications for philosophical research into relationships between language and human agency, intersubjectivity and truth.

In the chapter of the *Phenomenology* entitled 'The Body as Expression and Speech', Merleau-Ponty had explored how embodied beings experience themselves as inhering in space and maintaining a sense of cohesiveness within change. He then proposed that another, related way of revealing what the body is, and is like, would be through a phenomenological investigation of the body's capacity to express itself gesturally and in speech: 'The analysis of speech and expression', he wrote, 'brings home to us the enigmatic nature of our own body even more effectively than did our remarks on bodily space and unity.'[63]

His argument had a doubled aspect. First, he believed that through such an analysis he could most effectively challenge the view of the body as an object in the traditional sense – also evidenced by Grosse's gestural work with spray paint – and illuminate its status as a mode of conscious, intentional being inhering in a world of which it is irreducibly a part and in relation to which it perceives itself simultaneously as an active, instituting entity and a responsive, instituted entity. Secondly, given his view that important affinities exist between the expressiveness of the gesturing, speaking body-subject and that of language in its various manifestations, he proposed that to examine the nature of the latter – language as he would reconceptualize it – would be to gain insight into the nature of the former, that is, embodied being and thought.

Although, as noted, a deep engagement with the writing of Saussure was of crucial importance to Merleau-Ponty at this stage, in 'On the Phenomenology of Language', he stated that he was following Husserl in making the study of language a central philosophical concern:

> In the philosophical tradition the problem of language does not pertain to 'first philosophy'. ... [Husserl] moves it to a central position, and what little he says about it is both original and enigmatic. Consequently, this problem provides us with our best basis for questioning phenomenology and recommencing Husserl's efforts. ... It allows us to resume, instead of his theses, the very movement of his thought.[64]

As Merleau-Ponty saw it, traditional philosophers tended to regard language *as they used it* as having the primary aim of merely re-presenting or reproducing, with transparency, a 'language of things themselves' using terms that had already been established for this purpose. In this way, a supposed world of reality as it exists in-itself, an objective, universal reality, was thought to be brought to 'complete expression', without reference to individual perspectives, inclinations or motivations.[65] In 'Indirect Language and the Voices of Silence'[66] – and in what follows I will move freely between it and 'On the Phenomenology of Language' – Merleau-Ponty wrote that language thus treated as 'the translation or cipher of an original text'[67] was regarded by such thinkers as philosophically unproblematic. On the other hand, language in its creative modes, as in poetry or in novels, tended to be regarded as philosophically irrelevant, a view that was informed by a phenomenologically inaccurate, dualistic understanding of the relationship between fantasy or illusion and reality. More broadly, non-empirical language, which was seen to refer only to the world as it appears to, and is interpreted by, specifically situated individuals – in both concrete and metaphorical terms – was identified as a mode of expression that is subjective and relative, serving only to throw up differences and introduce fragmentation.

In 'Indirect Language and the Voices of Silence', Merleau-Ponty criticized Sartre for adhering to such oppositional thinking in his writing on language – in fact, the essay was dedicated to Sartre. As Johnson has argued, Sartre was one of 'the implicit, sometimes explicit, provocateurs addressed by Merleau-Ponty' in this work. Indeed, in *What is Literature?* from 1947,[68] Sartre had made a sharp distinction between the function of prose and that of poetic language, which he took to be a primarily visual mode of expression. Prose, by contrast, he presented as referring to a world of ideas from which it was distinct. As Madison put it: 'The prose word is for Sartre ... something which does not have its own being and merely serves to represent an object which exists independently of it. The sign immediately transcends itself towards its meaning and is but a way of arriving at it.'[69] Poetic language, on the other hand, Sartre regarded as self-referential. In prose, what is opened up is a relationship between the reader and the world of things-in-themselves; in poetry, it is a relationship between the reader and the (imaginary) world of the poem.

Merleau-Ponty, by contrast, rejected both the notion that static realities exist in some accessible manner 'beneath' the flux of appearances[70] and the correlative idea that language is our means of re-presenting it. Elaborating on themes present in the *Phenomenology*, he emphasized what he saw to be the incomplete and the fundamentally creative – both responsive *and* instituting rather than mimetic – character of language in *all* its various manifestations, as used by the poet, the philosopher and, indeed, the reporter and the scientist. As he put it in 'Indirect Language and the Voices of Silence': 'Now if we rid our minds of the idea that our language is the translation or cipher of an original text, we shall see that the idea of complete expression is nonsensical, and that *all language is indirect or allusive*.'[71]

Concerning what he saw to be the at-once responsive and instituting power of language, Merleau-Ponty had already written in the *Phenomenology* that

> for pre-scientific thinking, naming an object is *causing it to exist or changing it*; God creates beings by naming them and magic operates upon them by speaking of them. These 'mistakes' would be unexplainable [*sic*] if speech rested on the concept, for the latter ought always to know itself as distinct from the former, and to know the latter as an external accompaniment.[72]

He expanded upon this view by describing language as 'a sort of being'[73] which, rather than translating thought, is itself thought-like:

> Language does not *presuppose* its table of correspondence; it unveils its secrets itself. ... It is entirely a 'monstration'. Its opaqueness, its obstinate reference to itself, and its turning and folding back upon itself are precisely what make it a mental power; for it in turn becomes something like a universe, and it is capable of lodging things themselves in this universe – after it has transformed them into their meaning.[74]

In 'On the Phenomenology of Language', Merleau-Ponty cited Husserl as reaching a position that anticipated and informed his own in this respect but did not coincide with it. In Husserl's early works,[75] he wrote, there was an emphasis on the notion of 'a universal grammar' – a transparent and 'essential' language – said to be constituted by consciousness in order that we might think with clarity about pre-existent, eternally valid truths and make them communicable. This universal grammar was presented as an ideal or *Ur*-language of which actual languages are derivations. Merleau-Ponty concluded that here language was presented as 'an object before thought [which] could not possibly play any other role in respect to thought than that of an accompaniment, substitute, memorandum, or secondary means of communication'.[76] However, he claimed that Husserl had abandoned this view in the late works, with language now no longer understood merely as a means of re-presenting the 'in-itself', but as itself having instituting (or in Husserl's terminology, constituting) power:

> In more recent writings, on the other hand, language appears as an original way of intending certain objects, as thought's body (*Formale und transzendentale Logik*), or even as an operation through which thoughts that without it would remain private phenomena acquire intersubjective value and, ultimately, ideal existence (*Ursprung der Geometrie*). According to this conception, philosophical thinking which reflects upon language would be its beneficiary, enveloped and situated in it.[77]

Although doubts have been raised about the accuracy of Merleau-Ponty's reading of Husserl,[78] and although, as here presented, Husserl's position would still have the defect of making language mediate from private to public, leaving it non-constitutional or secondary,[79] what Merleau-Ponty claimed to find in Husserl's work was the impetus to rethink the status of language in terms of its relationship with thought and its role in instituting and reinstituting the world for us. Within this context, it was of prime philosophical importance for him to examine the ways in which language is actively used by us in everyday life and how in this process already-established terms take on transformed meanings:

What the phenomenology of language teaches me is not just a psychological curiosity – the language observed by linguistics experienced in me and bearing my particular additions to it. It teaches me a new conception of the being of language, which is now logic in contingency – an oriented system which nevertheless always elaborates random factors, taking what was fortuitous up again into a meaningful whole – *incarnate logic*.[80]

Two points are important. First, this new conception of language applies as much to the way language is experienced and used by philosophers as it does to anyone else. Philosophers are mistaken in thinking they can acquire and use language in a pure form. Secondly, language is productive in revealing how coherent meanings emerge from within the contexts of our lived interactions with the world. This is what Merleau-Ponty meant by its incarnate logic. In contrast to that stable and completed order which is the object of the disembodied intellect, the order associated with incarnate logic has the capacity to incorporate and adjust to factors that are unanticipated by it. Hence his reference to random factors. Its mode of being is not that of imposing its own order on the world, but of facilitating the emergence of order within given contexts. At issue is not the application of already existing principles or already prescribed manners of interrelating, but the discovery of appropriate patterns of meaning and interactive functioning within the specificities of our everyday modes of inhering in the world. Any formal logical rules and norms are derivative reflections on this lived process.

Syntax

In 'Indirect Language and the Voices of Silence', Merleau-Ponty began by directly referencing and reflecting on the lessons to be learned from Saussure's *Cours de linguistique generale*. First published in 1916,[81] and disseminated through the work of Claude Lévi-Strauss, the so-called father of structuralism, and others, the *Cours* would be crucial to the rise of structuralism which would increasingly dominate the interpretation of art, architecture, folklore, literary criticism and philosophy from the 1950s into the 1990s. Here, particularly impactful would be the writing on semiotics produced by Merleau-Ponty's compatriot Roland Barthes a little later on in the 1950s. Barthes's essays, also influenced by Saussure, were first published in the popular press and later collected in the 1957 volume *Mythologies*, together with his contextualizing theoretical text 'Myth Today'.

The accuracy of Merleau-Ponty's reading of Saussure's *Cours de linguistique generale* has also been called into question.[82] However, his position seems to have been that he saw Saussure explicitly upholding but implicitly undermining traditional dichotomous views of language. On the one hand, in 'On the Phenomenology of Language', he criticized Saussure for juxtaposing a synchronic linguistics of speech and a diachronic linguistics of language without considering their relationship – that is, for insisting on 'the duality of the two perspectives' and thus making them mutually exclusive.[83]

But, on the other hand, he concluded from Saussure's emphasis on the context-dependent[84] meaning of signs that, contrary to the classical position, here *all* language should properly be regarded as enigmatic, allusive or mysterious.[85] The fact that meaning, for Saussure, was dependent not on a relationship of resemblance between a given linguistic sign and a non-linguistic referent (the word 'vase', and the vase standing on my table), but on the relationships of divergence between signs,[86] suggested to Merleau-Ponty that language, whether as a system (Saussure's *la langue*) or as it is spoken by us (*la parole*), is neither finite nor complete but in constant reorganization in its concepts, their reciprocal boundaries and their scope. As he put it in 'Indirect Language and the Voices of Silence': 'As far as language is concerned, it is the lateral relation of one sign to another which makes each of them significant, so that meaning appears only at the intersection of and as it were in the interval between words.'[87] Returning to the field of recent painting, Grosse's work is again worth considering: her *The Poise of the Head und die anderen folgen*, referenced earlier, for instance, which, as noted, was installed in the Kunsthalle Düsseldorf in 2004. The work, described as consisting of 'acrylic on wall, floor, soil and canvas' was distributed within and across one of the gallery's corner spaces with the dimensions 900 × 900 × 1100 cm. Basically, it consisted of a mound of soil and two differently sized canvases, one of which had been spray-painted in colourful stripes while leaning, in a landscape orientation, against one of the walls, the sprayed colours also extending onto the wall behind and adjacent to it. The canvas was then moved – this is where the theme of rearrangement, repositioning and thus syntax comes into play; the notion of the painting as transportable and transposable, somewhat like a phoneme. It was rotated and positioned in 'portrait' mode against the adjacent wall, with a negative space of white wall now marking where it had been. Into this vacancy a significantly smaller canvas was positioned. It was painted, using a very different idiom, with two large, abbreviated circular forms. Grosse described the space against which it was framed as having the appearance of 'a flat well-lit showcase'.[88]

The application of acrylic paint produced multiple effects. With respect to its application to the soil – which she described as 'an unaccountable mass' and which itself also referenced 'pigment as the basic ingredient of paint'[89] – Grosse wrote that

it could also be read as colored earth, contaminated nature or thickened paint. The color on the soil could be looked at as mere light reflections coming from the colored walls or as being artificially lit from above as the space had skylights. The soil connected the wall and floor planes establishing a new space on which the canvas sits.[90]

As such, the work is also in conversation with Robert Smithson's much-discussed experiments, from the 1960s and 70s, with practices of placement and displacement and notions of site and non-site. Indeed, in Grosse's piece we see this not only by means of the introduction of soil, but also through the shifting interplays of figure, or object, and ground, of abstraction as addition and subtraction and of positive and negative space. At issue here was not only the unsprayed, rectangular wall space that was revealed following the transposition of the large canvas but also the effect created by the white paint that was sprayed with broad, sweeping strokes onto the floor: 'A white spray movement on the floor took up the soil's outline so that the earthen mass seemed to sit on a white field floating on the grey floor.'[91]

Grosse's piece is, of course, one of several such variations within contemporary art. Petersen, in her essay discussed earlier, also mentioned Torgny Wilcke's work in this regard but we might equally consider Rashid Johnson's modular constructions – *Within Our Gates*, for instance, installed at the Garage Museum of Contemporary Art, Moscow, in 2016 (Figure 5.4)[92] – or, indeed, to introduce a fresh reference, Tom Ellis' installation of modular, transposable paintings, alongside self-made furniture, entitled *The Middle*, which was shown at the Wallace Collection, London, in 2016.[93] Johnson's installation, we learn, was inspired by Moscow's modernist architecture, as well as by a visit to the islands of Turks and Caicos where architecture was overrun by organic growth. It also drew on the many other personally evocative and culturally and historically significant resources, discussed earlier, that are part of his vocabulary. Johnson described it as 'a brain'.[94] In it, geometry and the flexible, substitutional character of the grid provided an open-ended and potentially extendable matrix upon which an abundance of plants and objects were displayed. The geometry and grid notwithstanding, these objects-on-show were not subsumed under the logics of rationality, legibility or closure but of memory, association, intuition, curiosity and research. Ellis' installation consisted mainly of paintings (his own approximations of the baroque and rococo paintings that form the core of the Wallace Collection). But due to its overall schematic and modular character, it existed both as an exhibition in itself and at the level of a three-dimensional, inhabitable proposal *for* an exhibition. As such, it produced a space that could be experienced by viewers on multiple registers: as propositional, as provisional *and* as exhibitionary. It also seemed to ruminate more broadly on, and to bring into view, the museum and gallery as, behind-the-scenes, a working-space in which, to which, and from which objects are conveyed, unpacked and repacked, positioned, repositioned, circulated and recirculated. And here, thinking associatively, I cannot help but also recall what is to my mind one of the most visually and conceptually interesting curatorial strategies for installing an exhibition of paintings that I have seen: the 2015 exhibition *Artists imagine a nation: Pictures of people and places from the collections of Koh Seow Chuan and friends* at the Institute of Contemporary Arts, Singapore, 2015 (Figure 6.2), in which the curator, Bala Starr, worked collaboratively with the designer Helen Oja to design the exhibition architecture.[95] The outcome was a scene of grid-like stainless steel 'screens' arranged in 'corridors' upon which the paintings – figurative works, by thirty-six artists, dating from the 1930s to the present – were hung so that both the front and the back (verso) of each were visible and viewable. The verso, which normally remains hidden from view within exhibition contexts, is where often multilayered documentary evidence is to be found recording, for instance, where the work of art, or the materials from which it was made, came from, where the work was framed or cleaned, where it might have travelled. It also registers 'more recent signs ... of handling and safe-keeping, provenance, and the effects of time'.[96] This sense of history and provenance as well as ownership, and the status of these works as collectables, was further reinforced through the exhibition design. While the screens were described by Starr as following 'something of a modernist spirit consistent with the twentieth-century timeline of many of the works' and proposing 'an experimental, provisional approach to display that is contemporary',[97] intentionally or not, they also made reference to the systems and structures that are used for storing paintings. Thus they had the potential of reminding the viewer that Singapore, through the auspices of LE FREEPORT based at Changi airport – styled as 'the world's safest storage and trading platform for your valuables'[98] and thus 'heralding a new era in wealth protection and creation' – is a location where collectors can store, show and even sell works of art in a secure context, exempt from customs duty. But to return to Merleau-Ponty, again from the introduction to *Signs*:

> Language can vary and amplify inter-corporeal communication as much as we wish; it has the same spring and style as the latter. In language too, that which was secret must become public and almost *visible*. In inter-corporeal communication as in language, significations come through in whole packages, scarcely sustained by a few peremptory gestures. In both cases I envision things and others together. Speaking to others (or to myself), I do not speak *of* my thoughts; I *speak them*, and what is between them – my afterthoughts and underthoughts.[99]

As Merleau-Ponty saw it, then, Saussure's structuralist model of language could be appropriated by him for his own arguments in favour of language's fundamentally open and creative nature. Specifically, the claim that 'meaning appears only at the intersection of and as it were in the interval between words', confirmed his own Gestalt-informed views about the 'pregnancy' and fertility of language and directed him, in this essay, to explore the notion of language as 'silence'. 'All language', he wrote, 'is indirect or allusive ... if you wish, silence.'[100] The openness of language, manifested in the gaps, spaces, intervals and silences within it, pointed to the fact that that which is expressed is always a whole comprising indefinably more than the sum of its isolable parts. The gaps or intervals between words signal the possibility that

that which has been articulated can be re-formed, expanded or transformed. Indeed, they anticipate such reformation, expansion or transformation.[101] Silence, as he put it, has a 'voice'. Thus, silence and utterance should not be understood as diametrically opposed. Indeed, Merleau-Ponty provided an example of the way in which silence can 'speak' in his discussion of the power of tacit expression in Stendhal's novelistic analysis of French society published in 1830, *The Scarlet and the Black*:

> Julien Sorel's trip to Verrières and his attempt to kill Mme de Rênal after he has learned that she has betrayed him are not as important as that silence, that dream-like journey, that unthinking certitude, and that eternal resolution which follow the news. Now these things are nowhere said. ... In order to express them, Stendhal had only to insinuate himself into Julien and make objects, obstacles, means, and hazards appear before our eyes with the swiftness of the journey. ... The desire to kill is thus not in the words at all. It is between them, in the hollows of space, time, and signification they mark out.[102]

In clarification, then, at issue was *not* that identifiable, possible meanings exist in-themselves in 'cold-storage', as it were, in a depository underneath utterance and distinct from it. Rather, it was through the arrangement of signs that these meanings take form and become perceptible.

As Merleau-Ponty understood it, language, in its broadest sense, was a primordial reality. As with the realm of the perceptible, the realm of language is one from which we can never extricate ourselves. It is the 'universe' we inhabit and, as such, both defines us *and* is open to redefinition by us. In order to communicate this, he used the following illustration:

> Since the sign has meaning only in so far as it is profiled against other signs, its meaning is entirely involved in language. *Speech always comes into play against a background of speech; it is always only a fold in the immense fabric of language.* To understand it we do not have to consult some inner lexicon which gives us pure thoughts covered up by the words or forms we are perceiving; we only have to lend ourselves to its life, to its movement of differentiation and articulation, and to its eloquent gestures.[103]

As well as presenting language as the primordial 'universe' in which we are immersed, in 'Indirect Language and the Voices of Silence' Merleau-Ponty gave primacy to the phenomenology of speech (*la parole*), that is, language as it is lived and used by us. Thus in the first section of the essay, he distinguished two manifestations of speech. One, which he called 'empirical' language, refers to language operating *as if* it is a closed system of expression. It is characterized by the conventional use of expressions which have the appearance of being fixed in their meanings. The other, 'creative' language, is an open and inventive system of expression, involving repeated departures from convention.

These two modes of speaking, while distinguishable, were again not regarded by Merleau-Ponty as diametrically opposed. They interrelate and are mutually dependent, and he treated both as incomplete modes of expression. Empirical language, as he saw it, arises from creative language which is prior to it: 'The empirical use of already established language should be distinguished from its creative use. Empirical language can only be the result of creative language.'[104] Therefore, 'empirical' language cannot exist in a pure sense. Having emerged from creative language, far from becoming stable and fixed, its meanings continue to shift and alter, albeit gradually and often imperceptibly. An example he provided was the gradual transformation from Latin to French.[105] He concluded:

> Speech in the sense of empirical language – that is the opportune recollection of a pre-established sign – is not speech in respect to an authentic language. It is, as Mallarmé said, the worn coin placed silently in my hand.[106]

The metaphor within this text is suggestive in two ways. On the one hand, referencing the *silence* with which the worn coin is placed in my hand, empirical (or conventional) language tends to flow from person to person without introduction and without comment. It has a lack of distinctiveness that makes it unobtrusive and its currency and meaning are regarded as self-evident. A painterly intervention into such a state of affairs was discussed earlier in this book, in relation to Leah Durner's series *Texts*. On the other hand, the continued use of anything, words or expressions as well as objects like coins, necessarily and inevitably causes erosion and alteration, which leads to the gradual emergence of new significations.[107]

Just as there is no purely empirical language, there is no wholly creative language in the sense of a language that is utterly disconnected from convention or law-likeness. This is apparent from the way in which linguistic expression is learned: the child, while still unable to speak, finds itself from the very first immersed into 'an already-speaking world', that is, into language as it is used by others. Here, as Merleau-Ponty put it, language as 'a unique manner of handling words is anticipated by the child in the first phonemic oppositions'.[108] Creative and empirical language, then, seem to operate in two ways, depending on our vantage point. On the one hand, to repeat, Merleau-Ponty indicated that creative language is *prior* to empirical language. On the other hand, they are experienced as interrelating in a dialectical fashion and as mutually dependent. Creativity, however – even in the first scenario – is displayed always within the context of certain constraints; here we find echoes of themes already opened up in *The Structure of Behavior*.

By examining the structure of empirical and creative language as they occur in speech, and by describing their relationship one to the other, Merleau-Ponty saw himself as reconciling, literally bringing into conversation, two perspectives upon language which other writers at the time generally treated as mutually exclusive.[109] In 'On the Phenomenology of Language', he referenced the Dutch linguist and philosopher Hendrik J. Pos who, in his 'Phenomenology and Linguistics' ('Phénoménologie et linguistique') of 1939,[110] had set side by side an objective and a phenomenological attitude towards language but failed to address the question of their interrelationship. As already indicated, Merleau-Ponty also wrote that Saussure had failed on an explicit level to explore the relationship between what he saw to be the structural conditions of language, on the one hand, and the activity of speaking and thinking with language, on the other – that is, our creativity within it rather than our restriction by it. Nonetheless, as Merleau-Ponty's reading of Saussure reveals, he saw such a connection to be implied in Saussure's thought and set out to articulate it.

Language, truth and 'universality'

So far, four key points have been made. All are connected with Merleau-Ponty's rejection of language conceived of as bringing things that purportedly exist in-themselves to complete expression. In the first place, language is not merely something we make use of, but a 'universe' in which we are immersed and from which we cannot extricate ourselves. In the second place, language is incomplete. In the third place, precisely because it is incomplete, it is full of potentialities. The gaps in language function as pointers to a realm of possible meanings which language itself, through its internal reorganizations, may bring into actuality. As such, language can no longer be regarded as a passive mimetic tool; it has instituting power. And in the fourth place, creative language is prior to, and not an elaboration upon, empirical language.

From this account the following questions arise. First, if language does not give us access to the world in-itself, what is happening when we speak or write, listen or read? What *does* language give us access to? Specifically, what is the relationship between language and truth? Secondly, since speaking, writing, listening and reading imply the involvement of more than one person, what are the implications of Merleau-Ponty's view of language for intersubjectivity? I begin with the question of truth.

As already discussed, Merleau-Ponty rejected the objectivist idea that truth exists in-itself and is communicable only through our use of an objective language whose terms and structure correspond with it exactly. Rather, truth – the only truth that is available to us as perceptual beings – is contingent but, as Merleau-Ponty insisted, *not relativistic*. It resides within the specifics of our lived relationships with others and with the world as we perceive it. Further, just as this world is perceived by us both in its actual and virtual aspects, so it is through language, understood as allusive, full of potentialities and creative, that its truths are illuminated and shared. To cite Madison, who purposefully used sacred references to try to illuminate this paradoxical scenario: 'The narrow gate leading to truth is the linguistic reflection of language. That Logos which is language is light for those who speak and listen, and this light, as St. John said, is the life of men.'[111] Madison's allusions to biblical terminology are appropriate. As discussed earlier, John's Christ is 'The Word' through whom 'all things were made'.[112] But this creative Word is both transcendent *and* imminent. Christ *already was* in the beginning, before the world was made. He (the historical, incarnated Christ) *was in* the world which was made through him (the eternal, Cosmic Christ). And he *is in* the world now, incarnated in everyone who receives him, which means that he continues to create in collaboration with them. Similarly, for Merleau-Ponty, that 'Logos which is language' was an incarnated, creative Logos. It was not merely expressive of our existence and that of the world, but inextricably tied to them – indeed, bringing them into being. The relationship between language and truth was thus an internal and reciprocal one.

Merleau-Ponty also rejected the assumption that properly intersubjective communication – whether between individuals belonging to a single culture and historical period or occurring trans-historically or transculturally – required access for all to a common reality in the form of an unshifting 'original text' or universal language of which real languages are the translation. One of his tasks during this period, then, was to reassess the preconditions for intersubjectivity, for which he used the (now problematically loaded) term universality.[113]

In Merleau-Ponty's use of the term 'universality' – significantly, he insisted on keeping it within his philosophical vocabulary – it referred not merely to the fact that we are beings who are capable of altering our perspectives, indeed, of perceiving and communicating *as if* from the point of view of all potential others. It also involved the paradoxical but lived certainty that our interactions in the world are shared with other, embodied, consciousnesses, even though we are unable to point to *objective* assurances that this is the case. At issue, however, was not only a sense of connection or communication between all our individual, situated experiences of world, but also the sense that we experience ourselves as inhering in a common world. In 'On the Phenomenology of Language', again taking what he saw to be Husserl's lead, Merleau-Ponty wrote:

> If universality is attained, it will not be through a universal language which would go back prior to the diversity of languages to provide us with the foundations of all possible languages. It will be through an oblique passage from a given language that I speak and that initiates me

into the phenomenon of expression, to another given language that I learn to speak and that effects the act of expression according to a completely different style – the two languages (and ultimately all given languages) being contingently comparable only at the outcome of this passage and only as signifying wholes, without our being able to recognize in them the common elements of one single categorical structure.[114]

Merleau-Ponty's position seemed to be as follows. Universality is not presupposed by our capacity, ultimately, to coincide with one another linguistically. As situated beings, this is not an option for us. But this does not lead to a sceptical position whereby the non-coincidence of perspectives isolates each of us in non-communicable, private worlds of our own.[115] As embodied beings inhering flexibly in the world, we always have albeit incomplete perceptual access both to our own modes or styles of expression and to the different ways in which other beings convey their own experiences of themselves and the world. Bearing in mind discussions from *The Structure of Behavior* focused on the symbolic forms, and from the *Phenomenology* concerning the body's experience of itself as both subject and object, sensing and sensible, self and other, as well as the way in which this provided the model for our more general intersubjective interactions, we may perceive the world and bring it to expression from multiple perspectives, both our own and *not* our own – the two not being in an inevitable relationship of opposition – without losing a sense of its continuity. This was the basis for universality as Merleau-Ponty conceived of it. It was a term expressive of the way in which the 'not-us', to which, as irreducibly relational, multilingual beings we are nonetheless connected and in relation to which we find definition, provides us with different articulations of the 'same' self and 'same' world.

Returning to ideas referred to earlier, the sense of connectivity between these divergent articulations depends upon what Merleau-Ponty called 'logic in contingency' or 'incarnate logic', in which random factors – the non-predetermined but to some degree anticipated manifestations of self and other – are elaborated into a 'meaningful [and flexible] whole'. At issue are relationships of difference, in which communication is provoked by the non-coincidences between us. Merleau-Ponty's 'new conception of the being of language' gives us access to this understanding. As he had already put it in the *Phenomenology*, 'The intention to speak can reside only in an open experience.'[116] If we did not have potential as well as actual differences of idiom, viewpoint or experience, the desire to communicate would make no sense. We would perceive it as neither valuable nor necessary to adjust to the perspectives of others and learn from them. These themes will be developed in the next chapter.

FIGURE 6.1 André Malraux and His Imaginary Museum, Boulogne sur Seine, France, *1953 (the writer André Malraux poses in his house in Boulogne near Paris while working on his book* Le Musée Imaginaire *or* Imaginary Museum, *2nd volume,* Du bas relief aux Grottes Sacrées, *in 1953). Photo by Maurice Jarnoux / Paris Match Archive via Getty Images.*

FIGURE 6.2 *Installation view:* Artists Imagine a Nation: Pictures of People and Places from the Collections of Koh Seow Chuan and Friends, *Institute of Contemporary Arts, Singapore, 2015. Photo by J. Andrews.*

CHAPTER SIX

Visual language and the 'unity' of painting

Modern painting and the paradoxes of communication

Modern painting presents ... the problem of knowing how one can communicate without the help of a pre-established Nature which all men's senses open upon, the problem of knowing how we are grafted to the universal by that which is most our own.

(*Maurice Merleau-Ponty*)[1]

In 'Indirect Language and the Voices of Silence', Merleau-Ponty revisited a theme first opened up in *The Structure of Behavior*: the question of what constitutes true versus false unity. In *The Structure of Behavior*, this was discussed in relation to El Greco's painting and revolved around the question of how the idiosyncrasies of style in his work should be interpreted. Was it merely symptomatic of a visual dysfunction that therefore detracted from the communicative potential of his work? Or, as Merleau-Ponty argued, did it express another profile that might be taken upon being which, by communicating differently, communicated all the more powerfully – affirming that true unity operates across differences and is fuelled by curiosity. In the *Phenomenology*, this notion of unity was represented as having its origins in our own experiences of what it means to be embodied. In both works, Merleau-Ponty had presented these arguments against the backdrop of his critique of empiricism and positivism as valid modes of understanding the workings of human behaviour. In 'Indirect Language and the Voices of Silence' when Merleau-Ponty addressed this broad matter again he did so most explicitly in relation to questions raised by painting – this time *modern* painting, again understood as a phenomenon characterized by radical idiosyncrasy and divergences of style. These discussions took place in the portion of the essay where he clarified his own thought in relation to his interpretation of key claims about art formulated by his compatriot, the writer, adventurer and influential statesman André Malraux.

During the war years, Malraux had grown close to Charles de Gaulle, the leader of Free France from 1940 to 1944. After liberation, between November 1945 and January 1946, Malraux had been appointed temporary minister of information in de Gaulle's provisional government of the French Republic. This government lasted until early 1946 when de Gaulle resigned. Later, upon de Gaulle's return to power in France in 1958, Malraux would serve as minister of cultural affairs in the first cabinet of the Fifth Republic, a position which he held for ten years. Already well known for his political novels, published from the late 1920s – including the world-famous *La Condition humaine (The Human Condition)* of 1933 – between 1947 and 1950 Malraux had published his three-volume *Psychologie de l'art (The Psychology of Art)*. This was a project on which he had been working since about 1935. In it, inspired by what he had seen on his own extensive travels, he attempted to account for the metamorphoses of art across world cultures from ancient to modern times. It was republished in an abridged but still substantial form in 1951. With the addition of a new chapter, it was now entitled *Les Voix du Silence (The Voices of Silence)* as referenced in the title of Merleau-Ponty's essay. As Galen Johnson put it with respect to Malraux's visual source materials for the book – the great 'imaginary museum', 'museum of the mind' or 'museum without walls' that he had assembled, the contents of which were also shareable due to photography (Figure 6.1):

> Malraux's imaginative bounds and the breadth of his gallery of reproductions is [sic] sweeping. He writes about the masks of New Guinea, the Ivory Coast, and Hopi Indians, the pottery of ancient China and Greece, the mummies and Sphinx of Egypt, Celtic and Germanic coins, the mosaics, frescoes, and stained glass of the cathedrals of Europe, Leonardo's *Mona Lisa*, Rembrandt's *Prodigal Son*, and Cézanne's many versions of Mont Sainte-Victoire. On the same page, one can move through the art of four cultures and three epochs, sometimes even in a subordinate clause.[2]

In 'Indirect Language and the Voices of Silence', then, having already summoned up the notion of silence 'having a voice' in the context of his introductory reflections on the theories of Saussure, Merleau-Ponty went on to position his own thought, as noted, in conversation with, and contradiction to, the aesthetic theories of both Sartre, in *What is Literature?* and Malraux in *The Voices of Silence*.[3] (Having said that, Merleau-Ponty cited Malraux's earlier, three-volume *The Psychology of Art* in his footnotes.) In this essay, Merleau-Ponty did not address specific paintings or painterly practices in a sustained manner as he had done in 'Cézanne's Doubt'. But philosophical reflections on the workings of art history and of art institutions – that is, the public display and circulation of art – *were* key points of focus. Also of note were the variety of ways in which, as I see it, Merleau-Ponty made vision, or visual experience, paradigmatic for language as bringing out something primordial and general.[4] As already indicated, a precedent for this was found in the *Phenomenology*. When discussing the body as 'expression and speech', Merleau-Ponty had associated the body's communicativeness primarily with its identity as a gestural being which displays its intentions visually by reaching out or pointing in as-yet-incomplete formulations towards an incompletely determined world. Verbal language was presented as a particular manifestation of this capacity:

> The spoken word is a gesture, and its meaning, a world. ... It is impossible to draw up an inventory of this irrational power which creates meanings and conveys them. Speech is merely one particular case of it.[5]

When, in 'Indirect Language and the Voices of Silence', Merleau-Ponty embarked upon a sustained commentary on those aspects of Malraux's *The Voices of Silence* that he found problematic, this earlier focus upon gesture was taken up in the context of a discussion of style.

According to the objectivist prejudice, perfection in terms of visual expression was first of all equated with a supposedly style-less mode of representation which bears no trace of its maker. Style, manifested through an idiosyncratic use of colour, line, form, texture or composition, concealed the 'real' or the 'true' through distortion or distraction. At issue again was the notion of a visual world-in-itself and the conception of a visual language whose aim was perfectly to represent it. This transparent visual language was seen to be epitomized in works constructed according to the model of classical, linear perspective. Merleau-Ponty attacked this position and followed Erwin Panofsky in describing this mode of representation merely as 'one of the ways that man has invented for projecting the perceived world before him' and not 'the copy of that world'.[6] Secondly, the objectivist prejudice presupposed a theory of perception in which all human beings receive and interpret sense data in the same way. As Merleau-Ponty put it, writing in an ironic mode: 'Don't we all have eyes, which function in the same way? And if the painter has known how to discover the sufficient signs of depth and velvet, won't we all, in looking at the painting, see the same spectacle, which will rival that of Nature?'[7]

In Merleau-Ponty's reading of Malraux's ideas, he took Malraux to have productively opposed objectivist assumptions when he challenged the idea that 'painting as creative expression' is a new conception, unknown to earlier generations of artists. Merleau-Ponty paraphrased Malraux as saying that this conception 'has been a novelty for the public much more than for the painters themselves, who have always practised it, even if they did not construct a theory of it'.[8] Nonetheless, Malraux remained somewhat indebted to objectivist presuppositions elsewhere in his book. As Merleau-

Ponty put it: 'Sometimes Malraux speaks as if "sense data" had never varied throughout the centuries and as if the classical perspective had been imperative whenever painting referred to sense data'.[9]

Where Merleau-Ponty took particular issue with Malraux, however, was in the absolute distinction he saw Malraux propose between the nature of expression found in classical painting and that associated with modern (non-illusionistic) art. Malraux had described the latter as 'a return to subjectivity – to the "incomparable monster"',[10] and as 'a ceremony glorifying the individual'.[11] According to this logic, classical painters used their creativity to express the world. Modern painters, on the other hand (those who are 'in the tribe of the ambitious and the drugged'[12]), had turned away from that world altogether. By expressing themselves, they were depicting 'a secret life outside the world'.[13] And here, it is worth repeating that for Merleau-Ponty – I am again citing Johnson:

> Malraux's incoherent swing between these subjective and objective notions of style is an analogue of Sartre's existentialist philosophy of the free for-itself subject over against the inert, determined in-itself object, as well as of the tension in Marx's thought between the humanism of proletarian action in conflict with the objective market forces of capital production and exchange.[14]

In Merleau-Ponty's view, Malraux's assertion that there are two distinguishable worlds of painterly expression, the classical and the modern, had its source in three errors. In the first place, Malraux underestimated the radical creativity and inventiveness of the classical project. In the second place, his claim that modern paintings constituted pure self-expression betrayed a misunderstanding of the nature of painterly style or expression and of the way in which it actually emerges in practice. Further, the assertion that such works depict 'a secret life outside the world' was derived from the fact that Malraux had 'too swiftly abandoned the domain of the visible world'.[15] Specifically, he had failed to perceive that paintings are themselves always part of the visible world with which painters are engaged and in which we are all, differently, situated. Here, we might also recall analogous indications in Osborne's *Anywhere or Not At All* (if I have correctly understood him) of an oppositional relationship, or relationship of radical irreconcilability, between 'contemporary' art defined as post-conceptual art and, in effect, all other art forms.

In the third place, Malraux's questioning of the communicability of modern paintings was founded upon a wrong understanding of the preconditions for communicability in general. In contrast to Malraux, therefore, Merleau-Ponty embarked upon an examination of classical and modern painting from within the context of a phenomenological understanding of what it is like to perceive the visual world and bring it to expression. He began by exploring how, albeit with different degrees of emphasis, *all* paintings testify to perception and expression as activities through which the world is both given to us *and* imaginatively constituted by us. Concerning the use of perspective in classical painting, he wrote that it was:

> much more than a secret technique for imitating a reality given as such to all men. It is *the invention of a world* which is dominated and possessed through and through in an instantaneous synthesis which is at best roughed out by our glance when it vainly tries to hold together all these things seeking individually to monopolise it.[16]

Far from depicting the world as it really presents itself to our sight, the inventiveness of classical painting resided in the degree to which it presented the world as it could *never* be seen by an embodied being. This did not mean, following Sartre, that such paintings were the expression of that which does not exist.[17] To repeat, as Merleau-Ponty put it, it schematized the ways in which we might attempt to stabilize and thus control perceptual experience.

Although it is fair to say that the emphasis in classical painting is towards presenting the world as it may be *thought* or imagined, rather than the way it is *seen* by us in our everyday modes of being, Merleau-Ponty wrote that 'the great painter [of the classical tradition] adds a new dimension to this world too sure of itself by making contingency vibrate within it'.[18] Take, for instance, a paradigmatic painting belonging to this tradition, Raphael's *The Marriage of the Virgin (Lo Sposalizio)* of 1504, an example that is independent of Merleau-Ponty's text.[19] At first sight, it may well initially appear that 'the whole scene is in the mode of the completed or of eternity. Everything takes on an air of propriety and discretion. Things no longer call upon me to answer, and I am no longer compromised by them'.[20] But a closer examination provokes a different response. If we pay attention to the painting's main point of emotional and narrative interest we see that it comprises a delicate *gap* evoked by the anticipated meeting of Mary and Joseph's hands as the marriage ring is given, a gap that is highlighted against the background of the priest's robe. When viewed in relation to the perfectly composed geometry of the architectural background, it is as if eternity is being eclipsed by less than a micro-second of time. In other words, the image 'no longer call[s] upon me to answer' only if I fail to look at it with unprejudiced eyes. For is there not something unsettling and intellectually challenging in the juxtaposition of background and foreground? And what of that point of contingency and anticipation immersed within that mathematically precise rendering of an eternal present which, once observed, seems to 'vibrate' outwards through the painting, destabilizing it?

Having reflected upon the inventiveness of classical painting, Merleau-Ponty turned to a more direct criticism of Malraux's definition of modern painting as radically subjective and thus incommunicable. His first point was that if '"objective" painting is itself a creation',[21] there is no justification in distinguishing classical from modern paintings by defining the latter as 'a passage to the subjective and a ceremony glorifying the individual'.[22] Rather, both are more appropriately considered in terms of their *particular* modes of inventiveness in relation to other works or acts of expression with which we may wish to compare them.

In the second place – and here we return specifically to the quotation with which this chapter opened – Merleau-Ponty challenged Malraux's position concerning the question of style in *modern* painting. He countered Malraux's statement about its exclusively, even aggressively, *subjective* character by arguing that style is not something artists are fully conscious of or something they knowingly or premeditatedly impose upon their works. Style, as Merleau-Ponty understood it, is not a project; it emerges gradually while the painter's attention is focused on expressing his or her particularized experiences of interaction with the visual world. Indeed, particular artistic styles are more easily recognized by third-party observers than by the artists themselves. Or it is recognized by artists themselves only retrospectively, when they take on the role of viewers of their own past productions. Style in painting is the expression, in paint, of the painter's general and only partially grasped modes of embodied inherence in the world, and thus it does not arise solely from a self, conceived of as an isolated entity. As Johnson put it: 'Style ... is an intersubjective and historical phenomenon. ... It is what goes on *between* the subject in relation to others and the world, what Merleau-Ponty calls "the allusive logic of the perceived world".'[23] He added that it 'begins as soon as any person perceives the world, and all perception stylises because embodiment is a style of the world. Our own living body is a special way of accenting the variants the world offers.'[24] Gary Brent Madison's commentary found in his 1981 exegesis of Merleau-Ponty's work is also worth citing:

> The artist's style exists for him in the same way his body does; it is not an instrument, a mere vehicle but his very way of inhabiting and taking up the world, his way of presenting himself to others, and, in short, his existence; like the body, it is as imperceptible to him as it is manifest to others. We can thus see that for the artist his style is not an *end* in itself. It is not what he seeks to express but is rather the operative, latent, silent meaning which animates him; this meaning is present in everything he sees or, rather, in his very way of seeing, of responding to the visibility of his world.[25]

Indeed, Merleau-Ponty made the further point that if the painter puts his style into his painting this must not be regarded as synonymous with him putting 'his immediate self – the very nuance of his feeling' into it.[26] Malraux examined the matter of style from the 'outside' (that is, as a viewer of art) but when it is considered from the 'inside' (that is, from the perspective of the painter's existential experience of creating works of art), a different picture emerges:

> The painter at work knows nothing about the antithesis of man and world, of signification and the absurd, of style and 'representation'. He is far too busy expressing his communication with the world to become proud of a style which is born as if he were unaware of it. It is quite true that style for the moderns is much more than a means of representing. It does not have any external model; painting does not exist before painting. But we must not conclude from this, as Malraux does, that the representation of the world is only a *stylistic means* for the painter, as if the style could be known and sought after outside all contact with the world, as if it were an *end. We must see it appear in the context of the painter's perception as a painter; style is an exigency that issues from that perception.*[27]

Two points are important. The first is Merleau-Ponty's insistence, in contrast to Malraux, that style or expression in modern painting is not a subjective but an intersubjective and, indeed, inter-corporeal phenomenon, deriving from the painter's perceptual involvement with the world. To cite Crowther: 'Style in painting … is focussed *not on intentions but on outcomes.*'[28] The second is that style 'appears in the context of the painter's perception as a painter'.[29] This implies that the visual world in which the painter is immersed must be acknowledged as including that which is opened up by paintings and, specifically, the particular work-in-progress with which the painter is at that moment involved. In other words, the painter's style is responsive to the exigencies of the emerging painting itself as it is brought to birth by the painter. The character of this responsiveness was revealed early on in 'Indirect Language and the Voices of Silence', when Merleau-Ponty described his response to a slow-motion recording of Matisse at work.[30] The film, a documentary called *Matisse* or *A Visit with Matisse*, was made in 1946 and showed Matisse drawing, first, a flower picked from his garden and, then, the head of his grandson. Matisse 'looked at the still open whole of his work in progress', wrote Merleau-Ponty, 'and brought his brush toward the line which called for it in order that the painting might finally be that which it was in the process of becoming'.[31]

Malraux's third error concerning the nature of expression in modern painting involved his questioning of its communicability. Underlying this, according to Merleau-Ponty, was Malraux's assumption that communicability required a relationship of sufficient similarity to be in place between the visual world as it is received by our senses and the visual world of the painting as it has been produced by the artist and is made available to its viewers. For Malraux, style in modern painting was so radically subjective as to make this impossible. What then of Merleau-Ponty's resistance to this position, namely, his view that modern painting presents 'the problem of knowing how one can communicate without the help of a pre-established

Nature which all men's senses open upon, the problem of knowing how we are grafted to the universal by that which is most our own'?[32]

One way of elaborating on this position is to consider our engagement with a work such as *Suburban Idyll (Garden City Idyll)* of 1926 (Figure 6.3) by Paul Klee, an artist Merleau-Ponty referenced in this essay. Observing this painting it is true that as well as the gestural qualities of the elements depicted – the tiny figures left of centre, the various architectural features and the waving tree branches – the artist's own mark-making gestures, and thus a strong sense of his style, are also communicated to us. As our eyes are attracted by the layered daubs of yellow, ochre, brown and pink that cover the painting's plaster ground, or as we follow the jerky, fragile lines incised into it, we have a sense of 're-living' or echoing in our bodies the variety of movements, first broad, then minute, that were made by Klee as he worked. However – and this is a vital point; Merleau-Ponty has been misunderstood in this regard – we would be wrong to think that we were reproducing the artist's movements with transparency in our own bodies. For this would be to discount the context-dependent nature of signs so insisted upon by Merleau-Ponty in this essay and, with respect to this particular painting as a sign-system, the divergent ways in which we, as specifically situated and contextualized viewers, will interpret the marks and gestures given to us in this instance. It would be to ignore the process of metamorphosis in which we are involved as we look at the painting. Further, it would be to ignore the incomplete nature of all language. Through our involvement, in this instance, with Klee's gestural being, we are initiated into his particular experience of inventive interaction with the visible world – but only partially. Our interactions with the work also involve, and provoke, our own inventiveness.

Works of art communicate, then, not because their content resembles the world as we have already seen it but because they present particular ways of perceiving and responding to the world, and of sustaining intentionality and inventiveness towards it, that arouse our interest. In them, we recognize connections with our own individual propensities for intentionality and invention and the urgency in ourselves to bring these to expression in one form or another. As Merleau-Ponty put it:

> The accomplished work is thus not the work that exists in itself like a thing but the work which reaches its viewer and invites him to take up the gesture which created it and, skipping the intermediaries, to rejoin, without any guide other than a movement of the invented line (an almost incorporeal trace), the silent world of the painter, henceforth uttered and accessible.[33]

The work of art does indeed allow some kind of connection to occur between the painter's gesture and that taken up by viewers. But the relationship is *not* one of reproduction or mimesis in the traditional sense but one which has, internal to it, the dynamics of both similarity *and* difference.

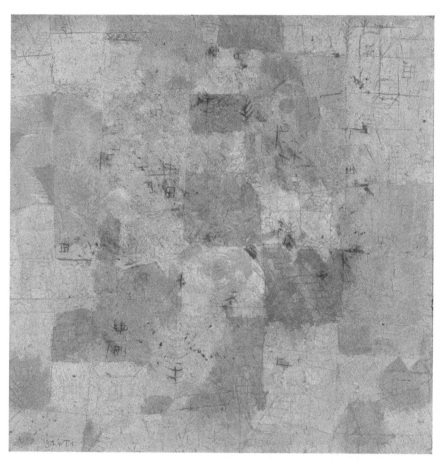

FIGURE 6.3 *Paul Klee*, Suburban Idyll (Garden City Idyll), *1926, oil and incised marks on oil-putty-sand primer on plasterboard. 42.5 × 39.5 cm. Kunstmuseum, Basel, Switzerland. Purchased with funds from the Birmann Foundation. Photo Credit: Kunstmuseum Basel, Martin P. Bühler. (Paul Klee, Vorstadt-Idyll (Gartenstadtidyll), 1926, 191 (T 1), Öl und Ritzzeichnung auf Ölkitt-Sand-Grundierung auf Gipsplatte; originale gefasste Rahmenleisten, 42.5 × 39.5 cm, Inv. 1794. Kunstmuseum Basel, Ankauf mit Mitteln des Birmann-Fonds. Photo Credit: Kunstmuseum Basel, Martin P. Bühler.)*

Merleau-Ponty made a further point about the communicativeness of works of art. He indicated that this was particularly tied to the degree of incompleteness the work itself displays: a work has intense communicative force when, through this openness, it calls upon the active participation of the viewer to bring it to a particular but temporary and contingent mode of completion. It leaves space for the viewer. This 'tolerance for the incomplete' he saw to be powerfully displayed in the works of modern artists such as Cézanne and Klee, in their presentation of 'sketches as paintings' and in their preoccupations with serial works: Cézanne's repeated, and by implication inexhaustible, explorations of Mont Sainte-Victoire, for instance.[34] Crucially, this capacity for provoking the participation of the viewer need not be associated only with modern works. As noted earlier, a mode of incompleteness was centrally embedded with that epitome of High Renaissance orderliness: Raphael's *Marriage of the Virgin*. A further example that is again independent of Merleau-Ponty's text, a painting that belongs to quite a different stylistic school, is also worth considering in this regard: Andrei Rublev's famous and much-reproduced fifteenth-century icon, *The Trinity*.[35] For in compositional terms the divine circle of Father, Son and Holy Spirit – all three are here presented in the form of almost identical, beautiful young men – is made whole only when the viewer has taken residence in the space left open at the base of the image, between the feet of the Father on the left and the Spirit on the right. The ways in which works of visual art may display incompleteness are various but they are correspondent. So too are the particular ways in which viewers become active participants in the worlds these works of art open up, thereby also transforming them.

As Merleau-Ponty saw it, then, when both classical and modern paintings are considered from the point of view of the practice of individual artists, the distinctions between them are distinctions of emphasis, not of kind. Modern painting does not introduce an entirely new agenda into the activity of painting but develops aspects that have always been integral to it albeit, in certain periods, in an understated or largely unrecognized manner, because cultural and historical conditions encouraged different prioritizations. In the classical period, one such prioritization would have been a different understanding of the relationship between painterly and literary or narrative expression and of the perceived social function of visual works.

Cultures of display and debate – Renegotiating particularity-generality

We must understand why what one culture produces has meaning for another culture, even if it is not its original meaning; why we take the trouble to transform fetishes into art. In short, the true problem is to understand why there is a history or a universe of painting.[36]

This conundrum was at the centre of Malraux's *The Voices of Silence*. Merleau-Ponty also treated it as crucial. Thus, having described the irreducibly communicative and intersubjectively significant nature of all works of art, whether classical or modern, Merleau-Ponty went on to raise questions about the category 'art' itself and about our shifting notions of what should and should not be included within it.[37] By what criteria do we group together a variety of often diverse cultural objects into a single category? Indeed, why is it that objects regarded in certain cultures or certain periods as non-art – stained-glass windows, for instance, or ritual objects – may, in another culture or period, find themselves grouped together and redefined precisely as art?

Malraux's position, as Merleau-Ponty understood it, was that while we might, at first glance, regard works which derive from a wide variety of cultures as radically different from one another in terms of their appearance, we are likely after careful scrutiny to observe that powerful similarities unite them.[38] Merleau-Ponty wrote:

> Malraux meditates upon miniatures and coins in which photographic enlargement miraculously reveals the very same style that is found in full-sized works; or upon works uncovered beyond the limits of Europe, far from all 'influences', in which moderns are astonished to find the same style which a conscious painter has reinvented somewhere else.[39]

Malraux accounted for a deep stylistic connection between such objects by invoking the notion of a universal 'Spirit' that directs all of these efforts: 'If one shuts art up in the most secret recess of the individual, he can explain the convergence of separate works only by invoking some destiny which rules over them.'[40] Merleau-Ponty continued: 'Thus Malraux meets, at least metaphorically, the idea of a History which reunites the most scattered efforts, of a painting which works behind the painter's back, and of a Reason in history of which he is the instrument.'[41]

Merleau-Ponty challenged this argument on two points, one being Malraux's notion that unity is based on stylistic resemblance. As indicated above, Merleau-Ponty's discussions in 'Indirect Language and the Voices of Silence' and, previously, in the *Phenomenology*, insisted that the meaning of any sign is context-dependent. A smile in one situation has a different connotation elsewhere. The same was true of the visual traces of those gestures and movements that are involved in the production of works of art. Where appearances are concerned, our understandings of similarity and therefore also of difference are unstable. Thus in his words, the nineteenth-century French painters Jean-Auguste-Dominique Ingres and Eugène Delacroix were those 'rival contemporaries' whom 'posterity recognises as twins'.[42]

Notions of some universal spirit that guides and unites the creation (and appearance) of diverse cultural objects, Merleau-Ponty referred to as 'Hegelian monstrosities'.[43] Such understandings could provide the basis for no more than an external and therefore a false unity. Nonetheless – and here again we witness Merleau-Ponty's refusal of easy oppositions or dichotomies – having reverted back to a discussion of painting, he wrote that since the painter's expressions are not self-projections, they *are* guided. Here again, it was the nature of the painter's engagement with his or her painting-in-progress as part of his visual world that was key. He wrote as follows:

> As long as he paints, his painting concerns visible things. ... *And that is why his labor, which is obscure for him, is nevertheless guided and oriented.* It is always only a question of advancing the line of the already opened furrow and of recapturing and generalising an accent which has already appeared in the corner of a previous painting or in some instant of his experience, without the painter himself ever being able to say (since the distinction has no meaning) what comes from him, and what comes from things, what the new work adds to the old ones, or what it has taken from the others and what is its own.[44]

For Merleau-Ponty, then, to speak of the unity of painting, understood here as the products of a collective, corporate or 'universal' endeavour, was not to speak of a community of similar cultural objects. Nor was it a matter of an imposed unity that had been brought to bear on a given selection of objects, as in a museum or art-gallery collection:[45]

> The unity of painting does not exist in the Museum alone; it exists in that single task which all painters are confronted with and which makes the situation such that one day they *will be* comparable in the Museum, and such that these fires answer one another in the night. The first sketches on the walls of caves set forth the world as 'to be painted' or 'to be sketched' and called for an indefinite future of painting, so that they speak to us and we answer them by metamorphoses in which they collaborate with us.[46]

The unity of painting, then, refers of a community of effort on the part of certain individuals to give visual expression to their experiences of being in, and open to, a world shared with others, past, present and future. These efforts, both 'obscure' to the artist concerned and yet 'guided and oriented', are also each time a kind of starting again. As Merleau-Ponty had already written in 'Cézanne's Doubt', at issue is the 'problem of the first word'. But this did not mean that the history of paintings was, therefore, a 'historicity of death' or cruel history in which 'each age [or each culture] struggles against the others as against aliens by imposing its concerns and perspectives upon them',[47] and in which a progression of artworks supersede and replace each other. This, he wrote, was the historicity encouraged by the art museums, certainly of his day, in which works of art were presented to viewers as autonomous things, cut off from the lived context of their creation – here his view differed to that of Malraux for whom, more fruitfully, the museum, imaginary or otherwise, was a place of metamorphosis. Rather, Merleau-

Ponty argued for a living history of painting. Here painting (*peindre*, to paint) was understood predominantly as a practice and a quest. Thus, it participated in a 'historicity of life' or 'cumulative history' in which the 'classical and the modern pertain to the universe of conceived painting as a single task stretching from the first sketches on the walls of caves up to our "conscious" painting'.[48] As he put it, this other history (this 'historicity of life'),

> is constituted and reconstituted step by step by the *interest* which bears us toward that which is not us and by that life which the past, in a continuous exchange, brings to us and finds in us, and which it continues to lead in each painter who revives, recaptures, and renews the entire undertaking of painting in each new work.[49]

Merleau-Ponty also suggested, in 'Indirect Language and the Voices of Silence', that the unity of painting had to do with the fact that the visible world, which is the common 'object' of interrogation, gives itself to the painter in ways that are both specific *and* general, replete with possibilities and associations. In making this observation, he anticipated what would become a central theme in his late writing. Referring to an anecdote recorded by Malraux in the section of *The Voices of Silence* translated as 'The Creative Process' (originally 'La Création esthétique'),[50] in which an innkeeper reports seeing Auguste Renoir at Cassis at work by the sea but painting 'some naked women bathing in some other place', Merleau-Ponty cited Malraux's comment that '"the blue of the sea had become that of the brook in *The Bathers*. His vision was less a way of looking at the sea than the secret elaboration of a world to which that depth of blue whose immensity he was recapturing pertained". Nevertheless', Merleau-Ponty continued:

> Renoir was looking at the sea. And why did the blue of the sea pertain to the world of the painting? How was it able to teach him something about the brook in *The Bathers*? Because each fragment of the world – and in particular the sea, sometimes riddled with eddies and ripples and plumed with spray, sometimes massive and immobile in itself – contains all sorts of shapes of being, and, by the way it has of joining the encounter with one's glance, evokes a series of possible variants and teaches, over and beyond itself, *a general way of expressing being*. Renoir can paint women bathing and a fresh water brook while he is by the sea at Cassis because he only asks the sea – which alone can teach him what he asks – for its way of interpreting the liquid substance, of exhibiting itself, and of arranging it. In short, because he only asks for a typical form of manifestations of water.[51]

Here again, Merleau-Ponty summoned up questions about how the specific relates to the general, and the particular to the universal. As such, we return yet again to the quotation with which this chapter opened: 'Modern painting presents ... the problem of knowing how one can communicate without the help of a pre-established Nature which all men's senses open upon, the problem of knowing how we are grafted to the universal by that which is most our own.'[52] Again there is that sense of affinity between how we, as embodied beings, experience ourselves and how we engage with cultural objects, in this case, modern paintings. And we see that when Merleau-Ponty asserted that the lesson of modern painting is that we are grafted to the universal by 'that which is most our own', he understood that this 'that which is most our own' has a doubled aspect. It refers to that which most differentiates us from others, to that which is exceptional *and* to that which has become generalized and dispositional: our habit bodies.

The scene at Cassis, with its crossings of places, vision, confusion and uncanny understanding, may also be regarded as metaphorical for the value of looking and thinking with works of art that are *not* contemporary (in Osborne's sense), that are experienced as being somehow out of time, or out of place. This is what Merleau-Ponty did, paradigmatically, with the work of Cézanne. To do so is to take seriously Merleau-Ponty's assertion that no painterly effort is devoid of relevance (actual or potential, present or future) either on its own terms, or because of when, where or by whom it was painted. Painting, precisely in and by means of its particularity, has a voice – 'of silence' – that nonetheless we are able to attend and potentially adjust to, and which we can share, even if only evocatively by pointing and being puzzled.

PART FOUR

Painting – Rethinking thought as 'secret science'

FIGURE 7.1 Merleau-Ponty at the Summit of Mont Sainte-Victoire, *summer 1960, photograph. © Archives Merleau-Ponty. Disclaimer: Every effort has been made to obtain permission to reproduce this image. The publishers will be pleased to make the necessary arrangement at the first opportunity.*

FIGURE 7.2 *Paul Klee,* Park bei Lu., *1938, 129* (Park near Lu., *1938, 129*), *oil and coloured paste on paper on burlap, original frame, 100 × 70 cm. Zentrum Paul Klee, Bern.*

CHAPTER SEVEN

Visibility, the 'flesh' of the world

'The common stuff ... is the *visible*'

During July and August of 1960, Merleau-Ponty had embedded himself in Le Tholonet, a village near to Aix-en-Provence in the south of France. With its dramatic views of Mont Sainte-Victoire (Figure 7.1), it had been one of Cézanne's favourite places to paint. Here, 'Eye and Mind' was written. It was completed during what would be the final year of Merleau-Ponty's life.

In 'Eye and Mind' and in the unfinished *The Visible and the Invisible*,[1] questions about our visual engagements with the world, particularly as foregrounded by practices of painting, were again central. But now Merleau-Ponty had radically reconceptualized his approach to this ongoing concern of his. In other words, once more he was beginning his thought all over again. As he had put it in 'Indirect Language and the Voices of Silence', each act of *authentic* expression, including his own, must be 'a recommencement of effort' in which, to paraphrase him, our image of the world is thrown out of focus, distended and drawn towards fuller meaning.[2] It is a process of pretending 'to have never spoken'.[3]

The Visible and the Invisible is a challenging but also an extraordinarily hospitable resource precisely due to its status as a work-in-progress. Inevitably, hard and fast judgements cannot be made; it is perhaps best approached as offering provocations about the need to rethink the nature and methods of philosophical interrogation. As it stands, the first three chapters, which are entitled 'Reflection and Interrogation', 'Interrogation and Dialectic' and 'Interrogation and Intuition', are organized around critiques of dominant philosophical positions. But a feature of this late work is the criticism that Merleau-Ponty also directed towards his own earlier thought which he described as still too-entangled in precisely those dualistic paradigms he had been challenging. Take his 'Working Note: "Dualism – Philosophy"', dated July 1959,[4] included in the book's final section: 'The problems posed in *The Phenomenology of Perception*', he wrote, 'are insoluble because I start there from the "consciousness" – "object" distinction.'⁵ An alternate starting point was required. Here then – and although perception would still be much discussed – the then-under-interrogated structures of the *visible* were to be foregrounded:

> The common stuff of which all the structures are made is the *visible*, which, for its part, is nowise of the objective, of the in itself, but is of the transcendent – which is not opposed to the for Itself, which has cohesion only for a Self – the Self to be understood not as a nothingness, not as something, but as the unity by transgression or by correlative encroachment of 'thing' and 'world'.⁶

A complex set of ideas are presented here and again of note is Merleau-Ponty's positioning of his ideas in contrast to Sartrean paradigms. But – as indicated by Merleau-Ponty's references to such notions as 'unity by transgression' and 'correlative encroachment of "thing" and "world"' – it is also clear that in order to progress his thought he regarded it as crucial to more emphatically relinquish the dualistically structured language of traditional, modern philosophy. This was the 'complex of Western philosophy',⁷ as he called it, with its focus on subjects and objects, minds and bodies, selves and worlds, seeing and being seen, terms that he had previously kept in play but attempted to redefine.⁸ Now, his philosophical vision required the formulation and use of an alternate set of terms more closely aligned to it. Not only that. Given the ambiguous nature of the territory he was entering and of the kinds of selfhood that might be associated with it – which neither conventional philosophical language could bring to expression nor the prosaic language of everyday currency – it is not surprising that Merleau-Ponty's terminology became increasingly poetic, allusive, metaphorical and characterized by neologisms: 'the flesh', 'chiasm', 'intermundane space', 'wild being' and so on. Significantly, and in contrast to notions such as 'subject', 'object', 'mind' and 'body', Merleau-Ponty's newly formulated terms all signal relations and relational structures.

Some commentators have regarded Merleau-Ponty's experiments with terminology as moving somewhat incomprehensively towards mystical or pseudo-mystical forms of expression, deemed additionally problematic given his asserted agnosticism. But with all its difficulties, this linguistic strategy could also be regarded as vital in that it eschewed one of the most enduring of Cartesian legacies: Descartes' association, in the 'First Meditation', for instance, of valid philosophical thought with clarity and distinction. Crucially, though, this eschewal on Merleau-Ponty's part was not for the sake of some obdurate immersion in obscurity. It was in order to best communicate the multivalent and ambiguous realities that characterize even the philosopher's fundamental embeddedness in the world as it presents itself to us and the need to cultivate orientations best able to acknowledge and cultivate this fact. Lefort, when introducing the English translation of *The Visible and the Invisible*, wrote of Merleau-Ponty's approach:

> Convinced that there is no privileged point whence nature, history, and being itself are unveiled, or, as he says so often, that high-altitude thinking detaches us from the truth of our situation, it was necessary at the same time that he forego the illusion of seeing his own work as a spectacle, oblige himself to make his way in semi-obscurity in order to discover the interior connection of his questions, and fully comply with what demands to be said here and now without ever giving himself over to the security of a meaning already traced out, already thought.[9]

It was, in any case, in the fourth and best-known chapter of *The Visible and the Invisible*, entitled 'The Intertwining – The Chiasm', that Merleau-Ponty's own rearticulations of philosophical thought and method were most emphatically and evocatively presented. This is followed by a fifth, abbreviated chapter called 'Preobjective Being: The Solipsist World' in which he described the philosophical task as an encounter with the 'brute world'.[10] It must originate 'not from the habitual world ... but from that present world which waits at the gates of our life'.[11] The book concludes with a substantial selection of working notes, the first dated January 1959 and titled 'Origin of Truth'. The final note included in the collection was dated March 1961 (thus it was not necessarily the final written note; Merleau-Ponty died two months later, on 3 May). As indicated in my introduction to this book, it was headed: 'My plan: I – The Visible, II – Nature, III – Logos.' Immediately thereafter, he had written that these three themes

> must be presented without any compromise with humanism, nor moreover with naturalism, nor finally with theology – Precisely what has to be done is to show that philosophy can no longer think according to this cleavage: God, man, creatures – which was Spinoza's division.[12]

As Lefort put it, fundamental to Merleau-Ponty's investigations in *The Visible and the Invisible* was 'a new ontology' which alone would 'permit a connection of the criticisms addressed to the philosophy of reflection, dialectics, and phenomenology – criticisms hitherto dispersed and apparently tributary of the empirical descriptions – by disclosing the impossibility of further maintaining the point of view of consciousness'.[13]

In the context of this penultimate chapter of *The Question of Painting*, I would like to foreground four issues, opened up in *The Visible and the Invisible*, that are pertinent to the notion of painterly interrogation and its philosophical implications. The first is a consideration of Merleau-Ponty's treatment of the visible/invisible relationship, a relationship which is in no sense dualistic or oppositional in nature. This attitude was in keeping with the orientation of his philosophical project as a whole. The second and third comprise explorations of the existential and philosophical implications of the types of visual primacy, and thus visual immersiveness, that Merleau-Ponty seemed to be emphasizing. In 'Eye and Mind', notably, these were presented as the particular remit of the painter. How, from such immersiveness, did Merleau-Ponty theorize the role played by the phenomena of illusion and deception that are aspects of visual expression, and how did he define their relation to truth? The fourth issue focuses on how, in his later writing, Merleau-Ponty powerfully equated visuality with the hospitalities of 'having at a distance' and not, as would increasingly become the norm in later-twentieth-century visual theory, with objectification and possession.

The visible and the *invisible*

Dualistic logics have so infiltrated our thinking and shaped our assumptions that when we are presented with two terms united by the word 'and' we are apt to define their relationship as oppositional, with one term generally regarded more positively than the other. This was not how Merleau-Ponty wished the relationship between the visible and the invisible to be understood. On the contrary. Just as in 'Indirect Language and the Voices of Silence', where he presented silence not as nothingness but as that as-yet-unformulated realm by which speech is enveloped, so here, the invisible is that which envelops the visible. For Merleau-Ponty it was painterly expression that was best able to open up and interrogate this territory and articulate this relationship, hence his repeated recourses to painting as a source of insight. But as a philosopher and a writer, his aim was to discover the means also to convey these realities linguistically.

As will be particularly explored in the following (and final) chapter of this book, one of the contrasts around which Merleau-Ponty organized his late thought was between what he described, on the one hand, as expansive painterly modes of interrogation into unknown territory and, on the other, the differently structured and regulated practices of what, in *The Visible and the Invisible*, he referred to as 'operational science' and, in 'Eye and Mind', as 'operationalism' and 'operational thought' – these again being associated with scientific thinking. However, Merleau-Ponty should not be misunderstood here as setting up a hard opposition between the arts and the sciences per se (this issue was discussed earlier, in the introduction to this book). Indeed, a now well-known visualization – a diagram – derived precisely from the sciences attests to Merleau-Ponty's understanding of the embedded nature of visibility within 'invisibility', even if it does so according to an un-Merleau-Pontean, linear format. I am referring to the readily available renderings of the electromagnetic spectrum[14] which demonstrate that visible light – light with wavelengths from about 390 or 400 to 700 nanometres that can be seen by unaided human sight – forms only a very small portion of the spectrum.

In other words, it underlines the fact that what we readily define as visible and what empirically minded persons regard as foundational for truth, on the one hand, and what we conventionally regard as invisible, on the other hand, are so only conditionally. Since the development, in the seventeenth century, of spectroscopy – which studies the interaction between matter and electromagnetic radiation or, put differently, studies objects based on the spectrum of colour they emit, absorb or reflect – increasing portions of the territory previously defined as 'invisible' have been made empirically available and have been visualized. Research in this field has also shown that various animals, including bees and other insects, can see light within frequencies that lie outside of the human visible spectrum. Significantly, with respect to the often intertwined histories of philosophical and scientific investigation into the visual, the origins of spectroscopy are conventionally associated with the work in optics carried out by Descartes's younger, near-contemporary, Sir Isaac Newton, during the later seventeenth century – Descartes's life (1596–1650) and Newton's (1642–1726) overlapped by just eight years. In particular, they are associated with Newton's observations of how visible light was dispersed, according to its wavelength, when passed through a prism. As a consequence, what was thought of as 'white' light, and thus colourless, was now understood to comprise all the colours in the rainbow. Possibly influenced by the power of number symbolism, Newton identified seven colours here: red, orange, yellow, green, blue, indigo and violet. Also of note with respect to the scientific opening up of the visible are subsequent discoveries, such as the discovery within the visual spectrum of so-called Fraunhofer lines, a set of spectral lines named after the German physicist Joseph von Fraunhofer (1787–1826). These had originally been observed as dark features, also known as absorption lines, within the optical spectrum of the sun. As Merleau-Ponty would argue, painters, too, are those who create techniques – alternate techniques – capable of entering into the realms of the not-yet-visible and discovering ways of making them so.

Nonetheless, given the assumptions that immediately come to mind when we hear the word 'invisible', and given Merleau-Ponty's experimentation with the introduction of new terms, it is perhaps surprising that he continued to use this word. Crowther, again in *Phenomenologies of Art and Vision*, made precisely this point. He first extracted four characteristics of the 'invisible' from Merleau-Ponty's writing: '1: that which is not actually visible but could be; 2: that which, relative to the visible could nevertheless not be seen as a thing'. By this Crowther meant 'the existentials of the visible, its dimensions, its non-figurative inner framework'; 3: that which exists only as 'tactile or kinaesthetically'; and 4: the Cogito. He argued, rightly, that 'to call all these factors the "invisible" is slightly misleading'.[15] Instead of defining these as 'invisible', he proposed the use of the term 'transperceptual':

We can only recognize visible things and states of affair insofar as they are contextualized by broader perceptual relations, beliefs and assumptions.

… Perceptual recognition involves demarcating it from that myriad of items, states of affairs, qualities, relations and imagined possibilities that constitute not only the immediate surrounding perceptual field but its continuance in new vectors of detail as we change our position. To call this the 'invisible' seems rather narrow. *It is both immanent in what we perceive, yet extends beyond it, in an unfathomable complexity.* The term *transperceptual* seems much more fitting in relation to all this.[16]

Indirect ontology and anonymous visibility

In *The Visible and the Invisible*, Merleau-Ponty described himself as moving beyond the parameters of the phenomenological explorations of perception, expression and thought that had occupied him for the last quarter of a century.[17] In this regard, he wrote of the 'necessity of a return to ontology'.[18] Hence, his focus on visibility. 'The common stuff of which all the structures are made', he had written, 'is the *visible*.'[19] Indeed, in his essay 'The Philosopher and his Shadow', also published in *Signs* and dating from 1959[20] – the year in which he started work on the material that would be incorporated into *The Visible and the Invisible* – he had referred to indications in the later Husserl of the 'continuing problematic nature of integral, self-contained, or self-supporting phenomenology'.[21] But if a turn to ontology was at issue in *The Visible and the Invisible*, it was an 'indirect ontology',[22] in which no attempt would – or could – be made to theorize about things-in-themselves or about some Being-in-Itself to which we might nonetheless hope to have direct and complete access. Nor would Being be treated as equivalent to a Hegelian *Geist*, for this would be to posit some thing or being external to us to which, knowingly or unknowingly, we are subject. As Merleau-Ponty put it:

> For us the essential is to know precisely what the being of the world means. Here we must presuppose nothing – neither the naïve idea of being in itself, therefore, nor the correlative idea of a being of representation, of a being for the consciousness, of a being for man: these, along with the being of the world, are all notions *we have to rethink with regard to our experience of the world*. We have to reformulate the sceptical arguments outside of every ontological preconception and reformulate them precisely so as to know what world-being, thing-being, imaginary-being, and conscious being are.[23]

This was an extraordinarily ambitious project and one that would only ever be sketched out roughly. Various indications are there but, as Lefort noted, readers of *The Visible and the Invisible* are left more or less 'ignorant of the route that would have been followed, the order of the stages, or the revolutions of the thought'.[24] Nonetheless, within the context of Merleau-Ponty's 'indirect ontology', Being[25] seems to have included a number of key characteristics. First, as indicated, Merleau-Ponty presented it as at once integrated and differentiated. Secondly, he presented it as itself displaying the self-reflexive characteristics of consciousness. Why? And how? Because it is that *of which* persons, as conscious entities, are irretrievably a part. In 'Eye and Mind' he wrote in this regard not of coincidence but rather in terms of varied processes of bodily donation, of which more in the next chapter. Thirdly, given this relationship of non-coincidence – and although Merleau-Ponty's ontology refused to incorporate classical notions of *a* '*transcendent*', that is, 'something which would have an existence in itself outside of our experience'[26] – Being was nonetheless to be understood as '*transcendence*'.[27] To repeat: in the 1959 working note already cited, Merleau-Ponty had described the visible, defined as the 'common stuff of which all the structures are made', as being 'of the transcendent'. This meant, among other things, that Being, for Merleau-Ponty, was both revelatory in nature *and* characterized by opacity and hiddenness.[28] In Madison's words, it is 'the original presence of that which could never be present in person; it is the non-dissimulation of that which is always dissimulated'.[29] Merleau-Ponty would elaborate upon its nature using the terms 'wild being', 'wild logos', 'visibility' and 'flesh'.[30] And it was to its opacity or hiddenness that Merleau-Ponty referred when he used the term 'invisible' in connection with the term 'visible'. Here again, Crowther's preference for the term 'transperceptual' is illuminating.

To reiterate, then, the main shift that occurred in Merleau-Ponty's thought as presented in *The Visible and the Invisible* was this: while perception and the experiences of self and world that it yields were still very much at issue, his starting point was the condition of visibility itself which, as noted, he treated as an inter- or, more properly, an intra-corporeal phenomenon.[31] In the *Phenomenology*, Merleau-Ponty had already presented the body's experience of itself as perceiving *and* perceptible, sensing *and* sensible, as the model according to which we understand the nature of our engagement with, and inherence in, the world – in this regard might not his later criticisms of his earlier phenomenological methods be regarded as too harsh? But now the connection would be formulated in terms that were deeper. Hence his need to tackle the problem of philosophical expression. This was vital since, for Merleau-Ponty, the vocation of philosophy was that it must not only say but do. It must have the capacity to initiate the reader into a given scenario. It must teach its own lessons. Turning again to the 'Editor's Foreword', Lefort cited Merleau-Ponty's words taken from the chapter on 'Interrogation and Dialectic':

the words most charged with philosophy are not necessarily those that contain what they say, but rather those that most energetically open upon Being, because they more closely convey the life of the whole and make our habitual evidences vibrate until they disjoin. Hence it is a question whether philosophy as the reconquest of brute or wild being can be accomplished by the resources of the eloquent language, or whether it would not be necessary for philosophy to use language in a way that takes from it its power of immediate or direct signification in order to equal it with what it wishes all the same to say.[32]

To reiterate, then, and as also expressed by Madison, without retreating from the primordial fact of the body's ambiguous experience of itself as visible seer, as tangible touch and thus as consciousness *and* object, in his late works Merleau-Ponty reformulated this embodied understanding, writing that when 'that visible which is the body sees itself, *it is the visible world which is seeing itself*'.[33]

As indicated, a second term used by Merleau-Ponty to define this 'transcendent stuff' was 'flesh'. One of its functions was to convey that the connection between self and world was not merely one of interaction and reciprocity – that model and its terminology he saw as still too indebted to the dualistic thinking he was seeking to overcome – but precisely of ontological status. In the chapter of *The Visible and the Invisible* entitled 'The Intertwining – the Chiasm' he wrote that

> he who sees cannot possess the visible unless he is possessed by it, unless he *is* of *it*,[34] unless, by principle, according to what is required by the articulation of the look with the things, he is one of the visibles, capable, by a singular reversal, of seeing them – he who is one of them.[35]

In *The Visible and the Invisible*, then, visibility or flesh, as the 'singular reversal' of seeing and seen, is a central concept and the basis for his 'indirect' ontology. In the introduction to *The Question of Painting* I tried to express this new sense of inversion and depth by referring to the differences of appearance and approach characteristic of Cézanne's late watercolours as compared to the robustness of his earlier work. Writing in 'The Intertwining – the Chiasm', Merleau-Ponty provided further clarification, using a different set of references. With respect to this 'Visibility' (presented here in capitalized form), in which 'the seer is caught up in what he sees, and it is still himself he sees',[36] he wrote of

> this generality of the Sensible in itself, this anonymity innate to Myself that we have previously called flesh, and one knows there is no name in traditional philosophy to designate it. ... The flesh is not matter, is not mind, is not substance. To designate it, we should need to old term 'element', in the sense of water, air, earth and fire, that is, the sense of a *general thing*, midway between the spatio-temporal individual and the idea, a sort of incarnate principle that brings a style of being wherever there is a fragment of being. The flesh is in this sense an 'element' of Being.[37]

Merleau-Ponty's definition of the flesh, or Visibility, as 'an "element" of Being' is suggestive. By this he was indicating, first of all, that the flesh is the fundamental constituent of all that is. Secondly, as Johnson pointed out in his essay 'Ontology and Painting: Eye and Mind', Merleau-Ponty was implying that, just as in the Milesian sense of the term, it is that 'which is always presupposed but always forgotten'.[38] In this regard, Madison had described the flesh – or, as Merleau-Ponty put it, 'the formative medium of the object and the subject'[39] – as:

> our medium and our element just as water is the element of fish. Water, for a fish, is an in-depth universe in which it lives and which allows it to encounter and be present to all other marine beings, but which, precisely because water is for the fish the possibility of all presence, is not itself something which is present. Being the medium of its life, water is what the fish never sees; it is for the fish something which is everywhere and nowhere. Similarly, the flesh is that element which unites us to things and which makes it be that the sentient body and the sensed thing are compatible within the same universe; the flesh is the latency and the depth and the possibility of all presence and, for this reason, is never itself present, never itself visible.[40]

Analogously, this time in his essay 'The Colours of Fire: Depth and Desire in Merleau-Ponty's "Eye and Mind"', Johnson wrote that

> the problem in the history of metaphysics to which Flesh responds is by no means new. ... It is the problem of the simultaneous oneness and plurality of Being, its unity-in-difference. It was Hegel's problem of the in-itself and the for-itself, equally stretching all the way back to Heraclitus' doctrine of the unity and strife of opposites. Merleau-Ponty believed that Flesh is a new word regarding this ancient problem.[41]

The other points made in the portion of *The Visible and the Invisible* cited above emphasize both the generality and the self-reflexivity implicit in Visibility, or Flesh, understood as an 'element' of Being. And it is in order to convey something of what I take Merleau-Ponty to mean that I turn to a further reading de Hooch's painting *A Woman Carrying a Bucket in a Courtyard* (Figure 1.2), discussed in the first chapter of this book. This time the point of focus is no longer the centrally positioned woman and the supposed nature of her perceptual and behavioural interaction with the patch of light that is depicted illuminating her space and touching her body. Of interest instead is the curved, eye-like container that is shown resting on its side on the bench to the right and slightly behind the woman. This container, open to the light and reflecting it, particularly on its interior surfaces, is depicted in such a way that it appears both to 'see itself' as part of the visible and to 'see' the woman and everything else that stands before it. In the shimmer of its external rim, we also anticipate its capacity to 'see' us as we view it. In this way, it seems to incorporate us into the visibility of which it is a part. Indeed, as an instance of 'visibility seeing itself', its 'seeing' appears to be more powerfully expressed in the painting than that of the woman who stands, head lowered and eyes in shadow, as if blind by comparison. Significantly, in 'Eye and Mind', Merleau-Ponty wrote of paintings and painterly interrogation – and pre-eminently those of the Dutch tradition of which de Hooch's painting is an instance – in terms of conveying a 'pre-human way of seeing':

> In paintings themselves we could seek a figured philosophy of vision – its iconography, perhaps. It is no accident, for example, that frequently in Dutch paintings (as in many others) an empty interior is 'digested' by the 'round eye of the mirror'. This pre-human way of seeing is the painter's way. More completely than lights, shadows, and reflections, the mirror anticipates, within things, the labor of vision. Like all other technical objects, such as signs and tools, the mirror arises upon the open circuit [that goes] from seeing body to visible body. Every technique is a 'technique of the body'. A technique outlines and amplifies the metaphysical structure of our flesh. The mirror appears because I am seeing-visible [*voyant-visible*], because there is a reflexivity of the sensible; the mirror translates and reproduces that reflexivity. ... Artists have often mused upon mirrors because beneath this 'mechanical trick', they recognised, just as they did in the case of the trick of perspective, the metamorphosis of seeing and seen which defines both our flesh and the painter's vocation.[42]

In the de Hooch, then, the shiny metallic container with its mirroring function may be taken to embody a 'pre-human way of seeing' in which we also partake. It conveys not merely that to see is also to be seen but also the understanding, key to Merleau-Ponty's late writings, that it is the general condition of visibility seeing itself that presupposes and preconditions our actual and various experiences of that intertwining of the sensible and the sensing in which we are inevitably immersed. In *The Visible and the Invisible* Merleau-Ponty explained that it was this generality at the heart of visibility – as the intertwining of seeing and seen – that presupposed the fact of intersubjectivity. As he put it – and the ethical implications of his words are clear – there, is, here

> no problem of the *alter ego* because it is not *I* who sees, not *he* who sees, because an anonymous visibility inhabits both of us, a vision in general, in virtue of that primordial property that belongs to the flesh, being here and now, of radiating everywhere and forever, being an individual, of being also a dimension and a universal.[43]

He continued, referring now also to the reversibility of the visible and the tangible, that what is open to us 'is – if not yet the incorporeal – at least an inter-corporeal being, a presumptive domain of the visible and the tangible, which extends further than the things I touch and see at present'.[44]

Chiasm, illusion, dis-illusion

Having referred to the 'I' as 'seeing-visible' (*voyant-visible*) and to 'the metamorphosis of seeing and seen which defines ... our flesh', Merleau-Ponty clarified his position and its implications by contrasting it with two viewpoints of which he was critical. In the first place, he insisted that the relationship between seeing and seen was not the Sartrean encounter of nothingness before Being.[45] Merleau-Ponty wrote:

> It has seemed to us that the task was to describe strictly our relation to the world not as an openness of nothingness upon being, but simply as openness: it is through openness that we will be able to understand being and nothingness, not through being and nothingness that we will be able to understand openness.[46]

In contrast to Sartre, and bearing in mind Merleau-Ponty's understanding of seeing and the seen as part of the same 'flesh', he wrote of their reciprocal relationship as an 'initial openness upon the world', but – as noted earlier – one which 'does not exclude a possible occultation'.[47]

The paradoxes and tensions at issue mean that, in the second place, the interrelationship of the self, understood as 'seeing-visible', and the visible cannot be understood as one of coincidence. He wrote in 'The Intertwining – the Chiasm' that

> the visible about us seems to rest in itself. It is as though our vision were formed in the heart of the visible, or as though there were between it and us an intimacy as close as between the sea and the strand. And yet it is not possible that we blend into it, nor that it passes into us, for then the vision would vanish at the moment of formation, by disappearance of the seer or of the visible.[48]

In a similar vein, in 'Interrogation and Intuition', he had stated:

> When I find again the actual world such as it is, under my hands, under my eyes, up against my body, I find much more than an object: a Being of which my vision is a part, a visibility older than my operations or my acts. But this does not mean that there was a fusion or coinciding of me with it: on the contrary, this occurs because a sort of dehiscence opens my body in two, and because between my body looked at and my body looking, my body touched and my body touching, there is overlapping or

encroachment, so that we must say that the things pass into us as well as we into the things.[49]

Thus the relationship between seer and seen as described here has two interconnected facets. In the first place, the seer's relative and unstable positivity of being, far from experienced as obliterated *before* the visible, as 'nothingness' in relation to Being, is rather maintained because the seer inheres *in* the visible as part of it. The body as 'seeing-visible' is experienced from two sides, as it were, such that its depth or *dimensionality* is brought into focus. Indeed, it was in order to emphasize this dimensionality that Merleau-Ponty used the terms 'intertwining' and 'chiasm', such that, to repeat, 'a sort of dehiscence opens my body in two' and in which 'there is overlapping or encroachment, so that we must say that the things pass into us as well as we into the things'. The term 'chiasm' was well-chosen. It was derived from the Greek sign *khi*, which takes the form of an 'X' in which the two elements from which it is constructed appear to oppose or rival one another and yet also to recline and incline 'mysteriously into one another'.[50] In anatomy, the term refers to the crossing-over of two parts or structures, such as the fibres of the optic nerves in the brain.

In the second place, the common inherence of seer and seen in the same 'flesh' does not obviate their relationship being one of distance and difference. This understanding is incorporated into the notion of chiasm. The dehiscence, intertwining and crossing-over of seer and seen do not culminate in the complete self-knowledge of Being, whether in individual or general terms, but involves openness and mystery and produces the ongoing genesis of new meanings and knowledges. This place of crossings-over that is the Visible, this 'flesh', is a place of transformation and generation. In 'Eye and Mind' Merleau-Ponty wrote in this regard of a 'spark' that 'is lit between the sensing and the sensible, lighting [a] fire that will not stop burning until some accident of the body will undo what no accident would have sufficed to do'.[51] And in a working note dated May 1960, under the heading 'Flesh of the world – Flesh of the Body – Being' he wrote:

> The *touching itself, seeing itself* of the body is itself to be understood in terms of what we said of the seeing and the visible, the touching and the touchable. I.e. it is not an act, it is a being at (*être à*). To touch *oneself*, to see *oneself*, accordingly, is not to apprehend oneself as an ob-ject, it is to be open to oneself, destined to oneself (narcissism) – Nor, therefore, is it to reach *oneself*, it is on the contrary to escape *oneself*, to be ignorant of *oneself*, the self in question is by divergence (*d'écart*), is *Unverborgenheit of the Verborgen* as such, which consequently does not cease to be hidden or latent.[52]

Merleau-Ponty's use of the term narcissism in *The Visible and the Invisible* and in 'Eye and Mind' is instructive with respect to the intertwined relationship between seer and seen. As he put it in 'The Intertwining – the Chiasm':

> Thus since the seer is caught up in what he sees, it is still himself he sees: there is a fundamental narcissism of all vision. And thus, for the same reason, the vision he exercises, he also undergoes from the things, such that, as many painters have said, I feel myself looked at by the things, my activity is equally passivity – which is the second and more profound sense of narcissism: not to see in the outside, as the others see it, the contour of a body one inhabits, but especially to be seen by the outside, to exist within it, to *emigrate into it, to be seduced, captivated, alienated by the phantom, so that the seer and the visible reciprocate one another and we no longer know which sees and which is seen.*[53]

Merleau-Ponty made an analogous point in 'Eye and Mind' about the inevitable role reversals between painters and the visible that take place during the activity of painting, such that 'so many painters have said that things look at them'.[54] He then cited the painter André Marchand, who – in an interview with the writer, academic, radio producer and interviewer Georges Charbonnier – had said, after Klee: 'In a forest, I have felt many times over that it was not I who looked at the forest. Some days I felt that the trees were looking at me ... were speaking to me. ... I was there, listening.'[55] And again: 'I think that the painter must be penetrated by the universe and not want to penetrate it. ... I expect to be inwardly submerged, buried. Perhaps I paint to break out.'[56]

In general terms, the myth of Narcissus and the phenomenon of narcissism can be interpreted as conveying a critique of the visual, especially its capacity to seduce, and of perceptual practices in which the visual is isolated and prioritized over the other senses such that, as in the myth, the warning cries of Echo are ignored. But Merleau-Ponty's engagement with narcissism here presents it as having a doubled aspect – whether it is understood in its most fundamental and general sense as the visible seeing itself or from the lived experience of a specific human inherence of the visible. On the one hand, it is to see oneself, to be 'open to oneself or 'destined' to oneself. But on the other hand, it is to experience oneself uncannily (*not* Merleau-Ponty's terminology) as a visible phenomenon and thus to be estranged from oneself. We are 'seduced, captivated, [and] alienated by the phantom'.[57] As in Ovid's myth, narcissism involves an entanglement less of self-recognition/obsession and more of mis-recognition and non-recognition: 'Himself he longs for, longs unwittingly. ... Not knowing what he sees, he adores the sight.'[58] Seers see themselves from the outside as 'other', are engrossed by that 'other', are filled with longing and plunge into that which they can never finally grasp hold of. Ultimately, however, this is a transformative act. Narcissus dies to one mode of being and is reborn into another:

but no body anywhere; / And in its stead they found a flower – behold, / White petals clustered round a cup of gold![59]

Hopefully, already evident from these descriptions of the integrated yet also disjunctive chiasmatic visibility of which we are a part, is a condition of visual immersiveness productively different to the deactivated and depoliticized model that was problematized within much post-Merleau-Pontean critical theory, paradigmatically in Guy Debord's *La Société du Spectacle* (*Society of the Spectacle*), which appeared in book form in 1967 and as a film in 1973. As performance scholars Margaret Werry and Bryan Schmidt have recently pointed out, and as phenomenological research, including Merleau-Ponty's, bears out, Debord's much-cited spectator – who was defined as a 'static witness and obedient consumer' and as 'a socially disembodied, ideologically and physically passive receiver of visual and aural messages'[60] – is a mythic figure. The 'spectral victim of Debord's *Society of the Spectacle*, paralyzed in the face of capital's domination of our image-world', they continue, culminates today in 'the contemporary denizen of a globalized information economy, supposedly alienated and isolated from "true" human contact by the devices that mediate his/her incessant communication'.[61] Merleau-Ponty's model, by contrast, presented an intertwining texture of give and take, alongside gestures of mutual 'self'-dispossession which only afterwards may be discovered to have been enhancing. Such highly engaged orientations within the visible, with their challenges, were explicitly opened up in *The Visible and the Invisible* in the context of Merleau-Ponty's discussions of imagination, another topic that had been extensively, but differently, treated by Sartre in *The Imaginary: A Phenomenological Psychology of the Imagination* of 1940.

Merleau-Ponty's position was that philosophical interrogation is an operation in which both perceiving and imagining are involved in the search for the 'real'. Thus interrogation is a process in which illusion and disillusionment – and what he had referred to earlier as 'sense and non-sense' – impinge upon each other and alter our understanding of that which we are seeking to know. 'Belief and incredulity', he wrote, 'are here so closely bound up that we always find the one in the other, and in particular a germ of non-truth in the truth: the certitude I have of being connected up with the world by my look always promises me a pseudo-world of phantasms if I let it wander.'[62] This does not mean that our interrogations of the visual world can never be regarded as veridical but rather that truth is never a finite concept. The challenge is to remain perpetually open to revelation and to adjust our positions accordingly. As Merleau-Ponty expressed it in 'Reflection and Interrogation':

> When an illusion dissipates, when an appearance suddenly breaks up, it is always for the profit of a new appearance which takes up again for its own account the ontological function of the first. I thought I saw

on the sands a piece of wood polished by the sea, and *it was* a clayey rock. The break-up and the destruction of the first appearance do not authorise me to define henceforth the 'real' as a simple probable. ... The dis-illusion is the loss of one evidence only because it is the acquisition of *another evidence*. ... What I can conclude from these disillusions or deceptions, therefore, is that perhaps 'reality' does not belong definitively to any particular perception, that in this sense it lies *always further on*; but this does not authorise me to break or ignore the bond that joins them one after the other to the real, a bond that cannot be broken with the one without first having been established with the following. ... Each perception, even if false, verifies, is the belongingness of each experience to the same world, their equal power to manifest it, as *possibilities of the same world*.[63]

Here, though, Merleau-Ponty is describing a material environment, inhabited by a viewer, who has the capacity and opportunity to explore that environment further. But what about an encounter with a painting, whether figurative or abstract? As Crowther has pointed out both involve us, differently, in illusion. Are encounters with an actual landscape you can enter with your body and with a painted landscape you can enter only with your eyes, 'possibilities of the same world', or are they fundamentally different in kind?

Here, a first reference to Vollemans' extended meditation on Philips Koninck's 1664 painting *An Extensive Landscape, with a River* (Figure 8.3) seems apt. Indeed, although Vollemans made no reference to Merleau-Ponty in his book, his series of short and each time differently inflected studies of Koninck's painting – which I will discuss in detail towards the end of the following chapter – were grounded in an adventurous, non-paranoid embrace of visual paradox akin to Merleau-Ponty's own sensibilities in this regard. Of particular interest to me now is a short section of Vollemans' book entitled 'Het voorrecht to worden bedrogen' ('The privilege of being deceived').[64] It occurs towards the middle of the book and acts as something of a diversion away from Koninck's painting but in so doing provides a further vantage point from which to consider Vollemans' idea that *An Extensive Landscape, with a River* might appropriately be defined as a 'treatise'. In 'The privilege of being deceived' we are reminded that Vollemans' study is resituating us in a seventeenth-century Dutch cultural scene in which the paradoxes of sight were being explored in multiple ways, not only philosophically and empirically but also in the realms of art-making, amusement and entertainment. On the one hand, the Dutch Republic was a centre for the production of advanced optical devices (magnifying glasses, microscopes and telescopes) intended to aid early scientific advancement. But on the other hand, it was also nurturing an artistic milieu in which, influenced by ideological, religious and political factors, longer-standing painterly priorities that had once been focused on religious, classical and historical themes were rapidly being expanded with the appearance of new genres, including ones in which the eye's capacity to be deceived was being actively and ingeniously exploited.

In this respect, Vollemans referenced such illusionistic devices as the much-discussed *Perspectival Cabinet with Dutch Interior*, 1656–62, constructed by the painter and writer Samuel van Hoogstraeten and now housed in the National Gallery, London in which, through the clever use of *tromp-l'oeil* and anamorphosis, the tiny painted figures depicted on the cabinet's interior, when viewed through peep holes, appear as though they are life-sized.[65] Vollemans also referenced works by the Dutch late-sixteenth- and early-seventeenth-century masters of pictorial illusionism, the architect, painter and engineer Hans Vredeman de Vries (1527–c. 1607) and his son Paul (1567–1617) who created extensive architectural trompe-l'oeil features for the famed castle of Rudolf II in Prague.[66] Vollemans referred to an account of their work in Carel van Mander's *Het Schilder-Boek* (*Book of Painters*) of 1603–4, including, for instance, an extraordinarily cunning perspective painted by Paul. It created the illusion of opening onto a gallery that in turn led to a courtyard with a fountain. Vollemans then asked his readers to dwell more deeply on this situation. Here, a painter was being commissioned to *deceive* his patron, an individual of the highest authority, and then to go on doing so: 'not to counter the illusion with dis-illusion, with relativizing and corrective insight',[67] but to continue cultivating the realm of illusion so that it might come to be acknowledged as self-standing and autonomous. The delight associated with these illusions, Vollemans added, was that the perspectives being fabricated pretended (convincingly) to provide access into worlds comprised of things that were able to manifest their own *non*-existence.[68]

It is unclear whether or not Vollemans believed that the creation of such self-standing realms of non-existence might indeed be fully possible. Certainly, he described practices, such as these, as culminating in the creation of a sense of rivalry between a world of illusion and a world of reality. But he also reminded his readers that just because a person may have been visually deceived – even to an extreme degree (and even such a sophisticated person as Rudolf) – this did not mean therefore that 'the real world has endured a loss of face'. In actuality, these worlds of extreme visual artifice were ones in which only the disembodied eye ruled supreme, and only, as already indicated, in order to be able to relish in the purported *privilege* of being deceived.[69] But this was a game that could turn against even such a man-of-power as Rudolf II. Why? Because, wrote Vollemans, illusion has the ultimate effect of annihilating the controlling gaze.[70]

In the end, even in the highly constructed, artificial illusory environments described by Vollemans, the non-oppositional, curiosity-provoking experiences of illusion and dis-illusion that Merleau-Ponty had described in *The Visible and the Invisible* as fundamental to genuine, whole-bodied pursuits of truth, hold true. This is because, phenomenologically speaking and in lived experience, sight is not disembodied. Even in the most extreme instances of pictorial illusion, the deceptive world that is constructed can be maintained only to the degree that sight (that is, prosaic sight) is operative and functioning *as if* more or less disembodied. But when vision is re-experienced as irrevocably interconnected with our entire bodily being and with motility, further exploration inevitably leads to *dis*-illusion, just as it did for Rudolf II, who – as van Mander tells us – *intending* to pass through a gallery leading to a courtyard with a fountain, simply walked into a wall.

Immersive thought and 'having at a distance'

In *The Visible and the Invisible* Merleau-Ponty presented the entangled inter- or intra-corporeal relationship between the sensible and the sensing, between seer and seen, and the modes of thought at issue, as involving inevitable paradoxes. A particular paradox where lived human experience is concerned, identified in the first chapter of his work, was the fact that we experience ourselves as open to a world of which we ourselves are part but which nonetheless also remains hidden from us and unfamiliar to us. Merleau-Ponty's earlier, phenomenological work provided the groundwork for understanding this. 'The world is what I perceive', he wrote in 'Reflection and Interrogation', 'but as soon as we examine and express its absolute proximity, it also becomes, inexplicably, irremediable distance.'[71] An important theme running throughout the first three chapters of the book is Merleau-Ponty's elaboration of a mode of philosophical interrogation capable of grappling with such paradoxes and making them understandable. Philosophy, he wrote:

> must tell us how there is openness without the occultation of the world being excluded, how the occultation remains at each instant possible even though we be [*sic*] naturally endowed with light. The philosopher must understand how it is that these two possibilities, which the perceptual faith keeps side by side within itself, do not nullify one another.[72]

Merleau-Ponty called the type of philosophical interrogation capable of grappling with this challenge a 'hyper-reflection' (*sur-réflexion*) which, rather than posit a distinction between investigator and investigated or between 'the perception and the thing perceived',[73] acknowledges the chiasmic nature of their entanglement. Indeed, it is worth noting the etymology of the word 'interrogation' here: the Latin *interrogare* – to question, examine, ask – which includes the Latin prefix *inter* – between, among, in the midst of, mutually, reciprocally, together and during. Accordingly, hyper-reflection is

> another operation besides the conversion to reflection, more fundamental than it ... that would also take itself and the changes it introduces into the

spectacle into account. It accordingly would not lose sight of the brute thing and the brute perception [in which the coexistence and intertwining of seer and seen are apprehended] and would not finally efface them.[74]

In hyper-reflection, then, that which traditional philosophy has regarded as external to the activity of interrogation is here apprehended as internal to it. Indeed, here the dyad internal/external loses its force and notions of 'within' and 'among' become more apt. In 'Eye and Mind' Merleau-Ponty wrote that this was something that painters, in their interrogations of the world, had long understood:

> Since things and my body are made of the same stuff, vision must somehow take place in them; their manifest visibility must be repeated in the body by a secret visibility. 'Nature is on the inside', says Cézanne. Quality, light, color, depth, which are there before us, are there only because they awaken an echo in our body and because the body welcomes them. Things have an internal equivalent in me; they arouse in me a carnal formula of their presence.[75]

By claiming that 'nature is on the inside', Merleau-Ponty was not reverting to a form of idealism in which the world is conceived of as a product or projection of consciousness and where the problem of the 'there is' of the world and of others becomes irresolvable.[76] Nor was he suggesting that the 'there is' of the world be regarded as the *equivalent* of our own experience of it – the notion of coincidence – nor again that nothing except our own individual experience can be known. Indeed, Merleau-Ponty declared in *The Visible and the Invisible* that the reason we interrogate our experience is 'precisely in order to know *how it opens us to what is not ourselves*'.[77] Thus two points are being conveyed. The first is the fact that we can only know that to which we are in some way connected or of which we are in some way a part. I experience nature as being on the 'inside' because 'first I was outside of myself, in the world, among the others [this is the internality and inter-corporeality to which he referred] and constantly this experience feeds my reflection' – because I admit 'the double polarity of reflection and ... that, as Hegel said, to retire into oneself is also to leave oneself'.[78] The second point, as indicated earlier, is that the 'there is' of the world has an irreducibly transcendent aspect. These are the understandings given us in the 'brute perception' characteristic of hyper-reflection *and*, as Merleau-Ponty saw it, the interrogations of painters.

Thus philosophical interrogation must not be understood as a mental operation in which a separated consciousness constitutes or posits an experientially unknowable world as it must be in itself. A key passage found in 'Interrogation and Dialectic' begins as follows:

> The philosopher's manner of questioning is therefore not that of cognition: being and the world are not for the philosopher unknowns

such as are to be determined through their relation with known terms, where both known and unknown terms belong in advance to the same order of *variables* which an active thought seeks to approximate as closely as possible.[79]

Indeed, a little earlier in this chapter, Merleau-Ponty had produced an impassioned critique of traditional dialectics or, as he called it, 'bad dialectic'. His words are so powerful, and so ethically significant, that they are worth reproducing at length: 'The bad dialectic', he wrote, 'is that which does not wish to lose its soul in order to save it, which wishes to be dialectical immediately, becomes autonomous, and ends up at cynicism, at formalism, for having eluded its own double meaning.'[80] By contrast, what he called, here, 'hyperdialectic' – a term analogous to but not necessarily coincident with 'hyper-reflection' – he described as a thought that 'is capable of reaching truth because it envisages without restriction the plurality of the relationships and what has been called ambiguity'.[81] He continued:

The bad dialectic is that which thinks it recomposes being by a thetic thought, by an assemblage of statements, by thesis, antithesis, and synthesis; the good dialectic is that which is conscious of the fact that every thesis is an idealization, that Being is not made up of idealizations or of things said, as the old logic believed, but of bound wholes where signification never is except in tendency, where the inertia of the content never permits the defining of one term as positive, another term as negative, and still less a third term as absolute suppression of the negative by itself. The point to be noted is this: *that the dialectic without synthesis of which we speak* is not therefore scepticism, vulgar relativism, or the reign of the ineffable. What we reject or deny is not the idea of a surpassing that reassembles, it is the idea that it results in a new positive, a new position. *In thought and in history as in life the only surpassings we know are concrete, partial, encumbered with survivals, saddled with deficits; there is no surpassing in all regards that would retain everything the preceding phases had acquired, mechanically add something more and permit the ranking of the dialectical phases in a hierarchical order from the less to the more real, from the less to the more valid.*[82]

Thus, rather than being 'an active thought', valid philosophical interrogation, for Merleau-Ponty, was a process in which that which is perceived as not us unfolds its meaning *in* us. The relationship between interrogator and interrogated is an internal one. Investigators experience themselves as 'porous' beings, such that, as indicated, 'things have an internal equivalent in me; they arouse in me a carnal formula of their presence'.[83] In 'Eye and Mind', we read that our questioning 'is addressed to a vision, a seeing ... which we do not make, for it makes itself in us'.[84] At issue, then, was the self-revelatory nature of visibility-in-general and thus the necessarily receptive nature of our particular experiences of interrogating the world. This receptiveness was further conveyed in the passage from 'Eye and Mind', with reference to painters' experiences of nature being 'on the inside', through Merleau-Ponty's use of the words 'repeated', 'echo' and 'welcomes' and through the phrase 'arouses in me'. All of these terms imply the intimately felt activity, in us, of that which must also be considered 'other'. Continuing his argument, in *The Visible and the Invisible*, about interrogation as a non-cognitive operation, he wrote:

> Just as we do not speak for the sake of speaking but speak to someone *of* something or *of* someone, and in this initiative of speaking an aiming at the world and at the others is involved upon which is suspended all *that which* we say; so also the lexical signification and even the pure significations which are deliberately reconstructed, such as those of geometry, *aim at a universe of brute being and of coexistence, toward which we were already thrown when we spoke and thought,*[85] and which, for its part, by principle does not admit the procedure of objectifying or reflective *approximation*, since it is at a distance, by way of horizon, latent and dissimulated. It is that universe that philosophy aims at, that is, as we say, *the object* of philosophy.[86]

The 'universe of brute being and of coexistence, toward which we were already thrown when we spoke and thought' is not a pre-existent object but a world that is coming into being and with which we are already in relationship. Thus the task of discovering what it is like requires that rather than posit it, we allow it 'to be' and follow its transformations:

> The effective, present, ultimate and primary being, the thing itself ... offer themselves therefore only to someone who wishes not to have them but to see them, not to hold them as with forceps, or to immobilise them as under the objective of a microscope, but to let them be and to witness their continued being – to someone who therefore limits himself to giving them the hollow, the free space they ask for in return, the resonance they require, who follows their own movement.[87]

The 'effective, present, ultimate and primary being' cannot be interrogated by the mind as it has been traditionally understood. Rather, as Merleau-Ponty wrote a little later in this passage, 'it is necessary to comprehend *perception* as this interrogative thought which lets the perceived world be rather than posits it, before which the things form and undo themselves in a sort of gliding, beneath the yes and the no'.[88] What we derive from such investigations is thus 'not an *answer* but a confirmation of ... astonishment'.[89] Here, as also indicated in my introduction to this book, the question/answer duality may be seen to be challenged.

Also of note is the fact that Merleau-Ponty prioritized not merely perception but 'the look' as interrogation. 'It is not only philosophy', he wrote, 'it is first the look that questions the things.'[90] The look is chiasmic: the intertwining of seeing and seen.[91] The reason for this prioritization of vision among the variety of chiasmic intertwinings of the sensing and the sensible, seems to be that the apparently paradoxical interdependence of distance and proximity characteristic of such intertwinings is here most powerfully in evidence: 'To see', he wrote in 'Eye and Mind', is *'to have at a distance'*.[92] In the intertwining of touching and touched, by contrast, the ungraspable aspect of the world is less clearly evident. It is in our visual explorations of the world that (paraphrasing him) we are best able to limit ourselves to giving things the hollow, the free space they ask for, the resonance they require and to follow their own movement. This is radical hospitality: the capacity at once to welcome someone or something and to leave them be.

Furthermore, the look, to a far greater degree than our other senses, reveals to us the transcendent nature of that which we are seeking to understand. By exposing the way in which things both show themselves to, and hide themselves from us, our visual interrogations of the world reveal the otherness that is intrinsic to it and, because we are of it, intrinsic to ourselves. As Alphonse de Waelhens put it: 'Only the visual *puts me in the presence of* what is not myself, as the unity of the world. The other senses either retain a dimension of radical immanence, or, like hearing, only bring us the other as a piecemeal or evanescent presence. ... Everything that is available to sight, although it is the exhibiting of an individual thing, manifests itself also as an express and adroit reference to other than itself.'[93] 'Vision', wrote Merleau-Ponty in 'Eye and Mind', is 'the means given me for being absent from myself, for being present at the fission of Being from the inside'.[94] As he saw it, painting par excellence is able to teach us this. Indeed, his position concerning the particular intertwinings of distance and proximity in 'the look' and its capacity to let the world be enable us to regard as less potentially problematic two statements regarding painting found towards the end of the first section of 'Eye and Mind'. As noted earlier – at the end of Chapter 4 – in the first place comparing painting with other forms of creative expression, he had written as follows:

> From the writer and the philosopher ... we want opinions and advice. We will not allow them to hold the world suspended. We want them to take a stand; they cannot waive the responsibilities of men who speak. Music, at the other extreme, is too far beyond the world and the designatable, to depict anything but certain outlines of Being – its ebb and flow, its growth, its upheavals, its turbulence. Only the painter is entitled to look at everything without being obliged to appraise what he sees.[95]

As he saw it, verbal forms of expression – those of the writer and the philosopher – are less able to immerse us into an experience of the vast dimensionality of the world's simultaneous distance from, and proximity to, us. Not in and of themselves but because we are uncritically predisposed to regard verbal expression as definitive. Music, on the other hand, he saw as too abstract and elusive in its interpretations to bring our understanding of the dynamics of 'Being' into some kind of balance. The first – verbal expression – has the appearance of bringing us too close to things, the second – music – takes us too far away from the world in its specificities.[96]

The second statement, which follows on directly from the first, had to do with Merleau-Ponty's understanding of the political implications of paintings and of the painter's role within society. At issue were again the dynamics of distance and proximity associated with vision as he understood it:

> For the painter, we might say, the watchwords of knowledge and action lose their meaning and force. Political regimes which denounce 'degenerate' painting rarely destroy paintings. They hide them, and one senses here an element of 'one never knows' amounting almost to a recognition. The reproach of escapism is seldom aimed at the painter; we do not hold it against Cézanne that he lived hidden away at Estaque during the war of 1870. ... It is as if in the painter's calling there were some urgency above all other claims at him. ... With no other technique than what his eyes and hands discover in seeing and painting, he persists in drawing from this world, with its din of history's glories and scandals, *canvasses* which will hardly add to the angers or the hopes of man – and no one complains.[97]

Nowadays, of course, precisely the complaints Merleau-Ponty thought no one would raise, have indeed been raised, often and loudly. But Merleau-Ponty – who, as a thinker and writer, was highly engaged politically throughout his career – had seen something, a possibility, attendant to the painter's position as he understood it. This position was *not* one of non-involvement with political events, although for those associating political efficacy with direct and immediate action, this might at first glance seem to be the case. At issue for Merleau-Ponty was a deeper, slower mode of involvement with such events – what might perhaps be described as a rarely engaged with pre-political and, arguably also, pre-personal mode of being – that was indirect, reflective and thus potentially profoundly subversive in terms of its capacity to search out, enter, keep open and extend existential possibilities that a given crisis was in the process of closing down. Indeed, our usual, urgent responses of immediate and direct action or reaction are generally ineffectual longer-term because the more difficult but diagnostically-nuanced modes of hyper-reflective thought Merleau-Ponty was advocating have been evaded. The prevalent direct and rapid response models – while often absolutely required – do nothing to challenge the prolongation of the problematic conditions and habituated patterns of social interaction that were likely to have caused the problem in the first place. More is needed. In this respect, Merleau-

Ponty advocated the painter's way because, as an at-once always intimately connected *and* productively distancing mode of being, it has the capacity, in the first instance, to let the world 'with its din of history's glories and scandals' be. Thus painters can have a particularly perceptive and unprejudiced kind of involvement with the world, the *general* articulations of this involvement being 'passed on' to those who become visually involved with their productions. Consequentially, such works can open up for us, albeit with varying degrees of effectiveness, previously unavailable spaces for reassessment concerning, firstly, our own complex implication in the world and its events and, secondly, the possibilities for transforming the world and our modes of interaction with it. To repeat: 'To see is *to have at a distance*.'[98] To which he added that 'painting spreads this strange possession to all aspects of Being'.[99] The implication here is that even the most overtly non-representational, imaginative or apparently non-ideological paintings – indeed, perhaps these in particular – have a vital social function.[100]

FIGURE 8.1 *Henri Matisse,* Baigneuse aux cheveux longs, *1942, lithographic crayon on transfer paper. Photo: Archives Henri Matisse, all rights reserved. Artwork: © Succession H. Matisse / DACS 2018.*

FIGURE 8.2 *Henri Matisse,* Artist and Model Reflected in a Mirror, *1937, pen and black ink on paper, 61.2 × 41.5 cm (24 1/8 × 16 5/16 inches). The Baltimore Museum of Art: Cone Collection, formed by Dr. Claribel Cone and Miss Etta Cone of Baltimore, Maryland. Photography by Mitro Hood. Courtesy Baltimore Museum of Art. Artwork: © Succession H. Matisse / DACS 2018.*

CHAPTER EIGHT

Visual treatises and the search for depth

Painterly thought as secret science

Galen Johnson has pointed out that by titling 'Eye and Mind' as he did, Merleau-Ponty was likely gesturing towards a recently published work of significant influence on him: Paul Klee's *Das bildnerische Denken* (literally, *Pictorial Thinking*).[1] This was the first volume of Klee's two-part *Pedagogical Notebooks*, drawn from his teaching at the Bauhaus during the 1920s. It had been edited and published in German only in 1956 and translated into French as *Contributions à la théorie de la forme picturale* in 1959.[2] Its English title is *The Thinking Eye*.

'Eye and Mind' appeared in three formats. It was first published in January 1961 in the inaugural issue of the journal *Art de France*. It was then republished posthumously, first in a special issue of *Les Temps Modernes* dedicated to Merleau-Ponty – along with articles reflecting on Merleau-Ponty's legacy by Jean Hyppolite, Jacques Lacan, Lefort, Jean-Bertrand Pontalis, Sartre, de Waehlens and Jean Wahl – and then as a book, published by Éditions Gallimard in 1964. Both the *Art de France* version of 'Eye and Mind' and the book contained images selected by Merleau-Ponty, one of which was by Klee: his *Park bei Lu.* of 1938 (Figure 7.2), to which I will return.

'Eye and Mind' opens with a warning. As already indicated in the previous chapter, it concerns the increasingly unchecked application of what Merleau-Ponty called 'operational thought', 'operational science'[3] or 'constructive scientific activities' to all fields of life and endeavour, colonizing them with their own limited principles and logics – factors that may well be absolutely apt within certain, highly specific or specialized contexts but should by no means be treated as generally applicable. 'Constructive scientific activities', he wrote,

see themselves and represent themselves to be autonomous, and their thinking deliberately reduces itself to a set of data-collecting techniques which it has invented. To think is thus to test out, to operate, to transform – on the condition that this activity is regulated by an experimental control that admits only the most 'worked-out' phenomena, more likely produced by the apparatus than recorded by it. From this state of affairs arise all sorts of vagabond endeavours. Today more than ever, science is sensitive to intellectual fads and fashions. When a model has succeeded in one order of problems, it is tried out everywhere else.[4]

Merleau-Ponty's stance, it must be remembered, was not anti-scientific per se; throughout his career, scientific works had formed an important backdrop for the formation of his own thought. Three things, in particular, were problematic though. The first was the condition, just described, of operational science radically overstepping its marks. The second – a problem already much referenced in his earlier writing – was its objectivism and thus its lack of critical self-reflexivity. And the third was what he described as its idealism and artificialism; its construction of reductive models to which all aspects of existence, in their diversity, were expected to conform. These operations Merleau-Ponty contrasted with the types of interrogation – the *secret* science – that he saw to be characteristic of painterly activity.

Just as the issue of philosophical interrogation was the main motif running through *The Visible and the Invisible*, so were these painterly modes of questioning, this 'secret science', recurrent themes in 'Eye and Mind'. 'Secret science' he described as a questioning that 'comes from one who does not know, and it is addressed to a vision, a seeing, which knows everything and which we do not make, for it makes itself in us'.[5] It is a questioning that seeks to 'make space and light, which are there, speak to us' – a questioning that he, therefore, described as endless, since 'the vision to which it addresses itself is itself a question'.[6] It is a questioning whereby territory that we thought of as closed is opened or reopened.[7] Painterly thinking, he wrote, is 'mute', sometimes leaving us 'with the impression of a vain swirl of significations, a paralyzed or miscarried utterance'.[8]

Above all, it is, as he put it, a search for depth which was, for him, none other than the dimensionality of his elementary being, the flesh.[9] As such, it was also a work of labour, that is, a bringing-to-birth, a bringing-to-visibility, of that which wishes to show itself but which nonetheless cannot be said to pre-exist the phenomenon of its emergence: being and coming-to-appearance are witnessed as inextricably intertwined. It is to the varied dimensions of the painterly search for depth and its implications that I now turn.

Intermundane space

Significantly, for Merleau-Ponty, it was modern painting that was most profoundly involved in that secret science, that search for depth that he felt was so existentially, and indeed by implication also so politically, vital.

His focus, in other words, was on precisely the kind of painting that was generally involved in a great effort to 'detach itself from illusionism and to acquire its own dimensions'.[10] Such works, such efforts, he described as having metaphysical significance: '"I believe Cézanne was seeking depth all his life", says Giacometti.[11] Says Robert Delaunay, "Depth is the new inspiration".'[12] 'Four centuries after the "solutions" of the Renaissance', he wrote, 'and three centuries after Descartes, depth is still new, and it insists on being sought, not "once in a lifetime" but all through life.'[13]

The paintings, and indeed also drawings, to which Merleau-Ponty turned in 'Eye and Mind' were those that were able to initiate him, time and time again, into differently articulated dimensions of 'depth'. As noted, he understood depth, not as a constructed *third dimension derived from the other two*'[14] but as the chiasmic realm of the 'flesh', in which interrelationships between what we *subsequently* regard as internal and external are given as elementary. These works visualized what Merleau-Ponty, writing in *The Visible and the Invisible*, had also named 'the intermundane space (*l'intermonde*) where our gazes are found to cross and our perceptions overlap':[15] This was 'a pell-mell ensemble of bodies and minds, promiscuity of visages, words, actions, with, between them all, that cohesion which cannot be denied them since they are all differences, extreme divergencies of one same something'.[16]

Modern painting was particularly able to access 'intermundane space' precisely because it was no longer aligned to the goals and methods of illusionism, and from the conception of space as a 'shell' in which objects are placed.[17] It was no longer concerned with the depiction of a world conceived of as a homogenous, extended and unambiguous space containing isolable things. Rather, it attended to the expressive power of so-called secondary qualities, particularly colour, which have the power par excellence of presenting things to us as distinguishable, yet without isolating them from their surroundings, fixing them in their place and making them discrete and autonomous. In making this shift, new modes of attention and sensitivity towards the visual had opened up. As de Waelhens put it, in his 1993 essay 'Merleau-Ponty: Philosopher of Painting', '*The thing* is therefore less important than *the qualities of things*, in that they *are at the origin of all appearances, composing them*.'[18] Contrasting the expressive capacities of colour with the 'prosaic conception of the line as a positive attribute and a property of the object itself',[19] and presenting the former, alone, as having the power to bring primary being to visibility, Merleau-Ponty wrote:

> what Descartes likes most in copper engravings is that they preserve the forms of objects, or at least give us sufficient signs of their forms. If he had examined that other, deeper opening upon things given us by secondary qualities, especially color, then – since there is no ordered or projective relationship between them and the true properties of things and since we understand their message all the same – he would have found himself faced with the problem of a conceptless universality and a

conceptless opening upon things. He would have been obliged to find out how the indecisive murmur of colors can present us with things, forests, storms. ... But for him it goes without saying that color is an ornament, mere coloring [*coloriage*], and that the real power of painting lies in design, whose power in turn rests upon the ordered relationship existing between it and space-in-itself as taught us by perspective-projection.[20]

For Merleau-Ponty, by contrast, and as Véronique Fóti has put it, modern painting shows 'the possibility of modulating space out of the instability of color and ... refuses to recognise the classical privilege of the "form-spectacle," without, for all that, seeking in color another privileged "key" to the visible'.[21] She continued: 'Merleau-Ponty notes thus that the confrontation of the universe of classical thought with the researches of modern painting generates an awareness of "a profound discordance, of a mutation in the relationships between man and Being".'[22]

Merleau-Ponty's inclusion of Klee's *Park bei Lu.* (Figure 7.2) among the illustrations to 'Eye and Mind' is of interest in this regard, both for its use of line and its use of colour. In the first place, rather than provide us with the external 'forms of objects', its black, hieroglyphic lines which schematically and gesturally signify trees, plants and people are immersed in, and emerge from, colours which at times themselves seem to function as outlines. As such, and unhindered by the image's flatness, these marks appear to reveal the deep, hidden structure of things and are suggestive of a certain effort on the artist's part to convey as interactive and fertile that which traditional thought had tended to make mutually exclusive: line versus colour, for instance, as well as writing versus painting, and reading versus looking. 'The effort of modern painting', wrote Merleau-Ponty, 'has been directed not so much toward choosing between line and color, or even between the figuration of things and the creation of signs, as it has been toward multiplying the systems of equivalences.'[23] Here, we might again recall Merleau-Ponty's responses to the paradigmatic painterly explorations of El Greco described in *The Structure of Behavior*, in terms of their capacity through their idiosyncrasies, to open up further 'profiles' of human existence.[24]

In the second place, this image testifies to the power of colour to open up a space which is not conceived of as extended and geometric: one that is without a defining measurable structure of that kind, without a rule of consistency, but is above all evocative, emotional and relational. What is given is not a park described in line and colour on a ground but painted marks (variously warm and cold; attractive and recessive) placed against other coloured marks and patches which become for us an *experience* of being in a park. Thus while the painting's calligraphic characteristics may seem to call for deciphering and appeal to cognition in this regard, its more profound effect is to reach out to that involved and committed *human* body that arises only when, in Merleau-Ponty's words, 'between the seeing and the seen, between touching and the touched, between one eye and another, between hand and hand, a blending of some sort takes place'.[25] Here we have, all mixed together – but not merged; still distinguishable – looking up (sky) and looking down (grass), play (the leaping, stretching stick-figures) and tranquillity (the ornate, tree-like form surrounded by a halo of orange). And we have visibility as the 'singular reversal' of seeing and seen (the inquisitive pair of 'eyes' that addresses us from the centre of the image). And yet there remains an inexplicable cohesion, a 'wild' cohesion. The black lines pull apart from one another only to become reconfigured with others. The contrasting colours both push away from and reach out to each other, competing with each other and yet, cumulatively, providing the eye with a kind of 'melodic' rest. Flows of energy and emotion are at issue here. In his essay 'Merleau-Ponty, Inhabitation and the Emotions', Glen A. Mazis described such spaces as 'topological' rather than Euclidean:

> Topological space is a space of places: it is varied, a patchwork of pulls and repulsions, of significances. It is not homogenous, not an indifferent medium to be arbitrarily designated by Cartesian co-ordinates. ... Merleau-Ponty states that, like Klee's touches of colour, the blue or green or red patches being more primordial than a colourless ground, the place where we go to play or to pray, or the house whose hostility I seek to avoid, or the forest as distinguished from the plains, are more primordial than a homogenous space. This patchwork is enveloping, the outer pattern within the landscape of my loves and hates, my preferences and my indifferences. It is in this entwining of oneself and the world, in which the emotions are played out, and play a vital role, that things matter, that a conflicting, cohering, flowing and always pulsating locus emerges.[26]

Having said all this, the character of intermundane space as it is presented here may nonetheless, appear removed from our everyday experiences of being in the world. And in a sense it is. Since it represents to us the flesh as 'our medium and our element' it is that which, as noted earlier, is 'always presupposed but always forgotten'.[27] Merleau-Ponty wrote in *The Visible and the Invisible* that 'it is at the same time true that the world is *what we see* and that, nonetheless, we must learn to see it'.[28] This brings me to my next point.

In 'Eye and Mind' Merleau-Ponty remarked that this learning-to-see may most effectively occur through the attentive viewing of our own reflections in mirrors. For, as he put it: 'The mirror itself is the instrument of a universal magic that changes things into a spectacle, spectacles into things, myself into another, and another into myself.'[29] In our everyday modes of being, we take a perfunctory approach to mirrors. Their transformative power eludes us. We fail to learn its lessons. However, over the centuries there has been an accumulation of works of visual art born precisely from artists' 'musings' upon these objects. This was a theme opened up in the previous chapter with respect to Dutch seventeenth-century paintings usually of, or involving, domestic interiors. There are also those works that bear witness to the fascination artists have had for placing themselves in front of mirrors and depicting themselves in the process of painting or drawing. Although Merleau-Ponty made no mention of a particular image, he did refer to the drawings of Matisse in this regard.[30] One of the most intricate of these, Matisse's *Artist and Model Reflected in a Mirror* of 1937 (Figure 8.2), may be seen to convey the complexities and paradoxes of Merleau-Ponty's 'intermundane space'. This drawing, originally part of the extensive private collection of Matisse drawings amassed in the first half of the twentieth century by the sisters Dr Claribel Cone and Miss Etta Cone of Baltimore, is now part of the Cone Collection housed at Baltimore Museum of Art.

As with Klee's *Park bei Lu(zern)*, here, too, it is first of all the drawing's flatness and decorativeness that is striking. This is significant because it reinforces that point made earlier: the picturing of depth and the search for depth that Merleau-Ponty associated with works such as these are emphatically not associated with linear perspective and its application.[31]

A reclining nude is immediately but not unambiguously discernible in the lower part of the image. Also immediately given is a surface covered with a confusion of broken lines. Some are longer than others, some are curved, some are scroll-like and others are straight. But all of them are more or less of the same width and tone, as if the pressure of pen on paper had remained consistent throughout. The central section of the drawing, with its fewer, longer lines, is the most open and ambiguous. Suddenly though, these lines appear to form a vortex, irresistibly drawing in the gaze. What was first perceived as flat becomes dimensional. It becomes apparent that in compositional terms the image falls into two halves along a diagonal axis running through the central area of openness from lower left to upper right, and that Matisse had depicted his model positioned directly in front of a mirror.[32] The upper diagonal of the picture becomes readable as that which the woman both sees (Matisse drawing) and does not see (the back of her own body) and in which she is presented as seeable. The two 'halves' of the image are thus expressive of the reversible intertwinings of visibility itself. Matisse sees himself as part of the visible, confusingly 'caught up in things'. And, as a viewer of the work, I have the further sensation that this Matisse who is before me, also 'sees' me, as does the woman who is both turned towards me *and* away from me. Thus I too experience the 'other side' of my power of looking.[33] The Matisse who is beside me, and yet not beside me, 'sees' *with* me. But while – to quote Merleau-Ponty again – 'our gazes cross and our perceptions overlap', they do not coincide. Matisse is in his studio; I am at home, and the image to which we are both open and in which we are both involved is lying in front of me on my desk, in the room in which I am writing, in the form of a reproduction. But I have the sense of Matisse as that 'other along *with* whom I haunt a single, present, and actual Being'.[34] As Merleau-Ponty put it, 'Essence and existence, imaginary and real, visible and invisible – a painting [or a drawing] mixes up all our categories.'[35] With this 'mixing up', vital conceptual and revelatory work is also being carried out. Concerning paintings-in-general, Madison has written:

> The picture … gets us under the skin of things in order to show us how 'things make themselves into things and the world into a world'. And it shows us how we see things by reintroducing our vision into the visible. The painter brings to expression and installs in the realm of the available the internal relation with things that for the most part we merely live. As a recuperative work, painting renders visible the phenomenon of visibility. … What a painting takes as its theme and recreates are the relations existing between 'light, illumination, shadows, reflections, colors', all those exchanges and performances which we do not normally see because we are too taken up by the thing which they present to us. For this reason, it can be said that painting is 'a central operation contributing to the definition of our access to Being'.[36]

Depth of being and body

> The painter 'takes his body with him', says Valéry. Indeed, we cannot imagine how a *mind* could paint. It is by lending his body to the world that the artist changes the world into paintings. To understand these transubstantiations we must go back to the working, actual body – not the body as a chunk of space or a bundle of functions but that body which is an intertwining of vision and movement.[37]

Merleau-Ponty placed immense value upon works of visual art (and non-illusionistic modern works in particular) because they made accessible for interrogation a space – the 'intermundane' space – that is *inaccessible* to the 'mind' as it is traditionally understood. This is a space with which idealism in its various manifestations, from the thought of Descartes onwards, is incapable of engaging. Because, within those positions, 'mind' it taken to be distinct from that which it is seeking to interrogate, because such thought 'wants no longer to abide in the visible'[38] and is an operation that purportedly occurs independently of the body, access to primary being is foreclosed. Mind, which in this system has become aligned with the disembodied perception of an all-seeing eye, is incapable of comprehending the primordial nature of self and world as that 'metamorphosis of seeing and seen which defines both our flesh and the painter's vocation'.[39] Starting from a point of initial separation between investigator and investigated, the problem of their subsequent connection must be approached through the route of intellectual problem-solving and model-building. Connection or relationship is thus a construct much as depth, within linear perspective, is that '*third dimension* derived from the other two'.[40] From such a position it comes as no surprise that the mirror's invitation into the realm of chiasmatic entanglement is habitually disregarded:

> A Cartesian does not see *himself* in the mirror; he sees a dummy, an 'outside', which, he has every reason to believe, other people see in the same way but which, no more for himself than for others, is not a body in the Flesh. His 'image' in the mirror is an effect of the mechanics of things. If he recognises himself in it, if he thinks it 'looks like him', it is his thought that weaves this connection. The mirror image is nothing that belongs to him.[41]

Picking up on an earlier point, Merleau-Ponty saw these interrogations of separated mind to inform the operationalism now dominating contemporary science, which he described as having lost the 'transcendent or transcendental foundation for its operations' and as having become autonomous.[42] Classical science, by contrast, had at least 'clung to a feeling for the opaqueness of the world, and it expected through its constructions to get back into the world'.[43] But for operational thought, the brute, existent world – the intermundane space which is our primary reality – had been denied its value as the source of knowledge and understanding. Thus 'it comes face to face with the real world only at rare intervals',[44] and claims for its 'blind operations that constituting value which "concepts of nature" were able to have for idealist philosophy'.[45] 'Thinking operationally', to repeat his words again, 'has become a sort of absolute artificialism.'[46]

For Merleau-Ponty, a primary distinction between the interrogations of the painter and those of the operational scientist revolved around the question of embodiment. The former, to repeat, 'takes his body with him' whereas the latter (behaves as though he) does not. This impacts upon space, world and self as they are inhabited, addressed and understood. Depth for operational scientists is not that 'to which we address ourselves as soon as we live',[47] but a realm from which their particular conception of interrogating mind has excluded them. Space is conceived of as a homogeneous container in which isolable objects are located. The disembodied, rational mind creates for itself a world that is unambiguous, given in transparency, purged of mystery and otherness. It is in principle wholly graspable, in which it is possible to say exactly *where* everything is.[48] As it was for the Cartesian, here too at issue was

> a space without hiding places which in each of its points is only what is it, neither more nor less. ... Space is in-itself; rather, it is the in-itself *par excellence*. Its definition is *to be* in itself. Every point of space is and is thought to be right where it is – one here, another there; space is the evidence of the 'where'. Orientation, polarity, envelopment are, in space, derived phenomena inextricably bound to my presence. *Space*

remains absolutely in itself, everywhere equal to itself, homogenous; its dimensions, for example, are interchangeable.[49]

Because operational thinkers fail to take their own embodiment into account, they fail to comprehend that space and content, world and body, investigated and investigator are given together. 'We must seek space and its content *as* together.'[50] For the painter, on the other hand, depth is precisely that lived, *relational* space which is inhabited by the body understood not as 'as a chunk of space or a bundle of functions but ... [as] an intertwining of vision and movement'. For such a body, the world is given in opacity and confusion. It is both visible and invisible (to use Merleau-Ponty's terminology), approachable and explorable, but never graspable:

> Immersed in the visible by his body, itself visible, the seer does not appropriate what he sees; he merely approaches it by looking, he opens himself to the world. And on its side, this world of which he is a part is not *in itself*, or matter.[51]

For painters, then, the question 'where?' never gives rise to an unambiguous, unproblematic 'there'. Here, neither interrogator nor interrogated can be assigned a definite place or a discrete identity; painterly interrogation is inevitably characterized by a certain porosity, openness or receptivity as well as density:

> The thinking that belongs to vision functions according to a programme and a law which it has not given itself. It does not possess its own premises; it is not a thought altogether present and actual; there is at its center a mystery of passivity.[52]

Merleau-Ponty expressed this receptivity by making a further distinction between the project of operational science and that of painting. The former, as a mode of disembodied, constructive thinking, deals with the object in general and 'makes its own limited models of things'.[53] Painting, on the other hand, 'looks toward this secret and feverish *genesis of things* in our body'.[54] As he expressed it in *The Visible and the Invisible*, 'Before the science of the body ... the experience of my flesh as the gangue of my perception has taught me that perception does not come to birth just anywhere, that it emerges in the recess of a body. ... Perception ... is nowhere else than in my body as a thing of the world.'[55] His use of the word 'gangue' here is instructive. Literally, it refers to rock or mineral matter that occurs with the metallic ore in a vein or deposit but is considered to be of no value.

In other words, then, painterly interrogations, being those of the embodied look, continually bring painters face to face with a world that is knowable only from the inside. *This* is Merleau-Ponty's definition of true thought. The world becomes a world and the thing becomes a thing only because the painter 'lends' his body to it, allowing it to express its being through him, albeit always incompletely; the relationship is never one of transparency. Indeed, Merleau-Ponty wrote of a reversal of roles between the interrogator and the interrogated:

> [The painter's question] is not a question asked of someone who doesn't know by someone who knows – the schoolmaster's question. The question come from one who does not know, and it is addressed to a vision, a seeing, which knows everything and which we do not make, for it makes itself in us. ... The painter lives in fascination. The actions most proper to him – those gestures, those paths which he alone can trace and which will be revelations to others (because the others do not lack what he lacks or in the same way) – to him they seem to emanate from the things themselves, like the patterns of the constellations. Inevitably the roles between him and the visible are reversed.[56] That is why so many painters have said that things look at them.[57]

Far from being a construction then, the painting presents precisely this self-revelation of being. It represents the 'inspiration and expiration of being'[58] – and Merleau-Ponty insisted that this notion of inspiration be taken literally.[59] It is the eye which enables this openness and the painter understands this, accepting 'with all its difficulties the myth of the windows of the soul'.[60] Citing Leonardo's *Treatise on Painting*, he wrote:

> We must understand the eye as the 'window of the soul'. 'The eye ... through which the beauty of the universe is revealed to our contemplation is of such excellence that whoever should resign himself to losing it would deprive himself of the knowledge of all the works of nature. ... Whoever loses them abandons his soul in a dark prison where all hope of once more seeing the sun, the light of the universe, must vanish.' The eye accomplishes the prodigious work of opening the soul to what is not soul – the joyous realm of things and their god, the sun.[61]

Furthermore, what is given to the eye is not pure generality but that which is both radically individual and specific and is at the same time incomplete and transcendent. 'All Flesh', wrote Merleau-Ponty, 'and even that of the world, radiates beyond itself.'[62] It is precisely in this way that both the ontological relatedness of seer and seen and their difference or otherness are confirmed:

> The world is in accordance with my perspective *in order* to be independent of me, is for me in *order to be* without me, and to be the world. The 'visual quale' gives me, and alone gives me, the presence of what is not me, of what *is* simply and fully. ... Every visual something, as individual as it is, functions also as a dimension, because it gives itself as the result of a dehiscence of Being. What this ultimately means is that the proper

essence [*le propre*] of the visible is to have a layer [*doublure*] of invisibility in the strict sense, which it makes present as an absence.[63]

The painter's effort and the fragility of the real

Merleau-Ponty wrote that the interrogations of the look, in contrast to the 'schoolmaster's question',[64] require a great and particular kind of effort. This effort was associated by Merleau-Ponty, again in *The Visible and the Invisible*, with an encounter with the fragility of the world as it presents itself to us; it is by means of the explorations of the look that 'we learn to know the *fragility* of the "real"' in which we are incorporated.[65] It is this which characterizes the difficulty of modern painting: the intermundane space it brings to expression is generative; it is 'the formative medium of the object and the subject'[66] where a 'spark is lit' between the sensing and the sensible, the seer and the seen. This also means that it is unstable and, as Cézanne knew only too well, can appear alien. It immerses us into the unprecedented and, as such, requires repeated interrogation and reorientation. Therefore, for those who are committed to its pursuit, 'depth is still new, and it insists on being sought, not "once in a lifetime" but all through life'.[67]

Johnson, again in his essay 'The Colours of Fire', emphasized the point that the painter's effort is understood by Merleau-Ponty to be intensely personal and *emotional*. At issue are also structures of feeling. Paintings reveal the spaces of desire and the dream residing within the depths of the self.[68] He wrote that 'Merleau-Ponty studied modern painting as the convergence of spatial depth and the depths of desire. He believed painting and philosophy share a natal ontological pact born of this double quest to express depth in self and world, which is the quest for transcendence.'[69] For Merleau-Ponty, this depth in self and world is the 'paradox of contact and distance, union and separation, presence and absence'. Therefore, the activity of painting is necessarily characterized by tension. On the one hand, it is fuelled by the desire to access that which, at the heart of ourselves, is 'not ourselves'.[70] On the other hand, this desire causes painters to discover, within themselves and within their culture, forces that would resist them in this task. With these they must do battle if they are to create.

The effort of the painter is to bring to visibility not that which already is but things that are not yet, things that are in the process of forming themselves within him or her.[71] Merleau-Ponty spoke of 'labor',[72] alluding above all to the labour of the pregnant woman in confinement:

> It can be said that a human is born at that instant when something that was only virtually visible, inside the mother's body, becomes at one and the same time visible for itself and for us. The painter's vision is a continued birth.[73]

Matisse's drawing *Baigneuse aux cheveux longs* (Figure 8.1), also reproduced in Merleau-Ponty's 'Eye and Mind', is a powerful mix of beauty and ugliness expressed through a certain awkwardness of line; in this regard, it contrasts with the eloquence of *Artist and Model Reflected in a Mirror*, discussed earlier. Before the *Baigneuse*, therefore, we may also speak of the *viewer's* labour as well as that of 'Being' itself. Merleau-Ponty wrote of Matisse's women that they 'were not immediately women; they became women'.[74] And of his use of line, that it 'is no longer a thing or an imitation of a thing'. The line – not the prosaic, but the *flexuous* line – 'no longer imitates the visible; it "renders visible"; *it is the blueprint of a genesis of things*'.[75] This is complex territory, and it is difficult to bring to expression. In fact, it is worth pointing out that Samuel B. Mallin, in his essay 'Chiasm, Line and Art', identified several areas of confusion in this section of 'Eye and Mind' with respect to Merleau-Ponty's notion and apparent understanding of 'genesis'. In Mallin's view, 'Merleau-Ponty is unsure whether the "flexuous line" is the "generating axis" itself (that is, a being's own emerging *phusis*) ... or merely the artist's painterly line that evokes it.'[76]

In *Baigneuse*, Matisse's lines are both fragmented and violent. They gouge and stab into and across the paper ground and in so doing force us to acknowledge that ground not as 'vacant' or transparent but as opaque, textured, dense: in part resistant; in part vulnerable. Here, though, a further area of confusion in 'Eye and Mind' must be noted. For Merleau-Ponty wrote of 'the indifference of the white paper' (*l'indifférence du papier blanc*).[77] Mallin also commented on Merleau-Ponty's terminology here, seeing it as evidence that he was not able 'to see that the line's relationship to other lines and its whole milieu is reciprocal'. He continued: 'The pre-established traits of the space bend the line as much as the reverse. The phrase "indifference of the white paper" continued to conceal and misrepresent this implication keeping it hidden and repressed.'[78]

What Merleau-Ponty did convey, however, was how the drawing, as representative of the effortful activity–passivity of the artist's body – understood as that 'intertwining of vision and movement' – enabled a woman to give birth to herself as she emerged from *his* watery womb. And how it also awakens in the viewer the sense of the body not as 'a self through transparence, like thought' but rather 'a self through confusion, narcissism ... a self, therefore, *that is caught up in things*, that has a front and a back, a past and a future'.[79] We are brought face to face with the dimensionality, the peculiar permanence, the fertility *and* the elusiveness of being. Matisse's woman reunites us with what the feminist psychotherapist and storyteller Clarissa Pinkola Estés has called the 'joyous body: the wild Flesh'.[80]

The effort of the painter, then, is not primarily an intellectual struggle to construct unshakeable 'models in thought' that are taken to reproduce the 'in-itself' of the world. Instead, it induces the emergence of a world that will always reach beyond our encounter with it and in which we are not certain of our own limits. These uncertainties characterize the 'being' of paintings.

Depiction – be it an image on canvas, a decorative device on a piece of kitchenware, or a piece of graffiti, be it figurative or abstract – always has the potential to destabilize and thus raise (productive) doubt:

> The animals painted on the walls of Lascaux are not there in the same way as the fissures and limestone formations. But they are not *elsewhere*. Pushed forward here, held back there, held up by the wall's mass they use so adroitly, they spread around the wall without ever breaking from their elusive moorings in it. I would be at great pains to say *where* is the painting I am looking at. For I do not look at it as I do at a thing; I do not fix it in its place. My gaze wanders in it as in the halos of Being. It is more accurate to say that I see according to it, or with it, than that I *see it*.[81]

The intermundane space is not a space *disconnected* from the 'there is' of the world – from the 'fissures and limestone formations', for instance.[82] It is not an idealized alternative; it is not the space of operational thinking. But neither is it a space of things or matter. It is this reality that painters force us to recognize through their commitment to that which is *only* visible – to colour, to shadows and reflections:

> Light, lighting, shadows, reflections, color, all the objects of his quest are not altogether real objects; like ghosts, they have only visual existence. In fact they exist only at the threshold of profane vision; they are not seen by everyone. The painter's gaze asks them what they do to suddenly cause something to be and to be *this* thing, what they do to compose this worldly talisman and to make us see the visible.[83]

'Painting', wrote Merleau-Ponty – and from a now-contemporary vantage point what follows is contentious as it seems to depart from his earlier insistence on the multisensorial and integrated nature of perceptual experience – 'Painting celebrates no other enigma but that of visibility. ... The painter's world is a visible world, nothing but visible: a world almost demented because it is complete when it is yet only partial.'[84] Nonetheless, the differences are more than evident between Merleau-Ponty's understanding of lived visuality as compared to the reductive ways in which the visual would be predominantly theorized during the second half of the twentieth century and into the present. In the scenario described by Merleau-Ponty, the world is given and yet not given. It is there and yet we can lay down neither its precise coordinates nor our own. The painter's gaze, as it interrogates 'light, lighting, shadows, reflections, color', will not find its questions answered with a definitive 'yes' or 'no'. Rather, as Merleau-Ponty had already written in the *Phenomenology*, 'attentiveness and wonder' will have been awakened.[85] But it is precisely because our interrogations are marked by this fundamental but energizing uncertainty that they are felt by us to be both meaningful and urgent.[86] In *The Visible and the Invisible*, this time evoking inter-sensorial experience, he used the tactile term 'palpate' in relation to vision to express this attentive but uncertain knowing:

> What there is then are not things first identical with themselves, which would then offer themselves to the seer, nor is there a seer who is first empty and who, afterward, would open himself to them – but something to which we could not be closer than by palpating it with our look, things we could not dream of seeing 'all naked' because the gaze itself envelops them, clothes them with its own flesh. Whence does it happen that in so doing it leaves them in their place, that the vision we acquire of them seems to us to come from them, and that to be seen is for them but a degradation of their eminent being? What is this talisman of color, this singular virtue of the visible that makes it, held at the end of the gaze, nonetheless much more than a correlative of my vision, such that it imposes upon me as a continuation of its own sovereign existence? How does it happen that my look, enveloping them [i.e. things], does not hide them, and, finally, that, veiling them, it unveils them?[87]

A little later, he restated that 'the look … envelops, palpates, espouses the visible things'.[88] The word *palpate* derives from the Latin *palpare*: to stroke. As a medical term it refers to a method of examining the body by the sense of touch and pressure. As Merleau-Ponty used it, bearing in mind his insistence in 'Eye and Mind' that vision must not be understood as modelled on touch in the Cartesian sense [since that model effectively closes down the transcendent aspects of visual experience that are crucial here], it suggests an intuitive mode of perceiving; the accessing of that which nonetheless remains hidden from us.

It is this mode of perceiving that must be recovered. Precisely because it retains germs of not-seeing and not-knowing, it is our means of accessing that transcendent or 'wild' being that is the flesh, for its deep, complex orders and patterns can be learned only receptively or, as it were, by 'faith'. 'Mind', by contrast, was for Merleau-Ponty a lesser form of consciousness. By believing it can see and know everything, it *fails* to see and know. As he wrote in *The Visible and the Invisible*, true interrogation must

> plunge into the world instead of surveying it, it must descend toward it such as it is instead of working its way back up toward a prior possibility of thinking it – which would impose upon the world in advance the conditions of our control over it. It must question the world, it must enter into the forest of references that our interrogation arouses in it, it must make it say, finally, what in its silence *it means to say*. … *We know neither what exactly is this order and this concordance of the world to which we thus entrust ourselves, nor therefore what the enterprise will result in, nor even if it is really possible.* But the choice is between it and a dogmatism of reflection concerning which we know only too well where

it goes, since with it philosophy concludes the moment it begins and, for this very reason, does not make us comprehend our own obscurity.[89]

Years earlier, in 'Metaphysics and the Novel', he had made analogous references to *plunging* in his discussions of the nature of 'true' communication: he wrote of our need to 'plunge into the time which both separates and unites us as the Christian plunges into God'.[90]

The insight arising from these Merleau-Pontean perspectives is that it is not by adopting an oppositional or antagonistic stance towards others that deep personal, social and political change-for-the-better is achieved. Ultimately, it is only from a place of immersion in the complex interstices, hollows and open-ended unities that characterize interrelational (or intermundane) space – where a plenitude of options may be seen to come into formation, albeit in often unanticipated forms – that it is possible to engage truthfully with broader social and political concerns. But such orientations have conventionally been confined to the realm of the aesthetic and, by and large, have been regarded as socially and politically redundant. Merleau-Ponty's orientation challenges us to declare that period of confinement over!

Visual treatises

I now emerge from more directly exegetical discussions of Merleau-Ponty's late treatments of painterly thought, intermundane space and depth, and turn to reflect on two visually oriented explorations of environments in which natural and man-made structures or systems are differently combined and in which – among other things – themes and practices of seeing, painting, drawing, filming, thinking, learning and relearning are presented for consideration. This territory was of course first introduced in the opening chapter of this book under the auspices of Merleau-Ponty's critique of conventional, philosophical nature–consciousness oppositions and has remained a differently articulated connecting theme throughout. The first case study is both painterly and historical: Koninck's *An Extensive Landscape, with a River* (1664) which, as already indicated, was the repeated point of focus for Kees Vollemans' 1997 book *The Puzzle of the Visible World*. The second is a recent work, Graham Ellard and Stephen Johnstone's 16mm film *For an Open Campus* of 2015 which was created over a number of months, in situ, at the Aichi Prefectural University of Fine Arts and Music, Nagakute, Japan.[91] Keeping Merleau-Pontean positions and perspectives in play, I approach them both in the light of Vollemans' examination of how visual works of art – in his case, a painting, and in the case of Ellard and Johnstone, a film – might offer viewers structures-for-thought akin to those of the treatise. Here it is important to underline that painting, film and treatise, with their differences, are all structures that are set up to be amenable to sight, although by no means exclusively so. As these explorations unfold, so too should their significance with respect to the issues central to *The Question of Painting*.

It may seem strange to deviate from a direct engagement with Merleau-Ponty's thought at this point. As indicated in the previous chapter, Vollemans' engagements with Koninck's painting did not draw upon Merleau-Pontean ideas. Instead, the concept of treatise of interest to him was derived from Benjamin's *The Origin of Tragic German Drama* (1928), specifically its 'Epistemo-Critical Prologue'. Arguably, though, this detour evidences precisely the complex and indirect ways in which thought operates, that is, thought understood in Merleau-Pontean terms as always embedded in and expressive of one or other *intermundane* encounter. In addition, this detour will help further illuminate the rationale for my own style of writing and thinking within the context of this book. Appropriately too, as I will show, immersion in the two visual works to be considered under the banner of 'treatise', *An Extensive Landscape, with a River* and *For an Open Campus*, will enable forms of far-seeing, deep-seeing and what Merleau-Ponty referred to as seeing-and-having-at-a-distance. Thus, useful vantage points will be provided upon the possible retrospective and prospective significance of *Merleau-Ponty's* writing and on why painting continued so powerfully to shape his thinking.

It is to Benjamin's text that I now turn. The 'Epistemo-Critical Prologue' opens with Benjamin's claim that 'it is characteristic of philosophical writing that it must continually confront the question of representation'.[92] As I have shown, this is a statement with which Merleau-Ponty would have agreed. Indeed, a major theme running through *The Question of Painting* has had to do with Merleau-Ponty's repeated attempts at reorganizing and rearticulating – that is, *re*-presenting – his own thought. In the late writing this included not only the invention and use of new terms but also his presentation of a structure – the chiasm – as that which best enabled, and best clarified, his claims about the inter- or intra-corporeal movements that are *fundamental* to viable philosophical thought. Significantly too, both Merleau-Ponty (notably at the beginning of, and throughout, 'Eye and Mind') and Benjamin – writing decades earlier, of course – had contextualized their arguments by issuing independently derived but similarly expressed warnings about the problematic, putatively all-embracing concept of 'system' that had dominated nineteenth-century thought and was continuing to inflect (and infect) then-contemporary thought. In the 'Epistemo-Critical Prologue' Benjamin wrote:

> Inasmuch as it is determined by this concept of system, philosophy is in danger of accommodating itself to a syncretism which weaves a spider's web between separate kinds of knowledge in an attempt to ensnare the truth as if it were something which came flying in from outside.[93]

What must be acknowledged instead is 'the uncircumscribable essentiality of truth in the form of a propaedeutic [that is, as a preliminary instruction

FIGURE 8.3 *Philips Koninck,* An Extensive Landscape, with a River (Vergezicht over een vlak land / literally: Vista over a Flat Terrain), *1664, oil on canvas, 95 × 121 cm, Museum Boijmans Van Beuningen, Rotterdam. Courtesy: Museum Boijmans Van Beuningen, Rotterdam / Photographer: Studio Tromp, Rotterdam.*

or introduction to further study], which can be designated by the scholastic term treatise'.[94] Merleau-Ponty, on his part, would similarly critique operational thought and constructive scientific activities. Having described the fundamentally impositional character of these techniques in that they invent investigative techniques 'regulated by an experimental control that admits only the most "worked-out" phenomena, more likely produced by the apparatus than recorded by it', Merleau-Ponty described a then-contemporary example of the 'vagabond endeavors' that emanate from such operations. 'Today, more than ever', he wrote:

> science is sensitive to intellectual fads and fashions. When a model has succeeded in one order of problems, it is tried out everywhere else. At the present time, for example, our embryology and biology are full of 'gradients'. Just how these differ from what tradition called 'order' or 'totality' is not at all clear. The question, however, is not raised; it is not even permitted. The gradient is a net we throw out to sea, without knowing what we will haul back in it. Or again, it is the slender twig upon which unforeseeable crystallizations will form. Certainly this freedom of operation will serve well to overcome many a pointless dilemma – provided only that we ask from time to time why the apparatus works in one place and fails in others.[95]

Benjamin, in an attempt to rectify the traps that he had identified in the field of philosophical thinking, had turned to the notion of 'treatise'. Merleau-Ponty would continue to draw insight from the testimonies and practices of painters. Vollemans' book, as I will show, is insightful for the way in which it brought 'treatise' and 'painting' into conversation one with the other. What then of 'treatise'?

In the 'Epistemo-Critical Prologue' at least seven defining characteristics of the treatise are in evidence. First, Benjamin argued that although treatises may appear didactic at first sight, their claims are relatively inconclusive and cannot properly be regarded as *instructive*. Secondly – and this is a point I referenced in the introduction – the treatise adopts as its persuasive methodology not the 'coercive proof of mathematics' but rather 'authoritative quotation'.[96] This makes the treatise polyvocal. Thirdly, its aim is to be educative, not didactic. According to Benjamin, its main concern is not to transmit specific facts or principles but to facilitate various modes of questioning. Fourthly, the treatise lacks an 'uninterrupted purposeful structure as its primary characteristic' but proceeds by means of digression: 'Representation as digression – such is the methodological nature of the treatise.'[97] This suggests that intrinsic to philosophical writing modelled after the treatise is a sense of never entirely hitting the mark. The lack of 'uninterrupted purposeful structure', wrote Benjamin, is also usually, but not always, marked by treatise sections that are numbered rather than titled; indeed, fifthly, thought is actively disabled from soldiering on in one direction or in one mode. Instead, as Benjamin put it, 'Tirelessly the process of thinking makes new beginnings, returning in a roundabout way to its original object.'[98] In this way, different levels of meaning can be elicited from the same point of interest. In the sixth place, and this follows closely from the fifth, at issue is a pursuit that is in some way fractured, involving stops and starts. It involves – and this is so evocatively worded – a 'continual pausing for breath'.[99] But this sense of fracture does not lead to fractured thought. For at issue in engaging with the treatise-format is allowing oneself to be caught up by and in the beauty and individuality of the details that compose its (open) whole – although without being swallowed up by them. In the seventh place, this mode of 'continual pausing for breath', defined also as a contemplative mode, disjunctive yet integrated, is presented as proper to the treatise. In order to clarify this point, Benjamin went on to make an analogy with a specific *visual* formation, that of the mosaic:

> Just as mosaics preserve their majesty despite their fragmentation into capricious particles, so philosophical contemplation is not lacking in momentum. Both are made up of the distinct and the disparate, and nothing could bear more powerful testimony to the transcendent force of the sacred and the truth itself.[100]

He continued:

> The value of fragments of thought is all the greater the less direct their relationship to the underlying idea, and the brilliance of the representation depends as much on this value as the brilliance of the mosaic does on the quality of the glass paste. The relationship between the minute precision of the work and the proportions of the sculptural or intellectual whole demonstrates that truth-content is only to be grasped through immersion in the most minute details of subject-matter. In their supreme, western, form the mosaic and the treatise are products of the Middle Ages; it is their very real affinity which makes comparison possible.[101]

How, then, did Vollemans carry over Benjamin's treatment of the treatise to Koninck's painting, which, indeed, was the product not of a medieval mindset but was produced in an early modern and proto-capitalist, mercantile context? How did he transfer Benjamin's points of concern about philosophical representation in the form of writing, to representation materialized and visualized in paint?

An obvious connector is the one just mentioned: Benjamin's own reference to the visual format of the mosaic and its effects. I will return to this. But a further evocation of the visual occurred in the 'Epistemo-Critical Prologue' when Benjamin contrasted the challenges attendant upon philosophical representation in its written form with those in its spoken forms. Specifically at issue were the ways in which speech might be amplified, embellished, expanded upon and undergirded by means of gesture, rhetorical or otherwise. Gesture might of course just as easily undermine or undo what was being said. Thus the capacities of the visual variously to illuminate and to waylay were being indicated, undergirding Benjamin's requirement that the treatise in its visual-pictorial format accord with the treatise in its visual–written form: it needed to operate in a way that *discouraged* the viewer from feeling carried away (or 'abducted', as before the pictorial mode of the trompe-l'oeil discussed in the previous chapter) and *encouraged* those processes of stopping and starting over:

> Whereas the speaker uses voice and gesture to support individual sentences, even where they cannot really stand up on their own, constructing out of them – often vaguely and precariously – a sequence of ideas, as if producing a bold sketch in a single attempt, the writer must stop and restart with every sentence. And this applies to the contemplative mode of representation more than any other, for is aim is not to carry the reader away and inspire him with enthusiasm. *The form can be counted successful only when it forces the reader to pause and reflect.*[102]

Turning, then, to *An Extensive Landscape, with a River* – and this is Vollemans' argument – we see that it presents itself in the form of a panorama (a format that we might assume intends to be exhaustive, comprehensive or complete) but has embedded into it precisely those modalities of the mosaic, the gesture and the digression as described by Benjamin. Considered within the broader rhetorics of Western landscape painting and landscape photography, the terrain presented in Koninck's painting registers as unmistakably Dutch. We see a large canvas which is divided in two, horizontally, with the earth (both land and water) represented in the lower half and the sky in the upper. Our eyes traverse fields, a cluster of tiny resting labourers, hillocks, an old farmstead and, further back, distant views of towns situated alongside a winding river. Looking up, we see a typically expansive and in this case also turbulent sky, the actions of which induce a lively interplay on the ground of golden light and deep shadow. Indeed, Vollemans remarked that the interplays of light and dark in the painting have somewhat the character of a checkerboard or chessboard, as if emitting a call to viewers to get absorbed in a clearly relational, comparative and negotiable structure. The 'artificiality' of this structure is important. Despite the painting's representational detail, it is not topographically accurate.[103] Rather, as tended generally to be the case with Dutch seventeenth-century landscape painting, it was produced from a combination of the seen, the remembered and the imagined. It was a synthesis – albeit *not* an attempt at a systemic syncretism of the kind Benjamin had critiqued and to which he presented the treatise-format as a vital counterpoint. Also of note, of course, is how the painting presents an interplay of surfaces that are experienced in life as variously reflecting or absorbing light and thus either multiplying or suppressing visual expressivity. Indeed here we may aptly recall references in the introduction to *The Question of Painting* to the variously matte and reflective surface qualities of Leah Durner's *Texts* paintings and their implications for vision and thought.

Shifting interpretative perspective slightly, and referencing a 1935 monograph on the work of Koninck by Horst Gerson, Vollemans also observed that – surprisingly perhaps, given the minute size of the human figures and man-made structures within *An Extensive Landscape, with a River*'s broader scene – the painting was not primarily a moralizing image about the fragility of human life in the face of powerful natural forces.[104] Despite the inclusion of details such as burgeoning storm clouds and a thunderous downpour, visible in the upper left-hand portion of the painting, the landscape presents itself as cultivated, domesticated and hospitable. Nor, thinking back to discussions in the previous chapter, is it primarily an invitation to viewers to become *lost* in a game of illusion: *An Extensive Landscape, with a River* is no trompe-l'oeil. Nonetheless, as Vollemans' painstaking analysis of the image revealed, Koninck *did* incorporate tropes of perspectival distortion deep within the structure of the painting so that *those* modes of visual engagement were not only alluded to but also partially elicited. For Vollemans argued that the horizon line of this 'flat' Dutch landscape is not entirely flat but takes the shape of a gentle curve, as if somewhat distorted by the implied use of a lens. Indeed, stretched across the middle of the composition, which includes the built-up areas – those towns surrounded by water – he identified what looks like an anamorphic form, an ellipse, that might offer who-knows-what further insights if seen from a vantage point other than the picture-plane/viewer orientation that is immediately proposed by this particular painting, or if viewed with the aid of an appropriate optical device.

But if the painting references a possible 'game' of pictorial illusion, more specifically, according to Vollemans, it prompts its viewers to delight in visual and mental digression, to get involved in the contemplative reflections that Benjamin had foregrounded as characteristic of the treatise. These are journeyings, in fact, akin to those also provoked by the interlocking and knotted routes embedded within the layers of ornamentation that are found in much medieval European manuscript illumination (paradigmatically in the *Book of Kells*) or provoked by the shimmering geometries of Islamic tile-work.

In *The Puzzle of the Visible World*, Vollemans followed Benjamin by making a further explicit connection between the treatise-format, the presentation of Koninck's painting and an often observed rhetorical aspect of Arabic architecture. He began by making a connection between the externally non-emphatic, non-self-aggrandizing character of this architectural mode and the non-emphatic, externally non-self-aggrandizing character of the treatise: 'The treatise', he wrote, 'is an Arabic form. ... Its

FIGURE 8.4 *Still from: Graham Ellard and Stephen Johnstone,* For an Open Campus *(16mm film, colour, sound, 29 mins) 2015. Courtesy of the artists.*

FIGURE 8.5 *Still from: Graham Ellard and Stephen Johnstone,* For an Open Campus *(16mm film, colour, sound, 29 mins) 2015. Courtesy of the artists.*

appearance is … unobtrusive, with its articulations and intricacies occurring only on the inside.'[105] He then described *An Extensive Landscape, with a River* in analogous terms. Above all, as modelled by the barely visible figures resting in one of the fields in the painting's foreground, Koninck's landscape presents itself as a structure in which the viewer is invited to become perceptually embedded by breathing deeply of its atmosphere *and* by taking the time to catch one's breath. Indeed, Vollemans argued that is only by being incorporated in *this* way that the painting's secretive inner rhythms begin to open up. As such, this painting, which at first sight presents a fascinating but nonetheless commonplace scene, starts to exhibit a strong sense of complex interiority. Here, the vista's setting up of great distances is at once also an invitation into the intimacies of drawing near: an investigative immersion in detail. And as the eye is exercised in these multifaceted ways so is the mind. This is also Merleau-Ponty's 'secret science'.

Much the same could be said of *For an Open Campus* which, thematically of course, directly refers us to a site created for the explicit purpose of learning, thinking, unthinking, rethinking and making: the campus of a university of the arts in Japan. Despite the film's obvious differences to Koninck's painting at the level of medium, it asks to be engaged with in a similar way. For as I will show, the manner in which *For an Open Campus* has been filmed and pieced together again institutes an invitation to wander, to digress and to ruminate, as well as continually to pause for breath – this time accompanied, even assisted, by the familiar but nonetheless non-humanly configured vision and insights of the film camera. Incidentally, and interestingly, given the site and subject of Ellard and Johnstone's film, it should also be noted that these phenomena, central to Benjamin's notion of treatise – that sense of unfolding vistas and of an aesthetically formatted call to pause and take in what is being presented – are also intrinsic to Zen Buddhism. As such, they are qualities that have long been intentionally cultivated in Japan at a lived, spatial level in large part through architectural means.[106]

The Aichi Prefectural University of Fine Arts and Music is situated on the outskirts of Nagoya, midway between Tokyo and Kyoto. Designed by Junzo Yoshimura and opened in 1966 – although construction continued until 1974 – it is recognized internationally as an iconic example of modern architecture; it also testifies to an alignment of traditional Japanese and mid-twentieth-century modernist architectural aesthetics. A remarkable feature of the campus is the strategically designed openness and transparency of its structures: its large, raised lecture building and canopied walkways, for instance. They seem to hover or float within an extraordinarily verdant natural setting, orchestrating divergent views onto and into it (Figure 8.4). According to the university's website, the campus was designed with two main aims. First, through formal and compositional means, it was intended tangibly to enable the school's founding educational rationale: 'to cultivate creativity, based on studies of art and applied art, that could contribute to the development of culture'.[107] In terms of the university's fine art programme, incidentally, here again traditional modes (classical Chinese landscape painting, for instance, and 'Nihonga' painting, which utilizes beautiful ground minerals and metals among other elements) intersect with the modern. Arguably, as repeatedly demonstrated by Ellard and Johnstone's film, the campus design served the university's educational rationale primarily by providing built structures which, due to their physical and visual transparency, ensure that physical works of art (including those positioned within buildings) and processes of art-making are viewable as sources of potential inspiration even from far afield. There is an evident sense, on campus, of art work (in both senses of the word) being glimpse-able from within a multiplicity of possible contexts and from varying vantage points. At issue in other words – now recalling Merleau-Ponty's *The Visible and the Invisible* – is the architectural orchestration of that intermundane space 'where our gazes are found to cross and our perceptions overlap',[108] that 'pell-mell ensemble of bodies and minds, promiscuity of visages, words, actions, with, between them all, that cohesion which cannot be denied them since they are all differences, extreme divergencies of one same something'.[109]

Secondly, and as importantly, the campus was designed to sit beautifully and as un-intrusively as possible in its natural setting, a wooded environment that includes several rare and endangered plant species as well as birds and a variety of small animals.[110] Thus, included in its architectural rationale were buildings that accommodate themselves to the contours of the ground. As such, the campus design could also be described as provoking, by example, varied embedded and sensitive considerations of the broader natural as well as human interactive structures that contextualize, condition and shape – as well as frame or contain – creative endeavour. This was a feature of the campus that was of great interest to the film-makers; as with several other of Ellard and Johnstone's projects, one of the things that *For an Open Campus* does is simultaneously explore relationships between natural and man-made space *and* – in terms of the visual traditions associated with their own craft – the conventions by which architectural spaces are represented in film.

Ellard and Johnstone, who have worked collaboratively since the 1990s, visited the Aichi campus with the intention of making a film during October and November of 2014. As they put it, however, they arrived 'at an extraordinary moment in its history'.[111] It was 'poised for change' as it awaited a major rebuilding programme, 'the estate in gentle neglect as plants, trees and wildlife slowly encroach, while academic and social life continues regardless'.[112] Almost fifty years after its inauguration, it was physically at risk. But it was also deemed unfit for purpose. It needed to undergo reconstruction and expansion, including the erection of a new music block – a controversial plan that had already generated opposition.[113] So the film asks us to enter a scene that is marked by uncertainty and imminent alteration, in which aspects of the campus's original architectural rationale might come under some degree of threat. All the more so since, upon their first encounter with it, Ellard and Johnstone observed that the campus – the openness and transparency of its structures notwithstanding – seemed to present itself as 'a world, with its own ecosystem ... a total environment ... a *Gesamtkunstwerk*'.[114] It was an entity that had a strong sense of physical and aesthetic cohesion. Indeed, a specific aspect of its visual rationale that might be disrupted was made particularly clear from Yoshimura's architectural plans for the site (four of which Ellard and Johnstone inserted among the film's end credits): the original layout of buildings was such that it established extensive sightlines. These enabled a sense of far-seeing within an overall visual environment which – again effected by the campus's open construction – might best be described as a constellation of shifting, mosaic-like fragments. To quote the film-makers with respect to the formal organization of the buildings and the centrality of orchestrated sightlines and paths of circulation:

> The emphasis here is on the way Yoshimura played with parallax, simultaneity and multiple and constantly changing views – constructed in particular through the frames provided by the canopied walkways and the piloti of the massive raised lecture building – in order to produce an experience of the campus as a set of ambiguous and changing relationships.[115]

Indeed – and this is a related point – Ellard and Johnstone understood that the success of Yoshimura's design was directly tied to the modes of actual and virtual circulation that it made possible; the realities of its usage not only as *lived* by students, faculty and visitors but also as made variously available to sight and indeed to the other senses. This focus on use was central to Yoshimura's architectural ethos in general:

> As an architect ... I am gladdened when I have completed a building and can see people having a good life inside it. To walk past a single house at twilight, with bright lights shining inside the house, being able to sense that the family enjoys their daily life; isn't that the most rewarding moment for an architect?[116]

Now, though, the campus faced sets of demands that it had not originally been designed to address. Not only did it require repair but also structural underpinning and infilling of some of its currently open architectural elements in order to be made earthquake-proof. Lifts also needed to be installed in order to make its upper levels fully accessible. Pragmatically, not only renovation but also the *restructuring,* recomposition and reorganization (or re-presentation) of aspects of the built environment were at issue.

How, then, did Ellard and Johnstone insert themselves into this scenario of institutional change? This was surely a pertinent question for the film-makers who, it should be emphasized, are also educators; both are professors in art schools: Ellard at Central Saint Martins (part of

University of the Arts London) and Johnstone at Goldsmiths, University of London. As teachers, then, they embedded themselves as participants in campus life as well as observers of it. In particular, and thanks to the facilitation of Aichi University of the Arts' faculty member Yoko Terauchi – a former student of sculpture at Saint Martin's School of Art, London (as it was then called) in the late 1970s – they worked closely with a group of students, discussing architectural topics with them and examining varied architectural plans and drawings. They then presented the students with a project brief: to collaborate for seven weeks on a large-scale visual response to the campus using a mix of 'found' as well as conventional drawing and painting materials. The students worked, on hands and knees, on an expanse of paper that had been spread out on the floor of the original, but now vacated, music building. The project – which was relatively open in terms of how it might be executed and thus contrasted with the usually more directed modes of instruction the students were accustomed to – resulted in a powerful work in which, significantly, strong geometric and abstract, thus structural and substructural, energies were evident (Figure 8.5). Filmed from a variety of angles, often in extreme close-up and often, too, from above, the students were shown working individually-yet-collectively and with a tremendous sense of quiet and prolonged absorption. The creation of the drawing was documented throughout the film in a chronological but nonetheless fragmentary fashion. Alongside the film's reflections on the campus-as-architecture and on the various ways in which the campus was navigated and used by the students, the progression of the drawing functioned as a one of the film's three important organizing features and points of recurring interest.

In terms of the film's own eventual structure and mode of presentation, *For an Open Campus* – which is just under thirty minutes in length – follows a broad, diaristic logic. It consists of seven 'entries' separated from one another by portions of black screen inscribed with simple white section titles. Here and there, shorter portions of black screen further subdivide the individual entries. Each entry references the film's three areas of thematic interest, identified earlier, but explores them with significantly different degrees of emphasis. The first is titled 'Week One: The Start of the Drawing'. Then comes 'Week Two: Landscape with a Festival' and 'Week Three: The End of the Festival'. These are focused on a student-run food and music festival on campus and on how the students had collaborated to build temporary and ad hoc cubicles and stalls, used to cook and serve food, by temporarily filling in the open, ground-level structures of the campus architecture. This is followed by 'Week Four: Landscape with a Strong Wind' and 'Week Five: Landscape with a Calm', foregrounding relations between the natural and built environment. Then comes 'Week Six: Landscape with Figures' in which an unobtrusive, static camera records the students moving along one of the college's main, raised, internal corridors in between classes. As I watched entries four, five and six I could not help but see remarkable structural and thematic affinities with two works discussed earlier on in this book: Johnson's *Within Our Gates* installation (Figure 5.4) and Klee's *Suburban Idyll (Garden City Idyll)* (Figure 6.3). The film's final portion, 'Week Seven: The End of the Drawing', is in the main a record of the carefully coordinated way in which the students roll up the large drawing, now scroll-like, and remove it from the building, the viewers of the film never really having been given an unobstructed view of the now completed piece. These entries, as I've called them, unfold between an opening sequence that combines somewhat jerkily filmed snatches of the campus and its life with previews of scenes that occur later on in the film, and between closing credits which, as already noted, are interspersed with examples of Yoshimura's original architectural plans.

The construction of the film itself with its constantly shifting visual presentations of vista and fragment – of note are mosaic-like effects conveyed not only through its patched-together filmic elements but also by the recorded play of glinting light through and upon an array of surfaces – brings me back to the characteristics and effects of the treatise-format already discussed. Overall, *For an Open Campus* is a film in which much is shown but (apart from the section titles) little is verbalized. It is non-didactic. Sound *is* important; vantages upon the campus and campus life are experienced alongside a soundtrack that sometimes consists of vocal and instrumental music and at other times comprises significant swathes of diegetic sound: bird and animal life, the wind blowing through the trees; the students talking, calling out, working, drawing and walking from place to place. But there is no narration or translation; there is no explanatory voice-over; there are no subtitles and no interviews. Therefore, in keeping with the compositional and communicative logics of the treatise and despite its own broadly chronological unfolding, the film does not forge ahead in one direction or attempt to lead the viewer towards a particular conclusion. Instead, through a mixed use of roving handheld as well as static film cameras, the film creates an atmosphere of digression or wandering – at once responsive and interrogative, following after that which has attracted attention. Its composition encourages its viewers to peruse the depicted space of the campus in stops and starts. Unobtrusively, it provides constant invitations to pause, to 'catch one's breath' and to look and indeed feel more closely. As it turns out, such associations with Benjamin's thought are not altogether surprising; his ideas have been of longstanding interest to the film-makers as witnessed not only thematically in their films but also overtly, some years ago now, in Ellard and Johnstone's academic contribution to Charlotte Pöchhacker's catalogue for the *film+arc.graz* biennale, 1995, which was on the topic of Benjamin's panorama.

My closing argument, then – and my reasons for concluding my Merleau-Pontean-focused interrogations in this book with Ellard and Johnstone's filmic reflection on a space of 'aesthetic education' undergoing imminent change – has to do with the orientational and reorientational structures that

Benjamin associated with the 'treatise' and which Merleau-Ponty associated with the figural and pictorial 'rationalities' he treated as paradigmatic for thought throughout his philosophical career. These structures are powerful because they create what we might call 'holding patterns' that are at once sufficiently situated and sufficiently open to help us inhabit meaningfully the kinds of intermediate situation that were of central concern to *For an Open Campus*. These are situations of change or imminent change, of potential identity-shift and thus of threat. As I have shown throughout this book, the capacity to create such structures (holding patterns) is vital because they allow us closely and discursively to interrogate phenomena that we might immediately want to insulate ourselves against. Furthermore, as already suggested, they do so in ways that respect the challenging sense of scale with which we might be confronted – the almost inevitable capacity of such situations to overwhelm us – while also enabling us to focus in on their points of detail, their specificities. Both of these orientations are vital in any quest to understand what could come next.

For an Open Campus (as a filmic instance of such an investigation) unobtrusively provokes large-scale philosophical questions about the spaces or structures that are required for thought, about when and how these might require reconstruction and to what ends. At issue here is the insistence, also central to Merleau-Ponty's writing, that just as space and content, world and body and investigated and investigator all evolve together and 'in confusion', so too are our capacities to learn intimately related to the spaces and places in which we attempt do so. Within such relatively unstable, transitional scenarios it is, to repeat, particularly important to attend to the *how* of our lives – to our ways of being and doing. Here, a crucial first question – but one that is perhaps rarely asked or acted upon – is this: To what degree are we able to compose or construct contexts in which to cultivate ongoing, openhanded connection within difficult circumstances without feeling immediately compelled to offer solutions? To recall Merleau-Ponty's words, again in *The Visible and the Invisible*, in such situations:

> The effective, present, ultimate and primary being, the thing itself … offer themselves therefore only to someone who wishes not to have them but to see them, not to hold them as with forceps, or to immobilise them as under the objective of a microscope, but to let them be and to witness their continued being – to someone who therefore limits himself to giving them the hollow, the free space they ask for in return, the resonance they require, who follows their own movement.[117]

For an Open Campus ends with a young woman, presumably a student, who has climbed onto the roof of one of Yoshimura's covered walkways. As Ellard and Johnstone's camera zooms in and out – as if scrambling to record an unanticipated but absolutely apt occurrence – we see that she is holding up her phone and filming or photographing aspects of the campus and campus life, which, for the viewers of *For an Open Campus*, are out of eyeshot. Like the contents of the students' rolled up collaborative drawing, at issue is a constellation of images that are, in Merleau-Ponty's non-dualistic understanding of the term, 'invisible'. Also suggested, of course, at the closure of one artistic and aesthetic interrogation of the world – Ellard and Johnstone's film – is the commencement of *a new effort*.

NOTES

Introduction

1   Véronique M. Fóti, 'The Evidences of Paintings: Merleau-Ponty and Contemporary Abstraction'. In Véronique M. Fóti (ed.), *Merleau-Ponty: Difference, Materiality, Painting*, Amherst, New York: Humanity Books, 1996 (2000), 137–68, 142–3.

2   Michel Tapié, *Un art autre où il s'agit de nouveaux dévidages du reel*, Paris: Gabriel-Giraud et fils, 1952.

3   Exhibition catalogue: *12 Peintres & Sculpteurs Américains Contemporains*, Paris: Musée National d'Art Moderne, 1953. René Magritte regarded Merleau-Ponty's engagement with art as valuable only to 'well-intentioned humbugs'. See 'Letter to Alphonse Waelhens' (28 April 1962). In Galen A. Johnson (ed.), *The Merleau-Ponty Aesthetics Reader: Philosophy and Painting*. Evanston, IL: Northwestern University Press, 1993, 336; Jean-François Lyotard later critiqued Merleau-Ponty's apparently dismissive assessments of Marey's photographs, and of the experimentations of the cubists and of Duchamp in 'Eye and Mind' (Maurice Merleau-Ponty, *The Primacy of Perception*, Evanston: Northwestern University Press, 1964, 185). See Jean-François Lyotard, 'Philosophy and Painting in the Age of their Experimentation: Contribution to an Idea of Postmodernity' (1984). In *The Merleau-Ponty Aesthetics Reader*, op. cit., 323–35, 331. In fact, Merleau-Ponty's assessments related specifically to the way movement was treated in these works. Merleau-Ponty's lack of engagement with surrealist art and writing – that of Bataille for instance – has also been commented on. Later in this chapter I will reference more positive and extended accounts of Merleau-Ponty's engagements with art. To those we might add: Remi C. Kwant, *De Stemmen van de stilte: Merleau-Ponty's analyse van de schilderkunst (The Voices of Silence: Merleau-Ponty's analyses of painting)*, Hilversum, Antwerp, 1968; Eugene F. Kaelin, *Art and Existence: A Phenomenological Aesthetics*, Lewisburg: Bucknell University Press, 1970; Dominique Rey, *La Perception du peintre et le problème de l'être*, University of Fribourg, 1978, and Linda Singer, *The Mystery of Vision and the Miracle of Painting: A Critical Examination of Merleau-Ponty's Philosophy of the Visual Arts* (unpublished doctoral thesis), Binghamton, New York: SUNY, 1991. Please see the bibliography for additional resources.

4   Anne Ring Petersen, 'Introduction'. In Pedersen et al. (ed.), *Contemporary Painting in Context*, Copenhagen: Museum Tusculanum Press, University of Denmark, 2010, 9–21, 10.

5   Terry R. Myers, 'Introduction: What has Already been said About Painting is Still not Enough'. In Terry R. Myers (ed.), *Painting: Documents of Contemporary Art*, London and Cambridge, MA: Whitechapel Gallery and MIT Press, 2011, 12–19, 12.

6   Paul Crowther, *Phenomenologies of Art and Vision: A Post-Analytic Turn*, London, New Delhi, New York and Sydney: Bloomsbury, 2013, 6.

7   Ibid., 5.

8   Ibid.

9   Ibid.

10 Ibid. Emphasis mine.

11 Erik Verhagen, 'The Horizon According to Jan Dibbets: An Endless Quest. A Childhood Memory', *Depth of Field*, Volume 2, Issue 1, June 2012. http://journal.depthoffield.eu/vol02/nr01/a02/en. Accessed 13 January 2018.

12 Marcel Vos, 'Conceptuele Kunst: Een Herinnering' in *Metropolis M*, December/January 2001-2032, No. 6, 13–15, 13. My translation.

13 Ibid., 14.

14 Erik Verhagen, op. cit.

15 Fosco Lucarelli, 'Perspective Corrections, by Jan Dibbets (1967-1969)', *Socks*, 25 April 2016. http://socks-studio.com/2016/04/25/perspective-corrections-by-jan-dibbets-1967-1969/ Accessed 13 January 2018.

16 Erik Verhagen, op. cit. See also Mary L. Coyne, *Correcting Perspectives: Jan Dibbets and an Optical Conceptualism*, Long Beach: California State University Press, 2013. http://journal.depthoffield.eu/vol02/nr01/a02/en. Accessed 13 January 2018.

17 See the 'Leon Golub, *Vietnam II*, 1973' entry on the Tate website. http://www.tate.org.uk/art/artworks/golub-vietnam-ii-t13702 for details. Accessed 3 February 2018.

18 Leah Durner, 'Artist's Statement', *Texts*, 1987. Durner wrote this statement in 1986 to accompany and contextualize the works in the series. The parenthetical instruction at the end ('See Ad Reinhardt') points to and reveals the underpinning of Reinhardt's practice for her painterly and conceptual concerns. Durner's statement on the *Texts* series also references Lawrence Wiener's *Statement of Intent* (1969).

19 Extracted from: Jorella Andrews and Leah Durner, 'Painting, Largesse, and Life – A Conversation with Leah Durner', 2018, online resource (forthcoming) an in-depth exploration of Durner's work and the philosophical and varied cultural sources that have influenced her.

20 Ibid.

21 Leah Durner in email correspondence with the author, 2 February 2018.

22 For more on this topic see Leah Durner, 'Gestural Abstraction and the Fleshiness of Paint'. In Anna-Teresa Tymieniecka (ed.), *Analecta Husserliana: The Yearbook of Phenomenological Research*, Volume LXXXI, Dordrecht, Boston, London: Kluwer Academic Publishers, 2004, 187–94. See also her more recent artist's statements as in the broadsheet Durner produced for her presentation 'Extravagant Painting: Outpouring and Overflowing' at the 2017 College Art Association Conference in New York. This was for the panel 'Immeasurable Extravagance: Proposals for and Economy of Abundance in an Age of Scarcity' which she co-chaired with the author. A copy is available on https://www.leahdurner.com/bibliography. Accessed 3 February 2018.

23 Georg Simmel, 'The Philosophy of Fashion', trans. Mark Ritter and David Frisby. In David Frisby and Mike Featherstone (eds), *Simmel on Culture*, London, Thousand Oaks, New Delhi: Sage Books, 1997, 187–206.

24 This painting and others from the Céline series may be viewed on the artist's website: https://www.leahdurner.com/paintings/1. Accessed 3 February 2018.

25 See Andrews and Durner, 'Painting, Largesse, and Life', op. cit.

26 A short but insightful account of Durner's working process may be found at Jake Lemkowitz, 'Studio Visit: Leah Durner' (Collaborators and friends). In *Front + Main: A Blog from West Elm*, 15 February 2013. Source: https://blog.westelm.com/2013/02/15/talking-with-leah-durner/ Accessed 2 February 2018.

27 Merleau-Ponty (b. 1908), died on 3 May 1961. For biographical information see Jean-Paul Sartre, 'Merleau-Ponty Vivant', *Les Temps Modernes*, 184, 1961, 304–76; Geraets, *Vers une nouvelle philosophie transcendantale: la genèse de la philosophie de Maurice Merleau-Ponty jusqu' à la Phénoménologie de la Perception*, The Hague: Martinus Nijhoff, 1971; André Robinet, *Merleau-Ponty, sa vie, son oeuvre, avec un exposé de sa philosophie*, 1963; Stephen Priest, *Merleau-Ponty*, London and New York: Routledge, 1998 and more recently Donald A. Landes, 'Chronology', *The Merleau-Ponty Dictionary*, London and New York: Bloomsbury Academic, 2013, 1–7.

28 Sara Hainämaa and Timo Kaitaro, 'Descartes' Notion of the Mind-Body Union and its Phenomenological Expositions'. In Dan Zahavi (ed.), *The Oxford Handbook of the History of Phenomenology*, Oxford: Oxford University Press, forthcoming. Draft: Available online at https://www.academia.edu/34005226/Descartes_notion_of_the_mind-body_union_and_its_phenomenological_expositions. Accessed 1 October 2017. They are citing Emmanuel Lévinas, *Totality and Infinity*, Boston, London: Kluwer Academic Publishers, 1961/1971: xx/210. For further detailed discussion of Descartes' thought in this regard, see also Thomas S. Vernon, 'Descartes' Three Substances', *The Southern Journal of Philosophy*, Volume 3, Issue 3, Fall 1965, 122–6 and J. Cottingham, 'The Role of God in Descartes' Philosophy'. In J. Broughton and J. Carriero (eds), *A Companion to Descartes*, Hoboken, New Jersey: Blackwell, 2008, 287–301.

29 It is important to note from the start that Merleau-Ponty's engagement with the writing of Descartes was prolonged and nuanced. Descartes' writing remained a crucial source for him. Again, see Sara Heinämaa and Timo Kaitaro, op. cit.

30 I will use the terms rationalism and empiricism.

31 Sartre, 'Merleau-Ponty Vivant', op. cit., 304.

32 Maurice Merleau-Ponty, 'The War Has Taken Place'. In *Sense and Non-Sense*, Evanston, IL: Northwestern University Press, 1964, 139–52, 139.

33 Ibid. Merleau-Ponty's own father had died in 1913, when he was just five years old.

34 Ibid.

35 Ibid., 139–40.

36 Again, see Gereats, Priest, Landes, and others for biographical information.

37 Alan Riding writes in *And the Show Went On: Cultural Life in Nazi-Occupied Paris*, London and New York: Duckworth Overlook, 2011, 290, that in or around April 1941, Merleau-Ponty had introduced Sartre, just released from prison camp, to Dominique Desanti and other students from the École Normale Supérieure with whom Sartre would set up *Socialisme et Liberté*. Since Autumn 1940 these students had published a tract titled 'sous la Bott' (Under the Boot) which they distributed in the metro or outside factories.

38 See for instance Robert Sokolowski's comment in his 'Appendix: Phenomenology in the Last One Hundred Years'. In *Introduction to Phenomenology*, Cambridge: Cambridge University Press, 2000, 226: 'One of the great deficiencies of the phenomenological movement is its total lack of any political philosophy'. A relatively early major exploration of Merleau-Ponty's relationship to politics is Sonia Kruks, *The Political Philosophy of Merleau-Ponty, Political Philosophy of Merleau-Ponty*, Harvester Press, 1981. For a more recent treatment see Diana Coole's *Merleau-Ponty and Modern Politics after Anti-Humanism*, Lanham, Boulder, New York, Toronto, Plymouth UK: Rowman and Littlefield Publishers Inc, 2007.

39 These were published under the direction of Stéphanie Ménasé, as *Causeries 1948* (Editions Seuil, 2002).

40 Carlos Alberto Sánchez, *Contingency and Commitment: Mexican Existentialism and the Place of Philosophy*, Albany, New York: SUNY Press, 2015, 32.

41 Sánchez, *Contingency and Commitment*. Sánchez is citing Villoro, 'Genesis y proyecto del existencialismo en Mexico', *Filosofía y Letras*, 18, no 36 (1949): 233–44.

42 Ibid.

43 See Wolfe May's article 'Merleau-Ponty's Visit to Manchester', *Journal of the British Society for Phenomenology*, Volume 25, Issue 1, 1994, 6. This was a special issue on the philosophy of Merleau-Ponty.

44 Translator's note: One is the translation of 'On' – the indefinite pronoun.

45 See Merleau-Ponty, Working Note dated 2 May 1959. In *The Visible and the Invisible*, (followed by working notes). Translated by Alphonso Lingis and edited by Claude Lefort. Evanston, IL: Northwestern University Press, 1968, 189.

46 It is worth saying at this point that Merleau-Ponty's consistent foregrounding of the 'how' rather than the 'what' of our being-in-the-world, alongside his explorations of inter- and intra-corporeality, has significance beyond the discussions in this book. For instance, I believe that it opens up a route into debates about identity and agency that are usefully positioned outside of the dualistically structured identity politics that would rise to prominence from the 1960s. For reference, selected feminist readings of Merleau-Ponty may be of interest. These include Luce Irigaray, *An Ethics of Sexual Difference*, Paris, 1984; translated by Carolyn Burke and Gillian C. Gill, London: The Athlone Press, 1993 (see, for instance, her chapter 'The Invisible of the Flesh: A reading of Merleau-Ponty, The Visible and the Invisible, "The Intertwining – The Chiasm"', 151–84); Judith Butler, 'Sexual Ideology and Phenomenological Description: A Feminist Critique of Merleau-Ponty's Phenomenology of

Perception'. In Jeffner Allen and Iris Marion Young (eds), *The Thinking Muse: Feminism and Modern French Philosophy*, Bloomington, IN: Indiana University Press, 1989; Elizabeth Grosz, *Volatile Bodies*, Bloomington, IN: Indiana University Press, 1994; and more recently Gail Weiss and Dorothea Olkowski, eds, *Feminist Interpretations of Merleau-Ponty*, University Park, PA: Pennsylvania State University Press, 2006.

47 The entire sentence is in fact: 'Ce que le Collège de France, depuis sa fondation, est chargé de donner à ses auditeurs, ce ne sont pas des vérités acquises, c'est l'idée d'une recherche libre'. From Merleau-Ponty's inaugural lecture at the Collège de France, reproduced in: Maurice Merleau-Ponty, *Éloge de la philosophie et autres essais*, Paris: Gallimard, 1989, 13. See http://www. college-de-france.fr/site/fr-about-college/index.htm Accessed 20 August 2016.

48 Maurice Merleau-Ponty, 'The Institution of a Work of Art' from his 1954-55 course Institution in Personal and Public History. In Maurice Merleau-Ponty (ed.), *Institution and Passivity: Course Notes from the Collège de France*, Evanston, IL: Northwestern University Press, 2010, 41–9, plus notes 95–101.

49 Claude Lefort, 'Editor's Preface'. In Maurice Merleau-Ponty, *The Prose of the World*. Translated by John O'Neill. Evanston, IL: Northwestern University Press, 1973, xi. The book contains material from Merleau-Ponty's Sorbonne courses La Méthode en psychologie de l'enfant and La Conscience et l'acquisition du langage and includes the following chapters: 'The Specter of a Pure Language', 'Science and the Experience of Expression', 'The Indirect Language', 'The Algorithm and the Mystery of Language', 'Dialogue and the Perception of the Other' and 'Expression and the Child's Drawing'.

50 Duane H. Davis and William S. Hamrick, *Merleau-Ponty and the Art of Perception*, New York: State University of New York Press, 2016.

51 Crowther, *Phenomenologies of Art and Vision*, op. cit.

52 Kees Vollemans, *Het Raadsel van de Zichtbare Wereld: Philips Koninck, of een landschap in de vorm van een traktaat*, Amsterdam: Uitgeverij Duizend & Een, 198.

53 Graham Ellard and Stephen Johnstone, *For an Open Campus*, (16mm film, colour, sound, 29 mins) 2015. http://www.ellardjohnstone.com/assets/ ForanOpenCampus.html. Password: campus.

54 Merleau-Ponty, *The Visible and the Invisible*, op cit., 274. See Diana Coole's essay 'The Inertia of Matter and the Generativity of Flesh'. In Diana Coole and Samantha Frost (eds), *New Materialisms: Ontology, Agency, and Politics*, Durham, NC: Duke University Press, 2010, 92–115, 96.

55 Christopher Pollard, 'Is Merleau-Ponty's Position in *Phenomenology of Perception* a New Type of Transcendental Idealism?', *Idealistic Studies*, Volume 44, Issue 1, Spring 2014, 119–38. Pollard is citing: Sebastian Gardner 2007. 'Merleau-Ponty's Transcendental Theory of Perception'. Available at http://sas-space.sas.ac.uk/375/. Pollard also makes references to assertions found in the 'Editor's Introduction' to *Merleau-Ponty: Basic Writings*, ed. Thomas Baldwin, London: Routledge, 2004. See also Sebastian Gardner, 'Merleau-Ponty's phenomenology in the light of Kant's Third Critique and Schelling's Real-Idealismus', *Continental Philosophy Review*, Volume 50, Issue 5, 2017. https:// doi.org/10.1007/s11007-016-9393-1 Accessed 26 September 2017.

56 Richard Kearney, 'Merleau-Ponty and the Sacramentality of the Flesh'. In
    Kascha Semionovitch and Neal DeRoo (eds), *Merleau-Ponty at the Limits
    of Art, Religion, and Perception*, London and New York: Continuum, 2010,
    147–66.

57 Joseph S. O'Leary's 'Merleau-Ponty and Modernist Sacrificial Poetics: A
    Response to Richard Kearney'. In Kascha Semionovitch and Neal DeRoo (eds),
    Merleau-Ponty at the Limits of Art, Religion, and Perception, London and
    New York: Continuum, 2010, 167–84.

58 Kearney, *Merleau-Ponty at the Limits of Art, Religion, and Perception*, 162.

59 O'Leary, Ibid., 169.

60 Ibid.

61 Semonovitch and DeRoo, 'Introduction', Ibid., 1–17, 1.

62 One of the courses taught here, during 1947–48, and at Lyon, was The Union
    of the Soul and the Body in Malebranche, Biran, and Bergson.

63 While at the University of Paris, Sorbonne, Hubert Damisch was among
    Merleau-Ponty's students. See Yve-Alain Bois et al., 'A Conversation with
    Hubert Damisch', *October*, Volume 85, Summer 1998, 3–17, 3–4.

64 Maurice Merleau-Ponty, *Sens et non-sens*, Paris: Les Éditions Nagel, 1948.

65 We see in the note appended to the title of 'An Unpublished Text by Maurice
    Merleau-Ponty: A Prospectus of His Work' that these pages were not written
    with an eye to publication but for the benefit of the French historian of
    philosophy Martial Gueroult in relation to Merleau-Ponty's candidacy to
    the College de France. Gueroult, who had himself just been awarded chair
    in the History and Technology of Philosophical Systems at the Collège de
    France, used it to write a report for the selection committee. The text was
    finally published in 1962 in the journal *Revue de métaphysique et de morale*
    (no 4, 1962, 401–09) and a translation was published two years later in
    an edited volume of his essays titled *The Primacy of Perception*, where
    the English translation of 'Eye and Mind' was also to be found. Indeed –
    these translations into English published by Northwestern University Press
    (alongside the 1962 translation of the *Phenomenology* by Colin Smith
    published by Routledge and Kegan Paul) were decisive in terms of the
    dissemination of Merleau-Ponty's work internationally, and its subsequent
    influence on the thought of various mid-century American artists, art
    historians and theorists.

66 See for instance the account in the Gospel of Saint Mark 15:33-39. This is
    reputedly the earliest account.

67 Five years earlier, in 1903, the Louvre had bought a smaller work, *Saint Louis,
    King of France, and a Page*, nd.

68 See Eric Storm's *El descubrimiento del Greco. Nacionalismo y arte moderno
    (1860-1914)*, Centro de Estudios Europa Hispánica, 2011.

69 Jean Cassou, *El Greco*, trans. Lucy Norton, Melbourne, London, Toronto:
    William Heinemann Ltd, 1956, v.

70 Ibid.

71 Ibid., viii.

72 Ibid., ix.

73 Steven M. Rosen, 'Bridging the "Two Cultures": Merleau-Ponty and the Crisis in Modern Physics', *Cosmos and History: The Journal of Natural and Social Philosophy*, Volume 9, Issue 2, 2013, 1–12, 1. The 'two cultures' refers to the scientist and novelist C. P. Snow's Rede Lecture titled 'The Two Cultures and the Scientific Revolution', presented in the Senate House in Cambridge on 7 May 1959.

74 Ibid., 1–2.

75 Ibid., 2.

76 Merleau-Ponty, *The Primacy of Perception*, 6.

77 Merleau-Ponty, *Phenomenology of Perception*, London: Routledge, 1962 (1989), xxi.

78 Maurice Merleau-Ponty, 'Eye and Mind'. In *The Primacy of Perception, 159-190, 190*, Evanston, IL: Northwestern University Press, 1964, 159–90, 190.

79 Merleau-Ponty, 'Eye and Mind'.

80 Ibid.

81 Merleau-Ponty, 'The Institution of a Work of Art' 41–9 plus notes 95–101, 48–9. In *Institution and Passivity*, op cit.

82 See the Gospel of Saint John, Chapter 1, especially verses 1–5 and 14.

83 Sin is an unfashionable word, and is not much used outside of religious circles. The writer Kathleen Norris has written that 'the most basic definition of sin [is] to comprehend that something is wrong, and choose to do it anyway'. (Kathleen Norris, *Acedia and Me: A Marriage, Monks and a Writer's Life*, New York: Riverhead Books, 2008, 204.) To this we might add: to know that something is right, and choose *not* to do it anyway.

84 Jn 3.16. The Holy Bible, New International Version.

85 See Josephus's reference and controversy. 'Josephus' Account of Jesus: The Testimonium Flavianum' available at: http://www.josephus.org/testimonium. htm Accessed 2 August 2016.

86 The Book of Revelation 13.8 *The Holy Bible*, New International Version.

87 Maurice Merleau-Ponty, *The Primacy of Perception*, 190.

88 The exhibition *The Forever Now: Contemporary Painting in an Atemporal World* was curated by Laura Hoptman, and took place at MOMA, New York. 14 December 2014–5 April 2015. Selected works from the exhibition are available on MOMA's website: https://www.moma.org/calendar/ exhibitions/1455?locale=en Accessed 17 July 2018.

89 Laura Hoptman, 'The Forever Now: Contemporary Painting in an Atemporal World'. In Laura Hoptman (ed.), *The Forever Now: Contemporary Painting in an Atemporal World*, New York: The Museum of Modern Art, 2014, 13–61, 14.

90 Ibid.

91 Ibid., 13.

92 Ibid.

93 Ibid. Emphasis in the original.

94 Ibid., 16.

95 Ibid., 39.

96 Ange-Aimée Woods, 'Five Questions: Brooklyn-based Visual Artist Rashid Johnson', *Colorado Public Radio News*, 12 February 2014. http://www.cpr. org/news/story/five-questions-brooklyn-based-visual-artist-rashid-johnson Accessed 25 September 2017.

97 Hoptman, *The Forever Now*, op. cit., 33.

98 Ibid., 24.

99 Ibid., 30.

100 Ibid., 35. She cities David Joselit's essay 'Painting Travesty'. In Elisabeth Sussman and Jay Sanders (eds), *Whitney Biennial 2012*, New York: Whitney Museum of American Art, 2012, 37, as the source for the notion of 'wearing the art of another'.

101 There is a growing literature on this topic. By way of example, see Sue Broadhurst, 'Merleau-Ponty and Neuroaesthetics: Two Approaches to Performance and Technology', *Digital Creativity*, 23:3–4, 2012, 225–38. Available online at http://dx.doi.org/10.1080/14626268.2012.709941. Accessed 27 September 2017.

102 Broadhurst, 'Merleau-Ponty and Neuroaesthetics', 232. She is citing Semir Zeki, *Inner Vision: An Exploration of Art and the Brain*, Oxford: Oxford University Press, 1999, 2.

103 Hoptman, *The Forever Now*, 18.

104 Ibid., 14.

105 Ibid., 15.

106 Ibid.

107 Ibid.

108 This too is a much-derided notion within today's theoretical circles.

109 Maurice Merleau-Ponty, *Sense and Non-Sense*, op. cit., 139–40.

110 This related to the idea that painters did no more than merely copy or imitate what is already there.

111 See for instance the article by Ted Loos, 'Blobs and Slashes, Interrupted by Forms: Amy Sillman Brings Together Abstraction and Figuration' in the *New York Times*, 26 September 2013. http://www.nytimes.com/2013/09/29/ arts/design/amy-sillman-brings-together-abstraction-and-figuration.html Accessed 3 February 2018.

112 Richard Kearney. 'Merleau-Ponty and the Sacramentality of the Flesh', op. cit., 149. Reputedly Merleau-Ponty *had* been a devout Catholic in his formative years.

113 Ibid., 148.

114 Maurice Merleau-Ponty, *Phenomenology of Perception*, 212.

115 See Merleau-Ponty, 'The Institution of a Work of Art'. In *Institution and Passivity*, op. cit., 41–9 plus notes 95–101, 41.

116 Maurice Merleau-Ponty, 'Summary for Thursday's Course: Institution in Personal and Public History'. In Ibid., 76–9, 77.

117 Merleau-Ponty, 'The Institution of a Work of Art'. In Ibid., 41.

118 Merleau-Ponty, 'Introduction'. In Ibid., 5–15 plus notes 80–3, 8. Constitution was of course also a key Husserlian theme.

119 Merleau-Ponty, 'Summary for Thursday's Course', Ibid., 76–9, 76.

120 See Claude Lefort, Foreword, Ibid., ix–xxxi, x.

121 Merleau-Ponty, 'Summary for Thursday's Course', 76. The emphasis at the end is my own.

122 Ibid., 48–9.

123 The theologian Eugene H. Peterson in *A Long Obedience in the Same Direction* (1980/2000) – the book's title references a saying of Nietzsche's – addressed this issue with particular clarity in a chapter titled 'Humility': 'For generations this story has been told and retold by poets and playwrights and novelists (Goethe, Marlowe, Mann) warning people against abandoning the glorious position of being a person created in the image of God and attempting the foolhardy adventure of trying to be a god on our own. But now something alarming has happened. There have always been Faustian characters, people in the community who embarked on a way of arrogance and power; now our entire culture is Faustian. (Peterson, *A Long Obedience*, 151–3). To this he added the point that ambition and aspiration (longing for something better, for things to be put right, etc.) often are confused. See also contemporary promethianism: http://www.prometheanmovement.org/index.html Accessed 2/8/2016.

124 Graham Harman, 'Vicarious Causation', *Collapse II*, 2007, 187–221, 192.

125 Merleau-Ponty, *Phenomenology of Perception*, xiii.

126 Merleau-Ponty, *The Primacy of Perception*, 9.

127 Merleau-Ponty, *Phenomenology of Perception*, ix.

128 Ibid., xi–xii.

129 Ibid., xv.

130 Ibid., xv–xvi. Aseity refers to an understanding of existence as originating from and having no source other than itself.

131 Merleau-Ponty, *The Primacy of Perception*, 189.

132 Merleau-Ponty, *Phenomenology of Perception*, xvi.

133 Ibid., 212.

134 Merleau-Ponty, *The Primacy of Perception*, 7.

135 Jean-Paul Sartre, 'Merleau-Ponty', *Situations, Les Temps Modernes*, Numéro spécial, October 1961; 17. année, no. 184–5, 322.

136 Ibid.

137 Paul Cézanne, *Mont Sainte-Victoire*, 1886–88. Oil on canvas, 66 × 92 cm, Courtauld Institute Galleries, London (Courtauld Collection). Viewable online at http://courtauld.ac.uk/gallery/collection/impressionism-post-impressionism/paul-cezanne-mount-sainte-victoire-with-a-large-pine

138 Gary Brent Madison, *The Phenomenology of Merleau-Ponty: A Search for the Limits of Consciousness*, Ohio University Press, 1981. Originally published as *La phénoménologie de Merleau-Ponty: une recherche des limites de la conscience*, Editions Klincksieck, 1973.

139 Martin Jay, *Downcast Eyes: The Denigration of Vision in Twentieth Century French Thought*, Berkeley, Los Angeles and London: University of California Press, 1993, 316.

140 Ibid.

141 Ibid., 323.

142 Merleau-Ponty, *The Primacy of Perception*, 11.

143 Crowther, *Phenomenologies of Art and Vision*, 79.

144 Merleau-Ponty, *The Primacy of Perception*, 3.

145 See, Maurice Merleau-Ponty, 'La Nature ou le monde du silence (pages d'introduction)'. In Emmanuel de Saint Aubert (ed.), *Maurice Merleau-Ponty*, Paris: Mermann Éditeurs, 2008, 41–53.

146 Merleau-Ponty, *The Primacy of Perception*, 3.

147 Ibid.

148 Merleau-Ponty, *Phenomenology of Perception*, 68. Emphasis in the original. I discuss this in *Showing Off: A Philosophy of Image*, London: Bloomsbury, 2014.

149 Maurice Merleau-Ponty, *The Primacy of Perception*, 7.

150 See *The Visible and the Invisible*, Working Note dated July 1959, 200.

151 I have chosen to draw on Colin Smith's 1962 translation, but readers may want to consult Donald Landes' more recent translation for the purpose of cross-referencing, not to mention, of course, the French originals.

152 Walter Benjamin, 'Epistemo-Critical Prologue'. In John Osborne (trans.), *The Origin of Tragic German Drama*, London and New York: Verso, 1998/2003, 28. First published as *Ursprung des deutschen Trauerspiels*, Suhrkamp Verlag, 1963.

153 Merleau-Ponty, *The Primacy of Perception*, 6.

154 Ibid., 7.

155 Ibid.

156 Ibid.

Chapter one

1 Barbara Kapusta, *The Bracket and the O*, 2016, poem, vinyl letters, pieces of jewellery.

2 *O's Vocalization*, 2016, HD 16:9 video transferred to PAL 4:3, sound Chra, 10:56 mins. Accessible via https://vimeo.com/154977040. Accessed 17 January 2018.

3   *The Promise of Total Automation*, Kunsthalle, Vienna, 11 March to 29 May 2016, curated by Anne Faucheret. http://kunsthallewien.at/#/en/exhibitions/promise-total-automation. Accessed 17 January 2018.

4   Norbert Wiener, *Cybernetics: Or Control and Communication in the Animal and the Machine*, Paris and Cambridge, MA: Hermann & Cie and MIT Press, 1948. In this book Wiener had famously defined cybernetics as 'the scientific study of control and communication in the animal and the machine' and written that 'if the seventeenth and early eighteenth centuries are the age of clocks, and the later eighteenth and nineteenth centuries constitute the age of steam engines, the present time is the age of communication and control' (Wiener, 39).

5   See Brett Buchanan, *Onto-Ethologies: The Animal Environments of Uexküll, Heidegger, Merleau-Ponty, and Deleuze*, New York: State University of New York Press, 2008. See also the useful review of Buchanan's book by Robert Vallier (DePaul University) in *Notre Dame Philosophical Reviews (an electronic journal)*, 2009, 06. 08. Available on http://ndpr.nd.edu/news/24045-onto-ethologies-the-animal-environments-of-uexk-252-ll-heidegger-merleau-ponty-and-deleuze/ Accessed 3 October 2016.

6   Maurice Merleau-Ponty, *The Structure of Behavior*, Boston: Beacon Press, 1963, 159. The source (not attributed by Merleau-Ponty) is F. J. J. Buytendijk, 'Les Différences essentielles des fonctions psychiques de l'homme et des animaux' *Cahiers de philosophie de la nature*, Vrin, IV (1930).

7   See my preliminary discussion of this in the introduction.

8   Merleau-Ponty, *The Structure of Behavior*, 3 and 4.

9   'Barbara Kapusta'. Entry in: *The Promise of Total Automation* (exhibition booklet), Kunsthalle Wien, 2016, 21.

10 The soundtrack is available at Spectral Sounds: Chra – Il_Liquid: https://soundcloud.com/spectral-sounds/christina-nemec. Accessed 18 January 2018. We are informed here that the title of the piece (Il-Liquid) refers to 'the state of a security or other asset that cannot easily be sold or exchanged for cash without a substantial loss in value. Illiquid assets also cannot be sold quickly because of a lack of ready and willing investors or speculators to purchase the asset. The lack of ready buyers also leads to larger discrepancies between the asking price (from the seller) and the bidding price (from a buyer) than would be found in an orderly market with daily trading activity'. Nemec cites Quincy Jones: 'If architecture is frozen music then music must be liquid architecture.'

11 Barbara Kapusta, *The Bracket and the O*, 2016, poem, vinyl letters, pieces of jewellery.

12 Author's email correspondence with the artist dated 23 June 2016.

13 Merleau-Ponty, *The Structure of Behavior*, 3 and 4.

14 I discuss this in Chapter 3. But see, for instance, Gary Brent Madison, 'Merleau-Ponty in Retrospect'. In Patrick Burke and Jan van der Veken (eds), *Merleau-Ponty in Contemporary Perspectives*, Dordrecht: Kluwer Academic Publisher, 1993, 183–95 and the discussions in Hugh J. Silverman, *Philosophy and Non-Philosophy since Merleau-Ponty*, Evanston: Northwestern University Press, 1988.

15 Graham Harman, 'On Vicarious Causation', *Collapse* II, 2007, 187–221, 188.

16 Harman on correlationism: 'I am a speculative realist who dislikes the correlationism that forever intertwines human and world as mutual correlates of one another … correlationism covertly bundles together two separate concepts. One of them is finitude, the idea that we cannot speak of reality outside its givenness to us. The other is the centrality of one kind of relation: that between human and world, such that we can only talk about the causal relation between two rocks insofar as we humans encounter this relation, so that humans always make up 50% of any philosophical situation.' A. Iliadis, 'Interview with Graham Harman', *Figure/Ground*, 2 October 2013. http://figureground.org/interview-with-graham-harman-2.

Quentin Meillassoux is also worth citing in this regard: 'In Chapter 1 of *After Finitude*, I define correlationism in general as an anti-absolutist thesis: one uses the correlate "subject-object" (broadly defined) as an instrument of refutation of all metaphysics to enforce that we would have access to a modality of the in-itself. Instead, for correlationism, we cannot access any form of the in-itself, because we are irremediably confined in our relation-to-the-world, without any means to verify whether the reality that is given to us corresponds to reality taken in itself, independently of our subjective link to it. For me, there are two main forms of correlationism: weak and strong [see Chapter 2, p. 42 for the announcement of this difference and p. 48 ff. for its explanation]. Weak correlationism is identified with Kant's transcendental philosophy: it is "weak" in that it still grants too much to the speculative pretension (e.g. absolutory) of thought. Indeed, Kant claims that we know something exists in itself, and that it is thinkable (non-contradictory). "Strong" correlationism does not even admit that we can know that there is an "in-itself" and that it can be thought: for this we are radically confined in our thought, without the possibility of knowing the in-itself, not even its taking place and logicity.

I then define correlationism's most rigorous contemporary opponent: the subjectivist metaphysician. The one who believes, unlike the strong correlationist (let's call him simply "the correlationist" from now on), that we can actually access an absolute: that of the correlate. Instead of saying, like the correlationist, that we cannot access the in-itself because we are confined to the correlate, the subjectivist metaphysician (let's call him the "subjectivist" alone) asserts that the in-itself is the correlate itself.' Source: Rick Dolphijn and Iris van der Tuin, '4: "There is contingent being independent of us, and this contingent being has no reason to be of a subjective nature": Interview with Quentin Meillassoux'. In *New Materialism: Interviews & Cartographies*, Open Humanities Press, 2012. Source: http://quod.lib.umich.edu/o/ohp/11515701.0001.001/1:4.4/--new-materialism-interviews-cartographies?rgn=div2;view=fulltext. Accessed 18 January 2018.

17 Harman, 'Vicarious Causation', 188.

18 Sara Heinämaa, 'Anonymity and Personhood: Merleau-Ponty's Account of the Subject of Perception', *Continental Philosophy Review*, Volume 48, 2015, 123–42, 125.

19 'James Edie Was Merleau-Ponty a Structuralist?', *Merleau-Ponty's Philosophy of Language: Structuralism and Dialectics*, 1987, 13–35, 14. The insertion in square brackets is my own.

20 Merleau-Ponty reflected on Montaigne and his legacy with great sensitivity in his essay 'Reading Montaigne' published in *Signs*, op. cit., 198–210.

21 See for instance Merleau-Ponty, *The Visible and the Invisible*, 8.

22 Ibid., 8.

23 Geraldine Finn, 'The Politics of Contingency: The Contingency of Politics. On the Political Implications of Merleau-Ponty's Ontology of the Flesh'. In Thomas Busch and Shaun Gallagher (eds), *Merleau-Ponty: Hermeneutics and Postmodernism*, Albany, New York: SUNY Press, 1992, 171–188. Finn discusses the difficulties and possibilities involved in such chiasmic interactions within the context of what she calls 'contingent' (in contrast to traditional) politics. She writes: 'From the standpoint of contingency (of chiasms, of the flesh, of subordination) politics encompasses the whole of one's life including its most personal and seemingly private moments. ... The skin, the genitals, the class, the language, the nationality, the education, the wealth, the good looks and their social and political meanings remain with us wherever we are and whatever we are doing, feeling or thinking. They *are* who we are and our struggles against the political hierarchies built upon them, against racism and sexism, for example, is one which is waged within and against ourselves and our own "subjectivity" and experience, as much as within and against the "objectivity" of the institutions which govern us and the "subjectivity" of those who rule' (Finn, 177).

24 Ibid., 181.

25 Merleau-Ponty, 'Eye and Mind', 189.

26 Hainämaa and Kaitaro, 'Descartes' Notion of the Mind-Body Union and its Phenomenological Expositions'. Draft: Available online at https://www.academia.edu/34005226/Descartes_notion_of_the_mind-body_union_and_its_phenomenological_expositions Accessed 17 July 2018.

27 Ibid., 8. Descartes' letter to Elizabeth, 28 June 1643, AT III: 691–2; CSM-K: 226–7.

28 Ibid., 12, 13. See also Endnote 12.

29 See my discussions of this in the introduction.

30 Princess Elizabeth to Descartes, The Hague, 6–16 May 1943. (Correspondence No. 301; *Oeuvres*, A. – T. Vol. III, p. 661.) Emphasis mine.

31 José Luis Bermúdez, Naomi Eilan and Anthony Marcel (eds), *The Body and the Self*, Cambridge, MA and London: MIT Press, 1995, 1.

32 John Bannan, *The Philosophy of Merleau-Ponty*, San Diego, CA: Harcourt, Brace and World, 1967, 5. Here, Bannan was making reference to material in Merleau-Ponty's 1935 review of Scheler's book *Ressentiment* entitled 'Christianisme et ressentiment' (*La Vie Intellectuelle*, 7e année, nouvelle série, T. XXXVI, 10 June 1935, 278–306).

33 Ibid.

34 Merleau-Ponty, 'Etre et avoir'. In *La Vie Intellectuelle*, 8e année, nouvelle série, T. XLV, 10 October 1936, 98–106.

35 In *The Structure of Behavior* Merleau-Ponty referred to the following texts by Husserl: 'Formale und transzendentale Logik: Versuch einer Kritik der

logischen Vernunft' [Formal and transcendental logic: an attempt at a critique
of logical reason.] In: *Jahrbuch für Philosophie und phänomenologische
Forschung*, 10, 1929. Halle a.d.S. v–xiii; 1–298; 'Ideen zu einer reinen
Phänomenologie und phänomenologischen Philosophie' [Ideas pertaining
to a pure phenomenology and to a phenomenological philosophy]. In
Jahrbuch für Philosophie und phänomenologische Forschung, 1 Halle a.d.S.
(1913), 1–323; *Méditations cartésiennes. Introduction à la phénoménologie*
[*Cartesian Meditations: Introduction to Phenomenology*]. Gabrielle Peiffer and
Emmanuel Levinas (trans), Bibliothèque de la Société française de Philosophie,
Paris: A. Colin, 1931; 'Vorlesungen zur Phänomenologie des inneren
Zeitbewusstseins' [On the Phenomenology of the Consciousness of Internal
Time.] *Jahrbuch für Philosophie und phänomenologische Forschung*, 9. Halle
a.d.S: Max Niemeyer, 1928, 367–498.

36 Merleau-Ponty, *The Structure of Behavior*, 3.

37 See also Jorella Andrews, 'The Virtual Intersection: A Meditation on Domestic
Virtue'. In Fran Lloyd and Catherine O'Brien (eds), *Secret Spaces, Forbidden
Places: Re-thinking Culture*, New York and Oxford: Berghahn, 2000, 171–83
where this painting was made a point of focus.

38 Ibid.

39 Merleau-Ponty, *The Structure of Behavior*, 4.

40 Ibid., 156.

41 By his use of the term *naïve*, Merleau-Ponty makes reference to Gestalt
terminology. For instance, Wolfgang Köhler in *Gestalt Psychology* wrote
that the starting point for psychology is 'the world as we find it, naively and
uncritically' and, again, that 'the whole development must begin with a naïve
picture of the world' (New York: Mentor Books, 1947, 3).

42 Merleau-Ponty, *The Structure of Behavior*, 7.

43 Emphasis mine.

44 Emphasis mine.

45 Merleau-Ponty, *The Structure of Behavior*, 7. Emphasis mine.

46 Ibid., 188.

47 As Madison put it: 'Merely descriptive thought is a thought which is still naïve'
(Madison, 1981, 146–7).

48 Merleau-Ponty, *The Structure of Behavior*, 189.

49 Ibid., 4.

50 Ibid., 7. A *vis a tergo* is a force acting from behind.

51 Emphasis mine.

52 Bannan, *The Philosophy of Merleau-Ponty*, 28. His definition of the
natural attitude or 'objectivist thinking' is sourced in the *Phenomenology
of Perception*, 320. He wrote that Merleau-Ponty's criticism of the natural
attitude 'leads to the restoration of the links between the thing and the
embodied subject, and the substitution of phenomena for nature. It is, in short,
a version of the *reduction* of the natural attitude'.

53 Merleau-Ponty, *The Structure of Behavior*, 188.

54 Gestalt theory, introduced to France by Aron Gurwitsch (Jay, 1993, 299) makes reference to 'images', 'goal-directed behaviour' and 'Ego' at a time when behaviourism, which was then dominant, had rejected from its descriptions and terminology such mentalistic terms typical also of everyday speech. See also David J. Murray, *Gestalt Psychology and the Cognitive Revolution*, New York, London: Harvester Wheatsheaf, 1995.

55 Max Wertheimer, 'Experimentelle Studien über das Sehen von Bewegung', *Zeitschrift für Psychologie*, LXI (1912). See Johan Wagemans, 'Historical and Conceptual Background: Gestalt Theory'. In Johan Wagemans (ed.), *The Oxford Handbook of Perceptual Organization*, Oxford: Oxford University Press, Forthcoming. http://www.gestaltrevision.be/pdfs/oxford/Wagemans-Historical_and_conceptual_background_Gestalt_theory.pdf Accessed 11 October 2017. Also of note is Viktor Sarris's earlier paper 'Max Wertheimer on Seen Motion: Theory and Evidence', *Psychological Research*, September 1989, Volume 51, Issue 2, 58–68. The nineteenth-century experimental psychologist Christian von Ehrenfels' essay 'On Gestalt qualities' of 1890 was an earlier founding document. Significantly, in Vienna, von Ehrenfels had been a student of Franz Brentano, one of the founding fathers of phenomenology.

56 Wagemans, 'Historical and Conceptual Background', 3.

57 Geraets, *Vers une nouvelle philosophie transcendantale*, 10.

58 Merleau-Ponty, 'Working Note: May 2, 1959'. In *The Visible and the Invisible*, 189. Gestalt theory therefore challenges the objectivist prejudice characteristic of empiricism. Madison wrote: 'Merleau-Ponty alludes to the work of German authors such as Weiszäcker and Goldstein in order to show that the reflex is not merely the result of independent, juxtaposed mechanisms and is not to be had by adding up elements, each of which would have its own reality. For the Gestaltists the reflex can be understood only by means of the notion of form. A reflex occurs only in response to a stimulus which "is not a sum of partial stimuli … but rather a constellation, an order, a whole"' (SB, 14; SC, 12). 'There are, therefore, no predetermined "reflex arcs". What exists is a reciprocal conditioning or constitution between stimulus and reaction where the reflex is a response to a global constellation of stimuli but also where the stimuli form a whole only by being subjected to "the descriptive norms of the organism" (SB, 28; SC, 28). A "cause" is therefore a cause only in regard to an organism which "constitutes" it as such. Thus, in order to describe the relations between the organism and its environment, one is led to give up the notion of a *linear causality* for that of a *circular causality*' (SB, 15; SC, 13). Madison, 1981, 8–9. Bannan (1967, 33) wrote: 'Merleau-Ponty recalls that physiologists have never been able to eliminate the response of the organism from the definition of the stimulus. The most familiar example of this is the "painful" stimulus. The inclusion of the organism in the definition of the stimulus offers an example of something that his discussion of rudimentary behaviour had indicated generally: the organism imposes its own conditions as variable between the given stimulus and the expected response, and therefore it *cannot be taken as passive*.'

59 Madison, op. cit., 148.

60 Ibid., 2–3.

61 Wagemans, 'Historical and Conceptual Background', 18. He cites R. Kimchi, M. Behrman, and C. R. Olson (eds), *Perceptual Organization in Vision. Behavioral and Neural Perspectives*, Mahwah, NJ: Erlbaum, 2003.

62 Ibid., 18. He references in this regard an essay by B. Pinna, 'New Gestalt Principles of Perceptual Organization: An Extension from Grouping to Shape and Meaning', *Gestalt Theory*, Volume 32, 2010, 11–78.

63 Ibid.

64 The nature of Merleau-Ponty's methodology thus constitutes an alternative to the Hegelian dialectical model (thesis-antithesis-synthesis).

65 Merleau-Ponty, *The Structure of Behavior*, 4.

66 Paul Ricoeur was critical of Merleau-Ponty's position, which he described as a 'philosophy of finitude': 'One can only wonder ... how the philosophical act [is] possible if man is so completely identified with his insertion into his field of perception, action, and life' (Ricoeur, 'Existential Phenomenology'. In. Edward Ballard and Lester Embree (trans.), *Husserl: An Analysis of his Phenomenology*, Evanston: Northwestern University Press, 1967, 209.) Cited by Thomas W. Busch in 'Perception, Finitude, and Transgression: A Note on Merleau-Ponty and Ricoeur'. In Thomas W. Busch and Shaun Gallagher (eds), *Merleau-Ponty: Hermeneutics and Postmodernism*, Albany, New York: State University of New York Press, 1992, 25–35, 25.

67 Such a philosophy, conceived of as having what Kaja Silverman calls 'an orientation towards openness' (openness to new formulations, new definitions and new orientations), has been termed 'non-philosophy'. (Silverman (ed.), *Philosophy and Non-philosophy since Merleau-Ponty*, 1–2.) This openness, arguably, is a defining characteristic of Continental Philosophy, understood as a generic term covering such modes of thought as phenomenology, existentialism, structuralism, semiology, post-structuralism, hermeneutics, deconstruction, and so on. Merleau-Ponty, in his lecture course Philosophy and Non-philosophy since Hegel, given at the *Collège de France* in 1960–61, opened by writing: 'No battles occur between philosophy and its adversaries. Rather what happens is that philosophy seeks to be philosophy while remaining non-philosophy, i.e. a "negative philosophy" (in the sense of a "negative theology" [he was citing Pseudo-Dionysius, and the practice of positing God in terms of what He is not]). "Negative philosophy" has access to the absolute, not as "beyond", as a positive second order but as another order which must be on this side, the double – inaccessible without being passed through. True philosophy scoffs at philosophy, since it is a-philosophical' (Silverman, *Philosophy and Non-philosophy since Merleau-Ponty*, 1988, 9). Such an outlook informs Madison's essay, 'Did Merleau-Ponty have a Theory of Perception?', Thomas W. Busch and Shaun Gallagher (eds), *Merleau-Ponty: Hermeneutics and Postmodernism*, 1992, 83–106.

68 Merleau-Ponty made frequent references in this work to findings from developmental psychology. His reason for doing so here appears to be to show that common features connect both the perceptual experiences of the naïve conscious and those of our earliest experiences of interaction with the world. This suggests to him to they are thus both primordial and persisting – and therefore, in his view, of first importance.

69 Jean Piaget, *Le Représentation du monde chez l'enfant*, Paris, 1926. Piaget (1896–1980), a Swiss psychologist, was the first to make a systematic study of the acquisition of understanding in children (developmental psychology). His basic view was that the mind of the child evolves through a series of set stages to adulthood. The child constantly creates and recreates his own model of reality, achieving mental growth by integrating simpler concepts into higher level concepts at each stage.

70 Merleau-Ponty, *The Structure of Behavior*, 188–9.

71 Merleau-Ponty referred in his notes to: Shinn, 'Notes on the Development of a Child', *University of California Studies*, I, 1–4, 1893–99.

72 Merleau-Ponty, *The Structure of Behavior*, 166. The words in the square brackets are my own insertion.

73 Ibid., 224. Emphasis mine.

Chapter two

1 Maurice Merleau-Ponty, Introduction to 'Institution in Personal and Public History'. In *Institution and Passivity: Course Notes from the Collège de France* (1954–55), 5–15, 6.

2 Maurice Merleau-Ponty, 'An Unpublished Text by Maurice Merleau-Ponty: A Prospectus of His Work'. In James M. Edie (ed.), *The Primacy of Perception*, Evanston, IL: Northwestern University Press, 1964, 7.

3 H. A. Ruger, 'Psychology of Efficiency': An Experimental Study of the Processes Involved in the Solution of Mechanical Puzzles and In the Acquisition of Skill in Their Manipulation. In *Archives of Psychology*, XV, June 1910. Columbia Contributions to Philosophy and Psychology, Col 19, No 2. New York, The Science Press.

4 Ibid., 2.

5 Merleau-Ponty, *The Structure of Behavior*, 103. It goes without saying that the piecemeal approach to teaching and learning that was adopted by Ruger, in order to evidence its unproductive character, still characterizes the educational regimes that are adopted in most mainstream and elite schools and universities.

6 Ibid.

7 Ibid.

8 Ibid., 104.

9 Bannan, *The Philosophy of Merleau-Ponty*, 39.

10 Merleau-Ponty, *The Structure of Behavior*, 104. Emphasis mine. (Source: Buytendijk, 'Les Différences essentielles des fonctions psychiques de l'homme et des animaux', *Cahiers de philosophie de la nature*, Vrin, IV, 1930, 46–7.)

11 Ibid., 45. (Source: Buytendijk, 'Le Cerveau et l'Intelligence', *Journal de Psychologie*, XXVIII, 1931, 257.)

12 Ibid., 45–6.

13 Ibid., 105.

14 Bannan, *The Philosophy of Merleau-Ponty*, 39.

15 Merleau-Ponty, *The Structure of Behavior*, 105.

16 Ibid., 104.

17 Ibid., 162. Merleau-Ponty indicated in the footnotes that he was making use of Husserl's terminology in 'Ideen zu einer reinen Phänomenologie und phänomenologische Philosophie' I, in *Jahrbuch für Philosophie und phänomenologische Forschung*, Halle, H. Niemeyer, I (1913) and in *Cartesian Meditation*s (the French edition of 1931).

18 Bannan (*The Philosophy of Merleau-Ponty*, 41) wrote: 'What is distinctive of the symbol, however, is its relatedness, not simply with the thing or event for which it stands, but *with other symbols ... .*' These lateral relations among symbols open up the 'possibility of varied expressions of a same theme... which is lacking in animal behaviour'.

19 Merleau-Ponty, *The Structure of Behavior*, 175–6. Emphasis mine.

20 Ibid., 173.

21 Ibid., 175.

22 Ibid., 120.

23 Ibid., 175.

24 This matter of perceiving a sense of continuity within change relates to discussions of the development of object constancy in infants in relation to things, other persons and the experience of self. Here, Merleau-Ponty implied that object constancy is an innate propensity. Recent treatments of this subject are found in Bermúdez, Marcel and Eilan's compilation. See, for instance, Andrew N. Meltzoff and M. Keith Moore, 'Infants' Understanding of People and Things: From Body Imitation to Folk Psychology', 43–69, and James Russell, 'At Two with Nature: Agency and the Development of Self-World Dualism', 127–51.

25 Referring to another experiment, Merleau-Ponty wrote: 'A dog which is trained to jump up on one chair on command, then to pass from it onto a second chair, will never use – lacking a chair – two stools and an armchair which are presented to him' (Merleau-Ponty, *The Structure of Behavior*, 120). (Sourced in Buytendijk and Fischel, 'Über die Reaktionen des Hundes auf menschliche Wörter', *Archives néerlandaises de physiologie*, XIX (1934); cf. Buytendijk, Fischel and Ter Laag, 'Über die Zieleinstellung von Ratten und Hunden', 455 sqq.) This is evidence of the dog's inability to generalize from a given concrete situation.

26 Merleau-Ponty, *The Structure of Behavior*, 118. Emphasis mine.

27 Ibid.

28 Ibid.

29 As Theodore F. Geraets put it, the animal's position is characterized by its inability to change its actual point of view for an alternative one (*le point de vue 'X'*). Thus, the animal cannot imagine itself from the (virtual or actual)

point of view of another object or organism in its world. Theodore F. Geraets, *Vers une nouvelle philosophie transcendantale*.

30 Merleau-Ponty, *The Structure of Behavior*, 175–6.

31 Ibid., 175.

32 When Merleau-Ponty used the term 'normal', here and elsewhere in his writings, he did so uncritically. What he meant by 'normal' is *integrated*. For a discussion of the concept of normality, see Anthony J. Steinbock, 'Phenomenological Concepts of Normality and Abnormality', *Man and World*, Volume 28, 1995, 241–60. Also relevant are Margrit Shildrick's discussions of the terms natural/unnatural in her essay 'Posthumanism and the Monstrous Body', *Body and Society*, 1996, 1–15.

33 Merleau-Ponty, *The Structure of Behavior*, 180.

34 Ibid., 130.

35 Ibid., 203.

36 See: Matthew Simunovic, '"The El Greco" Fallacy', *JAMA Ophthalmology*, Volume 132, Issue 4, April 2014, 491–4. doi: 10.1001/jamaophthalmol.2013.5684. He wrote: 'To what extent does an artist's work represent his or her perceptual world, and to what extent can attributes of his or her work be ascribed to sensory defects? These issues lie at the center of a conjecture more than a century old, which has been termed the El Greco fallacy. The El Greco fallacy posits that the elongation evident in El Greco's art reflects an underlying perceptual elongation of objects caused by astigmatism. The "logical" refutation of this theory argues that any perceptual elongation that El Greco might have experienced as a result of astigmatism would have caused not only his subjects to be elongated but also his canvas. Hence, it should have been unnecessary for him to elongate his paintings to match his perception. This objection is important because it warns us against drawing the erroneous conclusion that an artist's work represents a facsimile of his or her perception. However, an analysis of the effects of astigmatism on the retinal image suggests that this "logical" refutation of the El Greco fallacy promulgates another fallacy – that of astigmatism as a source of a constant perceptual error.'

37 Merleau-Ponty, *The Structure of Behavior*, 203. Emphasis mine.

38 Here I cannot help thinking, for instance, of the 're-branding' of disability within the realm of athletics, and specifically the Paralympics. See the UK campaign: 'We're The Superhumans' for the 2016 Rio Paralympics. Trailer'. Viewable at https://www.youtube.com/watch?v=IocLkk3aYlk. Accessed 19 January 2018.

39 Merleau-Ponty, *The Structure of Behavior*, 130.

40 Ibid., 203.

41 The source for this quotation is J. Cassou, *Le Greco*, Paris, Rieder, 1931, 35.

42 Merleau-Ponty, *The Structure of Behavior*, 203.

43 All communication, even when it occurs within an apparently homogenous group, should thus be regarded as cross-cultural. For example, experience shows that men and women who share the same language, and in this respect

may be regarded as a homogenous group, nonetheless tend to *use* it differently (shared terms have different connotations).

44 A further dimension to these discussions of genuine unity versus an 'apparent' or 'stereotyped' unity might be also to bring into play the notion of pseudo-unities. Here, Chris Hedges' comparison of stereotypes and pseudo-events in *Empire of Illusion: The End of Literacy and the Triumph of Spectacle* (New York: Nation Books, 2009) is insightful. 'Pseudo-events' are described as 'far more pernicious than stereotypes' because 'they do not explain reality, as stereotypes attempt to do, but replace reality' (Hedges, *Empire of Illusion*, 51). See also Endnote 48.

45 Merleau-Ponty, *The Structure of Behavior*, 203–4. Emphasis mine.

46 Ibid., 204.

47 Ibid., 177–8.

48 Merleau-Ponty discussed the matter of genuine versus superficial integration elsewhere in *The Structure of Behavior* within the context of ideology. Here, false unity occurs when the relationship between beliefs or values and a person's adherence to them is again of a purely external nature. In such cases, beliefs and values fail to become consistently, convincingly and flexibly dispositional. In his words: 'There is a vague love which attaches itself to the first object which it accidentally encounters; there is an art and a religion the whole true meaning of which is to compensate in a virtual world for real failures or constraints; there is finally, as Nietzsche said, an adherence to values of sacrifice which is only a form of vital impotence and of "impoverished life". These pseudo-solutions are recognisable from the fact that the being of the person never coincides with what he says, what he thinks, or even with what he does. False art, false sanctity and false love which *seek* like the seminary companions of Julien Sorel, to "perform significant acts" give to human life only a borrowed significance, effect only an ideal transformation, a flight into transcendent ideas. But there are other men, capable of integrating into their existence, by unifying it, what in the preceding ones was only ideological pretext, and these *would be* truly men. With respect to them, the causal explanations of Freud would always be anecdotal; they would account only for the most external aspects of a true love just as, according to Freud himself, physiological explanations do not exhaust the content of a dream. Mental acts would have their own proper meaning and their own internal laws' (Merleau-Ponty, *The Structure of Behavior*, 180).

Chapter three

1 Frances Morris, 'Introduction', *Paris Post-War: Art and Existentialism 1945-1955*, London: Tate Gallery Publications, 1993, 15–24, 16.

2 Ibid.

3 See also Alex Potts' discussions of Wols in *Experiments in Modern Realism: World Making in Postwar European and American Art*, New Haven and London: Yale University Press, 2013 and his 'Postwar Art and the

Psychoanalytic Imaginary' (In S. Alexander and B. Taylor (eds), *History and Psyche*, Palgrave Studies in Cultural and Intellectual History, New York: Palgrave Macmillan, 2012, 265–81) on broader issues relating to L'art informel, the significance here of the physicality of paint and of material process.

4   Jean-Paul Sartre, 'Doigts et non-doigts'. In Jean-Paul Sartre, Henri-Pierre Roché and Werner Haftmann (eds), *Wols en personne*, Paris, 1963, pp. 10–21.

5   Tate Gallery label, April 2008, relating to: Wols, *Untitled*, c 1944–5. http://www.tate.org.uk/art/artworks/wols-title-not-known-t04845. Accessed 13 October 2017.

6   Hector E. Henry van Loon, 'The Photography of Wolfgang Schulz'. In: *Filmliga: Onafhankelijk Maandblad Voor Filmkunst, Film, Smalfilm, Radio, Gramafoon, Foto*, Vol, 6 no 2, 20 Dec 1932, 48–9. See also: Christine Mehring, 'A Contemporary Look at Wols'. In *Wols Photographs*, Busch-Reisinger Museum, Harvard University Art Museums, Cambridge, Massachusetts, ex cat, 1999, 39–40. The exhibition took place from 13 February to 25 April 1999.

7   See: Frances Morris, 'Wols (1913–1951)' in *Paris Post War* (op. cit.) 181–2, 182. She references: Jean-Paul Sartre, 'Doigts et non-doigts'. In Jean-Paul Sartre, Henri-Pierre Roché and Werner Haftmann (eds), *Wols en personne*, op cit.

8   Crowther, *Phenomenologies of Art and Vision*, 35.

9   Fóti, 'The Evidences of Painting', 163. She is citing Claude Lefort, 'Qu'est-ce que voir?' In *Sur une colonne absente: Ecrits autour de Merleau-Ponty*, Paris: Gallimard, 1978, 140–55, 147.

10   Crowther, *Phenomenologies of Art and Vision*, 32. (He is citing Richard Wollheim, *Art and its Objects* (Second Edition, Cambridge: Cambridge University Press, 1980) 12–21. The first edition: Harper and Row, 1968.)

11   Ibid., 29.

12   All quotations from ibid., 29.

13   Ibid., 33.

14   He was not, however, alone in continuing to hold Cézanne in high regard. As Wilson has noted, Cézanne's legacy remained strong within the post-war period: 'A "school of Cézanne" was formed in Aix-en-Provence during and after the Second World War that affected the semi-abstract landscape paintings of "lyrical abstractionists" such as Pierre Tal-Coat' (Sarah Wilson, 'Paris Post War: In Search of the Absolute'. In Frances Morris (ed.), *Paris Post War: Art and Existentialism 1945-55*, London: Tate Gallery, 1993, 25–52, 30). Cézanne's legacy was particularly evident in the work of one of the most popular painters of the time, André Marchand. It was also a significant source for the Paris-based Dutch painter Bram van de Velde (1895–1981). Indeed, comparing the writing of Sartre and Merleau-Ponty, Wilson proposed that 'before Sartre's writings on the art of Wols or Giacometti, Merleau-Ponty produced a paradigm of the 'existentialist' artist full of contemporary resonances' (Wilson, 31).

15 Derek Taylor, 'Phantasmic Genealogy'. In Thomas W. Busch and Shaun Gallagher (eds), *Merleau-Ponty: Hermeneutics and Postmodernism*, Albany New York: State University of New York Press, 1992, 149–60.

16 Ibid., 150.

17 Ibid.

18 Madison, 'Merleau-Ponty in Retrospect', 183–95. At the end of this extract, Madison is citing Merleau-Ponty, *Phenomenology of Perception*, xx–xxi.

19 Originally published as *Phénoménologie de la Perception*, Paris, Gallimard, 1945. Translated into English by Colin Smith as *Phenomenology of Perception*, Routledge and Kegan Paul Ltd., 1962.

20 Interestingly, in her 'Paris Post War' essay, Wilson goes on to state that Merleau-Ponty's 'subsequent abandonment of the problems of the individual, the status of individual creation and individual failure, to concentrate on broader political dilemmas is telling. By considering "Cézanne's Doubt" in juxtaposition with *Humanism and Terror*, the relative claims of artist, philosopher and the discourse on art versus political writing and political engagement are firmly contextualized in the years 1945–47, with the latter, finally, prioritized' (Wilson, 'Paris Post War', 31).

21 Merleau-Ponty, *Phenomenology of Perception*, 3.

22 Ibid., 4.

23 Ibid., 63.

24 Ibid.

25 Ibid.

26 Ibid. Italics in the original.

27 Ibid.

28 Ibid., 3.

29 There are profound analogies here with Wollheim's description of the Ur-scene of painting as described by Crowther in his chapter 'Painting as an art'. Crowther writes that Wollheim's model of the fundamental constituents of (all) painting begins with 'an agent placed next to a support, who places marks on the support with a charged instrument' (Crowther, *Phenomenologies of Art and Vision*, 10).

30 Merleau-Ponty, *Phenomenology of Perception*, 3–4.

31 Ibid., 6. Emphasis mine.

32 It is important to note, however, that he did not consider his treatment of this matter to be sufficient in the *Phenomenology*. See his references to an intended work entitled *The Origin of Truth* in 'An Unpublished Text' (*The Primacy of Perception*, 8) and in 'The Metaphysical in Man', *Sense and Non-Sense*, 94, Endnote 13. Aspects of this work-in-progress would become incorporated into *The Visible and the Invisible*.

33 Also of relevance is the work of Heidegger, notably his *Being and Time* of 1927. However, Merleau-Ponty wrote in the preface to the *Phenomenology* that, as he saw it, 'the whole of *Sein und Zeit* springs from an indication given by Husserl and amounts to no more than an explicit account of the "natürlicher Weltbegriff" or the "Lebenswelt" which Husserl, towards the end

of his life, identified as the central theme of phenomenology' (Merleau-Ponty, *Phenomenology of Perception*, vii). Thus he made only a few direct references to Heidegger, these occurring mainly in the final section of this work, in the chapter entitled 'Temporality', and frequently only in the footnotes.

34 Merleau-Ponty's position concerning the embodied nature of perception and his attempts, in his various writings, to elaborate how the world is given to us in perception made his thought not dissimilar to that of the American experimental psychologist J. J. Gibson (*The Perception of the Visual World*, 1950, and *The Ecological Approach to Visual Perception*, 1979).

35 Merleau-Ponty, *Phenomenology of Perception*, x–xi.

36 This theme is explored by Gary Brent Madison in *The Phenomenology of Perception: A Search for the Limits of Consciousness*, 1981.

37 This is in contrast with the rationalist and empiricist positions. For rationalism, the world of perception is regarded as unintelligible, for empiricism it is an inchoate jumble of discrete sensations that can be assigned meaning only through the operations of a separated intellect, that is, through the operation of memory or the creation of associations between present and past configurations. As already discussed, Merleau-Ponty was influenced by insights drawn from Gestalt theory here. However, it is important to note that the German word 'Prägnanz' – as in the Gestalt 'Law of Prägnanz' – refers not to pregnancy but to the Gestalt theorists' observation that, when confronted with complex or ambiguous information, we tend to perceive it in the simplest possible way – often breaking complex figures as juxtapositions of simple, readable shapes. Prägnanz refers to a 'good', simple or concise form. The German equivalent of the English word 'pregnant' is 'schwanger'.

38 Merleau-Ponty, 'The Primacy of Perception and Its Philosophical Consequences' (a summary and defence of the *Phenomenology*) was presented to the Société française de philosophie on 23 November 1946. In *The Primacy of Perception*, 12–42, 15.

39 Ibid., 12.

40 To repeat: 'It is necessary that meaning and signs, the form and matter of perception, be related from the beginning and that, as we say, the matter of perception be "pregnant with its form"' (Ibid., 15).

41 Maurice Merleau-Ponty, 'The Film and the New Psychology'. In *Sense and Non-Sense*, Evanston, IL: Northwestern University Press, 1964, 48–59.

42 Ibid., 54.

43 Ibid., 58.

44 Ibid., 58 and 59.

45 Merleau-Ponty, 'The Primacy of Perception', 12.

46 Bannan, *The Philosophy of Merleau-Ponty*, 60.

47 Merleau-Ponty wrote: 'The meaning which I ultimately discover [in perception] is not of the conceptual order. ... In other words, the synthesis which constitutes the unity of the perceived objects and which gives meaning to the perceptual data is not an intellectual synthesis. Let us say with Husserl that it is a "synthesis of transition" [*synthèse de transition*] – I anticipate the

unseen side of the lamp because I can touch it – or a "horizontal synthesis" [*synthèse d'horizon*] – the unseen side is given to me as "visible from another standpoint," at once given but only immanently' (Merleau-Ponty, 'The Primacy of Perception', 15).

48 Ibid., 28. The presentation and discussion took place on 23 November 1946 and was first published in the *Bulletin de la société française de philosophie*, Vol. 49 (December 1947) 119–53.

49 In the first two chapters of this section he focused on empiricist accounts of perception and their shortcomings. In the third chapter, '"Attention" and "Judgement"', he turned to the traditional prejudices of rationalism. As before, the bases for rejecting the rationalist and empiricist positions are found in recent findings of Gestalt theory, contemporary psychology and psychopathology concerning the nature of perception.

50 Merleau-Ponty, *Phenomenology of Perception*, 6.

51 Ibid., 26, Final emphasis mine.

52 Merleau-Ponty, 'The Primacy of Perception', 15–16.

53 Merleau-Ponty, *Phenomenology of Perception*, 71.

54 Paul Cézanne, *Still life with Plaster Cupid*, circa 1894, The Samuel Courtauld Trust, The Courtauld Gallery, London. Viewable at: http://www.artandarchitecture.org.uk/images/gallery/872882ac.html Accessed 19 January 2018.

55 Merleau-Ponty, *Phenomenology of Perception*, 68.

56 Ibid.

57 Ibid., 57.

58 Ibid., xiii and xix.

59 Ibid., 63.

60 Also entitled 'Etre et avoir'. Published on October 1936 in *La Vie Intellectuelle*, Vol. XLV, 98–109. Marcel's text had appeared a year earlier in 1935.

61 Merleau-Ponty, *Phenomenology of Perception*, viii. Emphasis in the original.

62 Concerning Merleau-Ponty's early exposure to Husserl, Geraets (1971, 6) wrote that in the years 1928 to 1930, Georges Gurvitch taught a course at the Sorbonne on contemporary German philosophy, including Husserl and Heidegger, also that Merleau-Ponty had done some very selective reading of Husserl early on but that his use of his thought was very limited up to 1933. The *Phenomenology*'s bibliography also references several works by Eugen Fink (who had been Husserl's research assistant during the last decade of Husserl's life). James Schmidt, *Maurice Merleau-Ponty: Between Phenomenology and Structuralism*, London: Palgrave Macmillan, 1985, 35 ff., gives an account of Merleau-Ponty's use of Husserl's late thought. See also Herman Leo van Breda, 'Maurice Merleau-Ponty et les Archives-Husserl à Louvain', *Revue de Métaphysique et de Morale*, Paris, 1962 (67), 410–30. Madison is critical of Merleau-Ponty's interpretations of Husserl (see Endnote 67).

63 Husserl was born into an orthodox Jewish family but later converted to Protestantism.

64 The second is Husserl's notion of intentionality, which I discuss in Chapter 4.

65 The 'phenomenological reduction' is a procedure of 'bracketing' those conditions which, for traditional thought, presuppose our knowledge of the world, namely, the idea that there is an intelligible world in-itself that is prior to and presupposes the world of appearance, or world 'for us'.

66 Merleau-Ponty, *Phenomenology of Perception*, vii,

67 Martin Jay has written that '[Husserl's] later work, most notably *The Crisis of the European Sciences and Transcendental Phenomenology*, 1936, put the stress on the pre-reflective *Lebenswelt* (lifeworld) instead. Here both the cultural/historical variations of everyday life (the *doxa* of opinion prior to the *episteme* of science) and the lived body played a central role. Although most commentators deny that the *Lebenswelt* simply replaced the transcendental ego in Husserl's thinking, Merleau-Ponty in particular was able to seize on it as the means to strip phenomenology of its Cartesian residues' (Jay, *Downcast Eyes*, 268). Madison is critical of Merleau-Ponty's interpretation of Husserl: 'In my opinion, the trouble with the *Phenomenology of Perception* stems precisely from the relation that Merleau-Ponty maintains in regard to Husserl. ... Whereas Merleau-Ponty thought he discerned an "existential philosophy" in Husserl, all the evidence indicates that Husserl never gave up his desire to raise philosophy to the level of an absolute science. ... It is, moreover, highly significant that to a great extent, as Geraets shows, Merleau-Ponty read Husserl through the eyes of Fink. Fink's attempt to "existentialise" Husserl, without, however, breaking out of the framework of Husserlian thought must have been highly attractive to Merleau-Ponty. It is, however, precisely this attempt to bend Husserlian transcendental idealism to fit the demands of an existentialist thought that I find impossible' (Madison, *The Phenomenology of Merleau-Ponty*, 270–1).

68 Merleau-Ponty was referring here to Husserl's *Méditations cartésiennes*, 120 ff.

69 Merleau-Ponty, *Phenomenology of Perception*, vii. Merleau-Ponty inserted a footnote: 'See the unpublished *6th Méditatation Cartésienne*, edited by Eugen Fink, to which G. Berger has kindly referred us.'

70 In the chapter of the *Phenomenology* entitled 'Experience and Objective thought. The Problem of the Body', Merleau-Ponty wrote, '[My human gaze] can never come against previous appearances ... otherwise than through the intermediary of time and language. ... Even if, for example, the consciousness of my past which I now have seems to me to cover exactly the past as it was, the past which I claim to recapture is not the real past but my past as I now see it, perhaps after altering it. Similarly in the future I may have a mistaken idea about the present which I now experience' (Merleau-Ponty, *Phenomenology of Perception*, 69–70).

71 Thus the term 'primitive' as Merleau-Ponty used it refers to a situation of complexity and richness.

72 Merleau-Ponty wrote that this is how it has been interpreted 'for a long time, and even in recent texts' (Merleau-Ponty, *Phenomenology of Perception*, xi) but made no specific references.

73 Merleau-Ponty, *Phenomenology of Perception*, xi.

74 As Geraets tells us in *Vers Une Nouvelle Philosophie Transcendantale*, these late writings had not yet come to Merleau-Ponty's attention when he was writing *The Structure of Behavior*.

75 Merleau-Ponty, *Phenomenology of Perception*, xiv.

76 Ibid.

77 This is in contrast to objectivist notions of truths-in-themselves. Since these purport 'to be the same for everybody, valid in all times and places' (Merleau-Ponty, *Phenomenology of Perception*, 71), since they can, supposedly, be directly accessed by each individual, our utterances concerning them would not be seen to have this kind of revelatory status.

78 In the 'Preface', Merleau-Ponty described the quest for knowledge of the real not as 'the reflection of a pre-existing truth but, like art, the act of bringing truth into being' (Merleau-Ponty, *Phenomenology of Perception*, xx). This was a view of art he shared with Heidegger, who, in *The Origin of the Work of Art* (1936) wrote that 'in the artwork, the truth of beings has set itself to work. Art is truth setting itself to work'. Reproduced in *Martin Heidegger, Basic Writings*, David Farrell Krell (ed.), London: Routledge, 1978, 139–212, 165.

79 Originally published as 'Roman et Métaphysique', *Cahiers du Sud*, T. XXII, no. 270, mars-avril 1945, 194–207 and reprinted as 'Le Roman et la Métaphysique', in *Sens et non-sens*, 45–71. Translated as 'Metaphysics and the Novel'. In *Sense and Non-Sense*, Evanston: Northwestern University Press, 1964, 26–40.

80 Merleau-Ponty, *Sense and Non-Sense*, 28.

81 Written by Merleau-Ponty in 1945. It first appeared in the publication *Fontaine*, 4e année, T. VIII, no 47, 80–100 in December of that year. It was reprinted in *Sens et Non-sens*, 15–44. Translated as 'Cézanne's Doubt', the English-language version may be found in in *Sense and Non-Sense*, 9–25.

82 Merleau-Ponty, *Sense and Non-Sense*, 19.

83 Ibid., 26–7. The insertion in square brackets is my own.

84 Ibid., 27.

85 He refers in his notes to Péguy's *Notre Jeunesse* (Péguy: 1873–1914).

86 Merleau-Ponty, *Sense and Non-Sense*, 28.

87 Merleau-Ponty, 'An Unpublished Text', 7.

88 Reproduced in *Cézanne, by himself,* Richard Kendal (ed.), London: Guild Publishing, 1988, 31–3. *Mes Confidences* was first published in A. Chappuis, *The Drawings of Paul Cézanne*, 2 Volumes, London, 1973. This reference is not found in 'Cézanne's Doubt'.

89 Merleau-Ponty, *Sense and Non-Sense*, 13–14. Emphases mine.

90 Merleau-Ponty, *The Structure of Behavior*, 3.

91 The title of this essay may be read as suggesting that Merleau-Ponty was comparing Cézanne's search for certainty-through-doubt with that of Descartes.

92 Merleau-Ponty, *Sense and Non-Sense*, 16.

93 Ibid., 13. Seemingly, an implicit critique of conceptualism.

94 Ibid., 13–14. Emphases mine.

95 Cézanne destabilized certainty, but without resorting to irrationalism, another point of similarity Merleau-Ponty saw to exist between the painter's researches and his own. He wrote in the *Phenomenology*: 'Experience of phenomena is … the making explicit or bringing to light of the pre-scientific life of consciousness which alone endows scientific operations with meaning and to which these latter always refer back. It is not an irrational conversion, but an intentional analysis' (Merleau-Ponty, *Phenomenology of Perception*, 58–9).

96 Merleau-Ponty wrote: 'If the painter is to express the world, the arrangement of his colors must carry with it this indivisible whole, or else his picture will only hint at things and will not give them in the imperious unity, the presence, the insurpassable plenitude which is for us the definition of the real. That is why each brushstroke must satisfy an infinite number of conditions' (Merleau-Ponty, *Sense and Non-Sense*, 15).

97 Merleau-Ponty, *Sense and Non-Sense*, 13.

98 Ibid., 15. The insertion in square brackets is my own.

99 Ibid., 14–15. Emphasis mine.

100 A theme throughout this essay, seen later in his discussion of Freud's interpretation of Leonardo da Vinci's work ('Leonardo da Vinci and a Memory of his childhood', 1910, reproduced in Sigmund Freud, *Art and Literature*, The Pelican Freud Library Vol. 14, Penguin Books, 1988 edition, 151–231), is his criticism of causal explanations of art of a psychological nature.

101 Merleau-Ponty, *Sense and Non-Sense*, 16. See for example: Paul Cézanne, *Lac d'Annecy*, 1896, Oil on canvas. 81 × 65 cm. The Courtauld Gallery. Viewable at: http://www.artandarchitecture.org.uk/images/gallery/5586c3ce.html. Accessed 19 January 2018.

102 Ibid., 11–12.

103 Ibid., 11.

104 Paul Cézanne, *La Femme à la Cafetière*, ca. 1890-95, oil on canvas, 130 × 97 cm. Musée d'Orsay, Paris. Viewable at http://www.musee-orsay.fr/fr/collections/oeuvres-commentees/recherche/commentaire/commentaire_id/la-femme-a-la-cafetiere-2551.html?no_cache=1. Accessed 19 January 2018.

105 Merleau-Ponty, *Sense and Non-Sense*, 10.

106 Ibid., 9.

107 Paul Cézanne, *Portrait of Victor Chocquet*, 1877, oil on canvas, 36.8 × 45.7 cm. Private Collection.

108 Merleau-Ponty, *Sense and Non-Sense*, 16.

109 Ibid., 11.

110 Ibid., 25.

111　Ibid., 11.

112　Ibid.

113　Ibid.

114　Ibid., 12. The wording 'behind the atmosphere' could be suggestive of an unhelpful dualism.

115　Duccio, *Madonna Enthroned* 1308–11, part of the Maestà Altarpiece. Panel height 206 cm. Siena, Museo dell' Opera del Duomo.

116　Merleau-Ponty, *Sense and Non-Sense*, 16.

117　Ibid., 19. A little earlier, Merleau-Ponty had written: 'Cézanne's … artist is not satisfied to be a cultured animal but assimilates the culture down to its very foundations and gives it a new structure: he speaks as the first man spoke and paints as if no one had ever painted before' (Ibid., 18–19).

118　Also indicated here, is the affective (that is, emotional) nature of this primordial communication. Selected texts that explore Merleau-Ponty's treatment of our emotional being include Mary Rose Barral, 'Self and Other: Communication and Love', *Review of Existential Psychology and Psychiatry*, 1982–83, 155–80; Glen A. Mazis, 'Merleau-Ponty, Inhabitation and the Emotions' (1986), Henry Pietersma (ed.), *Merleau-Ponty: Critical Essays*, 1989, 251–68 and William S. Hamrick, 'Perception, Corporeity, and Kindness', *Journal of the British Society for Phenomenology*, 1994, 74–84.

119　Merleau-Ponty, *Sense and Non-Sense*, 17.

120　Ibid., 19.

121　Ibid.

122　Sol LeWitt, 'Paragraphs on Conceptual Art', *Artforum*, June 1967.

123　Merleau-Ponty, *Sense and Non-Sense*, 19.

124　Ibid., 18.

Chapter four

1　Merleau-Ponty, *Phenomenology of Perception*, 150.

2　Merleau-Ponty, *The Primacy of Perception*, 4–5.

3　Ibid., 5.

4　Bannan, *The Philosophy of Merleau-Ponty*, 59.

5　Merleau-Ponty, *Phenomenology of Perception*, 71. Emphasis mine. The passage from which this is taken runs as follows: 'The whole life of consciousness is characterised by the tendency to posit objects, since it is consciousness, that is to say self-knowledge, only in so far as it takes hold of itself and draws itself together in an identifiable object. And yet the absolute positing of a single object is the death of consciousness, since it congeals the whole of existence, as a crystal placed in a solution suddenly crystallises it. We cannot remain in this dilemma of having to fail to understand either the subject or the object.'

6　Ibid., 71.

7   This phrase is taken from the *Phenomenology of Perception*, 80.

8   These discussions are a development of those in *The Structure of Behavior* concerning the thing-like nature of the body which occur in Merleau-Ponty's discussion of the symbolic forms.

9   Merleau-Ponty, by contrast, writes that 'my body itself I move directly, I do not find it at one point of objective space and transfer it to another' (Merleau-Ponty, *Phenomenology of Perception*, 94).

10   Merleau-Ponty, *Phenomenology of Perception*, 90. The insertion in square brackets is my own.

11   Ibid.

12   As defined by Merriam-Webster dictionary: https://www.merriam-webster.com/medical/anosognosia. Accessed 16 October 2017.

13   Merleau-Ponty, *Phenomenology of Perception*, 76.

14   Ibid., 80.

15   Ibid.

16   Ibid.

17   Ibid., 78.

18   Ibid., 79.

19   Ibid., 81.

20   Ibid.

21   Ibid., 80.

22   Thus my reading of Merleau-Ponty differs from that of Shildrick in 'Posthumanism and the Monstrous body' (*Body and Society*, 1996, 1–15, 3), when she writes: 'Even in the phenomenological tradition of Merleau-Ponty, which stresses the unity of matter and mind expressed through the being-in-the-world of bodies, the healthy body, far from being consistently present to us, is scarcely experienced at all. It is what Drew Leder refers to as the "absent body" (1990). Once, however, it is broken – that is diseased or damaged – the body forces itself into our consciousness and that comfortable absence is lost. The body is now perceived but is experienced as other. ... In consequence, embodiment, in being symbolically associated with the disruption of the subject, is no less ontologically devalued in phenomenology than it is in more conventional philosophies.'

23   Concerning an inadequate or incomplete mode of integration between the two, Merleau-Ponty wrote: 'New perceptions, new emotions even, replace the old ones, but this process of renewal touches only the content of our experience and not its structure. Impersonal time continues its course, but personal time is arrested' (Merleau-Ponty, *Phenomenology of Perception*, 83).

24   Later in the *Phenomenology* (106), Merleau-Ponty also wrote of the doubling of the body in terms of the 'objective body' and the 'phenomenal body'.

25   Merleau-Ponty, *Phenomenology of Perception*, 87. Emphasis mine.

26   Ibid., 83.

27 For discussions of Merleau-Ponty's notion of 'anonymous being' see, for
    instance, Gail Weiss, 'The Anonymous Intentions of Transactional Bodies',
    Hypatia, Volume 17, Issue 4, Autumn 2002, 187–200 and Heinämaa,
    'Anonymity and personhood', 123–42.

28 This matter is taken up by Merleau-Ponty in his discussions of reflection in
    The Visible and the Invisible, the project with which he was engaged at the
    time of his death in 1961. I should add that in my 2014 book *Showing Off!
    A Philosophy of Image*, which is again focused on Merleau-Ponty's work, I
    introduced a third term into this doubled definition of the body as sensing/
    sensible, that is – where the visual is concerned – I introduced (and indeed
    prioritized) the notion of the self-showing body alongside those of the body as
    seeing and being-seen.

29 In the chapter 'The Body as Object and Mechanistic Physiology', within the
    context of a discussion of the phantom limb, Merleau-Ponty introduced the
    notion of 'organic thought'. He wrote: 'In order to describe the belief in the
    phantom limb and the unwillingness to accept mutilation, writers speak of
    a "driving into the unconscious" or "an organic repression." [Here he cited
    Paul Schilder *Das Körperschema*, 1923 and Jean Lhermitte, *L'image de notre
    Corps*, 1939 as two sources] These un-Cartesian terms force us to form the
    idea of an organic thought through which the relation of the "psychic" to the
    "physiological" becomes conceivable' (Merleau-Ponty, *Phenomenology of
    Perception*, 77).

30 Merleau-Ponty, *Phenomenology of Perception*, 93. Merleau-Ponty cited
    Husserl, *Méditations cartésiennes*, 81.

31 See my comments in Endnote 28 above, concerning a third concept, not
    discussed here, namely that of phenomenological self-showing.

32 For a somewhat more recent investigation of the body from these perspectives
    see Paul Rodaway, *Sensuous Geographies: Body, Sense and Place*, Abingdon,
    Oxfordshire and New York: Routledge, 1994.

33 Merleau-Ponty, *Phenomenology of Perception*, 221.

34 Ibid., 225. The words in square brackets are my own.

35 Ibid., 373.

36 Madison (*The Phenomenology of Merleau-Ponty*, 33) saw Merleau-Ponty's
    attempts at overcoming the antinomies of the objective and the subjective, in
    such cases, to be not only unclear (ambiguous) but also to be still too weighted
    towards the subjective: 'Merleau-Ponty tends to idealise or subjectivise the
    world, that is, to define it solely in relation to (bodily) subjectivity.' He wrote
    that it is only in his later works that his treatment of this problem becomes
    more convincing. Merleau-Ponty would later express similar concerns with
    respect to the *Phenomenology* and, if I have understood him correctly, he saw
    the corrective to lie both in an altered use of terminology and an increased
    focus on the body as an expressive being, indeed, on the issue of expression
    itself. Nonetheless, in my view (as I have tried to show in my discussions of
    the doubled body, or body already experienced as both subject and object,
    both self and world) Merleau-Ponty need not be read here as idealizing or
    subjectivizing the world in the way Madison suggests.

37 Merleau-Ponty, *Phenomenology of Perception*, xi.

38 This term was used by Heidegger to refer to the 'active transcendence of the subject in relation to the world' (Translator's note, *Phenomenology of Perception*, 70). In the French original, *Phénoménologie de la Perception*, Merleau-Ponty used either this form or the French word *extase*.

39 Merleau-Ponty, *Phenomenology of Perception*, 87.

40 Ibid., 75. Emphasis mine.

41 See for instance Merleau-Ponty, *The Structure of Behavior*, 118.

42 Merleau-Ponty, *Phenomenology of Perception*, xvii–xviii.

43 Emphasis mine.

44 Merleau-Ponty, *Phenomenology of Perception*, 108.

45 Ibid., 109.

46 F. Fischer, 'Raum-Zeitstruktur und Denkstörung in der Schizophrenie', *Ztschr. f. d. ges. Neurologie u. Psychiatrie*, 1930, 250. Merleau-Ponty wrote: 'The life of consciousness – cognitive life, the life of desire or perceptual life – is subtended by an "intentional arc" which projects round about us our past, our future, our human setting, our physical, ideological and moral situation, or rather which results in our being situated in all these respects. It is this intentional arc which brings about the unity of the senses, of intelligence, or sensibility and motility. And it is this which "goes limp" in illness' (Merleau-Ponty, *Phenomenology of Perception*, 136).

47 Merleau-Ponty, *Phenomenology of Perception*, 136.

48 R. Buccheri, Metod Saniga and W. M. Stuckey, *The Nature of Time: Geometry, Physics & Perception*. NATO Science Series II: Volume 95, Dordrecht, Boston, London: Kluwer Academic Publishers, 2003.

49 Metod Saniga, 'Unveiling the Nature of Time: Altered States of Consciousness and Pencil-Generated Space-Times'. An invited workshop presentation at 'Scienza e Trascendenza', Rome, 8 May 1998. Available online at http://www.ta3.sk/~msaniga/pub/ftp/unveil.pdf Accessed 6 August 2017.

50 Merleau-Ponty, *Phenomenology of Perception*, 137.

51 Ibid., 111. Emphasis mine.

52 Gelb and Goldstein, *Psychologische Analysen hirnpathologisher Fälle*, Leipzig, Barth, 1920 and Goldstein, 'Über die Abhängigkeit der Bewegungen von optischen Vorgängen', *Monatschrift für Psychiatrie und Neurologie*, Festschrift Liepmann, 1923.

53 Merleau-Ponty, *Phenomenology of Perception*, 105.

54 Ibid.

55 Ibid., 104.

56 Merleau-Ponty discussed the difference between *Zeigen* (pointing) and *Greifen* (grasping) in relation to abstract and concrete movement as follows: 'A patient, asked to point to some part of his body, his nose for example, can only manage to do so if he is allowed to take hold of it. If the patient is set the task of interrupting the movement before its completion, or if he is allowed

to touch his nose only with a wooden ruler, the action becomes impossible. [Here he cites Goldstein, *Zeigen und Greifen*, 1931, 453–66] It must therefore be concluded that "grasping" or "touching", even for the body, is different from "pointing"' (Merleau-Ponty, *Phenomenology of Perception*, 103). There is a link, here, with Merleau-Ponty's comment in 'Metaphysics and the Novel' (Merleau-Ponty, *Sense and Non-Sense*, 28) referred to in my Chapter 3, concerning the task of phenomenology as that of pointing to the world, thus indicating the possibilities that the world may have for us, rather than seeking to define it in certain limited or dogmatic terms.

57   Merleau-Ponty, *Phenomenology of Perception*, 109.

58   Ibid., 102. Mazis ('Merleau-Ponty, Inhabitation and the Emotions', 251–68, 252) wrote: 'For Merleau-Ponty, it was essential to see that the body *is* space, and not *of* space.'

59   Ibid., 382.

60   Emphases mine.

61   Merleau-Ponty, *Phenomenology of Perception*, 111.

62   Ibid., 111–2. Emphasis mine.

63   He wrote concerning such patients (Merleau-Ponty, *Phenomenology of Perception*, 112): 'Knowing that the month is March and the day a Monday, they will have difficulty in saying what the previous month and day were, though they may well know by heart the days and months in their correct order. They are incapable of comparing the number of units contained in two sets of sticks placed in front of them: they may count the same stick twice over, or else include in one set of sticks some which belong to the other.' Here he cited Van Woerkom, *Sur la notion de l'espace (le sens géometrique)*, 1910, 113–9.

64   Ibid., 110.

65   Ibid., 112.

66   That is, not merely the content of God's imagination, as in Berkeley.

67   Merleau-Ponty, *Phenomenology of Perception*, xii.

68   Ibid., xii.

69   Ibid., 150.

70   Merleau-Ponty, *The Primacy of Perception*, 3.

71   Here he refered to P. Lachièze-Rey, *Le Moi le Monde et Dieu*, Paris: Boivin, 1938, 83.

72   P. Lachièze-Rey, *L'Idealisme kantien*, Paris: F. Alcan, 1932, 472.

73   Merleau-Ponty, *Phenomenology of Perception*, 373.

74   Merleau-Ponty, *The Primacy of Perception*, 16.

75   Emphasis mine.

76   Merleau-Ponty referred in the footnotes to *Die Krisis der europäischen Wissenschaften und die transzendentale Phänomenologie, III* (unpublished).

77   Merleau-Ponty, *Phenomenology of Perception*, xii–xiii.

78   Merleau-Ponty, *The Primacy of Perception*, 26.

79 Stephen Watson in 'The Ethics of Ambiguity' (Patrick Burke and Jan van der Veken, eds, *Merleau-Ponty in Contemporary Perspectives*, Dordrecht, Boston, London: Kluwer Academic Publishers, 1993, 147–70, 155) wrote that 'Merleau-Ponty refused from the outset a certain "existential nihilism". ... The ambiguity affecting values neither negates their validity nor the responsibility required in the art of their interpretation.'

80 Merleau-Ponty, *Sense and Non-Sense*, 28.

81 For a concise and useful overview and bibliography, see Professor of Jurisprudence Panu Minkkinen's 'Hostility and Hospitality', *NoFo* 4, October 2007, 53–60. See also Richard Kearney and Kascha Semonovitch (eds), *Phenomenologies of the Stranger: Between Hostility and Hospitality*, New York: Fordham University Press, 2011 and Richard Kearney, *Anatheism*, New York, Chichester, West Sussex: Columbia University Press, 2011.

82 I also discussed *L'Invitée*, and Merleau-Ponty's engagement with it, in my earlier book, *Showing Off! A Philosophy of Image* but I did so within a different context of debate and focused on different sections of it.

83 Merleau-Ponty, *Sense and Non-Sense*, 28.

84 He wrote: 'Pierre, Françoise and Xavière are totally ignorant of the holy natural law of the couple and ... try in all honesty – and without moreover, any hint of sexual complicity – to form a trio' (Merleau-Ponty, *Sense and Non-Sense*, 39).

85 Again, see my *Showing Off! A Philosophy of Image* for a longer discussion of this essay. De Beauvoir's *The Ethics of Ambiguity* would be published in 1948 (trans. Bernard Frechtman, New York: Citadel, 1948).

86 Merleau-Ponty, *Sense and Non-Sense*, 40. Emphasis mine.

87 Merleau-Ponty, *The Primacy of Perception*, 161.

88 Ibid.

Chapter five

1 Merleau-Ponty, 'Introduction', *Signs*, Evanston: Northwestern University Press, 1964, 3–35, 19.

2 See Galen Johnson's essay 'Structures and Painting: "Indirect Language and the Voices of Silence"' in *The Merleau-Ponty Aesthetics Reader*, op cit.

3 Merleau-Ponty, *Signs*, 84–97. Presented at the first *Colloque international de phénoménologie*, Brussels, 1951, and published the following year: Brouwer, 1952, 89–109.

4 James Edie, 'Foreword', In *Consciousness and the Acquisition of Language*. Trans Hugh J. Silverman, Evanston: Northwestern University Press, 1973, xi–xxxii, xiii.

5 Published texts dealing with language include 'Language and Communication' (1948), 'Consciousness and the Acquisition of Language' (1949), 'The philosopher and sociology' (1951), 'Phenomenology and The Sciences of Man'

(1951–52), 'On the Phenomenology of Language' (1951), 'Indirect Language and the Voices of Silence' (1952) upon which I focus in this chapter, 'An Unpublished Text' (written in 1952 but first published in 1962), 'The Sensible World and the Value of Expression' (1953), 'Studies in the literary use of language' (1953), 'The problem of speech' (1954) and 'From Mauss to Claude Levi-Strauss' (1959). Also, *The Prose of the World* (1969), half-finished by 1953 but, according to Edie, abandoned in 1959.

6   Rosalind Krauss, 'Sculpture in the Expanded Field', *October*, Volume 8 (Spring 1979), 30–44.

7   In *Passages in Modern Sculpture* (1977) Krauss had drawn on Merleau-Pontean phenomenology (as she understood it) when attempting to come to terms with the phenomenon of minimalist art.

8   Petersen, 'Introduction', 14–15. Emphases mine.

9   Crowther, *Phenomenologies of Art and Vision*, op cit., 69.

10   Ibid., 176, footnote 21.

11   See Paul Crowther, *Phenomenology of the Visual Arts (even the Frame)*, Stanford, CA: Stanford University Press, 2009, 12.

12   Ibid.

13   Ibid.

14   Hoptman, *The Forever Now*, op cit., 22. She was referencing David Joselit, 'Signal Processing', *Artforum*, Summer, 2011, 356.

15   Peter Osborne, *Anywhere or Not at All: Philosophy of Contemporary Art*, London and New York: Verso, 2013.

16   Ibid., 1.

17   Ibid., 2.

18   See Ibid., 3 – but this is a point carefully developed and argued throughout the book.

19   Ibid., 48.

20   Ibid.

21   Ibid.

22   Ibid., 10.

23   This reference, and those above are from Ibid., 48.

24   Ibid.

25   Ibid., 104.

26   Anne Ring Petersen, 'Painting Spaces'. In Anne Ring Petersen with Makkel Bogh, Hans Dam Christensen and Peter Nørgaard Larsen (eds), *Contemporary Painting in Context*, Museum Tusculanum Press, University of Copenhagen, 2013 edition (2010), 123–38.

27   See: Mark Sinclair 'Spray paint and sea spray – *Rockaway*! installation unveiled in New York', *Creative Review*, 8 September 2016. Source: https://www.creativereview.co.uk/spray-paint-anpd-sea-spray/. Accessed 21 August 2017.

28 Petersen, *Contemporary Painting in Context*, 129.

29 Ibid., 125–6. A translation of this essay is also reproduced in *Contemporary Painting in Context*, 43–64.

30 The exhibition took place at the Neue Galerie am Landesmuseum Joanneum and the Künstlerhaus Graz, in Graz, Austria.

31 Petersen, *Contemporary Painting in Context*, 126.

32 Ibid., 126.

33 Petersen's essay opens with a quotation by Julian Opie, in Mikkel Bogh and Charlotte Brandt, *Fact and Value: nye positioner i skulptur og maleri/ New Positions in Sculpture and Painting*, Copenhagen: Charlottenborg Udsillingsbygning, 2000, 49: 'What I would really like to do is make a painting and then walk into it.'

34 Petersen, *Contemporary Painting in Context*, 132.

35 Ibid.

36 Ibid., 133.

37 Katharina Grosse, '*The Poise of the Head und die anderen folgen*'. In Anne Ring Petersen with Makkel Bogh, Hans Dam Christensen and Peter Nørgaard Larsen (eds), *Contemporary Painting in Context*, Museum Tusculanum Press, University of Copenhagen, 2013 edition (2010), 97–122, 103.

38 Ibid., 103.

39 Ibid.

40 Ibid.

41 Ibid.

42 Ibid.

43 Merleau-Ponty, *Signs*, 3.

44 Merleau-Ponty, 'On Madagascar' (1958), *Signs*, 328–36, 328, footnote 1.

45 'On News Items', 1954. In *Signs*, 311–3, 311.

46 Ibid., 312. Emphases mine.

47 Ibid., 311.

48 Ibid.

49 Ibid., 312. Emphases mine.

50 Ibid., 311.

51 Ibid., 312–3.

52 'An Analysis of Stendhal,' *The Spectator*, 26 September 1952, 21. Available via the *The Spectator Archive*, http://archive.spectator.co.uk/article/26th-september-1952/21/the-analysis-of-stendhal. Accessed 22 October 2017.

53 Merleau-Ponty, *Signs*, 312.

54 He made particular reference here to Swigonski's essay 'The Logic of Feminist Standpoint Theory for Social Work Research', *Social Work*, Volume 39, Issue 4, 1 July 1994, 387–93. The reference to 'stepping outside of patterns of assumed privilege and superiority' was taken from 'For the White Social Worker Who Wants to Know How to Work with Lesbians of Color'. In Hilda

Hidalgo (ed), *Lesbians of Color: Social and Human Services*, The Harrington Park Press, an imprint of The Haworth Press Inc 1995, 7–21.

55   Standpoint theory was developed in contradistinction to traditional research where the general outcome is 'a propensity toward encouraging generalizations on the basis of "scientific" findings with representative samples of subjects' (Mark P Orbe, *Constructing Co-Cultural Theory: An Explication of Culture, Power and Communication*, Thousand Oaks, London, New Delhi: Sage, 1998, 25), an approach that tends to be insensitive to the diversity within co-cultural groups.

56   Also of note is phenomenological interpretative analysis, which was developed by Jonathan A. Smith and his colleagues. See Jonathan A. Smith, Paul Flowers and Michael Larkin, *Interpretative Phenomenological Analysis: Theory, Method, Research*, Los Angeles, London, New Delhi, Singapore, Washington, DC: Sage, 2009.

57   Orbe, *Constructing Co-Cultural Theory*, 28.

58   Ibid. Emphasis mine.

59   Merleau-Ponty, *Signs*, 312. Emphases mine.

60   Orbe, *Constructing Co-Cultural Theory*, 28. Emphasis mine.

61   Merleau-Ponty, *Phenomenology of Perception*, xi.

62   In order to avoid confusion (given my discussions in the introduction about the distinction Merleau-Ponty was making during this period between institution and constitution), I have decided to use the word 'instituting' rather that 'constituting' here and below. See Merleau-Ponty's 'The Institution of a Work of Art', 41–9 plus notes 95–101.

63   Merleau-Ponty, *Phenomenology of Perception*, 197.

64   Merleau-Ponty, *Signs*, 84. Merleau-Ponty's position here reflects what he had already expressed in 'Metaphysics and the Novel', namely that before the rise of phenomenology and existentialism the issue of language had not been regarded as philosophically important.

65   In 'Indirect Language and the Voices of Silence' Merleau-Ponty cited the French writer la Bruyère (1645–96) as an exponent of this view (*Signs*, 47).

66   Originally published in two parts as 'Le langage indirect et les voix du silence' I & II, *Les Temps Modernes*, June and July 1952, nos. 80 & 81. Reprinted in *Signes* 49–104 with the English translation in *Signs*, 39–83. This essay was an altered version of the third chapter of his never completed work *The Prose of the World*, entitled 'The Indirect Language', published posthumously by Claude Lefort. Galen A. Johnson provides an analysis of the difference between both versions in 'Structures and Painting', 14–34, 15.

67   Merleau-Ponty, *Signs*, 43.

68   Jean-Paul Sartre, *Qu'est-ce que la littérature?*, Collection 'Idées', Paris: Gallimard, 1964. Originally published in 1947.

69   Madison, *The Phenomenology of Merleau-Ponty*, 111.

70   Merleau-Ponty's refusal of the classical point of view is underlined in 'Indirect Language and the Voices of Silence', when he makes reference to the notion

of God. God, to whom the characteristics of eternal stability and immutability are traditionally assigned, and to whom they were assigned by Descartes, is presented by Merleau-Ponty not merely as God who became man (that is, embodied and therefore intrinsically tied to the shifting and perspectival), but as a God who 'would not be fully God without becoming fully man' (*Signs*, 71). This underlines for Merleau-Ponty that philosophy has no recourse, through a theological conception concerning the nature of God, to a realm of static values (the notion of 'an original language'). Indeed, in its search for foundations it discovers that these foundations (exemplified here in the notion of God) are themselves shifting and allusive.

71   Merleau-Ponty, *Signs*, 43. Emphasis mine.

72   Merleau-Ponty, *Phenomenology of Perception*, 178. Emphasis mine.

73   Merleau-Ponty, *Signs*, 43.

74   Ibid.

75   He cites here the fourth of the *Logische Untersuchungen*.

76   Merleau-Ponty, *Signs*, 84.

77   Ibid., 84–5.

78   In note 1, in 'Was Merleau-Ponty a Structuralist?' (*Merleau-Ponty's Philosophy of Language: Structuralism and Dialectics*, 1987, 86), James Edie wrote as follows: 'Merleau-Ponty made four major attempts to explain Husserl's conception of "rational grammar", and to show that Husserl abandoned, in his later writings, his early proposal for an eidetics of grammar. [Edie then lists the sections on linguistics in 'Phenomenology of and Sciences of Man', 'On the Phenomenology of Language', 'The Philosopher and Sociology' and *The Prose of the World*.] I consider this attempt on the part of Merleau-Ponty to "push Husserl further than he wanted to go himself" to be not only historically unsound, given the fact that there is no evidence whatever that Husserl ever abandoned his early views on logical and universal grammatical invariants, but also phenomenologically misguided.' He then referred the reader to his article 'Can Grammar Be Thought?', in *Patterns of the Life-World, Essays in Honour of John Wild*, Evanston: Northwestern University Press, 1970, 315–45.

79   See Derrida's criticisms of Husserl, for instance, in *Speech and Phenomena* of 1967, trans. David B. Allison, Evanston: Northwestern University Press, 1973.

80   Merleau-Ponty, *Signs*, 87–8. Emphasis mine.

81   Saussure's *Course in General Linguistics* had been in publication since 1916. It was compiled after his death from notes taken by students of three courses on linguistics given at the University of Geneva between 1906 and 1911.

82   See Edie, 'Was Merleau-Ponty a Structuralist?', 88, footnote 15.

83   Merleau-Ponty, *Signs*, 86.

84   This understanding of the meaning of signs should not be regarded as a radical departure from Merleau-Ponty's observations on the nature of expression made in his earlier works. Rather, it would seem that the ideas (or terms) Merleau-Ponty took from Saussure concerning the structured context of a single utterance represented, for him, an enrichment and development of ideas

found in his earlier Gestalt-influenced texts. (The gestalt or whole is, firstly, that of the context of the particular utterance or sign, and, secondly, the place of that sign in the system of signs, the *langue*.) This connection (and here I am more interested in the connection than the differences) may be examined by comparing two passages, one from 'Indirect Language and the Voices of Silence' and the other from the earlier 'The Film and the New Psychology' op cit. In 'Indirect Language' he wrote that 'as far as language is concerned, it is the lateral relation of one sign to another which makes each of them significant, so that meaning appears only at the intersection of and as it were in the interval between words" (*Signs*, 42). However, an illustration used in 'The Film and the New Psychology' to demonstrate the importance of the figure/ground configuration for the construction of meaning (expressed here in temporal terms since film was being discussed) could just as readily serve to exemplify the Saussurian notion of the context-dependent meaning of signs: 'Let us say right off that a film is not sum of total images but a temporal gestalt. This is the moment to recall Pudovkin's famous experiment. ... One day Pudovkin took a close-up of Mosjoukin with a completely impassive expression and projected it after showing: first, a bowl of soup, then, a young woman lying dead in her coffin, and, last, a child playing with a teddy-bear. The first thing noticed was the Mosjoukin seemed to be looking at the bowl, the young woman, and the child, and next one noted that he was looking pensively at the dish, that he wore an expression of sorrow when looking at the woman, and that he had a glowing smile for the child. The audience was amazed at his variety of expression although the same shot had actually been used all three times and was, if anything, remarkably inexpressive. The meaning of a shot therefore depends upon what precedes it in the movie, and this succession of scenes creates a new reality which is not merely the sum of its parts' (Merleau-Ponty, *Sense and Non-Sense*, 54). Merleau-Ponty had already made reference to the arbitrary nature of signs, within the context of emotional and body languages in the *Phenomenology of Perception*: 'The angry Japanese smiles, the westerner goes red and stamps his foot, or else goes pale and hisses his words. ... It is no more natural, and no less conventional, to shout in anger or to kiss in love than to call a table "a table". Feelings and passional conduct are invented like words. Even those which, like paternity, seem to be part and parcel of the human make-up are in reality institutions. It is impossible to superimpose on man a lower layer of behaviour which one chooses to call "natural", followed by a manufactured cultural or spiritual world. Everything is both manufactured and natural in man, as it were, in the sense that there is not a word, not a form of behaviour which does not owe something to purely biological being – and which at the same time does not elude the simplicity of animal life, and cause forms of vital behaviour to deviate from their pre-ordained direction, through a sort of *leakage* and through a genius for ambiguity which might serve to define man' (Merleau-Ponty, *Phenomenology of Perception*, 189).

85 In the opening sentence of this essay he wrote: 'What we have learned from Saussure is that, taken singly, signs do not signify anything, and that each one of them does not so much express a meaning as mark a divergence of meaning between itself and other signs' (Merleau-Ponty, *Signs*, 39).

86 Taylor, 'Phantasmic Genealogy' (in Busch, Thomas W. and Gallagher, Shaun (eds.), *Merleau-Ponty: Hermeneutics and Postmodernism*, 1992, 149–60, 154), commented on Merleau-Ponty's reading of Saussure and on his use of the term 'divergence' in this context: 'It is [his] commitment to breaking down ontological dualism that marks out Merleau-Ponty's very particular reading of Saussure. Unlike others who discovered him at a later date, he was not tempted to overestimate Saussure's first principle: "the arbitrary nature of the sign" at the expense of his second principle: "the linear nature of the signifier." *Like* these others, Merleau-Ponty derives from Saussure the centrality of this relational concept of difference but never confers upon it a "purity" that would lend it any degree of autonomy. By writing difference as "divergence" (*écart*) Merleau-Ponty retains the temporal dimension of language that Saussure strongly affirms in principle II. Merleau-Ponty's "divergence" invokes a temporally contingent relation that is lost in the binary logic of difference as an ideal relation between "X" and "non-X". ... Merleau-Ponty's "divergence" avoids the static, synchronic characteristics of pure difference that is common to semiotics and structuralism in general. But what is most important about this "divergence" is that it does not designate any kind of absolute vector: it is dynamic but not teleological. In this way, through divergence, both meaning and expression are preserved without the sacrifice of history.'

87 Merleau-Ponty, *Signs*, 42.

88 Katharina Grosse, 'The Poise of the Head und die anderen folgen.' In *Contemporary Painting in Context*, 113.

89 Ibid.

90 Ibid.

91 Ibid.

92 See: Rashid Johnson, *Within Our Gates*, Garage Museum of Contemporary Art, Moscow, 2016. https://garagemca.org/en/event/rashid-johnson-within-our-gates. Accessed 24 October 2017.

93 Tom Ellis, *The Middle*, The Wallace Collection, 15th September–27th November, 2016. http://www.wallacecollection.org/collections/exhibition/120 Accessed 27 October 2017.

94 Johnson, *Within Our Gates*, op cit.

95 *Artists imagine a nation: Pictures of people and places from the collections of Koh Seow Chuan and friends*, Institute of Contemporary Arts, Singapore, 2015. Curator: Bala Starr. Exhibition architecture: Helen Oja. http://www.lasalle.edu.sg/events/artists-imagine-nation-pictures-people-places-collections-koh-seow-chuan-friends/ Accessed 24 October 2017.

96 Bala Starr, 'Foreword'. In *Artists Imagine a Nation: Pictures of People and Places from the Collections of Koh Seow Chuan and Friends* (exhibition catalogue), Singapore: Institute of Contemporary Arts Singapore, 2015, 8–9, 9.

97 Ibid., 8.

98 See: http://www.singaporefreeport.com/#/about Accessed 28 October 2017.

99 Merleau-Ponty, *Signs*, 19. Emphases are in the original.

100 Ibid., 43.

101 He wrote that 'a language sometimes remains a long time pregnant with
     transformations which are to come. ... Even when it is possible to date the
     emergence of a principle which exists "for itself", it is clear that the principle
     has been previously present in the culture as an obsession or anticipation, and
     that the act of consciousness which lays it down as an explicit signification is
     never without a residue' (Merleau-Ponty, *Signs*, 41).

102 Ibid., 76.

103 Ibid., 42. Emphasis mine.

104 Ibid., 44.

105 Ibid., 41.

106 Ibid., 44.

107 See M. C. Dillon's discussions around this subject in 'Temporality:
     Merleau-Ponty and Derrida'. In Busch and Gallagher (eds), *Merleau-Ponty:
     Hermeneutics and Postmodernism*, 1992, 189–212.

108 Merleau-Ponty, *Signs*, 40.

109 James Edie made this point in 'Was Merleau-Ponty a Structuralist?' op cit.

110 Hendrik J. Pos, 'Phénoménologie et linguistique', *Revue Internationale de
     philosophie*, (1), 1939, 354–365.

111 Madison, *The Phenomenology of Merleau-Ponty*, 109. John's expression is
     actually 'In him was life, and that life was the light of men.'

112 John 1 v. 1–3. *The Holy Bible*.

113 According to Madison, Merleau-Ponty regarded a commitment to the notion
     of (a kind of) universality to be a philosophical necessity. In *Merleau-Ponty in
     Retrospect*, 1993, 191, albeit with reference to Merleau-Ponty's later writings,
     Madison wrote: 'It is important to remember ... especially in the light of the
     anti-universalist stance taken by the post-Merleau-Pontean anti-humanists –
     that Merleau-Ponty was a staunch defender of the universalist claims of
     philosophy and, indeed, of the universalist notion of "humanity" itself.'

114 Merleau-Ponty, *Signs*, 87.

115 For a comparison of Merleau-Ponty's thought concerning language with
     that of Wittgenstein see Philip Dwyer, *Sense and Subjectivity: A Study of
     Wittgenstein and Merleau-Ponty*, Leiden, 1990.

116 Merleau-Ponty, *Phenomenology of Perception*, 196.

Chapter six

1 Maurice Merleau-Ponty, 'Indirect Language and the Voices of Silence', *Signs*,
   Evanston, IL: Northwestern University Press, 1964, 39–83, 52.

2 Johnson, 'Structures and Painting: "Indirect Language and the Voices of
   Silence"'. In Galen A. Johnson (ed), *The Merleau-Ponty Aesthetics Reader:
   Philosophy and Painting*, Evanston, IL: Northwestern University Press, 1993,
   14–34, 19.

3 The fourth part was entitled 'Les Metamorphoses d'Apollon'. *Les Voix du Silence* was published in one volume by Pléiade, Paris, 1951.

4 This is not to say that Merleau-Ponty was seeking to somehow conflate visual and linguistic experience. As Johnson put it (*The Merleau-Ponty Aesthetics Reader*, 34): 'The various forms of expression of meaning are not reducible one to the other.' In Johnson's view, for Merleau-Ponty language was neither primary not secondary to painting but rather 'both are different modes of signification for the expression of meaning'. My own view – I think – is that their interrelationship was, for him, rather more entangled.

5 Merleau-Ponty, *Phenomenology of Perception*, 184, 189.

6 Merleau-Ponty, *Signs*, 48.

7 Ibid.

8 Ibid.

9 Ibid. Merleau-Ponty doesn't cite Malraux so it is difficult immediately to judge whether or not he has correctly interpreted him.

10 Merleau-Ponty, *Signs*, 47.

11 Ibid.

12 Ibid., 51. Merleau-Ponty cited *La Création esthétique*, 144.

13 Merleau-Ponty, *Signs*, 47.

14 Johnson, *The Merleau-Ponty Aesthetics Reader*, 26.

15 Merleau-Ponty, *Signs*, 47.

16 Ibid., 50. Emphasis mine.

17 Sartre, in his writings on the imagination (*Imagination*, 1936, and *L'imaginaire*, 1940), regarded paintings as the product not of a perceptual relationship with the existent world but of a relationship between the imagination and an imaginary world that does not exist. As Galen A. Johnson wrote in 'Structures and Painting' (op cit., 29): 'In imagination, on Sartre's account, we find the exemplary case of a free, spontaneous act *ex nihilo* that is not bound to body, place, time, circumstance, or situation.' Merleau-Ponty, on the other hand, made no such dualistic split between imagination and perception. For him, as Johnson put it a little later, 'Imagination remains a variant of perception' (Johnson, *The Merleau-Ponty Aesthetics Reader*, 30).

18 Merleau-Ponty, *Signs*, 50.

19 Raphael, *The Marriage of the Virgin (Lo Sposalizio)*, 1504, Oil on panel, 67 × 46½", Brera Gallery, Milan. This was also briefly discussed in Andrews, *Showing Off*, op cit., 72.

20 Merleau-Ponty, *Signs*, 50.

21 Ibid.

22 Ibid.

23 Ibid., 57.

24 Johnson, *The Merleau-Ponty Aesthetics Reader*, 27.

25 Madison, *The Phenomenology of Merleau-Ponty*, op cit., 87.

26 Merleau-Ponty, *Signs*, 52. 'The painter does not put his immediate self – the very nuance of his feeling – into his painting. He puts his *style* there, and he has to master it as much in his own attempts as in the painting of others or in the world.'

27 Ibid., 53–4. Final emphases mine.

28 Paul Crowther, *Phenomenologies of Art and Vision*, 21. The emphasis in the original.

29 Merleau-Ponty, *Signs*, 54.

30 See Johnson, *The Merleau-Ponty Aesthetics Reader*, 20–1 for further details.

31 Merleau-Ponty, *Signs*, 45–6.

32 Ibid., 52.

33 Ibid., 51.

34 Ibid.

35 Andrei Rublev, *The Old Testament Trinity*, 1420s, levkas and tempera on wood, 142 × 114 cm, Tretyakov Gallery, Moscow.

36 Merleau-Ponty, *Signs*, 68. Merleau-Ponty is following Malraux in asking this question.

37 Although Merleau-Ponty did not make this point, it is well known that many cultures have no such term. This shows, more generally, that the ways we choose to categorize the world and things are culturally specific.

38 This argument for the stylistic unity between works of art from diverse cultures sits uncomfortably with Malraux's attempt to make a radical distinction between classical and modern painting.

39 Merleau-Ponty, *Signs*, 65.

40 There follows a quote from Malraux's *Le Musée imaginaire*, 52, where an 'imaginary spirit' is alluded to.

41 Merleau-Ponty, *Signs*, 65.

42 Ibid., 59.

43 Ibid., 65.

44 Ibid. 58–9. Emphasis mine.

45 A significant part of 'Indirect Language and the Voices of Silence' comprises an examination of the art-gallery system and the way in which this affects our conception of the meaning of works of art, and of art itself.

46 Merleau-Ponty, *Signs*, 60.

47 Ibid.

48 Ibid.

49 Ibid.

50 See Malraux, *The Voices of Silence*, trans Stuart Gilbert, New York: Doubleday and Company Inc., 1953, 280.

51 Merleau-Ponty, *Signs*, 55–6. Emphasis mine.

52 Ibid., 52.

Chapter seven

1   Maurice Merleau-Ponty, *The Visible and the Invisible (followed by working notes)*, translated by Alphonso Lingis, Edited by Claude Lefort, Evanston, Northwestern University Press, 1968. Originally published as *Le Visible et l'invisible*, Editions Gallimard, 1964. It was begun by Merleau-Ponty in 1959. By the time of his death in May 1961, only the introductory section was complete – or somewhere near completion.

2   Merleau-Ponty, *Signs*, 78.

3   Ibid., 46.

4   Merleau-Ponty, *The Visible and the Invisible*, 200.

5   Ibid.

6   Ibid.

7   Lefort, *The Visible and the Invisible*, xxvii.

8   As indicated earlier, in *Showing Off! A Philosophy of Image* (London: Bloomsbury, 2014), I attempted to open up this seeing/being-seen dyad by drawing on a third phenomenon that I regard as central to Merleau-Ponty's writing and indeed to phenomenology itself: self-showing or self-presentation, that is, the condition of visibility. However, in many places (even in his late writing) Merleau-Ponty also consistently described visual experience in precisely those dyadic terms (that is, purely in terms of seeing and being seen). Where this is the case, in this book, I've simply tried to follow Merleau-Ponty's arguments as they are presented. However, readers who are especially interested in phenomenological self-showing, and Merleau-Ponty's treatment of it, may wish to consider my arguments in *Showing Off!* alongside those presented here.

9   Lefort, *The Visible and the Invisible*, xxviii.

10 Merleau-Ponty, *The Visible and the Invisible*, 156.

11 Ibid., 157.

12 Ibid., 274.

13 Lefort, *The Visible and the Invisible*, xxi.

14 See for instance: https://www.gamry.com/Framework%20Help/HTML5%20 -%20Tripane%20-%20Audience%20A/Content/SE/Introduction/ Overview%20of%20Spectroscopy.htm Accessed 9 September 2017.

15 All quotations and paraphrases in the section relate to Paul Crowther, *Phenomenologies of Art and Vision*, 34–5.

16 Ibid., 35. All but the last emphasis (on transperceptual) are my own.

17 In Madison's opinion (*The Phenomenology of Merleau-Ponty*, 167–8): 'The *Visible and the Invisible* is not merely a continuation of the *Phenomenology* and the author's other writings, but is rather a radical *calling into question* of them. ... It must ... be recognised that *The Visible and the Invisible* takes up a position on a much deeper level than the *Phenomenology* and constitutes a wholly new starting point. ... [It] appears as a *total taking up again* of the *Phenomenology*, transposing it in its entirety into a wholly other field.'

18 Merleau-Ponty, 'Working note, January 1959', *The Visible and the Invisible*, 165.

19 Ibid., 200.

20 'The Philosopher and his Shadow', in *Signs*, translated by Richard C. McCleary, Evanston, Northwestern University Press, 1964, 159–81. Originally published as 'Le Philosophe et son ombre', The Hague: Martinus Nijhoff, 1959. *Phaenomenologica* 4, 195–220.

21 Merleau-Ponty, *Signs*, 178.

22 Merleau-Ponty, *The Visible and the Invisible*, 179.

23 Ibid., 6–7. Emphasis mine.

24 Ibid., xxvii.

25 Merleau-Ponty sometimes capitalized this term, and something did not. For the sake of consistency, in my own references to it, I will capitalize it when it is used in this sense. Other terms, such as 'Visibility' and 'Flesh' were also variously capitalized by Merleau-Ponty, or not.

26 Madison, *The Phenomenology of Merleau-Ponty*, 197.

27 Ibid.

28 Heidegger made a similar point in the second section of *The Origin of the Work of Art*. He wrote, in the context of his discussions of the articulations of Being – the 'essential strife' between what he called 'world' and 'earth' – and the search for truth: 'The earth is the spontaneous forthcoming of that which is continually self-secluding and to that extent sheltering and concealing. ... Truth means the essence of the true. We think this essence in recollecting the Greek word *aletheia*, the unconcealment of beings. ... If here and elsewhere we conceive truth as unconcealment, we are not merely taking refuge in a more literal translation of a Greek word. We are reminding ourselves of what, unexperienced and unthought, underlies our familiar and therefore outworn essence of truth in the sense of correctness' (*Martin Heidegger, Basic Writings*, London: Routledge, 1978, 174, 176 & 177).

29 Madison, *The Phenomenology of Merleau-Ponty*, 198.

30 In this chapter, I focus on his discussions of 'visibility' and 'flesh'.

31 The term 'perception' was now regarded by Merleau-Ponty as a problematic one, due to its associations particularly with philosophies of reflection. As Françoise Dastur wrote in 'Perceptual Faith and the Invisible', *Journal of the British Society for Phenomenology*, Volume 25, Issue 1, January 1994, 44–52, 45: 'The word "perception" is now excluded because it involves the opposition between the visible thing and the invisible "state" or "act" of consciousness which is meant to reproduce it mentally, so that the invisible seems to be a mere correlative or counterpart of the visible.' However, Merleau-Ponty's explicit concern with visibility may be seen to have been already anticipated in 'Indirect Language and the Voices of Silence', as I have indicated in the concluding part of the previous chapter.

32 Claude Lefort, 'Editor's Foreword', *The Visible and the Invisible*, xxxi. Citing Merleau-Ponty, ibid., 102–3.

33 Madison, *The Phenomenology of Merleau-Ponty*, 99. Emphasis mine.

34 Merleau-Ponty, *The Visible and the Invisible*, 135: in a footnote he wrote that 'the *Uerpräsentierbarkeit* is the Flesh'.

35 Ibid., 134–5.

36 Ibid., 139.

37 Ibid.

38 Galen A. Johnson, 'Ontology and Painting: Eye and Mind'. In Johnson (ed.), *The Merleau-Ponty Aesthetics Reader: Philosophy and Painting*, 1993, 35–55, 50. He wrote: 'The Milesian sense of element meant that which is always presupposed but always forgotten, that from which everything comes and to which everything returns. The Greek elements were, therefore, eternal. Merleau-Ponty's term *Flesh* was meant to convey a genesis and growth in contrast to this eternality. In the "Working Notes" to *The Visible and the Invisible*, Merleau-Ponty was quite direct on this point. "I call the world flesh", he wrote, "in order to say that it is a *pregnancy* of possibles" (*The Visible and the Invisible*, 250). Paired with this term "pregnancy" we also find the birthing term "labor": "in the patient and silent labor of desire, begins the paradox of expression" (*The Visible and the Invisible*, 144). The painter's vision, "Eye and Mind" says, "is a continued birth" (*The Primacy of Perception*, 168)' (Johnson, Ibid., 50–1).

39 Merleau-Ponty, *The Visible and the Invisible*, 147.

40 Madison, *The Phenomenology of Merleau-Ponty*, 177.

41 Galen A. Johnson, 'The Colours of Fire: Depth and Desire in Merleau-Ponty's "Eye and Mind"', *Journal of the British Society for Phenomenology*, Volume 25, Issue 1994, 58.

42 Merleau-Ponty, *The Primacy of Perception*, 168. The quotations in this passage are from P. Claudel, *Introduction à la peinture hollandaise*, Paris, 1935. With respect to Merleau-Ponty's definitions of Being as 'seeing-visible', again see endnote 8.

43 Merleau-Ponty, *The Visible and the Invisible*, 142.

44 Ibid., 143.

45 A large element of *The Visible and the Invisible* (particularly the chapter 'Interrogation and Dialectic') involves Merleau-Ponty's response to Sartre's *L'Etre et le néant*, Paris, 1943.

46 Merleau-Ponty, *The Visible and the Invisible*, 99. Merleau-Ponty's position with respect to the notion of nothing(ness) thus appears to be closer to Bergson's nuanced notion of it, as expressed in *Creative Evolution* (1907). There, Bergson wrote that the idea of 'nothing' is a 'pseudo-idea': 'The void of which I speak ... is, at bottom, only the absence of some definite object, which was here at first, is now elsewhere, and, insofar as it is no longer in its former place, leaves behind it, so to speak, the void of itself' (from the English translation, 1911, 296–7).

47 Merleau-Ponty, *The Visible and the Invisible*, 28.

48 Ibid., 130–1.

49 Ibid., 123.

50 Johnson, 'The Colours of Fire', 58.

51 Merleau-Ponty, *The Primacy of Perception*, 163–4.

52 Merleau-Ponty, *The Visible and the Invisible*, 249.

53 Ibid., 139. Emphasis mine.

54 Merleau-Ponty, *The Primacy of Perception*, 167.

55 Ibid. 167. Charbonnier's *Le monologue du peintre*, Volume One, 1959 which Merleau-Ponty referenced, consisted of interviews with Braque, Singier, Ernst, Coutaud, Dewasne, Hartung, Lapicque, Villon, Bazaine, Prassinos, Miro, Picabia, Marchand, Soulages, Giacommetti, Masson. Volume Two contained interviews with Matisse, Tal Coat, Dali, Chagall, Viera Da Silva, Labisse, Le Moal, Manessier, Rouault, Dunoyer De Segonzac, Brianchon, Buffet, Gischia, Le Corbusier, Ubac, Music, Zao-Wou-Ki, Pignon, Leger.

56 Ibid.

57 Here, an important source for Merleau-Ponty, although not directly referred to, was Lacan's essay 'Le stade du miroir comme formateur du fonction du je', *Revue Française de Psychanaylse*, Volume 13 (October–December, 1949), 449–55. Merleau-Ponty discussed Lacan's mirror stage in his essay 'The Child's Relations with Others' (1950–51), *The Primacy of Perception*, 1964, 96–155. There, he wrote: 'Thus in this phenomenon of the specular image, so simple at first glance, will be revealed to the child for the first time the possibility of an attitude of self-observation that will develop subsequently in the form of narcissism. … From this moment on, the child also is drawn from his immediate reality; the specular image has a de-realising function in the sense that it turns the child away from what he effectively is, in order to orient him toward what he sees and imagines himself to be. Finally, this alienation of the immediate *me*, its "confiscation" for the benefit of the *me* that is visible in the mirror, already outlines what will be the "confiscation" of the subject by the others who look at him' (Ibid., 137).

58 Ovid, *Metamorphoses*, Translated by A. D Melville, Oxford and New York: Oxford University Press, 2008, 63 & 64.

59 Ibid. 66.

60 Margaret Werry, Bryan Schmidt, 'Immersion and the Spectator', *Theatre Journal*, Volume 66, Issue 3, October 2014, 467–79, 468.

61 Ibid.

62 Merleau-Ponty, *The Visible and the Invisible*, 28. Here, as an aside, are perceptually based, phenomenological resources that help us approach and understand the logic of recent debates regarding anatheism, by Richard Kearney and others.

63 Ibid., 40–1. The emphases are in the original.

64 Kees Vollemans, *Het raadzel van de zichtbare wereld. Philips Koninck, of een landschap in de vorm van een traktaat* (*The Puzzle of the Visible World. Philips Koninck, or a landscape in the form of a* treatise), Amsterdam: Uitgererij Duizend en Een, 1998, 60–4.

65 Ibid., 63.

66 For more on this see: Petr Uličný, 'Hans and Paul Vredeman de Vries in Rudolf II's Prague Castle', *Studia Rudolphina: Bulletin of the Research Center for Visual Arts and Culture in the Age of Rudolf II*, Institute of Art History, Czech Academy of Sciences, 2015, 48–63.

67 Vollemans, *Het raadzel van de zichtbare wereld*, 63.

68 See Ibid., 63.

69 Ibid., 64.

70 Ibid., 61.

71 Merleau-Ponty, *The Visible and the Invisible*, 8.

72 Ibid., 28–9.

73 Ibid., 38.

74 Ibid. The insertion in square brackets is my own.

75 Merleau-Ponty, *The Primacy of Perception*, 164.

76 As Françoise Dastur put it ('Merleau-Ponty and Thinking from Within', in Burke and van der Veken (eds), *Merleau-Ponty in Contemporary Perspectives*, 1993, 25–35, 26): 'Merleau-Ponty's thought, especially in his later period, is a thought of the living structure for which interiority no longer refers to a subject closed on itself.'

77 Merleau-Ponty, *The Visible and the Invisible*, 159.

78 Ibid., 49. The words in square brackets are my own insertion.

79 Ibid., 101.

80 Ibid., 94.

81 Ibid.

82 Ibid., 94–5. Emphases mine.

83 Merleau-Ponty, *The Primacy of Perception*, 164.

84 Ibid., 167.

85 Emphasis mine.

86 Merleau-Ponty, *The Visible and the Invisible*, 101. The emphases are in the original.

87 Ibid., 101.

88 Ibid., 102. Emphasis mine. Bernard Waldenfels ('Interrogative Thinking: Reflections on Merleau-Ponty's Later Philosophy'. In Burke and van der Veken (eds.), *Merleau-Ponty in Contemporary Perspectives*, 1993, 3–12, 5) has written as follows: 'The region of "wild Being" presents itself as a region where it is not yet settled once and for all if something is the case, what something is and what it is good for. This is a region where the portals of cultural order are not yet closed, where what something is implies more and other things than what it is.'

89 Here we see, again, affinities with Heidegger's thought. As Jay put it (*Downcast Eyes*, op cit., 271), Heidegger contrasted 'the early Greek attitude of wonder, which lets things be, with that of curiosity, which is based on the desire to know how they function'.

90 Merleau-Ponty, *The Visible and the Invisible*, 103.

91 Again, I would add to these the notion of self-showing. See endnote 8 above.

92 Merleau-Ponty, *The Primacy of Perception*, 166.

93 Alphonse de Waelhens, 'Merleau-Ponty: Philosopher of Painting' (1962), translated by Michael B. Smith. In *The Merleau-Ponty Aesthetics Reader*, 1993, 174–91, 189.

94 Merleau-Ponty, *The Primacy of Perception*, 186.

95 Ibid., 161.

96 For discussions of Merleau-Ponty's treatment of music see Elizabeth A. Behnke, 'At the Service of the Sonata: Music Lessons with Merleau-Ponty', *Somatics*, Volume 4, Issue 2, 1983, 32–4 and Michel Lefeuvre, 'Musique et peinture ou Lévi-Strauss et Merleau-Ponty', *Etudes*, Volume 140, May 1974, 727–35.

97 Merleau-Ponty, *The Primacy of Perception*, 161.

98 Ibid., 166.

99 Ibid.

100 I discuss further the kinds of space painting opens up in the following chapter.

Chapter eight

1 Paul Klee, *Das Bildnerische Denken: Schriften Zur Form- und Gestaltungslehre*, Jurg Spiller (ed), Basel: Benno Schwabe & Co. Verlag 1956. The English version was *The Thinking Eye. The Notebooks of Paul Klee. Volume I*. Jurg Spiller (ed) and Ralph Manheim (trans). London: Lund Humphries and New York: George Wittenborn, 1961.

2 In the footnotes to 'Eye and Mind' Merleau-Ponty's citation actually reads *Journal*, trans P. Klossowski (Paris, 1959).

3 This particular expression is found in a working note written by Merleau-Ponty dated Monday 4 January 1960. See Merleau-Ponty, *The Visible and the Invisible*, 225. The others are found in 'Eye and Mind': see in particular Merleau-Ponty, *The Primacy of Perception*, 159–60.

4 Ibid.

5 Ibid., 167.

6 Ibid., 178.

7 Ibid.

8 Ibid., 189.

9 In 'Eye and Mind' Merleau-Ponty seldom made reference to the term 'flesh', preferring instead the term Being.

10 Merleau-Ponty, *The Primacy of Perception*, 178.

11 Merleau-Ponty cited as his source G. Charbonnier, *Le monologue du peintre*, Paris, 1959, 176.

12 Merleau-Ponty, *The Primacy of Perception*, 179. He was citing Robert Delaunay, *Du cubisme à l'art abstrait*, Paris, 1957, 109.

13 Ibid., 179–80.

14 Ibid., 172.

15 Merleau-Ponty, *The Visible and the Invisible*, 48.

16 Ibid., 84.

17 Merleau-Ponty wrote of Cézanne's understanding that 'the external form, the envelope, is secondary and derived, that it is not that which causes a thing to take form, that this shell of space must be shattered'. Merleau-Ponty, *The Primacy of Perception*, 180.

18 Alphonse de Waelhens, 'Merleau-Ponty: Philosopher of Painting', translated by Michael B. Smith. In Johnson (ed.), *The Merleau-Ponty Aesthetics Reader*, 1993, 174–91, 176. The final emphasis is mine.

19 Merleau-Ponty, *The Primacy of Perception*, 182.

20 Ibid., 172. Véronique M. Fóti provided a useful discussion of Merleau-Ponty's treatment of Descartes' *Optics* in her essay 'The Dimension of Color'. In Johnson (ed.), *The Merleau-Ponty Aesthetics Reader*, 1993, 293–308.

21 Fóti, 'The Dimension of Color', 306. The quotation is from Merleau-Ponty, *The Primacy of Perception*, 179. She continued, however: 'Notwithstanding his important insight concerning this interpenetration … Merleau-Ponty's focus is trained on one side or one direction of this reciprocal movement, to the neglect of the other. … He therefore slights the lawlike and, to some extent, mathematically expressible traits which characterise not only the physical infrastructure of color but also its phenomenal manifestations, preferring an almost mystical discourse of "exhalations" and – in a cryptic quotation from Hermes Trismegistus – of "the inarticulate cry which seemed to be the voice of light" (Merleau-Ponty *The Primacy of Perception*, 182). The phenomena of color and color-vision, far from being inarticulate, exhibit lawlike traits of astonishing intricacy.' She referred the reader to such works as Johannes Itten's *The Elements of Color*, Faber Birren (ed.), New York, Van Nostrand, 1970, Edwin H. Land's 'Experiments in Color Vision', *Scientific American*, May 1959, 84–99, and his 'The Retinex Theory of Color Vision', *Scientific American*, December 1977, 108–30.

22 Ibid., 306.

23 Merleau-Ponty, *The Primacy of Perception*, 182.

24 Merleau-Ponty, *The Structure of Behavior*, 203.

25 Merleau-Ponty, *The Primacy of Perception*, 163.

26 Glen A. Mazis, 'Merleau-Ponty, Inhabitation and the Emotions', 1986. In Pietersma (ed.), *Merleau-Ponty: Critical Essays*, 1989, 251–68, 264.

27 These are Madison's and Johnson's words, to which I referred in Chapter 7.

28 Merleau-Ponty, *The Visible and the Invisible*, 4.

29 Merleau-Ponty, *The Primacy of Perception*, 168.

30 Ibid., 169.

31 For a development of these themes, with respect to the work of Matisse, see: Ed KrÄma, 'Lightning and Rain: Phenomenology, Psychoanalysis and Matisse's Hand', *Tate Papers*, no.18, Autumn 2012, http://www.tate.org.uk/research/publications/tate-papers/18/lightning-and-rain-phenomenology-psychoanalysis-and-matisses-hand, Accessed 17 September 2017.

32 Merleau-Ponty wrote that 'artists have often mused upon mirrors because beneath this "mechanical trick" they recognised ... the metamorphosis of seeing and seen which defines both our Flesh and the painter's vocation' (Merleau-Ponty, *The Primacy of Perception*, 168–9).

33 Ibid., 162.

34 Ibid., 161.

35 Ibid., 169.

36 Madison, *The Phenomenology of Merleau-Ponty*, 100–1. He was referencing Merleau-Ponty, *The Primacy of Perception*, 181 and 166.

37 Merleau-Ponty *The Primacy of Perception*, 162.

38 Ibid., 169.

39 Ibid.

40 Ibid., 172.

41 Ibid., 170.

42 Operational science, as Fóti pointed out, did not 'spring from Cartesianism by direct filiation, but is one of "two monsters born of its dismemberment"'. Fóti, 'The Dimension of Color', 304. She was citing Merleau-Ponty, *The Primacy of Perception*, 177.

43 Merleau-Ponty *The Primacy of Perception*, 159.

44 Ibid.

45 Ibid., 160.

46 Ibid.

47 Merleau-Ponty, *The Visible and the Invisible*, 81.

48 'The Cartesian concept of vision', wrote Merleau-Ponty, 'is modelled after the sense of touch' (Merleau-Ponty, *The Primacy of Perception*, 170).

49 Ibid., 173.

50 Ibid., 180.

51 Ibid., 162.

52 Ibid., 175.

53 Ibid., 159.

54 Ibid., 167. Emphasis mine.

55 Merleau-Ponty, *The Visible and the Invisible*, 9 & 10.

56 As Dillon pointed out in his essay 'Merleau-Ponty and the Reversibility Thesis' (Pietersma, ed., *Merleau-Ponty: Critical Essays*, 1989, 77–98), Merleau-Ponty should not be misunderstood as suggesting that the notion of reversibility is characterized by symmetry. The relationship between seer and seen is always asymmetrical.

57 Merleau-Ponty, *The Primacy of Perception*, 167.

58 Ibid.

59 'We speak of "inspiration," and the word should be taken literally. There really is inspiration and expiration of Being, action and passion so slightly discernible that it becomes impossible to distinguish between what sees and what is seen, what paints and what is painted' (Merleau-Ponty, *The Primacy of Perception*, 167).

60 Ibid., 187.

61 Ibid., 186.

62 Ibid.

63 Ibid., 187.

64 Ibid., 167. In *The Visible and the Invisible*, he wrote of this kind of questioning that it 'condemns itself to putting into the things what it will then pretend to find in them' (Merleau-Ponty, *The Visible and the Invisible*, 38).

65 Merleau-Ponty, *The Visible and the Invisible*, 40. My emphasis.

66 Ibid., 147.

67 Merleau-Ponty, *The Primacy of Perception*, 179–80.

68 In making this point, Johnson was challenging Lyotard's reading of 'Eye and Mind' in *Discours, Figure* (4th edition, Paris: Klincksieck, 1971, 1985, 18–23 and 53–9). He wrote: 'Jean-François Lyotard … completely missed both the difference and the desire in Merleau-Ponty's treatment of depth in "Eye and Mind". Merleau-Ponty's account does not overlook the gaps, splits, and disunities within world and self, eliminating what is strange, foreign and Other in favour of conceptual sameness, and Merleau-Ponty's account has much to do with desire, dreams, and Eros' (Johnson, 'The Colours of Fire', 61).

69 Ibid., 53.

70 Merleau-Ponty, *The Visible and the Invisible*, 159.

71 Merleau-Ponty *The Primacy of Perception*, 183.

72 Ibid., 168.

73 Ibid., 167–8.

74 Ibid., 184.

75 Ibid., 183. Emphasis mine.

76 Mallin, 'Chiasm, Line and Art.' In Pietersma, ed., *Critical Essays,* 1989, 219–50, 246.

77 Merleau-Ponty, *The Primacy of Perception*, 184 / *L'oeil et l'esprit*, Paris: Gallimard, 1964, 76.

78 Mallin, 'Chiasm, Line and Art', 249–50.

79 Merleau-Ponty, *The Primacy of Perception*, 162–3. Emphasis mine.

80 Clarissa Pinkola Estés, *Women who Run with the Wolves: Contacting the Power of the Wild Woman*, 1992. See again: Ed KrÄma, 'Lightning and Rain: Phenomenology, Psychoanalysis and Matisse's Hand', op cit.

81 Merleau-Ponty, *The Primacy of Perception*, 164. The emphases are in the original.

82 By way of example, see the works by unknown Early Magdalenian artist(s) entitled *Painted and Engraved Horses,* c. 15,000 BC, part of the Panel of the Black Cow, The Cave of Lascaux, France. They are beautifully reproduced in Mario Ruspoli, *The Cave of Lascaux: The Final Photographic Record,* London: Thames and Hudson Ltd., and New York: Harry N Abrams Inc., 1987, 136–9.

83 Merleau-Ponty, *The Primacy of Perception,* 166.

84 Ibid.

85 Merleau-Ponty, *Phenomenology of Perception,* xxi.

86 On this point, Merleau-Ponty concluded 'Eye and Mind' with a rhetorical question and its refutation: 'Is this the highest point of reason to realise that the soil beneath our feet is shifting, to pompously name "interrogation" what is only a persistent state of stupor, to call "research" or "quest" what is only trudging in a circle, to call "Being" that which never fully *is*?' (Merleau-Ponty, *The Primacy of Perception,* 190). However, referring specifically to the interrogations of painting, he continued: 'If no painting comes to be *the* painting, if no work is ever absolutely completed and done with, still each creation changes, alters, enlightens, deepens, confirms, exalts, re-creates, or creates in advance all the others. If creations are not a possession, it is not only that, like all things, they pass away; it is also that they have almost all their life still before them' (Merleau-Ponty, *The Primacy of Perception,* 190).

87 Merleau-Ponty, *The Visible and the Invisible,* 131. The insertion in square brackets is my own.

88 Ibid., 133.

89 Ibid., 39. My emphasis.

90 Merleau-Ponty, *Sense and Non-Sense,* 40.

91 Graham Ellard and Stephen Johnstone, *For an Open Campus, For an Open Campus* (16mm film, colour, sound, 29 mins) 2015. A link to extract of the film is available on: http://www.ellardjohnstone.com/assets/ForanOpenCampus.html.

92 Walter Benjamin, 'Epistemo-Critical Prologue', *The Origin of Tragic German Drama.* Translated by John Osborne, London and New York: Verso 1998/2003, 27.

93 Ibid., 28.

94 Ibid. The explanatory insertion is my own.

95 Merleau-Ponty, *The Primacy of Perception,* 160.

96 Walter Benjamin, *The Origin of Tragic German Drama,* 28.

97 Ibid.

98 Ibid.

99 Ibid.

100 Ibid., 28–9.

101 Ibid., 29.

102 Ibid, 20.

103 The contextualizing information accompanying this image in the museum's online version of its collection states that 'this painting is a wonderful example of the landscapes of Philips Koninck. They were probably inspired by the river areas of the Waal and the Rhine, but the location cannot be precisely identified. Undoubtedly, the paintings took shape in the studio based on the memories the painter had of the region'. http://collectie.boijmans.nl/en/object/2144/An-Extensive-Landscape,-with-a-River/Philips-Koninck. Accessed 12 February 2018.

104 This is in contrast with the commentary that accompanies this painting again in the museum's online version of its collection. Here we read: 'Nature is so predominantly present in Koninck's paintings that the insignificance and the mortality of man seems to be the real theme.' Ibid.

105 Vollemans , *Het raadzel van de zichtbare wereld. Philips Koninck, of een landschap in de vorm van een traktaat* (*The Puzzle of the Visible World. Philips Koninck, or a landscape in the form of a* treatise), Amsterdam: Uitgererij Duizend en Een, 1998, 34.

106 My thanks go to Bei Guo, a student on my 'Ornamentation' module (Goldsmiths, University of London) during 2017, who drew my attention to the following texts by Norris Brock Johnson: *Tenryu-ji: Life and Spirit of a Kyoto Garden*, Berkeley: Stone Bridge Press (2012) and his 'Temple Architecture as Construction of Consciousness: A Japanese Temple and Garden', *Architecture and Comport. I Arch. Behav.*, Volume 4, Issue 3, North Carolina: University of North Carolina, 1968.

107 See 'Founding Philosophy', Aichi Prefectural University of Fine Arts and Music Website: https://www.aichi-fam-u.ac.jp/english/about/about02/about02-01.html. Accessed 28 January 2018.

108 Merleau-Ponty, *The Visible and the Invisible*, 48.

109 Ibid., 84.

110 See 'The Nature of the Aichi Geidai's campus: The campus in Autumn', http://www.shinodanozomi.com/Aichi-Geidai/nature_of_the_campus.html. Accessed 29 January 2018.

111 Ellard and Johnstone, 'For an Open Campus' website entry: http://www.ellard johnstone.com/assets/ForanOpenCampus.html. Accessed 31 October 2017.

112 Ibid.

113 See for instance 'Architect Junzo Yoshimura's unique campus in danger' http://www.shinodanozomi.com/Aichi-Geidai/top.html. Accessed 28 January 2018.

114 Extracted from a conversation with Stephen Johnstone at Goldsmiths, University of London, 17 January 2018.

115 Ellard and Johnstone, 'For an Open Campus' website entry, op cit.

116 Ibid.

117 Merleau-Ponty, *The Visible and the Invisible*, 101.

BIBLIOGRAPHY

Andrews, Jorella. 'The Virtual Intersection: A Meditation on Domestic Virtue'. In *Secret Spaces, Forbidden Places: Re-thinking Culture*. Edited by Fran Lloyd and Catherine O'Brien, 171–83. New York and Oxford: Berghahn, 2000.

Andrews, Jorella. *Showing Off: A Philosophy of Image*. London: Bloomsbury, 2014.

Andrews, Jorella and Leah Durner. 'Painting, Largesse, and Life – A Conversation with Leah Durner', online resource (forthcoming).

Bannan, John. *The Philosophy of Merleau-Ponty*. San Diego, CA: Harcourt, Brace and World, 1967.

Barral, Mary Rose. 'Self and Other: Communication and Love'. *Review of Existential Psychology and Psychiatry*, 1982–3, 155–80.

Behnke, Elizabeth A. 'At the Service of the Sonata: Music Lessons with Merleau-Ponty'. *Somatics* 4, no. 2 (1983), 32–4.

Benjamin, Walter. *The Origin of Tragic German Drama*. Translated by John Osborne. London and New York: Verso, 1998/2003.

Bermúdez, José, Naomi Eilan Luis and Anthony Marcel (eds). *The Body and the Self*. Cambridge, MA and London: MIT Press, 1995.

Bois, Yve-Alain, Denis Hollier, Rosalind Krauss and Hubert Damisch. 'A Conversation with Hubert Damisch'. *October* 85 (Summer 1998), 3–17, 3–4.

Broadhurst, Sue. 'Merleau-Ponty and Neuroaesthetics: Two Approaches to Performance and Technology'. *Digital Creativity* 23, no. 3–4 (2012), 225–38. Available online at http://dx.doi.org/10.1080/14626268.2012.709941 (accessed 27 September 2017).

Buccheri, R., Metod Saniga and W. M. Stuckey. *The Nature of Time: Geometry, Physics & Perception*. NATO Science Series II: Volume 95, Dordrecht, Boston and London: Kluwer Academic Publishers, 2003.

Buchanan, Brett. *Onto-Ethologies: The Animal Environments of Uexküll, Heidegger, Merleau-Ponty, and Deleuze*. New York: State University of New York Press, 2008.

Burke, Patrick and Jan van der Veken (eds). *Merleau-Ponty in Contemporary Perspectives*. Dordrecht, Boston and London: Kluwer Academic Publishers, 1993.

Busch, Thomas W. 'Perception, Finitude, and Transgression: A note on Merleau-Ponty and Ricoeur'. In *Merleau-Ponty: Hermeneutics and Postmodernism*. Edited by Thomas W. Busch and Shaun Gallagher, 25–35. Albany, NY: State University of New York Press, 1992.

Busch, Thomas W. and Shaun Gallagher (eds). *Merleau-Ponty: Hermeneutics and Postmodernism*. Albany, NY: State University of New York Press, 1992.

Butler, Judith. 'Sexual Ideology and Phenomenological Description: A Feminist Critique of Merleau-Ponty's Phenomenology of Perception'. In *The Thinking Muse: Feminism and Modern French Philosophy*. Edited by Jeffner Allen and Iris Marion Young, 85–100. Bloomington, IN: Indiana University Press, 1989.

Buytendijk, F. J. J. 'Les Différences essentielles des fonctions psychiques de l'homme et des animaux' *Cahiers de philosophie de la nature*, Vrin, IV, 1930.

Cassou, Jean. *El Greco*. Translated by Lucy Norton. Melbourne, London and Toronto: William Heinemann Ltd, 1956.

Charbonnier, Georges. *Le monologue du peintre*, Volume One. Paris: Julliard, 1959.

Claudel, Paul. *Introduction à la peinture hollandaise*. Paris: Gallimard, 1935.

Coole, Diana. 'The Inertia of Matter and the Generativity of Flesh'. In *New Materialisms: Ontology, Agency, and Politics*. Edited by Diana Coole and Samantha Frost, 92–115. Durham, NC: Duke University Press, 2010.

Coole, Diana. *Merleau-Ponty and Modern Politics after Anti-Humanism*. Lanham, Boulder, New York, Toronto and Plymouth UK: Rowman and Littlefield Publishers Inc, 2007.

Cottingham, J. 'The Role of God in Descartes' Philosophy'. In *A Companion to Descartes*. Edited by Janet Broughton and John Carriero, 287–301. Hoboken, NJ: Blackwell, 2008.

Coyne, Mary L. *Correcting Perspectives: Jan Dibbets and an Optical Conceptualism*. Long Beach: California State University Press, 2013. http://journal.depthoffield.eu/vol02/nr01/a02/en (accessed 13 January 2018).

Crowther, Paul. *Phenomenologies of Art and Vision: A Post-Analytic Turn*. London, New Delhi, New York and Sydney: Bloomsbury, 2013.

Crowther, Paul. *Phenomenology of the Visual Arts (Even the Frame)*. Stanford, CA: Stanford University Press, 2009.

Dastur, Françoise. 'Merleau-Ponty and Thinking from Within'. In *Merleau-Ponty in Contemporary Perspectives*. Edited by Patrick Burke and Jan van der Veken, 25–35. Dordrecht, Boston and London: Kluwer Academic Publishers, 1993.

Dastur, Françoise. 'Perceptual Faith and the Invisible'. *Journal of the British Society for Phenomenology* 25, no. 1 (January 1994), 44–52.

Davis, Duane H. and William S. Hamrick. *Merleau-Ponty and the Art of Perception*. Albany, NY: State University of New York Press, 2016.

Derrida, Jacques. *Speech and Phenomena of 1967*. Translated by David B. Allison. Evanston, IL: Northwestern University Press, 1973.

Dillon, M. C. 'Merleau-Ponty and the Reversibility Thesis'. In *Merleau-Ponty: Critical Essays*. Edited by Henry Pietersma, 77–98. Lanham, MD: University Press of America. 1989.

Dillon, M. C. 'Temporality: Merleau-Ponty and Derrida'. In *Merleau-Ponty: Hermeneutics and Postmodernism*. Edited by Thomas W. Busch and Shaun Gallagher, 189–212. Albany, NY: State University of New York Press, 1992.

Dolphijn, Rick and Iris van der Tuin. 'Interview with Quentin Meillassoux'. In *New Materialism: Interviews & Cartographies*. Edited by Iris van der Tuin and Rick Dolphjin. Ann Arbor, MI: Open Humanities Press, 2012. Source: http://quod.lib. umich.edu/o/ohp/11515701.0001.001/1:4.4/--new-materialism-interviews-carto graphies?rgn=div2;view=fulltext

Durner, Leah. 'Gestural Abstraction and the Fleshiness of Paint'. In *Analecta Husserliana: The Yearbook of Phenomenological Research*, Volume LXXXI.

Edited by Anna-Teresa Tymieniecka, 187–194. Dordrecht, Boston and London: Kluwer Academic Publishers, 2004.

Durner, Leah. 'Extravagant Painting: Outpouring and Overflowing', 2017, broadsheet produced for the College Art Association Conference in New York, for the academic panel 'Immeasurable Extravagance: Proposals for and Economy of Abundance in an Age of Scarcity'. https://www.leahdurner.com/bibliography.

Dwyer, Philip. *Sense and Subjectivity: A study of Wittgenstein and Merleau-Ponty.* Leiden: Brill, 1990.

Edie, James. 'Can Grammar Be Thought?' In *Patterns of the Life-World, Essays in Honour of John Wild.* Edited by James M. Edie, Francis H. Parker, Calvin O. Schrag Evanston, 315–45. Evanston, IL: Northwestern University Press, 1970.

Edie, James. 'Foreword'. In *Consciousness and the Acquisition of Language.* Edited by Maurice Merleau-Ponty and Translated by Hugh J. Silverman, xi–xxxii. Evanston, IL: Northwestern University Press, 1973.

Edie, James. 'Was Merleau-Ponty a Structuralist?' *Merleau-Ponty's Philosophy of Language: Structuralism and Dialectics*, Centre for Advanced Research in Phenomenology & University Press of America Inc., 1987, pp. 13–35.

Ellis, Tom. *The Middle*, The Wallace Collection, 15 September–27 November 2016. http://www.wallacecollection.org/collections/exhibition/120

Eugene F. *Art and Existence: A Phenomenological Aesthetics.* Lewisburg: Bucknell University Press, 1970.

Exhibition Catalogue. 'Barbara Kapusta.' Entry in: *The Promise of Total Automation*, Kunsthalle Wien, 2016, 21.

Exhibition catalogue: *12 Peintres & Sculpteurs Américains Contemporains*, Paris: Musée National d'Art Moderne, 1953.

Finn, Geraldine. 'The Politics of Contingency: The Contingency of Politics. On the Political Implications of Merleau-Ponty's Ontology of the Flesh'. In *Merleau-Ponty: Hermeneutics and Postmodernism.* Edited by Thomas W. Busch and Shaun Gallagher. Albany, NY: State University of New York Press, 1992, 171–188.

Fischer, F. 'Raum-Zeitstruktur und Denkstörung in der Schizophrenie', *Ztschr. f. d. ges. Neurologie u. Psychiatrie*, 1930.

Fóti, Véronique M. 'Painting and the Re-organisation of Philosophical Thought in Merleau-Ponty'. *Philosophy Today* 24 (Summer 1980), 114–20.

Fóti, Véronique M. 'The Dimension of Color'. In *The Merleau-Ponty Aesthetics Reader: Philosophy and Painting.* Edited by Galen A. Johnson, 293–308. Evanston, IL: Northwestern University Press, 1993. Originally published in *International Studies in Philosophy* 22, no. 3 (1990), 13–28.

Fóti, Véronique M. 'The Evidences of Paintings: Merleau-Ponty and Contemporary Abstraction'. In *Merleau-Ponty: Difference, Materiality, Painting.* Edited by Véronique M. Fóti, 137–68. Amherst, NY: Humanity Books, 1996 (2000).

Gardner, Sebastian. 'Merleau-Ponty's phenomenology in the light of Kant's Third Critique and Schelling's Real-Idealismus'. *Continential Philosophy Review* 50 (2017), 5–25. https://doi.org/10.1007/s11007-016-9393-1 (accessed 26 September 2017).

Gelb, Adhémar and Kurt Goldstein. *Psychologische Analysen hirnpathologisher Fälle.* Leipzig: Barth, 1920.

Geraets, Theodore F. *Vers une nouvelle philosophie transcendantale: la genèse de la philosophie de Maurice Merleau-Ponty jusqu' à la Phénoménologie de la Perception.* The Hague: Martinus Nijhoff, 1971.

Goldstein, Kurt. 'Über die Abhängigkeit der Bewegungen von optischen Vorgängen'. *Monatschrift für Psychiatrie und Neurologie*, Festschrift Liepmann, 1923.

Grosse, Katharina. 'The Poise of the Head und die anderen folgen'. In *Contemporary Painting in Contex* (2010). Edited by Anne Ring Petersen with Makkel Bogh, Hans Dam Christensen and Peter Nørgaard Larsen, 97–122. Museum Tusculanum Press and University of Copenhagen, 2013 edition.

Grosz, Elizabeth. *Volatile Bodies*. Bloomington, IN: Indiana University Press, 1994.

Hainämaa, Sara. 'Anonymity and personhood: Merleau-Ponty's account of the subject of perception'. *Continental Philosophy Review* 48 (2015), 123–42, 125.

Hainämaa, Sara and Timo Kaitaro. 'Descartes' Notion of the Mind-Body Union and its Phenomenological Expositions'. In *The Oxford Handbook of the History of Phenomenology*. Edited by Dan Zahavi. Oxford: Oxford University Press, forthcoming. Draft: Available online at https://www. academia.edu/34005226/Descartes_notion_of_the_mind-body_union_and_its_phenomenological_expositions (accessed 1 October 2017).

Hall, Harrison. 'Painting and Perceiving'. *The Journal of Aesthetics and Art Criticism* 39 (Spring 1981), 291–5.

Hamrick, William S. 'Perception, Corporeity, and Kindness'. *Journal of the British Society for Phenomenology* 25 (1994), 74–84.

Harman, Graham. 'Vicarious Causation'. *Collapse II* 2007, 187–221.

Hedges, Chris. *Empire of Illusion: The End of Literacy and the Triumph of Spectacle*. New York: Nation Books, 2009.

Hoptman, Laura. 'The Forever Now: Contemporary Painting in an Atemporal World'. In *The Forever Now: Contemporary Painting in an Atemporal World*. Edited by Laura Hoptman, 13–61. New York: The Museum of Modern Art, 2014.

Iliadis, A. 'Interview with Graham Harman'. *Figure/Ground*, 2 October 2013. http://figureground.org/interview-with-graham-harman-2.

Irigaray, Luce. *An Ethics of Sexual Difference*, Paris, 1984. Translated by Carolyn Burke and Gillian C. Gill. London: The Athlone Press, 1993.

Itten, Johannes. *The Elements of Color*. Edited by Faber Birren. New York: Van Nostrand, 1970.

Jay, Martin. *Downcast Eyes: The Denigration of Vision in Twentieth Century French Thought*. Berkeley, Los Angeles and London: University of California Press, 1993.

Johnson, Galen A. 'Ontology and Painting: Eye and Mind'. In *The Merleau-Ponty Aesthetics Reader: Philosophy and Painting*. Edited by Galen A. Johnson, 35–55. Evanston, IL: Northwestern University Press, 1993.

Johnson, Galen A. 'Structures and Painting: "Indirect Language and the Voices of Silence"'. In *The Merleau-Ponty Aesthetics Reader: Philosophy and Painting*. Edited by Galen A. Johnson, 14–34. Evanston, IL: Northwestern University Press, 1993.

Johnson, Galen A. *The Retrieval of the Beautiful: Thinking Through Merleau-Ponty's Aesthetics*. Evanston, IL: Northwestern University Press, 2009.

Johnson, Galen A. 'The Colours of Fire: Depth and Desire in Merleau-Ponty's "Eye and Mind"'. *Journal of the British Society for Phenomenology* 25, no. 1 (1994), 53–63.

Johnson, Norris Brock. 'Temple Architecture as Construction of Consciousness: A Japanese Temple and Garden'. *Architecture et Comportement/Architecture and Behaviour* 4, no. 3 (1968), 229–49. North Carolina: University of North Carolina.

Johnson, Norris Brock. *Tenryu-ji: Life and Spirit of a Kyoto Garden*. Berkeley: Stone Bridge Press, 2012.

Joselit, David. 'Painting Travesty'. In *Whitney Biennial 2012*. Edited by Elisabeth Sussman and Jay Sanders, 34–7. New York: Whitney Museum of American Art, 2012.

Joselit, David. 'Signal Processing'. *Artforum* (Summer 2011), 356. Available online at: http://artarchives.net/texts/2011/joselit2011.html.

Josephus. 'The Testimonium Flavianum'. Available at: http://www.josephus.org/ testimonium.htm.

Kearney, Richard. *Anatheism*. New York, Chichester and West Sussex: Columbia University Press, 2011.

Kearney, Richard. 'Merleau-Ponty and the Sacramentality of the Flesh'. In *Merleau-Ponty at the Limits of Art, Religion, and Perception*. Edited by Kascha Semionovitch and Neal DeRoo, 147–66. London and New York: Continuum, 2010.

Kearney Richard and Kascha Semonovitch (eds). *Phenomenologies of the Stranger: Between Hostility and Hospitality*. New York: Fordham University Press, 2011.

Kendal, Richard (ed.). *Cézanne, by Himself*. London: Guild Publishing, 1988, 31–3.

Kimchi, R., M. Behrman and C. R. Olson (eds). *Perceptual Organization in Vision. Behavioral and Neural Perspectives*. Mahwah, NJ: Erlbaum, 2003.

Klee, Paul. *Das Bildnerische Denken: Schriften Zur Form- und Gestaltungslehre*. Edited by Jurg Spiller. Basel: Benno Schwabe & Co. Verlag, 1956.

Klee, Paul. *The Thinking Eye. The Notebooks of Paul Klee*, Volume I. Edited by Jurg Spiller and Translated by Ralph Manheim. London and New York: Lund Humphries/George Wittenborn, 1961.

Köhler, Wolfgang. *Gestalt Psychology*. New York: Mentor Books, 1947.

KrÄma, Ed. 'Lightning and Rain: Phenomenology, Psychoanalysis and Matisse's Hand'. *Tate Papers*, no.18, Autumn 2012, http://www.tate.org.uk/research/ publications/tate-papers/18/lightning-and-rain-phenomenology-psychoanalysis-and-matisses-hand (accessed 17 September 2017).

Krauss, Rosalind. 'Sculpture in the Expanded Field'. *October* 8 (Spring 1979), 30–44.

Heidegger, Martin. *Martin Heidegger, Basic Writings*. Edited by David Krell. London: Routledge, 1978.

Kruks, Sonia. *The Political Philosophy of Merleau-Ponty*. Atlantic Highlands and Sussex: Humanities Press and Harvester Press, 1981.

Kwant, Remi C. *De Stemmen van de stilte: Merleau-Ponty's analyse van de schilderkunst (The Voices of Silence: Merleau-Ponty's Analyses of Painting)*. Antwerp: Hilversum, 1968.

Kwant, Remi C. *From Phenomenology to Metaphysics: The Later Work of Merleau-Ponty*. Pittsburg: Duquesne University Press, 1966.

Kwant, Remi C. *The Phenomenology of Expression*. Pittsburg: Duquesne University Press, 1970.

Lacan, Jacques. 'Le stade du miroir comme formateur du fonction du je'. *Revue Française de Psychanaylse* 13 (October–December 1949), 449–55.

Lachièze-Rey, P. *Le Moi le Monde et Dieu*. Paris: Boivin, 1938.

Land, Edwin H. 'Experiments in Color Vision'. *Scientific American* (May 1959), 84–99.

Land, Edwin H. 'The Retinex Theory of Color Vision'. *Scientific American* (December 1977), 108–30.

Landes, Donald A. *Merleau-Ponty and the Paradoxes of Expression*. London: Bloomsbury Academic, 2013.

Landes, Donald A. *The Merleau-Ponty Dictionary*, London: Bloomsbury Academic, 2013.

Lefeuvre, Michel. 'Musique et peinture ou Lévi-Strauss et Merleau-Ponty'. *Etudes* 140 (May 1974), 727–35.

Lemkowitz, Jake. 'Studio Visit: Leah Durner' (Collaborators and friends). In *Front + Main: A Blog from West Elm*, February 15, 2013. https://blog.westelm.com/2013/02/15/talking-with-leah-durner/

Lévinas, Emmanuel. *Totality and Infinity* (1961) Translated by Alfonso Lingis. Dordrecht, Boston and London: Kluwer Academic Publishers, 1991.

Levine, Stephen K. 'Merleau-Ponty's Philosophy of Art'. *Man and World* 2, no. 3 (August 1969), 438–52.

LeWitt, Sol. 'Paragraphs on Conceptual Art'. *Artforum*, June 1967.

Lingis, Alphonso. 'Translator's Foreword'. In *The Visible and the Invisible*. Edited by Maurice Merleau-Ponty, xi–xxxiii. Evanston, IL: Northwestern University Press, 1968.

Loos, Ted. 'Blobs and Slashes, Interrupted by Forms: Amy Sillman Brings Together Abstraction and Figuration'. *New York Times*, 26 September 2013. http://www.nytimes.com/2013/09/29/arts/design/amy-sillman-brings-together-abstraction-and-figuration.html.

Lucarelli, Fosco. 'Perspective Corrections, by Jan Dibbets (1967-1969)'. *Socks*, 25 April 2016. http://socks-studio.com/2016/04/25/perspective-corrections-by-jan-dibbets-1967-1969/.

Lyotard, Jean-François. 'Philosophy and Painting in the Age of their Experimentation: Contribution to an Idea of Postmodernity'. In *The Merleau-Ponty Aesthetics Reader: Philosophy and Painting*. Edited by Galen A. Johnson, 323–35. Evanston, IL: Northwestern University Press, 1993.

Madison, Gary Brent. 'Did Merleau-Ponty have a Theory of Perception?'. In *Merleau-Ponty: Hermeneutics and Postmodernism*. Edited by Thomas W. Busch and Shaun Gallagher, 83–106. Albany, NY: State University of New York Press, 1992.

Madison, Gary Brent. 'Merleau-Ponty in Retrospect'. In *Merleau-Ponty in Contemporary Perspectives*. Edited by Patrick Burke and Jan van der Veken, 183–195. Dordrecht, Boston and London: Kluwer Academic Publishers, 1993.

Madison, Gary Brent. *The Phenomenology of Merleau-Ponty: A Search for the Limits of Consciousness*. Athens: Ohio University Press, 1981.

Magritte, René. 'Letter to Alphonse Waelhens' (28 April 1962). In *The Merleau-Ponty Aesthetics Reader: Philosophy and Painting*. Edited by Galen A. Johnson, 336. Evanston, IL: Northwestern University Press, 1993.

Mallin, Samuel B. 'Chiasm, Line and Art'. In *Merleau-Ponty: Critical Essays*. Edited by Henry Pietersma, 219–50. Lanham, MD: University Press of America, 1989.

Malraux, André. *The Voices of Silence*. Translated by Stuart Gilbert. New York: Doubleday and Company Inc., 1953.

May, Wolfe. 'Merleau-Ponty's Visit to Manchester'. *Journal of the British Society for Phenomenology* 25, no. 1 (1994), 6.

Mazis, Glen A. 'Merleau-Ponty, Inhabitation and the Emotions' 1986'. In *Merleau-Ponty: Critical Essays*. Edited by Henry Pietersma, 251–68. Lanham, MD: University Press of America. 1989.

Mehring, Christine. 'A Contemporary Look at Wols'. In *Wols Photographs*, Busch-Reisinger Museum, Harvard University Art Museums, Cambridge, MA, ex cat, 1999, 39–40.

Merleau-Ponty, Maurice, 'An Unpublished Text by Maurice Merleau-Ponty: A Prospectus of His Work' (1952). In *The Primacy of Perception*. Edited by James M. Edie, 3–11. Evanston, IL: Northwestern University Press, 1964.

Merleau-Ponty, Maurice. 'Cézanne's Doubt'. In *Sense and Non-Sense*. Edited by John Wild, 9–25. Evanston, IL: Northwestern University Press, 1964. Originally published in *Fontaine*, 4e année, T. VIII, no. 47, 80–100, December 1945. Reprinted in *Sens et non-sens*, 15–44.

Merleau-Ponty, Maurice. 'Christianisme et ressentiment'. *La Vie Intellectuelle*, 7e année, nouvelle série, T. XXXVI, 10 June 1935, 278–306. English translation in Maurice Merleau-Ponty, *Texts and Dialogues: On Philosophy, Politics and Culture*. Edited by Hugh J. Silverman and James Barry, Humanity Books, 1992, 85–100.

Merleau-Ponty, Maurice. *Éloge de la philosophie et autres essais*. Paris: Gallimard, 1989.

Merleau-Ponty, Maurice, 'Etre et Avoir', *La Vie Intellectuelle*, Vol. XLV, 10 October 1936, 98–109. English translation in Silverman and Barry (eds.), *Texts and Dialogues: On Philosophy, Politics and Culture*, 1992, 101–7.

Merleau-Ponty, Maurice. 'Eye and Mind'. In *The Primacy of Perception*. Edited by James M. Edie, 159–90. Evanston, IL: Northwestern University Press, 1964. Originally published as "L'Oeil et l'esprit," *Art de France*, vol. I, no I (January 1961) and reprinted after Merleau-Ponty's death in *Les Temps Modernes*, no 184–85. It was published in book form by Éditions Gallimard in 1964.

Merleau-Ponty, Maurice. 'Hegel's Existentialism'. In *Sense and Non-Sense*. Edited by John Wild, 63–70. Evanston, IL: Northwestern University Press, 1964.

Merleau-Ponty, Maurice. 'Indirect Language and the Voices of Silence'. Translated by Richard C. McCleary, Edited by John Wild, 159–81. Evanston, IL: Northwestern University Press, 1964, 39–83. Originally published in two parts as "Le langage indirect et les voix du silence" I & II, *Les Temps Modernes*, June and July 1952, nos. 80 & 81.

Merleau-Ponty, Maurice. *Institution and Passivity: Course Notes from the Collège de France (1954–1955)*. Evanston, IL: Northwestern University Press, 2010.

Merleau-Ponty, Maurice. 'Introduction'. In *Signs*. Translated by Richard C. McCleary and Edited by John Wild, 159–81, 3–35. Evanston, IL: Northwestern University Press, 1964.

Merleau-Ponty, Maurice. 'Introduction' to 'Institution in Personal and Public History'. In *Institution and Passivity: Course Notes from the Collège de France (1954–55)*. Edited by Maurice Merleau-Ponty, 5–15. Evanston, IL: Northwestern University Press, 2010.

Merleau-Ponty, Maurice. 'La Nature ou le monde du silence (pages d'introduction)'. In *Maurice Merleau-Ponty*. Edited by Emmanuel de Saint Aubert, 41–53. Paris: Mermann Éditeurs, 2008.

Merleau-Ponty, Maurice. 'Metaphysics and the Novel'. In *Sense and Non-Sense*. Evanston, IL: Northwestern University Press, 1964, 26–40. Originally published as 'Roman et Métaphysique', *Cahiers du Sud*, T. XXII, no. 270, mars-avril 1945, 194–207 and reprinted as 'Le Roman et la Métaphysique, in *Sens et non-sens*, 45–71.

Merleau-Ponty, Maurice. 'On Madagascar' (1958). In *Signs*. Translated by Richard C. McCleary and Edited by John Wild, 328–36. Evanston, IL: Northwestern University Press, 1964.

Merleau-Ponty, Maurice. 'On News Items', 1954. In *Signs*. Translated by Richard C. McCleary and Edited by John Wild, 311–13. Evanston, IL: Northwestern University Press, 1964.

Merleau-Ponty, Maurice. 'On the Phenomenology of Language'. In *Signs*. Translated by Richard C. McCleary and Edited by John Wild, 84–97. Evanston, IL: Northwestern University Press, 1964. First presented at the first *Colloque international de phénoménologie*, Brussels, 1951.

Merleau-Ponty, Maurice. *Phénoménologie de la Perception*. Paris: Gallimard, 1945.

Merleau-Ponty, Maurice. *Phenomenology of Perception*. Translated by Colin Smith. London: Routledge and Kegan Paul Ltd., 1962.

Merleau-Ponty, Maurice. 'Philosophy and Non-philosophy since Hegel' (lecture course: *Collège de France* in 1960–1). In *Philosophy and Non-philosophy since Merleau-Ponty*. Edited by Hugh J Silverman, 9–83. New York and London: Routledge, 1988.

Merleau-Ponty, Maurice. *Projet de travail sur la nature de la Perception*, 8 April 1933, reproduced in Geraets, *Vers une nouvelle philosophie transcendantale: la genèse de la philosophie de Maurice Merleau-Ponty jusqu' à la Phénoménologie de la Perception*, 1971, 9–10.

Merleau-Ponty, Maurice. 'Reading Montaigne'. In *Signs*. Translated by Richard C. McCleary and Edited by John Wild, 198–210. Evanston, IL: Northwestern University Press, 1964.

Merleau-Ponty, Maurice. *Sense and Non-Sense*. Edited by John Wild. Evanston, IL: Northwestern University Press, 1964. Originally published as *Sens et non-sens*, Paris, Les Éditions Nagel, 1948.

Merleau-Ponty, Maurice. *Signs*. Translated by Richard C. McCleary and Edited by John Wild. Evanston, IL: Northwestern University Press, 1964. Originally published as *Signes*, Paris, Gallimard, 1960.

Merleau-Ponty, Maurice. *Texts and Dialogues: On Philosophy, Politics and Culture*. Edited by Hugh J. Silverman and James Barry, Jr. London: Humanities Press, 1992.

Merleau-Ponty, Maurice. 'The Child's Relations with Others' (1950–51). In *The Primacy of Perception*. Edited by James M. Edie, 96–155. Evanston, IL: Northwestern University Press, 1964

Merleau-Ponty, Maurice, 'The Film and the New Psychology' (1945). In *Sense and Non-Sense*. Edited by Maurice Merleau-Ponty, 48–59. Evanston, IL: Northwestern University Press, 1964. Originally published as 'Le Cinéma et la nouvelle Psychologie'. *Les Temps Modernes*, 3, No. 26, November 1947, 930–43.

Merleau-Ponty, Maurice 'The Institution of a Work of Art' (41–49 plus notes 95–101). In *Institution and Passivity: Course Notes from the Collège de France (1954–1955)*. Edited by Maurice Merleau-Ponty. Evanston, IL: Northwestern University Press, 2010.

Merleau-Ponty, Maurice. 'The Philosopher and his Shadow'. In *Signs*. Translated by Richard C. McCleary and Edited by John Wild, 159–81. Evanston, IL: Northwestern University Press, 1964. Originally published as 'Le Philosophe et son ombre', The Hague: Martinus Nijhoff, 1959, 195–220.

Merleau-Ponty, Maurice. *The Primacy of Perception*. Edited by James M. Edie. Evanston, IL: Northwestern University Press, 1964

Merleau-Ponty, Maurice, 'The Primacy of Perception and Its Philosophical
    Consequences' (a summary and defense of the *Phenomenology*). In *The Primacy
    of Perception*. Edited by James M. Edie, 12–42. Evanston, IL: Northwestern
    University Press, 1964. Originally presented to the Société française de
    philosophie on 23 November 1946, and published in *Bulletin de la Société
    française de philosophie*, 41e année, 1947, 119–35.
Merleau-Ponty, Maurice. *The Prose of the World*. Translated by John O'Neill.
    Evanston, IL: Northwestern University Press, 1973. Originally published as *La
    Prose du monde*, Paris, Gallimard, 1969.
Merleau-Ponty, Maurice. *The Structure of Behavior*. Translated by Alden L.
    Fisher. Boston: Beacon Press, 1963. Originally published as *La Structure du
    Comportement*, Presses Universitaires de France, 1942.
Merleau-Ponty, Maurice. 'The War Has Taken Place'. In *Sense and Non-Sense*.
    Evanston, IL: Northwestern University Press, 1964, 139–52.
Merleau-Ponty, Maurice, *The Visible and the Invisible* (followed by working
    notes). Translated by Alphonso Lingis and Edited by Claude Lefort. Evanston,
    IL: Northwestern University Press, 1968. Originally published as *Le Visible et
    l'invisible*, Paris: Editions Gallimard, 1964.
Minkkinen, Panu. 'Hostility and Hospitality'. *NoFo 4* (October 2007), 53–60.
Morris, Frances. 'Introduction'. In *Paris Post-War: Art and Existentialism 1945–
    1955*. London: Tate Gallery Publications, 1993, 15–24.
Morris, Frances. *Paris Post War: Art and Existentialism 1945–55*. London: Tate
    Gallery, 1993.
Morris, Frances. 'Wols (1913-1951)'. In *Paris Post War: Art and Existentialism
    1945-55*. Edited by Frances Morris, 181–2. London, Tate Gallery, 1993.
Munchow, Michael. 'Painting and Invisibility: Merleau-Ponty's Line'. *Journal of the
    British Society for Phenomenology* (forthcoming, 1993).
Murray, David J. *Gestalt Psychology and the Cognitive Revolution*. New York and
    London: Harvester Wheatsheaf, 1995.
Myers, Terry R. (ed.). *Painting: Documents of Contemporary Art*. London and
    Cambridge, MA: Whitechapel Gallery and MIT Press, 2011.
Norris, Kathleen. *Acedia and Me: A Marriage, Monks and a Writer's Life*. New
    York: Riverhead Books, 2008.
O'Leary, Joseph S. 'Merleau-Ponty and Modernist Sacrificial Poetics: A Response
    to Richard Kearney'. In *Merleau-Ponty at the Limits of Art, Religion, and
    Perception*. Edited by Kascha Semionovitch and Neal DeRoo, 167–84. London
    and New York: Continuum, 2010.
Orbe, Mark P. *Constructing Co-Cultural Theory: An Explication of Culture, Power
    and Communication*. Thousand Oaks, London and New Delhi: Sage, 1998.
Osborne, Peter. *Anywhere or Not at All: Philosophy of Contemporary Art*. London
    and New York: Verso, 2013.
Ovid. *Metamorphoses*. Translated by A. D Melville. Oxford and New York:
    Oxford University Press, 1986.
Petersen, Anne Ring, et al. *Contemporary Painting in Context*. Copenhagen:
    Museum Tusculanum Press and University of Denmark, 2010.
Petersen, Anne Ring. 'Painting Spaces'. In *Contemporary Painting in Context*.
    Edited by Anne Ring Petersen with Makkel Bogh, Hans Dam Christensen and
    Peter Nørgaard Larsen, 123–38. Copenhagen: Museum Tusculanum Press and
    University of Copenhagen, 2013 edition (2010).

Peterson, Eugene H. *A Long Obedience in the Same Direction* (1980). Downers Grove, IL: Intervarsity Press, 2000.

Piaget, Jean. *Le Représentation du monde chez l'enfant*. Paris: Presses Universitaires de France, 1926.

Pinkola Estés, Clarissa. *Women Who Run with the Wolves: Contacting the Power of the Wild Woman*. London: Rider Books, 1992.

Pinna, B. 'New Gestalt Principles of Perceptual Organization: An Extension from Grouping to Shape and Meaning'. *Gestalt Theory* 32 (2010), 11–78.

Pollard, Christopher. 'Is Merleau-Ponty's Position in Phenomenology of Perception a New Type of Transcendental Idealism?' *Idealistic Studies* 44, no. 1 (Spring 2014), 119–38.

Pos, Hendrik J. 'Phénoménologie et linguistique'. *Revue Internationale de philosophie*, (1), 1939, 354–365.

Potts, Alex 'Postwar Art and the Psychoanalytic Imaginary'. In *History and Psyche*, Palgrave Studies in Cultural and Intellectual History. Edited by S. Alexander and B. Taylor, 265–81. New York: Palgrave Macmillan, 2012.

Potts, Alex. *Experiments in Modern Realism: World Making in Postwar European and American Art*. New Haven and London: Yale University Press, 2013.

Priest, Stephen. *Merleau-Ponty*. London and New York: Routledge, 1998.

Princess Elizabeth to Descartes, The Hague, 6–16 May 1943. Correspondence No. 301; *Oeuvres*, A. - T. Vol. III, 661.

Rey, Dominique. *La Perception du peintre et le problème de l'être*. Fribourg, Switzerland: University of Fribourg, 1978.

Ricoeur, Paul. 'Existential Phenomenology'. In *Husserl: An Analysis of his Phenomenology*. Translated by Edward Ballard and Lester Embree. Evanston, IL: Northwestern University Press, 1967.

Riding, Alan. *And the Show Went On: Cultural Life in Nazi-Occupied Paris*. London and New York: Duckworth Overlook, 2011.

Robinet, André *Merleau-Ponty, sa vie, son oeuvre, avec un exposé de sa philosophie*, 1963.

Rodaway, Paul. *Sensuous Geographies: Body, Sense and Place*. Abingdon, Oxfordshire and New York: Routledge, 1994.

Rosen, Steven M. 'Bridging the "Two Cultures": Merleau-Ponty and the Crisis in Modern Physics'. *Cosmos and History: The Journal of Natural and Social Philosophy* 9, no. 2 (2013), 1–12.

Ruger, H. A. 'Psychology of Efficiency: An Experimental Study of the Processes Involved in the Solution of Mechanical Puzzles and in the Acquisition of Skill in their Manipulation'. In *Archives of Psychology*, XV, June 1910. Columbia Contributions to Philosophy and Psychology, Vol 19, No 2. New York: The Science Press.

Ruspoli, Mario. *The Cave of Lascaux: The Final Photographic Record*. London and New York: Thames and Hudson Ltd and Harry N Abrams Inc, 1987.

Sánchez, Carlos Alberto. *Contingency and Commitment: Mexican Existentialism and the Place of Philosophy*. Albany, NY: SUNY Press, 2015.

Saniga, Metod. 'Unveiling the Nature of Time: Altered States of Consciousness and Pencil-Generated Space-Times'. An invited workshop presentation at 'Scienza e Trascendenza', Rome, 8 May 1998. Available online at http://www.ta3.sk/~msaniga/pub/ftp/unveil.pdf.

Sarris, Viktor. 'Max Wertheimer on Seen Motion: Theory and Evidence'. *Psychological Research* 51, no. 2 (September 1989), 58–68.

Sartre, Jean-Paul. 'Doigts et Non-doigts'. In Jean-Paul Sartre, Henri-Pierre Roché and Werner Haftmann (eds), *Wols en personne*, Paris and Cologne, 1963, pp. 10–21.

Sartre, Jean-Paul. 'Merleau-Ponty Vivant'. *Les Temps Modernes* 184 (1961), 304–76.

Sartre, Jean-Paul. 'Merleau-Ponty' (1964). In *Situations*. Translated by Benita Eisler, 230–2. New York: George Braziller, 1965.

Sartre, Jean-Paul. *Qu'est-ce que la littérature?* [1947], Collection 'Idées', Paris: Gallimard, 1964.

Schmidt, James. *Maurice Merleau-Ponty: Between Phenomenology and Structuralism*. London: Palgrave Macmillan, 1985.

Semonovitch, Kascha and Neal DeRoo. 'Introduction'. In *Merleau-Ponty at the Limits of Art, Religion, and Perception*. Edited by Kascha Semonovitch and Neal DeRoo, 1–17. London and New York: Continuum, 2010.

Shildrick, Margrit. 'Posthumanism and the Monstrous Body'. *Body and Society* (1996), 1–15.

Silverman, Hugh J. (ed.). *Philosophy and Non-Philosophy since Merleau-Ponty*. Evanston, IL: Northwestern University Press, 1988.

Simmel, Georg. 'The Philosophy of Fashion'. In *Simmel on Culture*. Translated by Mark Ritter and David Frisby and Edited by David Frisby and Mike Featherstone, 187–206. London, Thousand Oaks and New Delhi: Sage Books, 1997.

Simunovic, Matthew '"The El Greco Fallacy" Fallacy'. *JAMA Ophthalmology* 132, no. 4 (April 2014), 491–4.

Sinclair, Mark. 'Spray paint and sea spray — *Rockaway*! installation unveiled in New York'. *Creative Review*, 08 July 2016. Source: https://www.creativereview.co.uk/spray-paint-anpd-sea-spray/.

Singer, Linda. *The Mystery of Vision and the Miracle of Painting: A Critical Examination of Merleau-Ponty's Philosophy of the Visual Arts* (unpublished doctoral thesis), SUNY, 1991.

Smith, Jonathan A., Paul Flowers and Michael Larkin. *Interpretative Phenomenological Analysis: Theory, Method, Research*. Los Angeles, London, New Delhi, Singapore and Washington DC: Sage, 2009.

Sokolowski, Robert. *Introduction to Phenomenology*. Cambridge: Cambridge University Press, 2000.

Starr, Bala. 'Foreword'. In: *Artists Imagine a Nation: Pictures of People and Places from the Collections of Koh Seow Chuan and Friends* (exhibition catalogue). Singapore: Institute of Contemporary Arts Singapore, 2015, 8–9.

Steinbock, Anthony J. 'Phenomenological Concepts of Normality and Abnormality'. *Man and World* 28 (1995), 241–60.

Storm, Eric. *El descubrimiento del Greco. Nacionalismo y arte moderno (1860-1914)*. Madrid, Spain: Centro de Estudios Europa Hispánica, 2011.

Swigonski, Mary E. 'For the White Social Worker Who Wants to Know how to Work with Lesbians of Color'. In *Lesbians of Color: Social and Human Services*. Edited by Hilda Hidalgo, 7–21. The Harrington Park Press, an imprint of The Haworth Press Inc, 1995.

Swigonski, Mary E. 'The Logic of Feminist Standpoint Theory for Social Work Research'. *Social Work* 39, no. 4 (1 July 1994), 387–93.

Tapié, Michel. *Un art autre où il s'agit de nouveaux dévidages du reel*. Paris: Gabriel-Giraud et fils, 1952.

Taylor, Derek. 'Phantasmic Genealogy'. In *Merleau-Ponty: Hermeneutics and Postmodernism*. Edited by Thomas W. Busch and Shaun Gallagher, 149–60. Albany, NY: State University of New York Press, 1992.

The Holy Bible, New International Version. London, Sydney, Auckland and Toronto: Hodder and Stoughton, 1984.

Uličný, Petr. 'Hans and Paul Vredeman de Vries in Rudolf II's Prague Castle'. *Studia Rudolphina: Bulletin of the Research Center for Visual Arts and Culture in the Age of Rudolf II*, Institute of Art History, Czech Academy of Sciences, 2015, 48–63.

Vallier, Robert. *Review of Brett Buchanan, Onto-Ethologies: The Animal Environments of Uexküll, Heidegger, Merleau-Ponty, and Deleuze*. Albany, NY: State University of New York Press, 2008. In *Notre Dame Philosophical Reviews (an electronic journal)*, 08 June 2009. Available on http://ndpr.nd.edu/news/24045-onto-ethologies-the-animal-environments-of-uexk-252-ll-heidegger-merleau-ponty-and-deleuze/.

van Breda, Herman Leo. 'Maurice Merleau-Ponty et les Archives-Husserl à Louvain'. *Revue de Métaphysique et de Morale, Paris* 67 (1962), 410–30.

van Loon, Hector E. Henry. 'The Photography of Wolfgang Schulz'. *Filmliga: Onafhankelijk Maandblad Voor Filmkunst, Film, Smalfilm, Radio, Gramafoon, Foto* 6 no. 2 (20 December 1932), 48–49.

Verhagen, Erik. 'The Horizon according to Jan Dibbets: An Endless Quest. A Childhood Memory'. *Depth of Field* 2, no. 1 (June 2012). http://journal.depthoffield.eu/vol02/nr01/a02/en.

Vernon, Thomas S. 'Descartes' Three Substances. *The Southern Journal of Philosophy* 3, no. 3 (Fall 1965), 122–26.

Villoro, Luis. 'Genesis y proyecto del existencialismo en Mexico.' *Filosofia y Letras* 18, no. 36 (1949), 233–44.

Vollemans, Kees. *Het raadzel van de zichtbare wereld. Philips Koninck, of een landschap in de vorm van een traktaat*. Amsterdam: Uitgererij Duizend en Een, 1998.

Vos, Marcel. 'Conceptuele Kunst: Een Herinnering'. *Metropolis M*, No 6, December/January 2001–2, 13–15.

Waelhens, Alphonse de. 'Merleau-Ponty: Philosopher of Painting' (1962). Translated by Michael B. Smith. In *The Merleau-Ponty Aesthetics Reader: Philosophy and Painting*. Edited by Galen A. Johnson, 174–91. Evanston, IL: Northwestern University Press, 1993.

Wagemans, Johan. 'Historical and Conceptual Background: Gestalt Theory'. In *The Oxford Handbook of Perceptual Organization*. Edited by Johan Wagemans. Oxford: Oxford University Press, Forthcoming. http://www.gestaltrevision.be/pdfs/oxford/Wagemans-Historical_and_conceptual_background_Gestalt_theory.pdf (accessed 11 October 2017).

Waldenfels, Bernard. 'Interrogative Thinking: Reflections on Merleau-Ponty's Later Philosophy'. In *Merleau-Ponty in Contemporary Perspectives*. Edited by Patrick Burke and Jan van der Veken, 3–12. Dordrecht, Boston and London: Kluwer Academic Publishers, 1993.

Watson, Stephen. 'The Ethics of Ambiguity'. In *Merleau-Ponty in Contemporary Perspectives*. Edited by Patrick Burke and Jan van der Veken, 147–70. Dordrecht, Boston and London: Kluwer Academic Publishers, 1993.

Website: Anonymous. 'An Analysis of Stendhal'. *The Spectator*, 26 September 1952, 21. http://archive.spectator.co.uk/article/26th-september-1952/21/the-analysis-of-stendhal.

Website: 'Architect Junzo Yoshimura's unique campus in danger' http://www.shinodanozomi.com/Aichi-Geidai/top.html.

Website: The Collège de France: http://www.college-de-france.fr/site/fr-about-college/index.htm

Website: 'Founding Philosophy', Aichi Prefectural University of Fine Arts and Music. https://www.aichi-fam-u.ac.jp/english/about/about02/about02-01.html.

Website: Ellard, Graham and Stephen Johnstone, 'For an Open Campus' website entry: http://www.ellardjohnstone.com/assets/ForanOpenCampus.html.

Website: Johnson, Rashid. *Within Our Gates*, Garage Museum of Contemporary Art, Moscow, 2016. https://garagemca.org/en/event/rashid-johnson-within-our-gates.

Website: Leah Durner: https://www.leahdurner.com/paintings/1.

Website: 'Leon Golub, *Vietnam II*, 1973', Tate. http://www.tate.org.uk/art/artworks/golub-vietnam-ii-t13702

Website: Merian Webster dictionary: https://www.merriam-webster.com/medical/anosognosia.

Website: Promethean Movement: http://www.prometheanmovement.org/index.html

Website: Spectral Sounds: Chra - Il_Liquid: https://soundcloud.com/spectral-sounds/christina-nemec.

Website: 'The Nature of the Aichi Geidai's campus: The campus in Autumn', http://www.shinodanozomi.com/Aichi-Geidai/nature_of_the_campus.html.

Website: 'We're The Superhumans' for the 2016 Rio Paralympics. Trailer'. Viewable at https://www.youtube.com/watch?v=IocLkk3aYlk.

Weiss, Gail. 'The Anonymous Intentions of Transactional Bodies'. *Hypatia* 17, no. 4 (Autumn 2002), 187–200.

Weiss, Gail and Dorothea Olkowski (eds). *Feminist Interpretations of Merleau-Ponty*. University Park, PA: Penn State University Press, 2006.

Werry, Margaret and Bryan Schmidt. 'Immersion and the Spectator'. *Theatre Journal* 66, no. 3 (October 2014), 467–79.

Wertheimer, Max. 'Experimentelle Studien über das Sehen von Bewegung'. *Zeitschrift für Psychologie*, LXI, 1912.

Wiener, Norbert. *Cybernetics: Or Control and Communication in the Animal and the Machine*. Paris and Cambridge, MA: Hermann & Cie and MIT Press, 1948.

Woods, Ange-Aimée. 'Five Questions: Brooklyn-based Visual Artist Rashid Johnson'. *Colorado Public Radio News*, 12 February 2014. Accessed on http://www.cpr.org/news/story/five-questions-brooklyn-based-visual-artist-rashid-johnson (accessed 25 September 2017).

INDEX

Note: Page numbers followed by "f" indicate figures.

Lightning Source UK Ltd.
Milton Keynes UK
UKHW022341171222
413964UK00019B/324

9 781472 574275